BRITANNIA OVERRULED

STUDIES IN MODERN HISTORY

General Editors: John Morrill and David Cannadine

This series, intended primarily for students, will tackle significant historical issues in concise volumes which are both stimulating and scholarly. The authors combine a broad approach, explaining the current state of our knowledge in the area, with their own research and judgements; and the topics chosen range widely in subject, period and place.

Titles already published

BRITANNIA OVERRULED

British Policy and World Power in the Twentieth Century

David Reynolds

Longman
London and New York

Longman Group UK Limited,
Longman House, Burnt Mill, Harlow,
Essex CM20 2JE, England
and Associated Companies throughout the world

Published in the United States of America
by Longman Inc., New York

First published 1991

British Library Cataloguing in Publication Data
Reynolds, David
    Britannia overruled: power and policy in the twentieth-century world. - (Studies in
modern   history).
    1. Great Britain. Political power, history
    I. Title II. Series
    320.941

    ISBN 0-582-08427-X
    ISBN 0-582-55276-1 pbk

Library Of Congress Cataloging in Publication Data
Reynolds, David, 1952–
    Britannia overruled: power and policy in the twentieth-century world / David Reynolds.
    p. cm. -- (Studies in modern history)
    Includes bibliographical references and index.
    ISBN 0-582-08427-X (cased). -- ISBN 0-582-55276-1 (paper)
    1. Great Britain--Politics and government--20th century. 2. Great Britain--Foreign
relations----20th century. 3. History, Modern--20th century. I. Title. II. Series: Studies
in modern history (Longman (Firm))
    DA586.7.R479 1991
    941.085--dc20   90-26872
                                                                                     CIP

Set in 10/11 Point Times

Produced by Longman Singapore
Printed in Singapore

Contents

Tables and Maps

TABLES

MAPS

Abbreviations

The following abbreviations are used in the text or bibliography. Those italicised are periodicals or collections of documents.

AA	*African Affairs*
ACDN	FCO, *Arms Control and Disarmament Newsletter*
ACDQR	FCO, *Arms Control and Disarmament Quarterly Review*
AHR	*American Historical Review*
BD	*British Documents on the Origins of the War, 1899–1914*
BEF	British Expeditionary Force
BJPS	*British Journal of Political Science*
CAB	Cabinet minutes, memoranda and papers (PRO)
CAP	Common Agricultural Policy
CBI	Confederation of British Industries
Commons	House of Commons, Debates
CND	Campaign for Nuclear Disarmament
CR	*Contemporary Record*
DBPO	*Documents on British Policy Overseas*
DEFE	Ministry of Defence papers (PRO)
DH	*Diplomatic History*
DRC	Defence Requirements Committee
EC	European Community
EcHR	*Economic History Review (2nd series)*
ECSC	European Coal and Steel Community
EDC	European Defence Community
EEC	European Economic Community
EHR	*English Historical Review*
EMF	European Monetary Fund
EMS	European Monetary System
ERDF	European Regional Development Fund
ERM	Exchange Rate Mechanism (of EMS)

FBI	Federation of British Industries
FCO	Foreign and Commonwealth Office (after 1968)
FO	Foreign Office. (FO + number indicates FO papers in PRO)
GDP	Gross Domestic Product
GNP	Gross National Product
GO	*Government and Opposition*
HJ	*The Historical Journal*
HZ	*Historische Zeitschrift*
IA	*International Affairs*
IHR	*International History Review*
IMF	International Monetary Fund
INS	*Intelligence and National Security*
JAS	*Journal of American Studies*
JCMS	*Journal of Common Market Studies*
JCH	*Journal of Contemporary History*
JEEH	*Journal of European Economic History*
JFKL	John F. Kennedy Library, Boston, Massachusetts
JICH	*Journal of Imperial and Commonwealth History*
JMH	*Journal of Modern History*
JSS	*Journal of Strategic Studies*
Keesing's	*Keesing's Contemporary Archives*
Lords	House of Lords, Debates
MAS	*Modern Asian Studies*
NATO	North Atlantic Treaty Organisation
NC	Neville Chamberlain papers (Birmingham University Library)
PP	*Past and Present*
PREM	Prime Minister's papers (PRO)
PRO	Public Record Office
PUS	Permanent Under-Secretary
RIS	*Review of International Studies*
SDI	Strategic Defense Initiative
T	Treasury Papers (PRO)
TA	Territorial Army
VAT	Value Added Tax

Acknowledgements

This book grows out of my own research and teaching over a number
of years, but, as with any work of synthesis, it draws heavily on the
scholarship of others. My debts are indicated specifically in the cita-
tions but I should particularly mention Paul Kennedy, Correlli Barnett
and Bernard Porter. Although I dissent from some of their interpretations, their insightful arguments have been an essential spur to my own
thought.

I presented earlier versions of the book in Cambridge in 1989 first
as a graduate seminar and then as an undergraduate lecture course. The
themes of chapter five were aired in a paper to the Prinz Albert Seminar at Coburg in September 1989. I am grateful to these audiences for
their comments. The later chapters have benefited from conversations
with several Whitehall and Westminster 'insiders'. Although not identified by name, their personal experiences provided valuable background and saved me from some of my misconceptions.

I should also like to acknowledge the assistance of numerous Cambridge librarians – at the University Library, the History Faculty and
Christ's College – and of staff at the Public Record Office. Crown
copyright documents at the PRO are quoted by permission of the
Controller of HM Stationery Office and Neville Chamberlain's papers
by permission of Birmingham University Library. Liz Ottaway of the
University of Kent Cartoon Study Centre helped to find a suitable
cover illustration.

Several scholars have spared time from their own work to read
drafts of the book. Zara Steiner and John Thompson – as ever generous friends and constructive critics – soldiered through the whole
manuscript and prodded me repeatedly to clarify my arguments. David
Feldman helped with the earlier chapters and Geoffrey Edwards
offered a trenchant commentary on the later ones.

I owe a particular debt to the Master and Fellows of Christ's College. Use of the word-processing facilities has been a great boon. But, even more, I appreciate the stimulus of a large and lively body of colleagues, with whom I have pondered my ideas. Two in particular have helped greatly. To David Cannadine I owe the original invitation to write this book, hours of animated discussion about modern history, and editorial comment delivered with his customary brio and insight. After David's transatlantic translation, Susan Bayly took on his role as a sympathetic sounding board, as well as reading the manuscript with a sharp eye for my ethnocentricities and for the 'French connection'.

As usual my greatest debt is to my wife Margaret. Not only did she act as a keen 'general reader', but she suffered the process of composition with just the right mixture of support, interest and impatience. Her mother, Jean M. Ray, helped both by reading the manuscript and by providing baby-sitting at a crucial time. The book is dedicated to my grandmother, whose repertoire of historical anecdotes, related with caustic Lancashire wit, stretched back to her brother returning home from the Boer war, and to my son, who was absolutely no use as a historical source but who put everything in its true perspective.

Cambridge   D.J.R.
December 1990

The publishers would like to thank the following for permission to reproduce copyright material: Royal Institute of International Affairs for table 2.1 from *The Foreign Policy Process in Britain*, William Wallace (1975); Oxford University Press for table 1.3 from *British Economic Growth 1856–1973: Postwar Period in Historical Perspective*, R.C.O. Matthews et al. (1982); Berg Publishers Limited for table 10.1 from *1992: The Struggle for Europe*, Tony Cutler et al. (1989).

Prudence Kay

her past

James Ray Reynolds

his future

Introduction

In the 1870s Great Britain possessed more battleships than the rest of the world combined. It directly controlled about a fifth of the earth's surface, including India, Canada and Australasia. It was the world's largest economy, accounting for nearly a quarter of total manufacturing output and a similar proportion of world trade. The first industrial nation had become the greatest power the world had ever seen. A century later, however, Britain had lost nearly all its overseas possessions, its manufacturing base had collapsed and it was on a par with Italy in per capita output and income. The first 'post-industrial' nation was struggling to find its post-imperial role. Explaining this 'decline' has been a national obsession. Economic sclerosis, imperial nostalgia and insular parochialism have all been blamed. Even those trying to combat the mood have often been backward-looking. In 1987 Margaret Thatcher campaigned on the slogan 'Britain Is Great Again'.

Yet Britain's erstwhile greatness has been misunderstood. Power is a more complex phenomenon than the possession of large navies or vast empires, and chapter one explores the changing character of British power in the nineteenth and twentieth centuries. Moreover, power is relative: it is not simply that Britain changed, but, even more, that the world changed around it. Explanations of Britain's fate that concentrate on its internal history[1] can undervalue this fundamental point. As the poet Rudyard Kipling asked a century ago 'what should they know of England who only England know?'.[2] The first chapter therefore also surveys the transformation of the modern world through the spread of industrialisation, the emergence of new powers and the reaction against imperialism.

In other words, broad trends in the world at large helped shape Britain's fate. Understanding this may make it easier to come to terms with what has happened. But important recent studies of British foreign policy push this insight to the point of being almost determinist in tone. Paul Kennedy (1981, 1988) and Bernard Porter (1987) take as their major theme the problems of an economy surpassed by rivals and enervated by military spending – part of a perennial rhythm of rise and decline among great powers. Yet the specific course of events was far from being pre-determined, certainly not by economic performance alone. Moreover, other European countries, notably France, went through similar experiences – economic decline, loss of empire, eclipse by the superpowers – and their responses were significantly different. Thus, it is too simple to claim that 'power determines policy'.[3]

After looking in chapter two at the concept of policymaking and at Britain's policymaking institutions, the remaining chapters therefore examine the reactions of British leaders to the upheavals of the twentieth-century world. Of central importance are the crises of two world wars, although these are sometimes depicted (and even dated) in unfamiliar ways. The chapters evolve chronologically, and, although in no sense constituting a comprehensive account of British overseas policy in the twentieth century, they provide an overview of the whole story.

Thinking in this way about power and policy has implications not merely for the explanation of Britain's twentieth-century fate but also for the way in which we describe it. Much of the debate assumes that Britain has lost a position which in reality it never had. Conventional wisdom postulates a steady decline from a position of 'primacy' at the beginning of this century,[4] with only 'delusions of grandeur'[5] keeping Britain going as a would-be great power after 1945. Such an account exaggerates Britain's nineteenth-century strength. Moreover, it also overstates Britain's weakness for much of the twentieth century. By understanding power in eclectic and relational terms and by looking at some of the crucial turning-points, we can see this more clearly. Contrary to some historians, Britain was never a nineteenth-century 'superpower'.[6] Nor was its 'decline' in the first half of the twentieth century as abrupt and pronounced as is often implied by those who treat the era after 1945, or 1956, as merely an elegiac finale.[7] The decade after the Second World War ended saw Britain, as never before, trying to act as a superpower. Although that strategy was shortlived, the country is still living with its consequences today. And by paying close attention to the second half of this century, we can see the nature of both power and policy have changed significantly. The story is not just one of 'decline' but of transformation.

These, then, are the main themes of the book. To examine them takes us beyond diplomacy in a narrow sense, to look at imperial, industrial and financial policy, at the armed forces, at government institutions and at domestic politics. In the now highly-specialised historical profession these too often form discrete sub-disciplines – separate compartments insulated by jargon and incomprehension. This book tries to transcend some of these barriers and allow the wealth of recent research in each area to enrich our understanding of the others and of the larger problem of Britain's changing place in the world. It also draws on the work of political scientists – especially theories of power, policymaking and the international system – to help give the analysis a firm conceptual base, while trying to avoid the aridity of much theoretical writing on international affairs.

In writing it I have become aware of many points at which the record remains unclear, especially when access to government archives is still barred under the thirty-year rule. I hope therefore that this overview will act as a stimulus to debate and further research. Equally important, I hope it will help to bridge the ever-widening gap between scholars and the public in an area of topical interest. It is therefore aimed at both students and general readers, particularly those, like myself, for whom the first half of this century is part of history not memory – for whom the Boers, the Kaiser, Appeasement, the Empire, 'Winston', the Commonwealth or Suez cannot simply be invoked but need explanation.

Thus, I try to do justice to two central but distinct tasks of the historian. One is to analyse, with the benefits of hindsight, the long sweep of events – discerning patterns and demonstrating how we got from one point to another. But the danger of hindsight is that it may encourage a sense of inevitability: what happened seems the only thing that could have happened. The historian must therefore also recapture the openness of events, reminding self and readers that events now long in the past were once in the future, and seeing them as they were seen at the time. The two tasks cannot be totally disentangled, of course. We can never reconstruct the past except with hindsight; that alone makes it possible to identify putative turning-points for closer analysis. In fact, any intellectual framework used by historians is strictly artificial. Anthony Eden, Lord Avon, once exclaimed that 'there are no chapters in foreign policy, only chapters in books about it'.[8] These particular chapters are offered, then, as one historian's contribution to our understanding of Britain's place in the twentieth-century and of its prospects for the twenty-first.

REFERENCES

1. e.g. Barnett 1972
2. Kipling 1933 (ed.): 218
3. Farrar 1981: 199
4. Friedberg 1988: 303
5. Porter 1987
6. e.g. Jones 1980: 10
7. Kennedy 1981; Bartlett 1989
8. Dilks 1972: 38

CHAPTER ONE

Power

THE RELATIVITIES OF POWER

For the student of international relations few concepts are more important than that of 'power'. Yet its meaning is difficult to pin down. In common parlance we tend to judge a country's power by the size of its armed forces or the number of missiles it possesses. We also rank countries as greater or lesser powers. Yet scholars agree that we would be wiser to think of power not as a *possession* but as a *relationship*[1] – one in which A gets B to do something that B would not otherwise do. This can be effected in various ways. Outright war is obviously the most extreme form, but other modes of power include coercion, manipulation, inducements and influence, as we move toward the opposite end of the spectrum. The sources of a country's power are also diverse. It is customary to focus on those that translate easily into military might, particularly population, natural resources and, in the industrial age, economic strength. Aside from such 'tangible' elements, however, scholars also note the importance of 'intangibles' such as national unity and morale, the coherence of the governmental system, the quality of leadership or diplomatic skill.[2]

All these elements come into play in a particular power relationship between two states. A strong economy may not be decisive if the country's armed forces are ill-prepared for war. A large army may be irrelevant if the country has no will to fight, or if its leaders are distracted by other concerns at home or abroad. A state with limited economic resources may be able to secure unexpected advantage by diplomatic dexterity. And the reputation for being powerful may ensure influence long after economic and military strength has waned, particularly if war can be avoided.

There is a danger, therefore, in categorising countries as 'minor' or 'great' powers, as 'world powers', 'superpowers', and the like. Although useful shorthands, such language can lure us into a static understanding of power as a permanent possession. Conceiving, instead, of power in relative terms means recognising that it may vary from situation to situation: the United States played a decisive role in defeating advanced industrial nations like Germany and Japan in 1945, yet it could not overcome the third-world peasant state of North Vietnam. Likewise, the Soviet Union was able to coerce Eastern European satellites such as Hungary in 1956 or Czechoslovakia in 1968 but it could not defeat the Afghanistan guerrillas in the 1980s. Power is also relative across time: countries rise and fall in effective power, for reasons that are usually connected with the state of their economies and armed forces but which are by no means simply reducible to those factors. Often the perception of a country's power, at home and abroad, is as important as its actual capabilities[3] – as the Americans discovered in the 1970s after Vietnam.

Power, then, is relative not absolute; its sources are intangible as well as tangible. What matters is not abstract rankings of great powers but the complex balance of forces in each particular power relationship. These complexities of power must be kept in mind when examining the British case. But there is another important relativity. What happened to Britain was paralleled by the story of several other western European states in the twentieth century, notably France, but also Spain, Portugal and the Netherlands. The fate of the so-called 'Pax Britannica' cannot be understood through purely British-centred explanations, for it is tied up with the rise and fall of a 'Eurocentric' world.

For a millennium after the fall of Rome, Europe was on the periphery of 'civilisation'. The world's centre of gravity lay in the Near East, India, and China – technological pioneer of gunpowder, canals and the mechanical clock. The world's most dynamic ideological force in this millennium was not Christianity but Islam, whose expansion reached its apogee in the great early-modern empires of the Mughals in India, the Safavids in Persia and the Ottomans in the Near East. For centuries the Islamic tide lapped around the Mediterranean, leaving an indelible mark on the Balkans and southern Spain. As late as 1683 Ottoman armies were at the gates of Vienna.

But by this time the Europeans were reaching out around the globe, using the sailing ship which they had developed to a state of unequalled sophistication. As traders and as settlers they expanded into Asia and the Americas, with the countries of Northwest Europe, strategically located on the Atlantic seaboard, taking the lead. Although conventionally dated from around 1500, this was a slow process: in 1700 much of the world's production and trade remained concentrated in Asia and the crisis of the three great Islamic empires came only in the eighteenth century.[4] The process of European expansion was accelerated by five great bouts of European war in the period 1689–1815, during which French hegemony was destroyed as part of a world-wide struggle for trade and colonies. Although by the end of these wars most of the Americas – North and South – had thrown off colonial rule, European outreach intensified throughout the world in the nineteenth century with the spread of industrialisation. European manufactures and non-European primary products became part of a global trading system, and a new struggle for colonies broke out in the last quarter of the nineteenth century, centred now on Africa.

By 1900 the Europeans seemed supreme. They occupied one-third of the earth's land surface in 1800, two-thirds by 1878 and 84 per cent in 1914.[5] Yet within fifty years the tide of history had ebbed dramatically. In the eighteenth century the wars over French hegemony had helped spread European influence around the globe. In the first half of the twentieth century two great German bids for domination sapped Europe's wealth and brought the Continent under the influence of two new 'superpowers', America and Russia. The first of these was a veritable economic giant in 1945, producing half the world's manufactured goods. At the same time the process of decolonisation accelerated dramatically and by the late 1960s most of the European empires had disappeared. In their wake all the European powers faced a painful process of re-definition, which increasingly focused on the development of the European Community. By the 1990s the economic centre of the world was again shifting away from Europe, this time to the Pacific basin, which is likely to have two-thirds of the world's population and to generate half of its total gross domestic product by the year 2000.[6] And Islam was once more a world force, both in population and ideological vigour. The collapse of the 'iron curtain' in 1989 gave Europe the prospect of a new unity and its western part remains a significant force in international affairs, but its three centuries of world dominance are over – at least for the foreseeable future.

Any account of Britain's changing place in the world over the last century must therefore recognise that it is part of this larger metamorphosis of European power. Purely British-centred explanations are inadequate. Yet in the nineteenth century Britain did achieve a remarkable international position and, in order to understand how and why it was lost, we must begin by identifying what this was.

BRITANNIA RULES

Britain stood in the vanguard of the great movements of European expansion – commerce and conquest in the eighteenth century, industry and empire in the nineteenth. Its principal advantage was probably an island position. Unlike rivals such as France or Prussia, sharing land borders with often hostile powers, Britain could shelter behind what Shakespeare called its 'moat defensive', the English Channel. This did not guarantee immunity – in the 1690s and again in 1804–5 the threat of invasion seemed acute – but it did mean that normally the British did not need the sort of large standing army that became familiar on the Continent. The Royal Navy, however, was both popular and necessary – a trend also encouraged during the Civil War years when the service was placed on a properly-funded footing. The navy was Britain's main barrier against hostile forces crossing the Channel. It was also important because, as an island, increasingly dependent on the import of food and key raw materials such as cotton, Britain needed to protect its seaborne commerce from privateering and wartime enemies.

Britain's insular position left it well-placed to capitalise on the five great rounds of warfare against France. While French leaders from Louis XIV to Napoleon had to fight their primary battles on land against continental foes, Britain was able to divert more of its resources to the struggle for trade and colonies. The Seven Years War of 1756–63 left the British in control of most of North America, and, although they lost nearly all their American colonies in the new world war of 1776–83, they held on to what became Canada and also the British West Indies. The Revolutionary and Napoleonic wars of 1793 to 1815 brought long periods of isolation and economic crisis for the British but also, eventually, overwhelming victory. French seapower was shattered and Britain was left as the world's main colonial power, paramount in India but also well-entrenched in Australasia and southern Africa. Its fleet, previously based mostly at home and in the Baltic and Mediterranean, was now spread around the globe. In 1848 only 35 warships were in home waters and 31 in the Mediterranean. There were 27 on the West Africa station, 10 at the Cape of Good Hope, 25 in the East Indies and China, 10 in the West Indies, 14 in South America and 12 in the Pacific.[7] Their ability to command the seas depended on holding what Admiral Sir John Fisher was later to call the 'five strategic keys' that 'lock up the world' – the great British bases at Dover, Gibraltar, Alexandria, the Cape of Good Hope and Singapore.[8]

Established in key points around the globe, able to reach out through a strong navy and merchant marine, Britain after 1815 also enjoyed the advantage of being the world's first industrial nation. This position was intimately bound up with commercial hegemony. From the late eighteenth century the country's initial industrial surge was stimulated by cotton manufacture. All the raw material was imported and most production was for export. By 1830 half the value of British exports came from cotton goods and raw cotton made up 20 per cent of net imports. As the cotton boom waned by the 1840s so iron and steel became the new growth sector, stimulated particularly by the railway-building manias of the 1830s and 1840s and then by British dominance in the construction and financing of railways around the world. By 1860 a country with only 2 per cent of the world's population was generating about one-fifth of Europe's total gross national product (GNP), producing half the world's iron and steel and accounting for 40 per cent of world trade in manufactured goods. It had the highest GNP in the world and its population enjoyed the highest average per capita income. Britain's dominance of the world economy in the mid-nineteenth century was greater than that of the USA at its peak a century later.[9]

So, in the mid-Victorian era Britain seemed truly great. It was the dominant sea power, the leading colonial power and the world's industrial giant. Economic strength and a well-grounded system of national debt had enabled it to see off the challenge from Napoleon. In the decades after 1815 the Royal Navy did seem to rule the waves, sweeping piracy from the Indian Ocean and China Seas, combatting the slave traders in the Caribbean and South Atlantic, and advancing British mercantile interests, particularly in the 'Opium War' of 1839–42 to open up China to British trade. Many foreign leaders had no doubt that British power was decisive. 'Only England, mistress of the seas, can protect us against the united force of European reaction,' exclaimed Simon Bolivar, the liberator of South America, as he contemplated the threat of Spanish reconquest, while Muhammad Ali, the Ottomans' unruly viceroy of Egypt, observed, 'with the English for my friends I can do anything: without their friendship I can do nothing'.[10] Like Rome, Britain seemed to rule or shape much of the world, what Tennyson celebrated in 1886 as

. . . the mightiest Ocean-power on earth
Our own fair isle, the lord of every sea.[11]

Politician Joseph Chamberlain simply called it the 'Pax Britannica'.
The sensation of national power seemed most palpable during the

celebrations for Queen Victoria's Diamond Jubilee in June 1897. A week of festivities ended with a vast naval pageant off the Isle of Wight when the Queen reviewed 165 of her ships manned by 40,000 men. But the highpoint was 22 June when Her Majesty processed in state through six miles of London streets amid cheering crowds. The capital had spent a quarter of a million pounds on street decorations, many of them illuminated by the latest miracle of British industrialism, the electric light bulb. For most observers the theme of the celebrations was 'the world-wide Empire of Britain . . . the exultant expression of a power the greatest in the world's history'.[12] Of particular fascination were contingents of troops from the Queen's territories all over the world. G.W. Steevens of the new popular newspaper *The Daily Mail* depicted them marching up Ludgate Hill to St Paul's –

> white men, yellow men, brown men, black men, every colour, every continent, every race, every speech – and all in arms for the BRITISH EMPIRE AND THE BRITISH QUEEN. Up they came, more and more, new types, new realms at every couple of yards, an anthropological museum – a living gazeteer of the British Empire. With them came their English officers, whom they obey and follow like children. And you began to understand, as never before what the Empire amounts to.[13]

The rhetoric of the week was extravagant, often implausible. A Jubilee mug, inscribed with portraits of the seventy-eight-year-old Queen, carried the legend 'The Centre of a World's Desire'.[14] A Canadian poet penned his own tribute:

> Here's to Queen Victoria
> Dressed in all her regalia
> With one foot in Canada
> And the other in Australia[15]

A remarkable posture indeed, but one that was difficult to sustain for long. In July 1897 the popular bard of empire, Rudyard Kipling, offered his own more sober verdict on the Jubilee. His 'Recessional' reminded readers of the obligations of empire and also carried intimations of its mortality:

> Far-called our navies melt away –
> On dune and headland sinks the fire –
> Lo, all our pomp of yesterday
> Is one with Nineveh and Tyre![16]

The mood of 1897 – of present power and anticipated decline – has often been used by historians as a benchmark for the twentieth century. It is claimed for instance that 'Britain alone had dominated world affairs in the years following 1815',[17] that in this period Britain was 'the only superpower, whose intervention was decisive for the balance of power, not only in Europe but in the world',[18] and that the end of British naval supremacy in the early twentieth century meant the loss of 'the nation's unique role as the independent, detached arbiter of world affairs'.[19] Such language is misleading. British power was more limited in the nineteenth century than appearances suggested.[20] The nature of that power – economic, international and imperial – is the theme of the next three sections of this chapter.

WEALTH

It is an axiom of international affairs that 'wealth is usually needed to underpin military power'. There is 'a very significant correlation *over the longer term* between productive and revenue-raising capacities on the one hand and military strength on the other'.[21] And, in the long run, the British case seems to support that claim. In 1880 Britain produced nearly 23 per cent of total world manufactured goods, only 10 per cent in 1928 and 4 per cent in 1980 (table 1.1). As a trading nation Britain's decline was longer-delayed, but the end result was similar. At the beginning of this century Britain generated one-third of the world's exports of manufactured goods, a quarter in 1950 and less than 10 per cent by 1980 (table 1.2).

While Britain's share of the world's wealth was declining, the cost of military armaments rose exponentially. In 1893–5 Britain's *Majestic* class warships each cost on average £1 million, the *Dreadnoughts* of 1905–6 averaged £1.79 million and the *Queen Elizabeth* of 1912–13 required £2.5 million.[22] In the 1980s the cost of 385 Tornado fighters for the RAF was greater in real terms than that of all the 21,000 Spitfires produced before and during the Second World War.[23] With the increasing complexity of modern weapons you got less bang for your buck, year by year. Yet a nation that fell behind in the spiral of sophistication – be it *Dreadnought* battleships or nuclear missiles – risked eclipse as a first-rank power.

Scholars, politicians and pundits have agonised over the reasons for Britain's economic decline. Yet in the broadest terms, what happened is hardly surprising: 'it is a mistake to think that England's supremacy was normal and her decline abnormal'. On the contrary, original 'supremacy' rather than subsequent 'decline' is more in need of explanation.[24]

Table 1.1 Relative shares of total world manufacturing output, 1860–1980 (in percentages)

	1860	1880	1900	1913	1928	1938	1953	1963	1973	1980
UK	19.9	22.9	18.5	13.6	9.9	10.7	8.4	6.4	4.9	4.0
Germany/ W. Germany	4.9	8.5	13.2	14.8	11.6	12.7	5.9	6.4	5.9	5.3
USA	7.2	14.7	23.6	32.0	39.3	31.4	44.7	35.1	33.0	31.5
Russia/USSR	7.0	7.6	8.8	8.2	5.3	9.0	10.7	14.2	14.4	14.8
Japan	2.6	2.4	2.4	2.7	3.3	5.2	2.9	5.1	8.8	9.1
France	7.9	7.8	6.8	6.1	6.0	4.4	3.2	3.8	3.5	3.3

Source: Bairoch 1982: 296, 304. Annual figures except for 1860, 1880, 1900, 1928 and 1938, which are triennial averages.

Table 1.2 Percentage of world exports of manufactures 1899–1980

	1899	1913	1929	1937	1950	1960	1970	1980
UK	33.2	30.2	22.4	20.9	25.5	16.5	10.8	9.7
Germany/ W. Germany	22.4	26.6	20.5	16.5	7.3	19.3	19.8	19.9
USA	11.7	13.0	20.4	19.2	27.3	21.6	18.5	17.0
Japan	1.5	2.3	3.9	6.9	3.4	6.9	11.7	14.8
France	14.4	12.1	10.9	5.8	9.9	9.6	8.7	10.0

Sources: Balfour 1982: 285; Chalmers 1985: 126

In 1860 20 per cent of the world's manufactured goods was being produced by a country with only 2 per cent of its population. Once the process of industrialisation spread, particularly through America and Germany in the last third of the nineteenth century, Britain's advantage would certainly be reduced. The USA – a country the size of a continent, blessed with booming population growth, abundant natural resources and a vast, tariff-free internal market – was especially likely to surpass Britain. Furthermore, those countries trying to catch up, assuming they had crossed a basic threshold of socio-economic capacity, could benefit from a leader's technological innovations, copying them directly rather than learning by trial and error. Indeed 'followers tend to catch up faster if they are initially more backward'.[25] Thus, leaders of a particular stage of industrialisation tend be caught in the long-run. In the last century, this has happened twice – for Britain around 1900 and America since 1945 (at a more advanced stage of industrialisation).

The 'catch-up' phenomenon in part explains Britain's fate.[26] The advantages of an 'early start' faded as others caught up: indeed they became disadvantages because the country was tied to outdated technology and working practices. But this points to a deeper problem. It is customary to think of Britain as an erstwhile industrial leader who gradually lost both its place and its skills. Recent historiography, however, has argued that in crucial respects Britain was never truly industrialised in the first place. Its advantage in the early nineteenth century did not stem from high growth rates, impressive productivity, substantial investment or advanced technology. It was narrowly based in a few industries geared to exports and reliant on Britain's coal reserves and abundant unskilled labour. In the history of industrialisation Britain was unique in the size of its industrial workforce at a very early stage of its economic development. In 1840 British per capita income was equivalent to US\$550 (at 1970 values). By then only 28.6 per cent of the male workforce remained in agriculture. When most European countries crossed the \$550 income threshold later in the century, around half their workforce was still in agriculture.[27] In other words their industrial sector was far more efficient than was Britain's at the same stage.

It is therefore true to say that Britain had an industrial revolution in a *structural* sense, meaning a massive transfer of workers from agriculture to industry and from countryside to town. But its experience of industrial revolution was much slower and more limited in the *technological* sense, that is to say involving far-reaching changes in productivity, technology and industrial practices.[28] Nor did nineteenth-century businessmen visualise themselves as part of an industrial *revolution*, creating a culture of continuous change. Instead they 'saw the changes wrought by the innovations largely as once-for-all events. . . . They certainly did not see themselves as heralds of a new order that in the twentieth century would increasingly call upon scientific understanding in an ever-deepening search for the means of economic survival'.[29]

Thus, to lament 'the decline of the industrial spirit'[30] misses the fact that, in significant respects, the British never had it in the first place. The problems of twentieth-century British industry have their roots in the partial and idiosyncratic character of its early industrialisation. The easiest scapegoat has been Britain's patchwork of competing trades-unions, defending over-manning, resisting new technology and exercising a unique hold over local workplace practices. Yet the union problem is only the tip of the iceberg. 'Well into the twentieth century employers in many British industries remained reluctant to assume direct control over the production process through the introduction of deskilling technology and more systematic management'.[31] Both unions and employers exhibited the small-scale 'competitive capitalism' that was typical of nineteenth-century British industry.[32] Most manufacturers were compact family firms, who relied on personal wealth and ploughed-back profits for new investment. They were run directly, without a managerial structure, and their technology relied on trial and error for much innovation. In the prosperity of the Victorian era, these small firms made accommodations with the many specialist craft unions that emerged to protect workers' rights, allowing them considerable autonomy at the workplace level rather than engaging in prolonged strife that would endanger production and profits.

This pattern was slow to change. In the USA and Germany large industrial combinations were established in the late nineteenth century, bringing in their train a specialist management system and encouraging mass production of standardised goods. The equivalent British merger movement did not begin until the 1920s and even then was mainly a defence against the US and German giants. The result was usually a large holding company, such as Imperial Chemical Industries (ICI) or Associated Electrical Industries (AEI). Not until the 1950s did they begin to fuse the separate component companies into a fully-integrated structure with modern methods of accounting and control. 'Normally, it took a British firm three generations to reach the size and managerial structure that a comparable American enterprise achieved in one'.[33] Even so, the old patchwork union structure persisted, with a plethora of rival unions exerting substantial if divisive influence over the local workplace.

Likewise, the much-lamented deficiencies of British technological education have their roots in the period of industrialisation. In the heyday of the industrial revolution from 1770 to 1830 there was little need for educational skills among most of the workforce. Technology was crude and much was achieved by mere muscle-power.[34] Consequently, 'in Britain, where technological change came early, a new industrial society had already taken shape by the time the schools were built'. These embodied 'not only the prejudices and cleavages of the established order, but the material inequalities'. In contrast, 'the Germans developed their schools in advance of and in preparation for industrialization' which came near the end of the nineteenth century.[35] On this foundation of basic education, Germany reared an excellent system of secondary technical training. But British education at all levels remained inherently biased against technical subjects. In 1976 only 5.7 per cent of British eighteen-year-olds were in technical and vocational education outside the higher education structure. In Germany and Switzerland the figure was around 50 per cent.[36] Managers were consistently picked for 'leadership' qualities rather than expertise, and as late as 1987 only 24 per cent of senior British managers were graduates, compared with 85 per cent in the USA and Japan.[37] Britain has also generally lagged behind in research and development. Of the top 200 firms in the USA in 1948, 164 had their own industrial laboratories, compared with 40 of the top 200 in Britain.[38]

To say that Britain was never as radically industrialised as, say, the USA or Germany, is not, however, to say that it was 'anti-capitalist'. What was distinctively British was the strength of non-industrial forms of capitalism, particularly financial, and their association with the members and ethos of Britain's landed élite – what has been called 'gentlemanly capitalism'.[39] Rather than seeing finance as a putative handmaiden of industry that failed to play its appointed role, historians are recognising that it has always been an autonomous sector in Britain, with its own rationale and national utility. Indeed it pre-dates the industrial revolution. The Bank of England (1694) was established as a private corporation and given special privileges in return for managing the government debt – mainly the result of wars for empire against the French. Loans were raised through the City, and the Treasury serviced the national debt by income from customs and excise duties.[40] That corrupt system was destroyed by the early nineteenth-century 'economical' reformers, but investors shifted from British government stock to foreign investment and the City found a new raison d'être in servicing the booming world economy. Its interests lay not in industry, nor even investment per se, but in trading in money (and in any other commodity in which it could make a market). The greatest gains were realised outside Britain rather than within it.

The City's priority gradually became clear as the nineteenth century progressed: to maximise the scope of the international economy. This entailed free trade, free markets in money, goods and capital, and above all the preservation of the value of sterling as an earnest of

Britain's financial integrity. These goals made good sense, both for the City's profits and for the country's balance of payments. Furthermore, trade often flowed to areas opened up by British investment. But the City's objectives were divorced from, and increasingly conflicted with, the demands of a separate and struggling sector of British capitalism – productive industry – where a policy of selective tariffs and flexible exchange rates backed by restructuring investment might have been desirable. And its hold over national life was aided by the fact that City, Bank and Treasury were peopled by a small, well-acquainted elite who usually came through the funnels of the major public schools and Oxbridge. Thus, Britain *was* a capitalist country, but one dominated to a unique degree by 'commercial capitalism'[41] and run by 'gentlemanly capitalists' who had little interest in modernising the 'competitive capitalism' of British industry.

The effect of 'catch-up' on an economy that was never radically industrialised, and whose most precocious sector was finance, explains much of the British economic performance. (Why the old practices were so tenacious is another question – to which some possible answers will be offered in due course.) What needs emphasis here is that the British evaded rather than confronted the challenge of new industrial rivals. Britain responded to competition 'not by modernizing her economy, but by exploiting the remaining possibilities of her traditional situation'.[42] In the late nineteenth century, as industrialisation spread and a truly international economy emerged, British exports moved away from the developed markets of Europe and North America to concentrate on countries in Asia, Australasia and Latin America which lacked their own industries in textiles, iron or steel and which were already exporting their own food and raw materials to Britain. And, with its strong pre-existing financial sector, Britain was well-placed to act as banker, shipper and insurer of the new world economy.[43]

This pattern was formalised by Depression, World War and Cold War. In the 1930s the open, multilateral world economy fragmented into several semiclosed economic blocs, tied to the major currencies. As the world's major trader and investor, Britain was particularly hard hit. But it made the best of the situation by consolidating relations with its closest trading and financial partners. The principle of free trade – open access to the British market for virtually all foreign goods – was now abandoned in favour of protective tariffs. But preferentially lower tariff rates were accorded to countries of the British Empire ('imperial preference'). An embryonic sterling area also began to emerge, embracing those countries who traded heavily with Britain and kept their currencies pegged to sterling. From 1939 this was rein-forced by formal exchange controls which continued after the war was over. The Sterling Area overlapped with the Empire but was by no means coterminous – Canada, for instance, was outside, while coun-tries in Latin America and Scandinavia were included. Nevertheless, the increased importance of the Empire to Britain was striking. During the interwar years it attracted far more new British foreign investment than nonimperial countries – a contrast with the pre-1914 story – and between 1913 and 1938 the Empire's share of British exports rose from 22 per cent to 47 per cent.[44] The Empire/Commonwealth and the Sterling Area became the framework for British economic policy from the 1930s to the 1960s – a privileged market for goods and capital which insulated an increasingly backward economy from inter-national competition. The collapse of this framework by the 1960s and the difficulties of British accommodation in a new one – the European Community – were at the heart of the economic malaise from which Britain has still not recovered.

None of this denies the genuine growth of Britain's economy dur-ing this century. In 1950 British industry produced twice as much as in 1913 and in the period from the mid nineteenth century to 1970 the gross domestic product (GDP) grew *on average* at nearly 2 per cent each year. Average incomes are now more than three times what they were in 1900 and the real wages of manual workers have doubled every thirty years during the century. But, although Britain grew, other economies grew faster, gradually overtaking Britain as an indus-trial producer and squeezing its share of the world's wealth. This re-duced Britain's capacity to maintain large armaments and safeguard its foreign commitments. Often the mechanism whereby diminishing wealth was translated into reduced power was via the balance of pay-ments. For most of the nineteenth and early twentieth centuries Bri-tain ran a deficit on visible trade but offset this by a surplus on invisible income from shipping, insurance and overseas investments. The only peacetime exceptions to that pattern occurred in 1919 and 1926 – both aberrant years because of immediate postwar commit-ments and then the General Strike. But from 1931 the country ran persistent peacetime balance of payments deficits, reflecting both its weakening competitive position industrially and the reduction of its invisible earnings. Frequently it was pressure on the balance of pay-ments and especially on sterling which hobbled defence policy – re-tarding rearmament in the 1930s, helping force decisions to withdraw from India and Palestine in 1947–8 and from 'east of Suez' in 1968, and bringing the Suez operation to an abrupt end in November 1956.

Thus it is clear that in a broad sense wealth does determine power. Britain's declining ability to shape world affairs owes much to the diminution in its relative economic strength. Yet the latter was no steady, inexorable slide from 1900. Had it been, arguably, Britain's decline would have come much more quickly because many of the problems of economic uncompetitiveness were apparent in the early years of this century, as Britain's especially poor growth figures indicate (table 1.3). What distorted the ruthless logic of the international market was the effect of two world wars.

Table 1.3 Relative growth of GDP per man-year, 1873–1973

	Annual percentage growth rates					
	UK	USA	France	Germany	Italy	Japan
1873–1899	1.2	1.9	1.3	1.5	0.3	1.1
1899–1913	0.5	1.3	1.6	1.5	2.5	1.8
1913–1924	0.3	1.7	0.8	−0.9	−0.1	3.2
1924–1937	1.0	1.4	1.4	3.0	1.8	2.7
1937–1951	1.0	2.3	1.7	1.0	1.4	−1.3
1951–1964	2.3	2.5	4.3	5.1	5.6	7.6
1964–1973	2.6	1.6	4.6	4.4	5.0	8.4
1873–1973	1.2	1.8	2.0	2.0	2.4	2.6

(Source: Matthews et al. 1982: 31)

It is customary to focus on their deleterious effects for Britain, and rightly so. The country lost nearly 15 per cent of its total assets in 1914–18 and nearly 28 per cent of what remained in 1939–45. So great was this decline 'that over a period of nearly 40 years from the beginning of World War I the total real wealth of the United Kingdom scarcely increased at all – a phenomenon that must have few parallels in the history of an advanced economy'.[45] In both wars, the USA was the prime economic beneficiary. Yet, remembering that power is relative, we can see that the wars were not uniformly disastrous for Britain. Tables 1.1 and 1.2 show how both conflicts retarded the German economic challenge to Britain's position, while Japan, an economic beneficiary of the First, was seriously damaged by the Second. Indeed because of the vast devastation wrought by the war on all of continental Europe, including Germany and the USSR, around 1950 Britain was probably second only to the USA in total GNP.[46] It

was not until the late 1950s that economic recovery and open international trade produced a competitive Western economic market of the
sort not seen since 1913. In this context the root problems of Britain's
uncompetitive industry came to the fore again with renewed urgency,
as the relative growth figures indicate (table 1.3).

Thus, the timing of events is as important as their causes. The parameters of power comprise more than economic strength. In particular, we need to look more closely at the rhythms of war, peace and
international rivalry.

RIVALS

Power is relative. Britain's strength in the half-century after 1815
depended partly on its own resources but also on the weakness of its
opponents. Such weakness was unusual – a far cry from the struggles
against Spain and France in the days of Philip II, Louis XIV and Napoleon. Moreover, it proved only a brief hiatus. From the late nineteenth century Britain faced a wider range of enemies, no longer
confined to Europe, and with greater military strength. They would
eventually capitalise on new technologies of warfare to render its
'moat defensive' irrelevant and erode its independence.

Contrary to common belief, 'European peace in the nineteenth
century did not derive to any great degree from Britain's maintaining a
continental balance of power'.[47] It owed far more to the exhaustion of
Europe after two decades of war and the satisfaction of all the continental powers with the ensuing peace – except for defeated France,
which was isolated. In trying to avoid further horrific wars, the five
major powers – Austria, Britain, France, Prussia and Russia – looked
beyond a mere balance of military might. They consulted regularly
together in what became known as 'the Concert of Europe' to maintain the territorial settlement of 1815 or at least to try to ensure that
changes, such as the creation of Belgium in 1830, took place by agreement rather than force.[48] Rather than the Pax Britannica sustaining an
era of European peace, it was peace which sustained the Pax. Indeed
Britain was almost a 'free rider' – allowed to concentrate its resources
on global expansion because of the European equilibrium.[49] When
continental states chose once more to use war as an instrument of
policy – with the unification of Italy and Germany in the 1860s –
Britain could do little to affect the outcome.

These wars revealed the limits of British military power. The country's great strength lay in its navy, transformed from wooden sailing ships to steampowered ironclads by the 1860s. Lord Palmerston justly boasted that 'diplomacy and protocols are very good things, but there are no better peace-keepers than well-appointed three-deckers'.[50] Yet it was also Palmerston who admitted that 'ships sailing on the sea cannot stop armies on the land'.[51] Seapower could be used to real effect in areas adjacent to the oceans, from Portugal to China, particularly where there were few hostile vessels in the offing, but the Royal Navy was impotent in the great crises in the interior of Europe, such as the revolutions of 1848–9 or Bismarck's wars of 1864–70. Moreover, these conflicts effected a military revolution on the continent. The new 'Prussian way of war'[52] – conscript armies, superior firepower, a centralised General Staff and railways for rapid mobility – was gradually emulated by the other continental powers. But in Britain conscription remained politically unacceptable, and as a military force 'Britain was simply not in the same league as the major continental powers'.[53] In 1871 Lord Salisbury estimated that whereas the Austrians and Germans could each put over a million men into the field and the Russians nearly 1.5 million, Britain's 'utmost strength . . . for the purpose. . . of foreign action' was 100,000.[54] Little wonder that Bismarck reportedly scoffed that if the British army landed on the German coast he would send the local police force to arrest it.[55]

Thus, in part because of geopolitics, in part because of policy, the military power of Victorian Britain was of limited use in deciding continental quarrels. By 1871 Bismarck's new German empire was the greatest military power on the continent, dominating Central Europe. Disraeli called the Franco–Prussian war 'a greater political event than the French revolution. . . . The balance of power has been entirely destroyed, and the country which suffers most. . . is England'.[56] Moreover, by the late nineteenth century the balance of forces globally was also shifting against Britain. After the post-Napoleonic interlude, European imperial rivalries had been renewed with the scramble for Africa in the 1880s and 1890s and the attempted partition of China at the end of the century. Britain's naval supremacy disappeared. In 1883 the Royal Navy possessed thirty-eight battleships; the rest of the world had forty. By 1897 Britain was outnumbered, sixty-two against ninety-six.[57] By this time the Russian empire had spread across Asia to the Pacific and the borders of India. And new powers were emerging outside Europe to contest the European dominance of world affairs. Japan industrialised and built up its armaments, defeating China in 1894–5 and, more strikingly, Russia in 1904–5. Even more important, the

United States had survived the trauma of civil war in 1861–5. Instead of two separate and rival states vying for control of the American continent, a united, if federal, government held sway from the Atlantic to the Pacific – a distance equivalent to that from the Pyrenees to the Urals. Already in 1866 the French economist Michel Chevalier was urging Europe to unify in the face of the 'political colossus that has been created on the other side of the Atlantic' because 'within thirty years North America will be a rival to Europe, competing with her in everything'.[58]

In the first half of the twentieth century Britain tried to defend a global position consolidated after the Napoleonic wars at a time when the continent was stable and at peace. Rivals now were numerous. The old fears of French hegemony had not disappeared and were particularly significant in the 1920s and 1960s. Outside Europe the Japanese challenge was acute in the 1930s and early 1940s. But the main threats were threefold. Within Europe the status quo was challenged by Germany's economic power and its bids for a continental empire – the root cause of two devastating wars in which the old Europe committed suicide. Outside Europe the fundamental challenge, albeit peaceful, came from America, Britain's rival for global economic leadership. And in the wings Russia played a Janus-like role – half European, half Asiatic – a threat to Britain's Indian empire in the early part of the century, an imperial power in Europe itself for four decades after the Second World War.

The first German bid for hegemony, in 1914–18, was repulsed but at great cost, not just in lives and wealth but also through the shift of power to the Pacific, as Japan and particularly America were confirmed as major naval and economic powers. Moreover, Germany was not crushed and its bitter resentment formed the seed of a future conflict. This found fertile soil in the chaos of Eastern and Southeastern Europe where the collapse of the Habsburg empire left a patchwork of unstable, feuding successor states, many with German minorities. Equally important was the fact that while two of the great Eastern empires – the Habsburgs and the Ottomans – had collapsed in the war, the third – the Romanov empire across Russia and Asia – survived revolution and civil war to re-emerge under new Bolshevik leadership. In future this would pose a double danger for Britain – the old geopolitical rivalries in southern Asia were now coupled with the ideological challenge of a power ostensibly bent on world revolution.

The second European war grew out of the first – part of a thirty years war for German hegemony.[59] Yet 'round two' assumed a more menacing form for Britain because of the latest revolution in military technology. In the 1900s the main German challenge to Britain had been by sea; in the 1930s the bomber replaced the battleship as *the* strategic weapon. Now geography was no longer a major British asset: in the air-age an enemy could simply leap-frog the Channel. 'The old frontiers are gone', warned Stanley Baldwin, soon to become Britain's Prime Minister, in 1934. 'When you think of the defence of England you no longer think of the chalk cliffs of Dover; you think of the Rhine'.[60] Indeed Britain was peculiarly vulnerable to the new weapon because the pre-eminent position of London – centre of government, finance, trade and transportation, home for a fifth of the country's population – made it a more significant target than anywhere else in Europe. Not only was seapower less important for British security, it was also less effective in protecting Britain's empire and trade. Heavily-armed battleships, designed for set-piece engagements between rival fleets, were now vulnerable from below and from above. In 1917 and again in 1941–2 Germany's submarines nearly severed Britain's Atlantic lifelines, while the importance of naval airpower was dramatically demonstrated in December 1941 when Britain's only two capital ships guarding her Asian empire, the *Prince of Wales* and the *Repulse*, went down in two hours before Japanese torpedo-bombers.

In 1940–2 the European and global threats and the end of the sea-power era conjoined in the great crisis of British power. In the decade before 1914 the global challengers had been kept at bay as Britain concentrated on Germany. The war of 1914–18, though involving the Middle East and sporadically East Asia, was primarily a European conflict. The war of 1939–45 took a very different course. First, in 1940 Hitler defeated France and overwhelmed western Europe, achieving in six weeks a continental empire that had eluded the Kaiser in four years of fighting. Isolated, Britain was dependent to a far greater extent than in 1914–18 on the USA and, after Hitler turned east in 1941, the Soviet Union. Secondly, Italy and Japan took advantage of the collapse of Europe to press their own claims for empire in North Africa and East Asia respectively, each of which threatened central interests of a beleaguered Britain. To recover their position in both areas the British were also reliant on the United States.[61]

By 1945 Germany's second bid for hegemony had ended in disaster, but Hitler had brought the old Europe down in ruins around him. Such was the extent of his early successes that he had, in effect, called the superpowers into existence to redress the balance of the Old World. At the end of the war the American and Soviet armed forces each totalled between 11 and 12 million men, more than double those of Britain. American troops occupied Japan and western Germany, while the Red Army's victory over the Nazis had brought it control of much of east and southeast Europe as well as eastern Germany. Yet Britain was still a major power in the post-war world, third in military and industrial terms to the USA and USSR even in the early 1950s. Had the world reverted to the pattern of the previous post-war era, with Russian and American withdrawal, Britain's eclipse would not have been so complete. But out of the war came bitter Soviet–American rivalry, over the division of Europe, the future of Germany and the ideological struggle between capitalism and communism. This time, then, these two extra-European powers maintained vast military establishments. Once they had 'decided' to do so, the great disparity in resources between them and Britain told against the latter in a way it had not after the war of 1914–18, even though the British kept their armed forces 'artificially' high until the end of the 1950s by the unprecedented device of peacetime conscription. In 1953, Britain's peak post-war year, its armed forces totalled 900,000 compared with 3.5 million for the USA and an estimated 4.75 million for the USSR.[62]

The Cold War – the absence of stable peace and the spiralling Soviet–American rivalry – was one reason why the British could not maintain their international position. But equally important was the revolution in military technology associated with nuclear weapons. Given the Soviet conventional superiority and the growing fear of war over Berlin, the British could not hope to stop a possible Red Army advance. They had little choice but to rely on the American monopoly of the atomic bomb, developed at the end of the war, as their main deterrent. The NATO alliance of 1949 reflected this new strategy. But later that year the USSR tested its own atomic device. Geography, Britain's great ally in the seapower age, told against it in the nuclear age even more than in the 1930s. A small, densely-populated island, it was more vulnerable to nuclear devastation than the continent-wide superpowers. A few bombs could effectively finish it off, and, unlike the USA, it was well within range of Soviet airpower. Although Britain tried initially to maintain its own nuclear capability, since the 1960s its small strategic nuclear force has been US-made and the fundamental principle of its defence policy has been to shelter under NATO's American nuclear umbrella.

The other main orbit for modern British foreign policy has been the European Community (EC). Since its creation in 1958 this has become the framework for western European economic and political cooperation. Yet Britain did not join at the beginning and its belated efforts to do so were frustrated by France: in the 1950s and 1960s the old Anglo–French rivalry was renewed in the battle over European integration. Initial British reluctance and France's subsequent veto ensured that Britain did not join the EC until 1973, *after* its basic shape was determined – a fundamental disadvantage for Britain ever since. The enlargement of Europe south in the 1980s and east in the 1990s shifted its centre of gravity farther away from Britain, while the renewed process of 'deepening', through economic and monetary union, accelerated the erosion of national sovereignty. Like it or not – and many Britons do not – the European Community is now a fact of British life, setting the framework for much of domestic and foreign policy.

Both NATO and the EC were in part attempts to solve the 'German problem'. A divided Germany with its western part integrated into the economy of its neighbours constituted a de facto peace settlement for a generation. Since the mid-1960s Germany has been the major continental partner in NATO and its efficient, export-led economy has dominated western Europe, but this revival took place within the constraints provided by NATO and the EC. By the end of the 1980s, however, the Soviet empire in eastern Europe had disintegrated, the future of NATO was uncertain as Soviet troops pulled back, and German unification proceeded apace. The potential dominance of the German economy seemed even greater with the addition of 17 million people and new access to markets and labour across eastern Europe. For Britain the German problem had been re-opened, bringing the century around in full circle, except that now the German challenge was primarily economic and Britain was in no position to compete. In 1989 two-thirds of its substantial deficit on trade in manufactured goods within the EC was with the Federal Republic.[63]

To sum up: in an era of seapower the British had enjoyed greater security than most continental powers, thanks to their insular position and strong navy. Nevertheless, Britain could never be indifferent to radical changes in the European balance, and its high-Victorian sense of security and power owed much to the unusual stability of the Continent at that time. In the twentieth century, new technologies of airpower and then nuclear weapons placed Britain in unprecedented potential danger. At the same time new foes emerged to contest its extended international position, proving especially menacing when they challenged simultaneously, as in 1940–2. While Germany hammered away at the old Eurocentric order from within, Japan, Russia and, more insidiously, America pushed it over from without. Both world wars, particularly the second, greatly accelerated the changes in the technology of warfare and in the relative positions of the great powers. And after 1945 the Cold War and nuclear arms race hastened

Britain's eclipse by, and dependence on, powers with greater resources than itself.

Yet this discussion of international rivalries points us to another consideration. In its heyday, Britain did not stand alone. The rise and fall of Britain's empire constitutes another changing parameter of power.

EMPIRE

It was the empire which made Britain great. At the beginning of this century the United Kingdom had only 42 million people, whereas the United States had 76 million and Russia 133 million. When one added in the population of Britain's overseas territories, however, the arithmetic was very different. At its peak in 1933 the British Empire covered nearly a quarter of the earth's land surface and embraced a similar proportion of its population, over 500 million in all. France, with the next-largest empire if one excludes Russia, accounted for only 9 per cent of the earth's land surface and 108 million of its people.[64] At times of crisis the Empire could be a vast resource of material and manpower. In the First World War Britain mobilised 6.7 million men, but 3 million more came from the Empire, nearly half of them from India.[65] In 1939–45 the imperial contribution was even more substantial: while Britain mobilised 5.9 million, the so-called 'white dominions' – Canada, Australia, New Zealand and South Africa – raised 2 million and India 2.5 million.[66] With such statistics in mind, some historians have chastised British leaders for 'losing' the Empire. Correlli Barnett, for example, argues that, had the British not lost their nerve, they could have held India by 'resolute autocracy'.[67] Yet that is to miss the tenuous nature of British imperial power.

Britain's global base as a great power was very different from that of its rivals. In the late nineteenth century the concept of a 'world power' was much in vogue, meaning a state with the interests and the capability to act on a global scale. On these criteria the USA and Russia, both vast continental empires that survived the crises of civil war in 1861–5 and 1917–21, had the potential to be world powers. In 1914–45 Germany tried and ultimately failed by military means to establish its own continental base for world power through domination of Europe, though in the process it helped make real the world-power potential of America and Russia. The only existing world power in the late nineteenth century was Britain but, in the words of the German commentator Constantin Frantz in 1882, it was really 'an artificial worldpower' (eine künstliche Weltmacht), 'because the territorial basis of this power was just a European country'. Its resource-base lay across the seas in far-flung colonies which lacked a natural unity. They were only held to Britain 'through the threads of the fleet, and these threads could all be broken or cut'.[68]

Britain's lack of a contiguous empire was its basic weakness as a world power, but almost as significant was the diversity of its colonial possessions. Although not acquired 'in a fit of absence of mind',[69] the empire did emerge piecemeal and haphazardly, with little coordination from London. It was a ragbag of possessions – leftovers in Canada and the Caribbean from the pre-1776 American colonies; spoils, particularly in India, from the wars against France; creeping imperialism in West Africa as weak tribal government caved in before the advance of European commerce and culture; pre-emptive strikes in south and east Africa in the late nineteenth century to stop European rivals; the post-1918 carve-up of the old Ottoman empire in the Middle East.

Nor did Britain 'own' these diverse 'possessions'. In most cases British control was skin-deep, although the forms varied from place to place.[70] In colonies settled by white emigrants from Britain, successive governments in London generally followed the path of ever-greater devolution. The pattern was pioneered in Canada, where, after disturbances in the late 1830s, it was decided to transfer some areas of domestic administration to an elected government, while 'reserving' defence and foreign policy for the imperial authorities. This principle of 'diarchy' – a division between transferred and reserved powers – was applied to the other white settler colonies in Australasia and southern Africa during the late nineteenth and early twentieth centuries. By 1931, when the British Parliament's remaining authority was abrogated, the Dominions, as the white settler colonies were known, were effectively independent in all domestic affairs. Increasingly the main bond linking them with Britain was that of loyalty to the country from which many of them or their families had only recently come in the great waves of migration in the 1900s. This was a potent force in mobilising support for Britain in two world wars. In the 1930s, for instance, perhaps 80 per cent of Australians were of British stock and 74 per cent of Canadians were of English or Scots origin.[71]

The policy of measured devolution was adopted in colonies where there was a large British settler community which had the capacity for fiscal independence. Non-white colonies were treated differently because, until well after 1945 in many cases, they were regarded as incapable of self-government. There, more autocratic and paternalistic methods were employed, with an unelected government headed by a British Governor exercising certain devolved powers under supervision from London. Much of the dependent empire was run in this way as Crown Colonies. Even where there seemed no great benefit to Britain – as in West Africa, the West Indies or the Falklands – London hung on for fear that a rival power would acquire them or because they lacked a natural ethnic or political viability of their own. But at the same time the British tried to minimise the costs. The result was an attitude of what might charitably be called benevolent neglect, as London turned a blind eye to the problems of poverty and underdevelopment, except and until, as in the Caribbean in the 1930s, they exploded in serious disorder. This was cut-price empire – Britain was getting little out, but putting little in.

Between the Dominions and the Crown Colonies stands the special case of India. There the British succeeded the old Mughal emperors and their tributaries as the paramount power.[72] In 'British India' they ruled directly through a European-led civil service. In some six hundred princely states, covering a third of the sub-continent – some tiny, others, like Hyderabad, as large as England – they ruled indirectly through hereditary lords and princes who handled all but defence and foreign policy under the eye of a British 'resident'. Even in British India, however, imperial rule was only superficial. At its peak in 1900 the European (or Covenanted) elite of the Indian Civil Service numbered only 1,300, in a population of around a quarter of a billion. British influence depended on alliances with local landed and commercial leaders and on the western-educated Indians who filled the clerical grades of British administration. They mediated between the British raj and the lower levels of provincial and village society – effecting British wishes, collecting revenue and gathering intelligence. Despite early Victorian waves of evangelical and reforming zeal, the prime object of British rule was not to Anglicise or even 'improve' India. As elsewhere in the Empire, Indians were left to their own religious, social and economic devices, except where order was threatened or British interests jeopardised.

In the case of India those interests were considerable.[73] At the beginning of the century Britain provided sixty per cent of India's imports, particularly textiles, machinery and iron and steel products, and used the surplus to balance its deficits on trade with continental Europe and North America. Even more important was the Indian army. In 1914 its strength of 160,000 fighting troops, one-third of them British, represented half Britain's peacetime worldwide military strength – essential manpower for a country that did not have conscription. Cost as well as numbers was important. India, in Lord Salisbury's phrase, was regarded 'as an English barrack in the Oriental seas from which we may draw any number of troops without paying for them'.[74] More precisely, the general principle was that the Government of India paid out of its own tax revenues for the peacetime army in India and for the basic costs of troops serving overseas. In this way the Indian army was employed repeatedly in a great arc from China to East Africa around the turn of the century. During the 1914–18 war nearly one million men were sent overseas, half of them to spearhead Britain's effort in the Middle East.

In retrospect, the great British empire seems something of a con trick. How could so many be ruled for so long by so few? There *were* forces promoting genuine acceptance of British rule – the ties of kinship in the Dominions, the networks of clientage created in India and elsewhere among indigenous elites. Yet empire rests ultimately on force or the threat of force and for much of the nineteenth century this could be exerted easily through the superiority of British military technology.[75] Here is another instance of the axiom that power is relative. The Royal Navy may have faced growing European challengers, but it needed only a few steam-driven gunboats to overwhelm the Chinese junks and open up that country to European trade in mid-century. The British army may have been irrelevant to the European balance of power in the 1860s but it was quite sufficient to handle most threats on the periphery of empire. At the battle of Omdurman in 1898 General Kitchener won control of the Sudan with the loss of only 368 men. His adversary, the Khalifa, lost 11,000, massacred by 3,500 shells and half a million bullets. As Hilaire Belloc's 'modern traveller' comforted himself that same year:

Whatever happens we have got
The Maxim Gun, and they have not.[76]

Underpinning superior force in the non-white empire was racial prestige. Lord Curzon, Viceroy of India in 1903, would not allow the hymn 'Onward, Christian Soldiers' to be sung at the Imperial Durbar because it contained the potentially subversive lines 'Crowns and thrones may perish, Kingdoms rise and wane'.[77] In 1890 Lord Lugard, a leading colonial administrator of the period, clouted a native servant in East Africa for a misdemeanour. When the man made as if to retaliate, Lugard smashed his eye in, believing that any lesser response would have been disastrous. Lugard explained that

no one who has not been in Africa or India can fully appreciate the full force of this. The native looks on it as a sacrilege to touch a Sahib, and also expects little short of death from the Sahib if he should try conclusions. To this prestige the white man owes his ascendancy, and it *must* at any price be maintained, just as one would with a brute beast.[78]

This incident is perhaps extreme. But most British policymakers, even those remote from imperial administration, knew that British power rested on the 'intangibles' of prestige, fear and credibility. When Sir Alexander Cadogan, Permanent Under-Secretary at the Foreign Office, rebelled against Hitler's terms for Czechoslovakia in September 1938, he noted in his diary: 'I *know* we . . . are in no condition to fight: but I'd rather be beat than dishonoured. How can we look any foreigner in the face after this? How can we hold Egypt, India and the rest?'.[79]

Throughout the empire, then, the British were generally a paramount not a dominant power – controlling the upper echelons of government to extract revenue and safeguard economic and strategic interests, rather than trying to reshape indigenous societies. Dominion devolution, more-or-less benign neglect in the Crown colonies and the superstructure of the Raj all testify in their different ways to this principle. Indeed it has become conventional to argue that the British were reluctant imperialists and that much of the Empire was acquired almost as a by-product of the larger process of British economic expansion around the world. The degree of imperial control depended significantly on the internal cohesion of the societies affected by British outreach.[80] In some places, such as India or Egypt, this expansion resulted in formal political rule. Elsewhere, for instance in Latin America, where local polities were more stable, the consequence was only 'informal' empire, whereby British interests were protected by agreements with supportive clients, reinforced, as in China, with the judicious use of force. Formal empire was more costly and burdensome, entailing British troops and administrators, and so 'British policy followed the principle of extending control informally if possible and formally if necessary'.[81] Or, as Lord Palmerston put it with typical directness: 'All we want is trade and land is not necessary for trade; we can carry on commerce on ground belonging to other people'.[82]

Yet this is not to imply that the empire had a clear economic rationale. Britain was of course a major trading nation, unusually dependent among great powers on world trade for its markets, raw materials and invisible income. For instance, in 1913 imports accounted for all its consumption of cotton and copper, 90 per cent of its tin, 80 per cent of its wheat and nearly half its meat and dairy products.[83] Yet that did not mean that the empire itself was essential to the British economy. It accounted for no more than a third of

Britain's exports and a quarter of its imports in the early twentieth century, attracting only a quarter of British investment (1865–1914) and one-third of its emigrants.[84] With this in mind, some historians have gone on to argue that the defence of empire was a significant net burden for late-Victorian Britain – that, instead of supporting Britain, the colonies were actually being subsidised by it.[85] They have estimated that in the period 1860–1912 the average Briton was paying nearly ten times as much for defence as his counterpart in Canada, Australia, New Zealand and South Africa, and over eleven times the amount paid by every Indian. On a European scale, Britons were paying double the average Frenchman or German.[86]

These claims are the subject of lively debate. For instance, France and Germany had conscription, so the money costs of military manpower were much less than those for Britain's professional forces. And what of the larger benefits, very difficult to quantify, of the British presence in protecting trade and investment and keeping open the sea-lanes for Britain's essential imports?[87] On the other hand, against the claim that, say, British rule in India was vital to maintain an orderly framework for trade and investment, historians of India can point to that region's capacity for lively and diversified foreign trade before British monopoly became a reality.[88] At root in this continuing argument is a fundamental issue: how far was the British empire a case study of the dictum that 'military power is usually needed to acquire and protect wealth'.[89] The cost-benefit analysis of British imperialism is only in its infancy. What is clear is that the economic utility of the empire and imperial defence is not to be taken for granted.

Without prejudging the outcome of this debate, two points can be made here. First, the purely economic motivations for acquiring colonies should not be exaggerated. Against the 'imperialism of free trade', recent historians have drawn attention to the 'authoritarian and ideological' strand of British imperialism, involving periods of deliberate empire-building, racist nationalism and calculated social control. This, after all, was the empire of Curzon, Milner and Churchill as well as that of Cobden, Gladstone and Attlee.[90] The period of mid-Victorian liberal imperialism was an interlude in a long sequence of imperial wars, sandwiched as it was between the conquest of India during the Napoleonic struggle and the scramble for Africa of the 1880s, the near-partition of China around 1900 and the division of the Ottoman empire in the First World War. Thus, in empire as in economy and foreign policy, the mid-Victorian era is not so much a benchmark as an aberration.

Secondly, whether or not empire was a burden or a benefit for the

Victorians, the costs of its defence were only 1 or 2 per cent of national income at a time when Britain was the wealthiest nation in the world and there was no serious opposition to imperial rule. In Uganda, for instance, after the southern kingdoms came under British rule in 1896, three million people were governed by an administrative structure headed by only twenty-five British officials.[91] In these circumstances it was not very burdensome to hang on to, say, the West Indies, even though their eighteenth-century value as sugar exporters had largely disappeared. Cost-benefit analysis, whether formal or instinctive, began to matter when it became harder to hold on to empire. As it took more effort to keep the natives down and the rivals out, so hard questions were asked about whether the gains of empire outweighed its mounting costs.

In the nineteenth century Britain struck out. In the twentieth century the empire struck back. In many British dependencies political organisation coalesced, both peaceful and violent, forcing concessions from the colonial authorities that progressively reduced their control over local policy and resources. The pattern of Dominion devolution was followed, more reluctantly, elsewhere as Britain tried to deal with the new forces of nationalism. The Indian case was particularly important. Fiscal autonomy, conceded in the post-war disturbances of 1919, led to a growing Indian tariff wall against British goods which helped ruin the Lancashire cotton industry, and, when war began again in 1939, London agreed to pay for the extraordinary costs of using Indian troops – resulting in a £1.3 billion British debt to India, equivalent to roughly one-fifth of Britain's GNP.[92] Meanwhile, the diffusion of military technology evened up the military imbalance between rulers and ruled. For instance, in 1946, less than half a century after Omdurman, a handful of Jewish insurgents, using seven milk churns packed with TNT, blew up the King David Hotel in Jerusalem, nerve-centre of British power in Palestine. Ninety-one died, and with them much of Britain's will to hang on to its troubled Mandate.

Relations with the white Dominions also changed. The positive ties of kinship weakened after 1945, as British migration tailed off, other nationalities flocked in and a keener sense of national identity emerged. This was true even in Australia and New Zealand – previously the most loyal of the Dominions. In South Africa the bonds had been weakened much earlier, because of the dominance of the ex-Dutch Afrikaaners, while in Canada the French community and the neighbouring USA had long exerted their own countervailing pulls. In Ireland, English rule was particularly resented, and independence for most of the country was granted after the First World War. Ireland was a unique problem because it lay on the borders of imperial and domestic politics. Irish MPs were a substantial and unsettling force in the Westminster Parliament before independence, and the place of Protestant-dominated Ulster within the United Kingdom became a bitter domestic- and foreign-policy issue from the late 1960s as it became locked into a new spiral of terror and counter-terror.

The growing centrifugalism of empire in the twentieth century was exacerbated by the resumption of great-power rivalry. The scramble for Africa was the first indication of how international relations had reverted to 'normal'.[93] The great wars in the first half of the twentieth century required far greater exertions by Britain to safeguard global possessions, particularly the second because it was truly a global crisis. Japan's victories in 1941–2 were especially damaging, not just because much of British Southeast Asia was temporarily lost but because Japan had exposed the myth of white invincibility. In February 1942 130,000 British troops *surrendered* at Singapore. 'The British Empire in the Far East depended on prestige', wrote the Australian minister to China. 'This prestige has been completely shattered'.[94] And the ensuing Cold War further undermined the empire. Russia and China supplied crucial modern weaponry to opponents of Britain such as Nasser in Egypt or the communists in Malaya and, in the 1960s, Indonesia. Meanwhile, the Americans, vying with communism as they saw it for the hearts and minds of the Third World, became more vocal in their critique of colonialism, pressing the British hard over India in 1942 or Egypt in 1956, and casting doubt from their side on the morality of imperialism. This changed international climate chilled Britain's sense of imperial mission. In 1853 Lord Grey, a former Colonial Secretary, spoke for most Victorian politicians in affirming that the 'superiority of the British Crown . . . assists in diffusing amongst millions of the human race the benefits of Christianity and civilisation'.[95] By the 1940s, however, non-white inferiority was no longer axiomatic. The post-war Labour Government conceded Indian independence – a momentous precedent – and transmuted the British Empire into a Commonwealth of international equals.

Formal empire therefore 'represented only a particular phase in the ever-changing relationship of Europe with the rest of the world'.[96] In the British case it was made necessary by the temporary weakness of local power structures. It was made possible by Britain's vast superiority in military technology and by the brief absence of serious great-power rivals. Acting as justification were underlying notions of racial superiority and 'the white man's burden'. Yet the British never 'owned' the Empire, they merely utilised some of its resources, relying heavily on local collaborators, and its value to them depended on a delicate balance of burden and benefits. As the twentieth century progressed, indigenous political power made it harder to exploit the empire's resources. At the same time local protest and international rivalry made it more expensive to hang on. The British were not simply pushed out, they often pulled out because the game of formal empire was no longer worth the candle – as it had been in the Victorian era. As with Britain's economic and international leadership, the British Empire was a product of peculiar and ephemeral circumstances.

'IN THE LONG RUN . . .'

To a significant degree, then, the changes in Britain's place in the world over the past century should not be surprising. Instead of being mesmerised by the trappings of power at Victoria's Diamond Jubilee in 1897, we can see that the underlying realities were less impressive. Britain was a great power in the late Victorian era, but power is relative and that position reflected the weakness of others as well as Britain's own strengths. Economic leadership was largely the result of an early start and was compromised from the beginning by Britain's idiosyncratic industrialisation. The Pax Britannica was the product of a brief era in which Europe was unusually stable and seapower was the dominant military technology. The empire rested not on armed might but on a delicate balancing act of coercion and persuasion, all done on the cheap at a time when rival European empires had temporarily been eclipsed. When other nations industrialised, great powers re-emerged and empire became harder to retain, in consequence Britain's position changed for the worst. It was unlikely that a nation with only 2 per cent of the world's population could control over a fifth of its land surface, maintain half its warships and account for 40 per cent of its trade in manufactured goods for very long.

Re-stating the problem in this way may help make Britain's twentieth-century metamorphosis less surprising. To a considerable extent what happened was determined by the changing parameters of power – wealth, rivals and empire. Yet to say that some measure of decline was almost inevitable in the long run does not tell us very much. As Keynes observed of economists' penchant for long-term cycles: 'this *long run* is a misleading guide to current affairs. *In the long run*, we are all dead. Economists set themselves too easy, too useless a task if in tempestuous seasons they can only tell us that when the storm is long past the ocean is flat again'.[97]

In fact, the story of Britain's 'decline' as a great power is not a steady twentieth-century slide. Economically the two wars weakened Britain's position compared with that of the USA, while in the short-term, at least, improving it relative to Germany and, after 1945, Japan. In military terms, Britain was unquestionably the leading European power for a decade or so after 1945, achieving a nuclear capability years earlier than France. Likewise, the story of the 'end of empire' in the twentieth century is not simple. Britain's colonial empire reached its largest extent not under Victoria but through the carve-up of the Middle East after the First World War. And the late 1940s, usually identified with Indian independence, actually saw a determined reassertion of British *informal* imperialism through financial controls and economic development in Africa and the Middle East.

Although this chapter has highlighted some intrinsic weaknesses of British power, that does not mean that Britain should be dismissed as an international force after 1918 or even 1945. On the contrary, because power in most cases could be exerted cheaply in the mid-nineteenth century, there was a good deal of 'slack' to be utilised when Britain's position was challenged in the twentieth. What follows, therefore, is not a history of inexorable decline, but an account of how a major power with intrinsic weaknesses *and* under-utilised potential tried to consolidate and retain its exposed position. And in that story the decade after 1945 is of particular moment for understanding where Britain stands today.

In other words, how Britain reacted to its international predicament mattered as much as the predicament itself. All this leads us on to policy. Take the relationship between wealth and military power, for instance. In 1938 the USA produced 31 per cent of the world's manufactured goods (table 1.1) yet in 1940 its armed forces by size ranked twentieth in the world, with the Dutch in nineteenth place.[98] In the 1980s the Soviet Union, despite its primitive industrial base, maintained itself as a rival superpower by choosing to devote some 15 per cent of GNP to defence – more than double the American proportion.[99] In other words, there has to be a decision to translate economic strength into military strength: the relationship between wealth and power is not automatic. The same is true for Britain. At certain points in their twentieth-century history (and not exclusively in wartime) the British chose to divert a much larger proportion of national wealth (including manpower) into military forms of power. This involved decisions about taxation, borrowing and military conscription.

These were complex *political* choices, impinging on domestic as well as foreign policy.

If we bear in mind that the story of Britain's diminishing international influence is part of a wider pattern of the rise and decline of a Eurocentric world, we can see other ways in which policy choices were important. The contrast with post-1945 France is particularly instructive. Both countries experienced economic, international and imperial decline at much the same time. The British responded by constructing a close alliance with the Americans and only joined the European Community belatedly and reluctantly. The French, by contrast, were assertive anti-Americans and calculating pioneers of the EC. Obviously geography and language explain the differences in part, but the two sets of responses were not pre-determined. Again we enter the realm of political choice.

Thus, the broad parameters of Britain's international position are clear and they form a *necessary* part of any explanation of what happened to the country's place in the world during this century. Yet, by themselves, they are not *sufficient*. For one thing, the story itself is more complex than one of linear decline. Furthermore, the determinants of power were mediated through the choices of policymakers. Delineating the pattern of the story – the precise interaction of power and policy – will be the task of the chronological chapters of the book. But first we must look more closely at what is meant by 'policy'.

REFERENCES

1.   Frankel 1979: 101
2.   Reynolds 1989b: 483
3.   Berridge and Young 1988
4.   Bayly 1989: 13–14
5.   Fieldhouse 1973: 3
6.   Kennedy 1988: 442–3
7.   Kennedy 1983a: 169–71
8.   Marder 1961: 41
9.   Crouzet 1982: 4–8
10. Bartlett 1963: 68, 95n.
11. Ricks (ed.) 1969: 84
12. *Manchester Guardian*, 23 June 1897: 5
13. *The Daily Mail*, 23 June 1897: 5
14. Longford 1964: 549

15. Beloff 1969: 20–1
16. *The Times*, 17 July 1897, p. 13
17. T. Smith 1981: 184
18. Crouzet 1982: 1
19. Friedberg 1988: 152
20. Dilks (ed.) 1981: i, 1; Chamberlain 1988: 6
21. Kennedy 1988: xvi
22. Kennedy 1983a: 193
23. Chalmers 1985: 23–4
24. Crouzet 1982: 379
25. Abramowitz 1986: 387
26. cf. Pollard 1989: 270
27. Crafts 1985: 54–60
28. Ibid., 6–8, 69, 86
29. Coleman and Macleod 1986: 601–2
30. Wiener 1985
31. Zeitlin 1987: 173
32. Elbaum and Lazonick (eds) 1986: 3–4
33. Chandler 1980: 408; also Chandler and Daems (eds) 1980; Hannah 1976
34. Sanderson 1983: 16
35. Landes 1969: 347–8
36. Sanderson 1988: 45
37. Ackrill 1988: 69–71
38. Mowery 1986: 192–3
39. Cain and Hopkins 1986, 1987
40. O'Brien 1988a
41. Ingham 1984: 6
42. Hobsbawm 1969: 151
43. cf. Floud and McCloskey (eds) 1981: chs 1, 3, and 4
44. Drummond 1972: 18
45. Matthews et al. 1982: 129–30
46. Bairoch 1982: 301
47. Schroeder 1972: 401
48. Elrod 1976
49. Mandelbaum 1988: 357
50. Bartlett 1963: 58
51. Wilson (ed.) 1987: 11
52. McNeill 1983: 242
53. Bond 1984: 39
54. 3 Hansard, Lords, 204: 1364–5
55. Kennedy 1983a: 201
56. Ghosh 1984: 289
57. Kennedy 1983a: 209
58. Chevalier 1866: 784–5
59. cf. P. Bell 1986
60. Commons 292: 2339

61. Reynolds 1990a
62. IISS 1972: 74
63. Cutler et al. 1989: 20
64. Fieldhouse 1982: 242, 303
65. Judd and Slinn 1982: 38
66. Mansergh 1982: ii, 94
67. Barnett 1972: 143; cf. Lowe and Dockrill 1972: ii, 379
68. Frantz 1966 edn.: i, 106–7
69. Seeley 1883: 8
70. Fieldhouse 1982: chs 11–12
71. cf. Lloyd 1984: 403
72. Brown 1985
73. Tomlinson 1979
74. Ibid., 179
75. Headrick 1979; Howard 1984
76. Belloc 1970 edn.: 184
77. Mansergh 1982: i, 3
78. Hyam 1976: 158
79. Dilks (ed.) 1971: 104
80. Doyle 1986: chs 8–9
81. Gallagher and Robinson 1953: 13
82. Hyam 1976: 54
83. Harley and McCloskey 1981: 52
84. O'Brien 1988b: 166–75
85. Davis and Huttenback 1986; O'Brien 1988b
86. Davis and Huttenback 1986: 164
87. A. Porter 1988
88. Kennedy and O'Brien 1989
89. Kennedy 1988: xvi
90. Bayly 1989: 250
91. Low 1974: 29
92. Tomlinson 1979: 140
93. Doyle 1986: ch. 10
94. Thorne 1978: 206
95. B. Porter 1984: 14
96. Fieldhouse 1982: 381
97. Keynes 1971 edn.: iv, 65
98. Thorne 1986: 211–12
99. IISS 1987: 215–16

CHAPTER TWO

Policy

Books on international relations are full of such phrases as 'Britain did this' or 'the French feared that', as if whole countries and their peoples were acting with one mind and voice. Without these shorthands the process of writing would be impossible, but it is essential to pause occasionally and spell out their implications. This chapter takes a broad look at the concept of 'policymaking' over the whole century. After starting with the pressures of 'public opinion', it considers the role of 'bureaucratic politics' within Whitehall. Closer examination is reserved for the policy areas of taxation, expenditure and diplomacy whereby national wealth is translated into international power. The final section asks just how considered and rational foreign policy really is.

INFLUENCES FROM OUTSIDE GOVERNMENT

Who makes British foreign policy? The short answer, in the 1990s as in the 1890s, is 'the Executive branch of government'. Over the past four centuries, albeit erratically, the prerogatives of the monarch in governing the country have been shared with and gradually appropriated by Parliament. The conduct of foreign affairs, however, remains the undivided preserve of the Crown and its ministers – a constitutional doctrine that has been invoked, for instance, to excuse the lack of accountability of the intelligence services to Parliament.

This formal independence of the Executive in the making of foreign and defence policy stands in contrast, say, to American practice. Under the US Constitution the Senate must ratify all treaties and approve the appointment of ambassadors and heads of government departments. Both houses of Congress also have vigilant and well-staffed committees in foreign affairs and defence. Particularly since the 1930s US presidents have found ways of evading these restrictions, but the broad contrast between America and Britain remains clear. Parliament has no formal right to ratify treaties – the so-called Ponsonby rule, dating from the 1920s, is simply 'a self-denying ordinance on the part of government', allowing Parliament three weeks to debate a treaty if it wishes.[1] In contrast with the US Congress there was no foreign affairs committee in Parliament until 1979, and even thereafter its (limited) ability to investigate government policy has depended on the voluntary cooperation of ministers and civil servants. Although there have been a few occasions when a parliamentary vote has been of decisive importance in shaping foreign policy – notably in May 1940 when it brought down Neville Chamberlain – it remains true that 'Parliament is in no sense a regular participant in the [foreign-policy] process, either by right or by custom'.[2]

Nor has overseas policy usually been determined by differences between the political parties. In Britain, as elsewhere, foreign policy has frequently been represented as an issue of national security around which all patriotic citizens should close ranks. The principle of 'continuity of policy' between the parties was stated classically by the Liberal Lord Rosebery. 'Whatever our domestic differences may be at home, we should preserve a united front abroad', he declared in 1895, insisting even more forthrightly ten years later that 'the second rate foreign policy which is continuous is better than the first rate foreign policy which is not'.[3] Such continuity has been facilitated since the 1870s by a career civil service, largely untouched by the ebb and flow of elections, able to guide politicians along established grooves.

Apart from the constraints of patriotism and bureaucracy, however, the party leaderships have generally agreed on the main lines of policy. For all the anger of Radical Liberals about the Boer War and Tory imperialism in the early 1900s, the dominant party voices on foreign affairs were Liberal Imperialists such as Sir Edward Grey and R.B. Haldane, who assumed key posts in the Liberal governments of 1905–16. Likewise, between the 1940s and the 1960s Labour leaders did not differ fundamentally from their Tory counterparts on the need for Britain to remain a great world power or to maintain the value of sterling. The sharpest differences of view have generally occurred within the parties rather than between them. Arguments over tariff reform in 1903–5 wrecked Balfour's Conservative government, and the Labour party feuded interminably over unilateral nuclear disarmament in the early 1960s and early 1980s. Of the two parties, Labour has tended to be the more brittle and argumentative, whereas Tory party conferences have become notorious for their well-drilled displays of assent and adulation. In addition to the endemic nuclear debate, Labour had been split over rearmament in the 1930s, Cold War alignments in the late 1940s and the EEC from the 1960s to the early 1980s. Faced with recurrent revolts over defence spending in the 1960s, Prime Minister Harold Wilson told his backbenchers: 'Watch it. Every dog is allowed one bite, but quite a different view is taken of a dog that goes on biting all the time'.[4] His warnings had little effect. With some exceptions, such as the 'Suez Group' opposing Eden's withdrawal from Egypt in 1954–6, Labour leaders have always had much more difficulty than their Conservative counterparts in carrying their own party with them on defence and foreign policy and in maintaining their general bias towards bipartisan continuity.

What of public opinion? At the end of the nineteenth century Lord Salisbury frequently commented to the effect that 'the action of an English ministry must depend on the national feeling of the moment',[5] but this was usually for the benefit of foreign diplomats – to maintain his freedom of manoeuvre in the face of their pleas for firm British commitments. Modern scholars make a distinction between the 'mass public' and the 'informed public' – the former being the proverbial men in the street, the latter the 10 or 15 per cent of the population who follow foreign affairs in the media and express opinions through interest groups. Among the public as a whole it is notorious that foreign affairs normally seem complex, remote and unimportant. One MP in 1957 asked some of his constituents who *were* concerned about foreign policy

> which they would rather I did – endeavour to catch Mr Speaker's eye in
> the grand foreign affairs debate tomorrow or raise the question of their
> bus shelter, which is only a local problem. They told me that any fool can
> speak on foreign affairs and no doubt several would, but that if I did not
> speak about their local bus shelter, then nobody else would.[6]

Such judgements have been confirmed by opinion poll data repeatedly indicating the low salience of foreign policy for the general public.[7]

At times, however, the proportion of the population interested in and vocal about foreign affairs can expand dramatically. This is particularly true over the issue of peace or war – in August 1914, for instance, or in the 'Munich', Suez and Falklands crises of 1938, 1956 and 1982. In the twentieth century, when total war has necessitated the mobilisation of all the nation's resources and manpower, sustained public support in wartime has been essential. And even at other times it can be important, for instance to operate the unprecedented practice of peacetime conscription for some fifteen years after 1945.

Usually, however, public attitudes have much less effect on specific policies than in setting the broad ideological framework within which foreign policy must operate. This was particularly true of the League of Nations Union between the world wars, boasting over 400,000 members at the peak of its popularity in 1931,[8] which obliged successive British governments to conduct themselves in ways that did not seem egregiously at odds with the principles of collective security and national self-determination. When they failed to do so, as in the case of the Hoare–Laval pact to divide up Abyssinia in 1935, public outcry forced a rapid U-turn. Since the Second World War that kind of mass movement has been less potent, with the exception of the Campaign for Nuclear Disarmament (CND). At its height in the early 1960s and early 1980s CND obliged Tory governments to pay close attention to the packaging, if not the content, of their defence policy.

The point at which public concerns have set the tightest parameters for foreign and defence policy is over the question of public spending. Inexorably during this century governments of all political hues have accepted an obligation to divert national resources to promote the wellbeing of their citizens – health, education, social services – and not just to support the traditional function of the state, defence. This tension between national security and social security has been an important constraint on the conduct of external policy, and it has been intensified for much of the century by the party political struggle between Labour, dedicated to advancing living standards through government control of the economy, and the Conservatives, for whom empire, defence and international status have long been ideological imperatives. How this struggle has influenced decisions about the allocation of Britain's decreasing share of international wealth will be discussed in more detail later in this chapter.

Sustained non-governmental involvement in decisions usually comes not from the population at large but from a smaller group, the 'interested public'. Frequently its influence is exerted informally and discreetly, through the network of social channels available to a remarkably homogenous ruling elite who came from the same public schools (especially Eton and Harrow), attended the same universities (overwhelmingly Oxford and Cambridge) and who frequent the same few London clubs. Pressure group politics in Britain have always been more circumspect than in Washington, where organised lobbyists,

poised to mobilise their supporters across the country, have proliferated to press their concerns on Congressmen and bureaucrats. But in
the course of this century the number and activity of organised pressure groups in Britain have grown considerably. In the 1900s one
thinks of the Navy League or Tariff Reform League; in more recent
times of the Federation (later Confederation) of British Industries,
closely linked to the Tory party, and the Trades Union Congress,
Labour's principal paymaster, which exerted a powerful influence over
the Wilson and Callaghan governments in the 1960s and 1970s. In
foreign affairs such groups have occasionally played a significant role:
the National Farmers' Union reinforced Whitehall's opposition to entering the EEC in the 1950s, whereas the FBI added momentum to
the change of direction in 1961–2. And from the late 1960s the Falklands lobby in and around Parliament blocked every attempt to negotiate with Argentina over the islands, contributing substantially to the
diplomatic impasse which the Argentines tried to resolve by force in
1982.

Playing a central role in the process of influence are the mass media
– partly a two-way channel between government and public, partly a
pressure group in their own right. In the first half of this century the
dominant medium was the press – uniquely centralised in London,
unlike the newspapers of France, Germany or the USA – which was
spreading its readership throughout the social strata following the
pioneering work of Alfred Harmsworth, Lord Northcliffe. His new
Daily Mail of 1896 was dubbed by the olympian Lord Salisbury as 'a
paper written by office boys for office boys'.[9] Most papers in the early
twentieth century were fiercely partisan on domestic politics, and some
took firm positions on foreign policy. Under Max Aitken, Lord
Beaverbrook, the *Express* newspapers were steadfastly isolationist in
their attitude to continental Europe from the 1920s to the 1960s. It is,
however, hard to document the influence of such press campaigns on
public attitudes or government decisions. An occasional article could
have explosive effect, such as the famous despatch from *The Times*
military correspondent, Colonel Charles Repington, which set off a
scandal about shell shortages in France in 1915 that helped force the
Asquith government into coalition. More often, however, the press
simply reflected the opinions of policy-makers. Repington's famous
message was in reality the result of a calculated leak by disgruntled
Army commanders in France.[10]

Britain is unusual among democracies in the restrictions placed on
access to government information. The cocoon surrounding the small
elite has been reinforced by the omnicompetent provisions of the Of-

ficial Secrets Act, rushed through all its Commons stages in less than an hour in July 1911 during a panic about a possible German invasion,[11] and used vigorously by subsequent governments of all parties until Margaret Thatcher found it inadequate in the Clive Ponting case of 1985. Given such constraints, mediamen have been ready to connive in the notorious lobby system, whereby a favoured few are given selective access via off-the-record briefings by government ministers and advisers. The Prime Minister's press secretary has often played a central role in these campaigns of disinformation, from George Steward blackening the anti-appeasers in the 1930s to Bernard Ingham denigrating anti-Thatcherites in the 1980s. The torrent of information released by both sides in the Heseltine-versus-Thatcher Westland affair in 1986 proved the sagacity of James Callaghan's definition: 'leaking is what you do; briefing is what *I* do'.[12]

Despite government restrictions on information, however, the media can often shape the agenda of public debate, by focusing on certain news items and giving them particular colouring and significance. This is especially true when events can be linked to fundamental patriotic values, as over German and British naval programmes in 1908–9, over withdrawal from empire in the 1950s and 1960s or over 'sovereignty' and the European Community. Even more potent in this regard were the radio and newsreels between the world wars and television since the 1950s, bringing the sounds and sights of the world to ordinary people, stimulating their imagination and passions. Yet, as with the press, governments have found ways of managing and utilising these new media, particularly through increasingly sophisticated use of public relations advisers to promote the desired image of politicians and their policies. Admittedly British society has become progressively more open – would it be possible in the 1990s for civil servants to persuade the press to conceal a prime minister's illness and to run the country without him for a month, as happened after Churchill's stroke in 1953? Nevertheless, governments are always 'economical with the truth',[13] to quote the phrase that ensured immortality for Margaret Thatcher's Cabinet Secretary, Robert Armstrong.

We are coming closer to a preliminary answer to the question 'who makes British foreign policy?'. Much depends on the level of policy in question.[14] For most of the time the Executive branch of government takes the essential decisions, often along well-worn paths of precedent. Few outsiders, even in Parliament, possess the information let alone the influence to have much impact. On the 'high policy' issues of peace or war, however, public acquiescence and even firm support are vital. More generally, MPs and public have a negative effect on foreign policy, reminding government of its ultimate accountability and setting the bounds of what is ideologically acceptable, even if they do not directly determine specific decisions. Between the routine issues of daily overseas policy, conducted by the Executive, and the problems of high policy, over which there is often brief but intense public debate, lie a range of what are called 'sectoral' issues, such as trade with particular countries, weapons procurement, and so on. Here government departments engage with a variety of interested pressure groups, usually behind the scenes. Issues can be moved from being purely sectoral to matters of high policy, for instance the EEC question, which was gradually recast between the 1950s and the 1960s as a subject of public and political debate involving principles of national identity and independence. In determining whether issues are matters of routine, sectoral or high policy – involving few or many of the population – media interest and treatment can often be decisive. But, despite the enlargement of non-governmental influences as the century has progressed, foreign policy is still largely made in Whitehall.

WHITEHALL: THE PROBLEMS OF COORDINATION

The question then arises, 'where in Whitehall?'. The 'central column of the policy-making machine' for most of this century has extended down from the Prime Minister, through the Cabinet and Foreign Office (FO) to British diplomatic missions around the world.[15] From these missions comes the information about foreign affairs which officials in the FO then use to recommend policy to ministers. The latter then take decisions for which they are ultimately responsible to Parliament and which the diplomats in turn implement. That at least is the constitutional fiction – the FO 'not so much a maker of policy as an instrument for its execution'.[16] In practice Parliament, and more specifically the Cabinet (Parliament's executive committee), have relatively little say most of the time. 'Collective Cabinet responsibility' is a means of spreading blame not taking decisions. 'Cabinets do not proceed by the counting of heads', Harold Wilson noted. He observed that a premier's 'power, when it comes to summing up a Cabinet discussion, is enormous . . . I had been trained by Attlee. He was usually able to sum up, as I was, by saying that the Cabinet view was thus and thus, and it was rarely challenged'.[17] In any case, few diplomatic issues reach Cabinet level and when they do, as radicals from Lloyd George to

Richard Crossman have complained, they usually come 'pre-cooked' by key officials and ministers.[18]

In foreign affairs the FO does most of the cooking.[19] Since the bureaucratic reforms of the early 1900s, most routine diplomatic problems are simply dealt with by the relevant FO department. Traditionally these have been divided on geographical lines – American, Far Eastern, Northern, and so on – but, more recently, functional departments have been created which transcend regional boundaries, such as UN affairs and Treaties. Most business therefore does not come near the Foreign Secretary or the Permanent Under-Secretary (PUS) – the most senior civil servant in the FO.

In determining major lines of high policy a strong PUS can often exert considerable influence on the Foreign Secretary – Charles Hardinge (1906–10) or Robert Vansittart (1930–8), for instance. But the crucial relationship is usually between the Foreign Secretary and Prime Minister. Sometimes the latter has almost totally abdicated responsibility, notably Stanley Baldwin. At the opposite extreme other PMs have tried to run their own foreign policy: Lloyd George was a particular offender in 1916–22 and so was Anthony Eden over Suez in 1956. In both cases it took the Foreign Office some time to recover its morale and authority. Usually, however, a premier chooses a Foreign Secretary whom he trusts and to whom he feels able to delegate substantial authority, as Clement Attlee did with Ernest Bevin (1945–51), on the grounds that 'you don't keep a dog and bark yourself'.[20] There have, however, also been bitter struggles – Ramsay MacDonald and Arthur Henderson in 1929–31, Neville Chamberlain and Anthony Eden in 1937–8, Churchill and Eden in 1951–5.

As a simple description of foreign-policymaking, this account is satisfactory. But features of Britain's international power – economic, military and imperial – do not fit within even a capacious definition of 'diplomacy'. For this reason some scholars prefer to talk about a country's 'external policy', to avoid the potentially limiting connotations of 'foreign policy' or 'diplomacy'. With this broader framework in mind we need to look at other Whitehall departments that have a say in British policy overseas.

In the imperial sphere the dominant force in the first half of this century was the India Office, linking Whitehall with the Indian subcontinent via a semi-independent Viceroy of often substantial authority and status. The Colonial Office dealt with Britain's other overseas territories but from 1925 a separate Dominions Office was established to handle relations with Canada, Newfoundland, Australia, New Zealand, South Africa and the Irish Free State. After Indian independence in

1947 the Indian and Dominion Offices were merged to form the Commonwealth Relations Office, which absorbed the Colonial Office in 1966 only to be subsumed in turn by the FO two years later to create the Foreign and Commonwealth Office (FCO). This process reflected the gradual contraction of Britain's territorial responsibilities as the empire became independent, but it should be stressed that for the first two-thirds of the century, when Britain's imperial commitments were at their most extensive and demanding, there was no single department coping with these problems.

The lack of unified focus is even more apparent in the field of defence. The armed forces have cherished their independence with an intensity born of bureaucratic self-interest and hallowed by a sense of patriotic duty. The Army and Navy, institutionalised in Whitehall for much of the century in the War Office and the Admiralty but often keeping civilian direction at arms length, were complemented from the end of the First World War by the Royal Air Force (RAF) and the Air Ministry. These three services were inveterate competitors for funds and for strategic supremacy, despite attempts at inter-service co-ordination such as the Committee of Imperial Defence (1904–39) and a Chiefs of Staff committee in 1924. During his Second World War premiership Churchill assumed the personal title of Minister of Defence and in 1946 a formal Ministry of Defence (MOD) was established. But this had very limited powers over the individual services, who retained direct access to the Cabinet, and it could do little to resolve conflicts over shares of a declining defence budget at a time when equipment costs were spiralling. Not until the 1960s was the MOD officially integrated – fusing the separate bureaucracies into one, eliminating the individual service ministers and setting up machinery to critique and cost the procurement programmes that the services advance.[21] Making these new structures work took another two decades.

Thus for all the period when Britain was a world power, two vital aspects of its external policy, the empire and defence, were handled by a plethora of rival departments, each with its own specialist career civil servants – an institutional arrangement that made it difficult for anyone to see the problems of British power as a whole.

In the economic sphere the institutional difficulty was the opposite, that of excessive unification. There was some division of labour, with the Board of Trade and its successors taking responsibility for commercial policy, but in general one department, the Treasury, has dominated economic policy. Yet the Treasury's traditional brief was narrowly defined. Its primary concerns until the 1960s were the control of public spending and the management of sterling. The latter was conducted in concert with the Bank of England whose foreign departments have traditionally been more generously staffed than the Treasury's Overseas Finance division and whose head, the Governor, enjoys direct access not merely to the Chancellor of the Exchequer but also to the Prime Minister. A simple indication of his weight can be gained from the fact that since 1920 there have been only seven Governors while 28 different politicians have held the Chancellorship.

The Treasury has fought jealously to preserve its stranglehold over economic policy. Twice, under post-war Labour governments, it killed off attempts to create a more domestically oriented ministry to manage the economy and promote growth – the shortlived Ministry of Planning in 1947 and the Department of Economic Affairs in 1964–9, intended to facilitate 'creative tension' with the Treasury.[22] Although the Treasury has construed its role more broadly since the 1960s, with its acceptance of economic management tasks and the demise of sterling as a reserve currency, it still views its central function as the control of public spending. Britain has never had a Bureau of the Budget separated from an economics ministry, as in the USA, Japan and many continental countries.

Thus, numerous government departments have interests in facets of British external policy. And over the last two decades, since British entry into the European Community, every part of Whitehall has developed a foreign policy to some degree, since issues as apparently domestic as agriculture, transport and health standards now involve consultation with Britain's EC partners and acceptance of EC regulations. The question then arises: does anyone harmonise these competing bureaucratic noises about Britain's place in the world?

The twentieth century has seen an underlying struggle between three departments, with influence gradually shifting away from the Foreign Office and the Treasury towards the Cabinet Office. Traditionally the FO has tried to coordinate foreign policy, ensuring that all contacts with other governments, or at least information about those contacts, passes through its departments and that officials of other Whitehall ministries serving abroad, such as military or commercial attachés, are under the authority of the local Ambassador. The FO has generally enjoyed greater success in keeping tabs on defence and commercial policy than on overseas financial policy. Good working relations with the Board of Trade and its successors and with the integrated MOD have not until recently been matched by close contacts with the more independent Treasury's Overseas Finance Division, let alone the Bank of England. Within the FO the main instrument of coordination has been the 'functional' departments, which have greatly increased in number, size and importance in the last quarter-century. Central now are the two European Community departments, but important newcomers include Arms Control and Disarmament; Information Technology; and Energy, Science and Space. Their task, in the Whitehall vernacular, is that of 'marking' (in the soccer sense) rival departments.

Despite this rather desperate effort by the FO to keep track of what the rest of Whitehall is doing abroad, its effective influence has gradually shrunk. Since the First World War the Treasury has been a powerful rival, extending its dominance over domestic economic policy into foreign and defence issues through its power of the purse. During the First World War Treasury lost control of Whitehall spending, with alarming inflationary consequences, and the post-war backlash gave the Permanent Secretary of the Treasury, Sir Warren Fisher (1919–39) a position of unrivalled authority through his right to scrutinise any proposal involving government spending.[23] Fisher saw the Treasury as a Whitehall 'general staff' forming 'independent views' and ready to intervene on issues of policy as well as public finance. In particular, he argued in 1936, the Treasury 'must concern itself with . . . foreign affairs (which are now largely economics, finance and armaments)'.[24] In the 1930s Fisher intervened to set priorities in defence spending for the service ministries and also tried, less successfully, to promote a more radical appeasement of Japan than the FO desired.

Treasury influence over defence and foreign policy reached its apogee in the 1930s.[25] The department has continued to impose limits on overseas spending and its influence at times of financial crisis, notably 1947 and 1967, has been considerable, but Fisher's grandiose claims for its coordinating role have never been echoed to the same extent again. Gradually power has shifted towards the Cabinet committees and the Cabinet bureaucracy, both of which date from the First World War.

The pre-1914 Cabinet itself had been a committee of leading politicians, meeting with little preparation and no secretarial assistance, to discuss political crises and legislative business. During the war much of the vital work was done by Cabinet committees and particularly, under Lloyd George from December 1916, by a small War Cabinet. Staff of the Committee of Imperial Defence, headed by Maurice Hankey, were utilised to service these committees and they went on to form the new Cabinet Office. In 1922 Hankey successfully fought off Fisher's attempt to subsume his staff in the Treasury, but during the interwar years the Cabinet Office's influence depended largely on Hankey's close *personal* relationship with successive Prime Ministers.

Institutionally he remained 'a floating kidney in the body of government'[26] because the Cabinet Office was mainly staffed by 'irregulars' rather than civil servants and because its coordinating role was still largely confined to matters of defence.

Since the Second World War Cabinet committees and the Cabinet Office have become the major forces working for coordination in Whitehall. This has been a slow process. Many of the wasteful battles over defence programmes in the 1950s, for instance, can be attributed to the failure of the Cabinet's Defence Committee to impose priorities on the services, as the Treasury had tried to do in the 1930s. Nevertheless, since 1963 the Defence and Overseas Policy Committee, chaired by the Prime Minister and including the Foreign Secretary, Chancellor and Minister of Defence, has exercised a decisive role, backed by related committees of civil servants that 'shadow' its work in specialist areas. The Cabinet Office itself, 1700-strong by the late 1980s, has become '*the* crucial junction box of the central government system'.[27] The internationalisation of all Whitehall work since Britain joined the EEC has played into its hands, as the only appropriate body to coordinate *all* government departments, unlike either the Treasury or the FCO. The Cabinet Office won a particularly momentous battle in the early 1970s with the decision that it, and not the FCO, should coordinate all EC policy in a secretariat headed by a home civil servant. (As consolation prize for the FCO, a diplomat would always head the British delegation to the European Commission in Brussels.) Cabinet Office dominance is by no means complete or clear-cut, but the trend is clear. Conversely, it is also apparent that for the first two-thirds of this century, as Britain was struggling with the dilemmas of declining relative power, there was no institution in Whitehall able to confront the diverse problems of Britain's international position as a unified whole.

One should remember, however, that bureaucratic rivalry and lack of coordination are familiar features of other Western governments. France's imperial possessions were divided up untidily between the colonial, war, navy and foreign ministries at the beginning of this century and there was nothing comparable to the Committee of Imperial Defence to essay a global view.[28] Likewise, in the post-war period, the US, French and Canadian governments are among those who have struggled to restrict the autonomy of the armed services, impose budgetary discipline and create strategic coherence.[29] What particularly distinguishes Whitehall from its foreign counterparts is the entrenched character of these bureaucratic divisions, thanks to the pre-eminence of a career civil service. Elsewhere in the West a change of ministry usually entails a turnover of many high-level posts in the bureaucracy, whereas in Britain these are retained by senior civil servants regardless of the political ebb and flow. Furthermore, this is an elite that was (and remains) deeply ingrown, meshed together by a web of contacts fostered through school, university and club.[30]

In terms of policy, the outcome of all this is continuity and compromise. Bureaucratic argument takes place behind the scenes and results usually in a messy lowest-common-denominator policy that satisfies most bureaucratic interests to some degree while frustrating new initiatives. In the 1930s foreign policy was half-hearted and muddled, in part because of unsatisfactory compromises between the Treasury, Foreign Office and the services which left Britain unable either to conciliate potential enemies or to confront them. Similarly, for two decades after 1945 persistent horse-trading between the three services meant that each got something, making it harder to advance radical solutions to Britain's defence dilemmas. Two vigorous attempts – the Sandys and Nott White Papers of 1957 and 1981 – were the result of ministers forcing through decisions themselves, over the heads of the Chiefs of Staff, with full prime-ministerial backing. Policy review was clearly not impossible, but the existence of entrenched bureaucracies, engaged in consensual competition, has militated against radical change and intellectual coherence. Collegiality breeds consensus, continuity and also 'muddle'.[31]

BETWEEN WEALTH AND POWER: THE ROLE OF POLICY

In chapter one we saw how Britain's share of the world's wealth has diminished during this century. Although this obviously has had broad implications for the country's ability to sustain military commitments around the world, I argued that it represents a long-term trend and that there is no exact and immediate correlation between changes in economic performance and shifts in international position, between wealth and power. An essential intermediary is 'policy' – the attitudes and decisions of government departments, particularly on taxation, defence and diplomacy, which we need to examine now. We shall also look more closely at how the lack of coordination among deep-rooted bureaucracies has made it harder to take clear-cut policy choices on defence and foreign policy.

With regard to fiscal policy, we should note that statistics about GDP do not automatically tell us much about a nation's military capability. Government must decide how much of the nation's income to extract through taxation and also how to allocate that money in public spending. In the late nineteenth century general government spending (by central and local governments) in Europe was around 10 per cent of GDP. In Britain itself the proportion was 11.9 per cent in 1840 and 9.2 per cent in 1890. By 1975 government's share of British GDP was around 50 per cent – a figure comparable with that for non-communist Europe as a whole. As for the direction of government spending: in Britain in 1840 roughly a quarter went on the army and navy and around 40 per cent on paying off the national debt, most of it accumulated during the Napoleonic wars and therefore directly related to Britain's military role. By 1975 defence was only about 10 per cent of total British government spending, and over half of the latter was taken up by social services and nearly a quarter by education and the environment. Spending on social services was the equivalent of 25.7 per cent of GDP, defence only 5 per cent.[32]

The same pattern was broadly true for most Western developed countries: a marked increase in government spending and, within that, a pronounced shift from defence-related expenditure to social services and education. This has reflected the growing acceptance by all these governments of a responsibility for social welfare, a case usually pressed on them and on the elites that controlled them through the growth of representative democracy and socialist parties. Thus defence, traditionally the main function of the state, has had to struggle for funding at a time of escalating armament costs. This, of course, was a problem for all Britain's rivals. But the British experience has exhibited some distinctive developments in economic philosophy and political priorities.

The critical shift in economic philosophy has been from liberalism to Keynesianism, a revolution that even Margaret Thatcher did not reverse. At root this means an acceptance of the idea that government can actually promote economic growth – increase national wealth – through its policies. The classic expression of economic liberalism was John Stuart Mill's dictum that 'as a general rule, the business of life is better performed when those who have an immediate interest in it are left to take their own course, uncontrolled either by the mandate of the law or by the meddling of any public functionary'.[33] In this philosophy the government was allowed limited tasks, particularly in defence and public order, but as small a role as possible in the economy. Taxation and government borrowing might be necessary to pay for wars but in normal times it was believed that they simply reduced the amount of money available for private investment and thus stifled the natural growth of the economy. Though axioms of Victorian public finance, these ideas were formalized during the Depression of the early 1930s into the celebrated 'Treasury view' of public spending.[34] This provided the justification to reject proposals for government borrowing to finance public works and, later, rearmament, of the sort that Hitler had practised with notable success in Germany. In other words, British attitudes to public spending changed more slowly than those of its major rival and this had a significant effect in retarding British rearmament in the 1930s.

Acceptance of Keynesian ideas came only with the Second World War. The 1941 budget was the first to attempt a form of national income accounting – setting projected expenditure in the context of an estimate of the country's likely income, rather than simply assuming a small, balanced budget as the ideal. The 1950s and 1960s saw successive governments trying to manage the economy by tax and credit policies, oscillating between the fear of recession and unemployment on the one hand and of overheating, excessive imports and balance of payments problems on the other. By the 1960s, under Tories and Labour alike, there was an explicit commitment to economic growth as a prime object of government policy. Indeed 'growth', a novel word, had become a major criterion of a government's success and a new basis of international comparison. Increasingly national strength was assessed in economic rather than military terms. With these perceptions in mind countries like West Germany and Japan no longer looked like the failures they had seemed in 1945. The currency of international power had changed – to Britain's detriment, exacerbating at home and abroad the sense of national 'decline'.

Britain's experience of the mounting pressures for greater domestic spending has also displayed distinctive features. Although a trend throughout the century, it has been especially associated with the aftermath of two world wars. At home as well as abroad, it was politically necessary to recompense British subjects for their wartime sacrifices. After all, the wars 'must' have been fought to some purpose. Defeat is its own reward; victory is not. Thus after the First World War, with the electorate trebled in size by the 1918 Reform Act (which enfranchised most women), the government embarked on what proved a lasting commitment to promote public housing – 'homes fit for heroes'. After the Second World War pledges about a welfare state (the Beveridge Plan) and the maintenance of high employment (the 1944 White Paper) seemed politically inescapable – taking precedence over industrial modernisation.[35] Those two commitments shaped government economic policy until the Thatcher era, but they were of particular moment in the 1950s and 1960s. The British Government was then making unprecedented military commitments on the continent as well as trying to defend the bulk of Britain's possessions overseas more tenaciously than at any other time outside the world wars. Yet it was also committed at home to ever-increasing levels of domestic spending at a time when Britain's lack of industrial competitiveness was beginning to handicap its economic performance.

Political choices have also affected the use of national resources in another respect – the issue of conscription. In an era of seapower Britain's insular position rendered it more secure than continental states. The policy of conscription, which became common across the continent in the wake of Bismarck's victories,[36] was resisted by the British as antipathetic to basic libertarian traditions, although it had been used in the Napoleonic wars. This left Britain, as Lord Salisbury put it in 1871, with 'an army which is too weak to fight any civilised nation except under the wing of a military ally',[37] even though its total population was the equal of France and not much less than Germany's. From 1916 and again from 1939 the demands of war made conscription unavoidable, but it was only after 1945 that its sustained use in peacetime was accepted. The crises of the Cold War and colonial upheavals enabled Labour and Tory governments to perpetuate the policy until the Sandys Defence White Paper of 1957.

There were of course plausible contrary claims that conscription did *not* enhance national power – immediately after 1945, for instance, it delayed the return of essential labour to the economy and contributed to the balance of payments crisis of 1947. Moreover, the regular armed forces always disliked it because it diverted skilled manpower into training sulky, inexperienced soldiers who were often limited assets. Much depended on the length of service – less than two years was barely worthwhile. But, as the continentals found, national service did at least ensure a pool of semi-trained reserves that could be more quickly made effective in the event of war. Precisely what role this deficiency played in Britain's problems is hard to estimate, but it does constitute an obvious contrast with the experience of all its major rivals, except the USA, and it certainly retarded Britain's ability to translate economic strength into effective armed forces at the beginning of both world wars. Given the rapidity with which the war of 1939–45 reached crisis point in 1940, that may have been of real historical significance.

Thus, British governments made distinctive choices about the allocation of national resources between defence, industry and social welfare. (Likewise, we have seen in chapter one how successive British governments gave unique importance to international monetary policy – the value of sterling – within economic policy as a whole.) With regard to defence spending itself the British experience had peculiar characteristics. Of course, all bureaucracies try to perpetuate themselves, all armed forces tend to exaggerate or even invent threats to strengthen their bids for scarce funds. But bureaucratic politics in Whitehall have been exacerbated by the unusual range of what could be deemed British interests and the difficulty of determining the most likely threats to them. This was a direct reflection of both the extent and the vulnerability of British power for the first two-thirds of this century under conditions of global as well as European rivalry.

Broadly speaking, for much of this century the army, navy and airforce have identified three principal military roles and have feuded over which service was best suited to fulfil them. First was the problem of policing and defending the empire. Around 1900 the Army cited the Russian threat to the borders of India as being of paramount importance, using it to justify demands for a massive increase in trained reserves and even for conscription.[38] In the 1920s and early 1930s, before the growth of the Luftwaffe, the RAF made much of the utility of airpower in coercing unruly tribesmen at minimal cost, while the Royal Navy repeatedly argued that seapower was the key to imperial defence, pushing the case for destroyers and frigates in the interwar years and for aircraft carriers 'east of Suez' in the late 1950s. The Sandys White Paper of 1957, reflecting navy advocacy, argued that the aircraft carrier was 'in effect a mobile air station' and the Navy constituted an 'effective means of bringing power rapidly to bear in peacetime emergencies or limited hostilities'.[39]

Secondly, the Navy and RAF vied for superiority as bearer of the nation's strategic deterrent. Until the 1930s the Royal Navy's position was unquestioned. Battleships seemed the acme of power, as indicated by the naval races against Germany in the late 1900s and against America after the First World War. But from the early 1930s the RAF made repeated claims for the bomber as the key deterrent weapon – an argument that was first weakened by the failure of strategic bombing in 1942–4 and then enhanced by the invention of the atomic bomb. Until the end of the 1950s the RAF's V-bomber force was the heart of Britain's nuclear deterrent and the main beneficiary of government funds, even at a time of increasing stringency. But when the British dropped out of the nuclear race on their own account and arranged to buy whatever the Americans had to offer, the advantage switched back to the Navy. Now the Polaris submarine force, updated by Trident in the 1990s, constituted the nuclear deterrent force and it was the RAF in the 1970s that was struggling to justify itself.

The third area of service competition was over the issue of war-fighting roles. For the Army the 'continental commitment' has been the best rationale for its existence, once the threat to India diminished after the 1900s. Repeatedly it has taken the lead in advocating alliance with France, most notably in the wide-ranging staff talks with the French from 1906 to 1914, but also in 1938–9 and again from the late 1940s, when the Army gained a major peacetime role through Britain's commitments to the Brussels Pact (1948) and NATO (1949), culminating in the 1954 commitment to keep four British divisions in West Germany. The end of the Cold War and the unification of Germany in 1990 struck at the army's principal rationale. As for the Navy, its role in war was axiomatic in the first half of the century – the protection of trade routes and the escort of convoys being its central function in both world wars. But the nuclear age called all this into question, *if* one assumed that there would be nothing left after the initial nuclear exchange. Consequently, the Navy keenly contested the latter assumption, arguing strongly in the early 1950s for the concept of 'broken-backed warfare' – continued global war by adversaries crippled but not exterminated by nuclear engagement. The RAF's problem was that war-fighting tended to relegate it to a purely tactical role – support for the army and the navy. (In America, for this reason, there was no independent air force until after the Second World War.) Consequently the RAF reiterated its claims to a strategic role and in the 1950s often questioned the need for an extensive British military commitment to NATO, but once it had lost its strategic role to the Navy from the 1960s it developed a new case for a strike role in NATO in order to save it from relegation to support and tactical duties. For all the services the end of the Cold War constituted a major threat to their size and status.

These various strategic and bureaucratic arguments had distinctive budgetary implications. Each putative role carried with it demands for appropriate weaponry, all of which took ever-longer to develop as the technological complexity of weapons systems increased. (Modern aircraft and missiles systems take perhaps a decade to produce.) Moreover, fundamental changes in the technology of warfare – the shift from battleships to aircraft carriers during the 1940s, the change from the V-bombers to Polaris in the 1960s – entailed vast wastage of funds. And these changes occurred frequently, especially in the quarter-century from 1945 – further increasing Britain's problems in coping with that particularly fraught period in overseas policy. Even after the end of empire strategic arguments still had bureaucratic implications. To say that Britain's contribution to NATO should be in continental Europe favoured the Army and RAF, while the case for concentrating on protecting reinforcement routes across the Eastern Atlantic benefited the Royal Navy.

We have looked at two sets of bureaucratic relationships – between finance and defence and between the three armed services. The other problematic interface in overseas policy is that between defence and diplomacy. As Sir Oliver Harvey of the FO observed in 1947, 'the Chiefs of Staff will always object to evacuating anything where they have been for some time'.[40] Indeed, military advice was deliberately ignored when the Attlee Government decided to pull out of India and Palestine. But, although in principle the military seek to protect British interests by armed force and the diplomats by negotiation, this does not preclude consensus. Frequently the armed services, conscious of British over-extension, have advocated the use of diplomacy to reduce the number of threats they had to confront. In the early 1900s alliance with Japan and the ententes with America and France received their blessing. Likewise, in 1937-8 it was the military planners, particularly Hankey and Admiral Chatfield, who took the lead in urging the appeasement of Italy to reduce the threats to Britain's exposed position.[41]

Usually the diplomats have also favoured diplomatic solutions to Britain's problems. In 1905–7, for instance, the Foreign Office sought an agreement with Russia to head off the impossible War Office demands for the reinforcement of India. And consistently it favoured negotiating away Britain's differences with America even when, as over naval parity in the 1920s, this was stoutly resisted by Navy diehards. But on significant occasions the FO has judged that diplomatic concessions would undermine the 'intangibles' (a favourite word) of Britain's international position. Given the fragility of British power – the degree to which it rested on appearances rather than substance – concessions that strengthened the reality of power could compromise its appearance. Thus, the FO was less ready than the Treasury or the military to appease Japan in the mid-1930s. Likewise in 1952 Foreign Secretary Anthony Eden argued that, although Britain was over-extended, rapid withdrawal anywhere could undermine its international prestige and 'once the prestige of a country has started to slide, there is no knowing where it will stop'. Even getting rid of something as minor as the Falkland Islands would be inadvisable, he warned, 'for public admission of inability to maintain these traditional possessions would cause a loss of prestige wholly out of proportion to the saving in money obtained. It might precipitate a scramble by the numerous claimants to various parts of British territory'.[42]

Indeed the Foreign Office has sometimes deemed it necessary for Britain to assume additional military burdens, whether or not the armed forces felt capable of assuming them. In the spring of 1939, after Hitler had broken the Munich agreement and taken the rump of Czechoslovakia, the Cabinet guaranteed the security of Poland, Romania, Greece and other east European countries. The military were not consulted and no staff talks ensued: these actions reflected not so much a plan 'to create a military alliance against Germany' as a hope that 'evidence of political determination would prevent further aggression'.[43] Yet some of these commitments later created considerable problems for Britain, particularly in its relations with Russia over Poland in 1943–5 – a stimulus for the Cold War. Likewise, Eden's sudden pledge in 1954 to keep British troops in Germany was made without reference to the military, in order to end the diplomatic crisis over German rearmament. He sought to reassure the French and Americans with evidence of British resolve. Indeed Britain's periodic continental commitments throughout this century have had as much to do with diplomatic as with military calculations – reassuring allies as well as deterring enemies. Yet they have significantly added to Britain's defence burdens.

POLICYMAKING: CHAOS, REASON, INSTINCT AND TRADITION

We have seen that foreign policy is made largely in Whitehall, within parameters set by public opinion and pressure groups, that many government departments have input and that, particularly in the years of maximum challenge to British power, from the 1930s through the 1960s, coordination between these departments was often inadequate. We have also seen how divisions between the entrenched staffs of the Treasury, the three services and the Foreign Office have complicated the already acute problems of how to make the best use of Britain's diminishing share of international wealth in the face of multitudinous challenges. The conclusion of this analysis is that there was rarely, if ever, a unified concept that we can call 'British foreign policy'. But there is a further problem. Not merely did different parts of Whitehall have different policies but to talk of 'policymaking', even for individual departments, conveys an exaggerated image of rationality, order and effectiveness.

Politicians, of course, naturally encourage the impression that they are in control. This is evident in their memoirs, written partly to make money (a perk of office they have often denied to civil servants under the Official Secrets Act) but also to get a head start on the historians by giving their shape to the muddle of politics. Lloyd George and Churchill were notorious as self-serving autobiographers, but another example was Harold Macmillan who, for instance, depicted the end of the British Empire in India as 'the culmination of a set purpose of nearly four generations', as the British worked 'to spread to other nations those advantages which through the long course of centuries they had won for themselves'.[44] That, of course, is nonsense. Not merely does it endow the British retreat from India, and elsewhere, with a spurious order and purpose, but it also distorts the way government 'decisions' are made.

These are often quick reactions to crises rather than considered verdicts based on comprehensive evaluation. Time constraints and the simultaneous pressure of other business often preclude sustained reflection about any one problem. This is an occupational hazard for all policymakers, but foreign affairs are particularly intractable for at least two additional reasons. Most politicians and government ministers naturally focus on domestic issues. It is these which usually determine their political survival. In July 1914 the Cabinet was pre-occupied with the danger of war in Ireland not on the Continent; in 1982 it was totally unprepared for the Argentine attack on the Falklands. Furthermore, foreign problems are intrinsically more difficult to manage than those at home. The individual nation state only has sovereignty over its internal affairs: foreign policy is, by definition, about dealing with those over whom one does not have direct control. Or as Herbert Morrison, briefly Labour's Foreign Secretary in 1951, put it: 'foreign policy would be okay except for the bloody foreigners'.[45] These 'bloody foreigners' have become more of a problem for Britain as its effective sovereignty has been eroded by membership of NATO and the EEC – witness Margaret Thatcher's battles with Jacques Delors and the European Commission.

Nor have policymakers enjoyed access to the range and quality of information available to later historians. Statistical data about national and government activities, which we now consider routine, have only become available in recent years. The Treasury did not have its own statistical unit until after the sterling crisis of 1947. Before that it relied on financial information from the Bank of England.[46] Also not to be taken for granted, as we look back from the era of satellites and electronic surveillance, is the quality of military intelligence about other powers. At certain points in its history, Britain enjoyed a decisive advantage, particularly through the ULTRA and MAGIC decrypts of Axis signals in 1940–5. The official British historian has argued that 'but for the superiority of their intelligence' the Allies might not have won the war until 1948 or 1949.[47] Yet at other times the inadequacies of British intelligence have had almost fatal consequences. Chronic over-estimation of German airforce strength played a significant part in the policy of appeasement in the 1930s[48] and failure to predict the Nazi–Soviet pact laid Britain open to war in 1939 and near-disaster in 1940.[49] The contribution of highly-placed British traitors in the 1940s and 1950s in accelerating the Soviet nuclear programme and in revealing details of NATO strategy and capability has yet to be quantified.

'Foreign policy' is therefore often a quick reaction to a surprise crisis, taken on the basis of inadequate information amid a mass of conflicting problems. Moreover, the pressures of business have grown inexorably during this century. When Paul Gore-Booth entered the FO in the 1930s the routine had changed little since the 1900s. Work did not begin until eleven in the morning, after the cypher officers, typists and clerks had prepared the incoming telegrams and despatches for attention by the relevant departments. The principle was to deal with each morning's work within the day. The Second World War saw the demise of 'eleven o'clock diplomacy'.[50] The young John Colville, seconded from the FO to 10 Downing Street in September 1939, was required to start work at 9.30 – which he considered 'a disgustingly early hour'.[51] In the 1990s, telexes, telephones and computer nets are used routinely for instant communication and the 8 a.m. meeting and the working breakfast are no longer worthy of comment. The vast increase in business can be quantified. In 1934 over 155,000 incoming papers were registered and filed by the FO, compared with just under 50,000 in 1900.[52] Between 1938 and 1949 the number almost trebled.[53] And the increase in telegrams alone between 1939 and 1972 – ninefold incoming, more than twentyfold outgoing – is documented in table 2.1. Staff levels have not increased proportionately to the growth of business. In fact, in the last twenty years the diplomatic service has been cut by 20 per cent and the FCO, with some 8,000 staff at home and abroad, is now one of the smallest departments of state.[54]

Table 2.1 Telegraphic traffic through the Foreign Office, 1939–72

	Incoming	Outgoing
1939	25,088	18,351
1962	75,391	155,020
1969	166,000	271,000
1972	231,269	391,859

Source: W. Wallace 1975: 62

One attempt to gain some perspective on the rush of events has been by creating a planning unit. In the FO there were precursors in the short-lived Economic and Reconstruction department of the Second World War and the Permanent Under-Secretary's committee (1949–55), but it was not until after the Suez debacle that a small policy planning staff was established, following US precedent, and this became a separate department within the FO from 1964. It has always been headed by a 'high-flyer' within the service and has benefited from the contemporaneous growth of similar departments elsewhere in Whitehall (the MOD's Policy Staff, for instance, dates from 1968). Nevertheless, the influence of foreign-affairs planners on daily policy remains limited. Not merely are their long-term projects frequently sacrificed to the exigencies of immediate crises, but effective planning is difficult without a stable, predictable environment, or at least one in which change is largely under your control. Demonstrably that has not been the case for Britain for much of this century. During the Suez crisis of 1956 Lord Bridges, Permanent Secretary of the Treasury *and* head of the Civil Service, was asked how he managed to cope. 'I don't', he replied, 'I just catch one ball in four'.[55]

Thus, Britain's ability to cope with the erosion of its real but often tenuous power has been compromised by continuity within individual departments and conflict between them, by lack of overall coordination and by the intrinsic difficulties of making any considered policy judgements. Often the reactions to events have been determined more by instinct than rationality, by temperament and not analysis. A number of these instinctive responses recur, and it is worth noting them briefly now.

The basic instinct, of course, was simply to hang on. As prime beneficiaries of the late Victorian status quo, British leaders naturally considered that any change was for the worse. This view was expressed with striking candour by the First Sea Lord, Admiral Chatfield, in 1934: 'we have got most of the world already, or the best parts of it, and we only want to keep what we have got and prevent others from taking it away from us'.[56]

Unfortunately, as Winston Churchill had put it equally frankly two decades before, 'our claim to be left in the unmolested enjoyment of vast and splendid possessions, *mainly acquired by violence, largely maintained by force*, often seems less reasonable to others than to us'.[57]* Given that war would be a disruption to Britain's trade and the world economic system on which its prosperity was founded, Britain's leaders repeatedly inclined towards appeasement – meaning attempts to resolve international disputes by 'satisfying grievances through rational negotiation and compromise'.[58] This was the approach of Lord Lansdowne at the beginning of this century and of Neville Chamberlain in the 1930s. Related to it was a preference for calculated withdrawal from excessive commitments – a policy adopted by the Royal Navy in the decade before 1914 and advocated forthrightly by Prime Minister Clement Attlee in 1945–6. The discrediting of appeasement in 1938–40 removed an important option from British policy in the period after the Second World War and helped negate Attlee's efforts to reduce British overstretch.

Appeasement and withdrawal seemed one way to bring Britain's resources and responsibilities into balance. Another spectrum of policy instincts, however, pointed in the opposite direction. For Joseph Chamberlain and his followers at the beginning of the century, the creation of a unified white empire would help redress the balance between Britain and the new powers like Germany and America. It was not a considered policy so much as an ethnic instinct – Anglo-Saxon race feeling – newly elevated to the level of pseudo-scientific dogma, and it had little chance of checking the centrifugal forces of Dominion nationalism. More promising was the instinct for bluff, for utilising the myths of British power and continued prestige to outface potential rivals. As W.H. Auden observed in 1957:

> Our race would not have gotten far
> Had we not learned to bluff it out
> And look more certain than we are
> Of what our motion is about . . . [59]

The supreme exponent of bluff was Winston Churchill, with famed success against Germany in 1940 and ignominious failure against Japan

---

* Churchill omitted the italicized phrases from his war memoirs – *The World Crisis* – one of many instances of his surreptitious editing.

in 1941–2. Churchill's most notable pupil in the diplomacy of bluff has been Margaret Thatcher.

The instincts towards appeasement and withdrawal on the one hand and towards imperial defence and plain bluff on the other all represented attempts to take the initiative in foreign affairs. But some British leaders have inclined towards a more quietist view of policy. This was epitomised by Lord Salisbury in 1880 – 'the utmost we can do is to provide halting-places where the process of change may rest awhile'.[60] Stanley Baldwin took much the same view in the 1920s and 1930s. And, it must be said, whether this was their instinct or not, many British 'policymakers' in this century have found themselves unable to control the sweeping tides of change, already described, in the economy, empire and international system.

To some extent, then, policy was irrelevant to power – much that happened was beyond London's control. But perhaps the clearest point at which policy *did* matter was the question of allies. That, after all, was the traditional way to enhance national strength, by drawing on the military resources of others. And for a country chronically unwilling to spend heavily on defence or maintain a standing army, the use of surrogates or proxies was a frequent way out. In the eighteenth-century wars against France Britain had made extensive use of mercenaries. It remained the preferred British way of war in the twentieth-century, when the country relied heavily on France and Russia in two world wars and tried to utilise the relationship with America to enhance itself after 1945. The acceptance of permanent alliances, NATO and the EC – though shocks to British pride and independence – can be seen as a continuation of these efforts to compensate for the limits of national power.

To guide its practice of alliance diplomacy in Europe, British leaders frequently invoked the principle of the balance of power. As scholars emphasise,[61] this is a slippery notion, much-used yet ill-defined. British leaders in the nineteenth and early twentieth centuries often employed it to identify Britain as the actual or potential balancing agent, shifting its diplomatic weight to ensure that no hostile power achieved hegemony in Europe. In 1936 Churchill called this 'the wonderful unconscious tradition of British Foreign Policy . . . to oppose the strongest, most aggressive, most dominating Power on the Continent, and particularly to prevent the Low Countries falling into the hands of such a Power'.[62] As noted in chapter one, it is doubtful whether Britain actually played such a balancing role in the nineteenth century, but it has been a frequent axiom of British diplomacy.

Foreign policymaking is therefore rarely the result of calm reflection on current problems. In circumstances of confusion and pressure, instinct or tradition frequently prevail. Moreover, these are often grounded in group experience. The concept of historical generations must be used with subtlety.[63] Differences in political allegiance frequently divide an age cohort, for instance the Labour left's innate suspicion of capitalist America. Professional experience could also shape attitudes in divergent ways – the British officer's road to promotion at the beginning of this century lay via service in India, Africa and the Middle East, whereas no diplomat gained seniority without extended spells in Paris and Berlin. Views of the Empire and Europe were shaped accordingly.

Despite these qualifications, however, the idea of a distinct generational outlook sometimes has utility. 'What is essential to the formation of a generational consciousness is some common form of reference that provides a sense of rupture with the past and that will later distinguish the members of that generation from those who follow them in time'.[64] The 'rupture' of the First World War scarred a generation, turning many against war as an instrument of policy. By contrast, the failure of policy in the 1930s made 'Munich' and the 'lessons of appeasement' watchwords for decades to come. And many of those who came to maturity in the 1940s – a decade straddled by the fall of France and the creation of NATO – were left with ingrained suspicions of the continentals and Russia and an underlying faith in America. Margaret Thatcher is an obvious example.

Thus, policy must be understood by reference to personalities as well as structures. Instincts and traditions played their part in shaping responses to Britain's overall international situation. Appeasement, withdrawal, empire-building, bluff, quiescence, and alliance diplomacy were all recurrent motifs of policy. Some were tried, others rejected. Some succeeded, others failed. The same strategy might be vindicated at one point, but not at another. Generational timelags could account for a delayed or inappropriate application. In short, successful policymaking entails thinking and acting *in time*.[65] Ultimately the dilemmas of power and policy must be understood as history – and it is to this that I now turn.

REFERENCES

1. Bradshaw and Pring 1973: 400
2. Vital 1968: 48
3. Matthew 1973: 195–6
4. Barber 1976: 80
5. C. Howard 1967: 77
6. W. Wallace 1975: 95
7. Frankel 1975: 40
8. Ceadel 1980: 317
9. Koss 1981: i, 369
10. French 1982: 146–7
11. Andrew 1985: 64
12. Hennessy 1989: 337
13. Ibid., 667
14. Wallace 1975: 11–14; Barber 1976: 125–6
15. Vital 1968: 49
16. Strang 1955: 20
17. H. Wilson 1971: 480–1
18. Crossman 1975: i, 198
19. cf. Cromwell 1982: 541–73
20. Bullock 1983: 75
21. M. Howard 1970
22. Sampson 1971: 282
23. Burk 1982: 84–107
24. Peden 1979a: 30–1
25. Peden 1983b
26. Turner 1982: 76
27. Hennessy 1989: 390
28. cf. Fieldhouse 1982: 309–10
29. M. Howard 1970: Appendix 3
30. Neustadt 1969; Steiner 1987
31. May (ed.) 1985: 17
32. Flora 1983: ii, ch. 8, esp. 442–3; Mitchell and Deane 1962: 396
33. Mill 1878: 575
34. P. Clarke 1988: 27–69
35. Barnett 1986
36. Bond 1984: 16–17
37. K. Wilson (ed.) 1987: 13
38. Friedberg 1988: ch. 5
39. Grove 1987: 203
40. Louis 1984: 225
41. Pratt 1975
42. CAB 129/53, C (52) 202
43. Gibbs 1975: 803
44. Macmillan 1972: 117

45. Donoughue and Jones 1973: 498
46. Cairncross 1985: 133
47. Hinsley 1987: 218
48. Wark 1986
49. Watt 1989: chs 24–25
50. Gore-Booth 1974: 51–2
51. Colville 1985: 39
52. Willert 1936: 403
53. Adamthwaite 1986: 22
54. Jenkins and Sloman 1985: 24
55. Hennessy 1989: 144
56. Reynolds 1981: 5
57. Marder 1961: i, 322–3
58. Kennedy 1983b: 16
59. Auden (ed.) 1976: 505
60. Cecil 1921–32: ii, 377
61. e.g., *RIS* 1989: vol. 15, no. 2
62. Churchill 1948: i, 162–3
63. e.g., D.C. Watt 1984: 13–20
64. Wohl 1980: 210
65. cf. Neustadt and May 1986

CHAPTER THREE
Cold War, 1899–1914

For historians of British foreign policy the early years of this century are overshadowed by the images of 1914. The impact of the 'Great War' was so immense that accounts of the previous two decades have centred on what has been called 'the rise of the Anglo–German antagonism'.[1] This story has been set, in turn, in the larger context of a *fin de siècle* mood of imperial decline and international isolation. Historians have often taken this as the first signs of imperial mortality, coinciding as it conveniently did with the end of the long Victorian age in January 1901. Joseph Chamberlain's famous phrase at the Imperial Conference of 1902 – 'the Weary Titan staggers under the too vast orb of his fate'[2] – is frequently used as the epigraph for an era and even the epitaph for a century.[3]

Chamberlain, however, was not speaking 'pathetically'[4] but theatrically – making a vivid appeal for imperial burden-sharing rather than an objective analysis of Britain's plight. We have seen that, Diamond Jubilee euphoria notwithstanding, Britain was never truly a 'titan' in the Victorian era. Conversely, even if weary and anxious in 1900, the country had recovered much of its balance and nerve within a few years, under the Conservative governments of Lord Salisbury and A.J. Balfour (1895–1902, 1902–5) and their Liberal successors, Sir Henry Campbell-Bannerman and H.H. Asquith (1905–8, 1908–15). In the more competitive environment of the 1900s Britain was neither superpower nor superfluous but merely one of several great powers, each with particular strengths and weaknesses, whose relationships and fate were by no means pre-determined.

Even conflict with Germany was not inevitable. Recent research has highlighted the ebb and flow of Anglo–German relations in these years and has emphasised Britain's continuing tensions with other powers, particularly France and Russia. This multiplicity of Britain's rivalries helps us to understand the relative British complacency about Germany after its defeat in 1918. How those rivalries were managed in the 1900s also provides interesting points of similarity and contrast with the story of appeasement in the 1930s. Above all, the complexity of Britain's foreign relations in the early twentieth century reminds us that the 'road to war' in 1914 was more circuitous than hindsight might suggest.

EMPIRE AND 'EFFICIENCY'

Nothing brought home the limits of British power more forcibly than the events of the Boer War of 1899 to 1902. 'The war has been the nation's Recessional after all the pomp and show of the year of Jubilee', wrote the journalist Leopold Amery in 1900.[5] The causes of the conflict were typical of Britain's reluctant empire-building. Having controlled the Cape Colony since 1815, it had allowed the descendants of the former Dutch settlers, the Boers, to establish their own republics (the Transvaal and the Orange Free State) in the hinterland without much interference, except for a brief period in the late 1870s. But the discovery of gold near Johannesburg in 1886 transformed the situation. Within twelve years the mines of the 'Rand' had become the world's largest single source of gold, accounting for 28 per cent of total output, and the centre of gravity of South Africa was shifting to the Transvaal at a time when Germany was extending its influence there. Aside from the economic consequences, anxiety was expressed about the security of the British naval base at Cape Town should these trends continue.

As in other imperial flashpoints the problems on the periphery were exacerbated by the actions of British agents on the spot. Cecil Rhodes, premier of the Cape and builder of a private-enterprise empire in central Africa, tried to overthrow the Transvaal government by force. His botched attempt, the Jameson raid of December 1895, seriously exacerbated Anglo–Boer tension. Thereafter Sir Alfred Milner, British High Commissioner in South Africa from May 1897, and the Conservative Colonial Secretary, Joseph Chamberlain, took up the demands of the 'Uitlanders', the British migrants into the Transvaal who were denied full political rights. Milner insisted that there had to be 'reform in the Transvaal or war'.[6] But this was really a pretext for the larger issue of who controlled southern Africa. 'What is now at stake', Chamberlain told the Cabinet in September 1899, 'is the position of Great Britain in South Africa – and with it the estimate formed of our power and influence in our Colonies and throughout the world'.[7] Faced with a growing British troop buildup the Boers declared war on 11 October.

What followed was a devastating shock for British imperial pride. Before the ill-organised and poorly-led British forces could be reinforced from London, the Boer armies had penetrated deep into British territory. In 'Black Week' in December 1899 they inflicted three separate defeats on the British. Sir Arthur Conan Doyle, the creator of Sherlock Holmes, wrote that 'the week which extended from 10 December to 17 December, 1899, was the blackest one known during our generation, and the most disastrous for British arms during the century'.[8] In early 1900 the tide began to turn. Reinforced and reorganised under the command of Roberts and Kitchener, the British drove the enemy back and by the summer the Boer field armies had disintegrated. But then followed nearly two years of guerrilla warfare. To isolate the Boers from local support the British instituted the notorious 'concentration camps' in which 26,000 Boer women and children, over a fifth of the inmates, died of malnutrition and disease.

By the end Britain had put 450,000 men into the field, the Boers probably no more than 60,000. It had taken the self-styled greatest empire in the world nearly three years to defeat two republics whose population, to quote the Radical Liberal David Lloyd George, 'did not exceed that of Flintshire and Denbighshire'.[9] How would Britain fare in a 'real' war against a great power? Over the next few years a series of reforms were undertaken to make British institutions more 'efficient' – the catchword of the day.

Some focused on the empire itself. Here the most influential text was *The Expansion of England* (1883) by the Cambridge professor J.R. Seeley. He called for an imperial federation of the white settler colonies – 'Greater Britain' – to meet the challenge of the great continental states, America and Russia. His book, which sold 80,000 copies in the first two years and was still selling 11,000 in 1919,[10] had considerable political appeal. Joseph Chamberlain, Salisbury's Colonial Secretary from 1895 to 1903, was a particular enthusiast, and A.J. Balfour, Salisbury's nephew and successor, shared his concern. Prominent 'Liberal Imperialists' included Lord Rosebery, H.H. Asquith, Sir Edward Grey and R.B. Haldane, who dissented from most of their party and supported the Boer war. All these politicians agreed on the need to strengthen the links between Britain and the white settler colonies in Canada, Australia, New Zealand and South Africa. This was facilitated by the federation of the Australian colonies in 1901 and of South African colonies in 1910. After Edward VII's coronation it was agreed to hold a conference of imperial prime ministers every four years. Pressure was also applied on these colonies, or Dominions as they were known from 1907, to contribute to the cost of the Royal Navy. The Australians and New Zealanders had been paying a small subsidy since 1887; the Cape Colony followed suit in 1897 and Natal in 1902.

More significant, however, was the creation of a proper military bureaucracy at home. A Cabinet Defence Committee had existed on paper since 1895 but it took the post-mortem after the Boer War to establish it securely. As premier, Balfour was persuaded of the need for a permanent advisory body, comprising ministers and service representatives, to 'survey as a whole the strategical and military needs of the Empire'.[11] In its new form as the Committee of Imperial Defence (CID) it sat for the first time in December 1902 and within two years had been strengthened by the addition of a permanent secretariat to record discussions and prepare relevant papers. This was the brainchild of Lord Esher, a zealous military reformer and close friend of Balfour and the King, who also argued that the 'experience of South Africa has proved to demonstrate that the army suffers from the want of a trained General Staff', on the German model.[12] This was remedied in late 1906.

The Boer war also sparked off calls for improved military fitness. To quote Rosebery, the Empire needed 'an imperial race – a race vigorous and industrious and intrepid'.[13] The National Service League was founded in February 1902 and by 1914 it boasted 270,000 members.[14] Ideally its leaders wanted conscription, arguing that Britain was disastrously out-of-date compared with her continental rivals. But even an ardent supporter such as Lord George Hamilton, the Secretary of State for India, admitted in 1902 that 'any Government that propose[s] it will fail, and probably be driven from office'.[15] The Liberals were firmly opposed and, although the Tory leader from 1911, Andrew Bonar Law, privately supported the League, he had no intention of pushing it publicly. The League, therefore, campaigned only for universal military training for all boys and young men. Even this made little progress but the general concern for national fitness was reflected in the youth movements of the period. The most celebrated was the Boy Scouts movement, 1908 brainchild of General Robert Baden-Powell, the somewhat fortuitous hero of the Boer siege of Mafeking. He feared that modern Britons might follow the example of the

Romans, who lost their empire, he said, by being 'wishy-washy slackers without any go or patriotism in them'.[16]

Probably the most important contribution to the efficiency of Britain's armed forces was the reform of the Navy by Sir John Fisher, First Sea Lord from 1904 to 1910. Notwithstanding the great Jubilee review of 1897, the Navy was qualitatively 'a drowsy, inefficient, moth-eaten organism' which 'had run in a rut for nearly a century'.[17] Training still cultivated skills from the age of sail; the technological revolution associated with the torpedo, mine and high-explosive shell was scarcely understood; and gunnery practice was regularly skimped for fear of dirtying the highly-polished paintwork! The relentless, Bible-quoting Fisher, loved and hated in equal measure, revolutionised the old Navy. He reformed recruitment and training, focusing particularly on the quality of officers and on gunnery skills. He scrapped 154 obsolete vessels – some wooden, some muzzle-loading – a 'miser's hoard of useless junk', he complained, which a modern enemy cruiser could lap up 'like an armadillo let loose on an ant-hill'.[18] He concentrated this modernised fleet in home waters – in the Channel, Atlantic and Mediterranean commands – instead of spreading it around in penny packets off China, North America, the West Indies, West Africa and the Cape. He pushed the Royal Navy towards converting its fuel from coal to oil. And, with most import for the future, he presided over the construction of a new generation of battleships. HMS *Dreadnought*, launched by the King amid cheering crowds at Portsmouth in February 1906, was the largest, fastest, most powerful battleship in the world – 18,000 tons, capable of 21 knots, armed with ten 12-inch guns and driven by modern turbine engines. Fisher's *Dreadnought*-era navy seemed a match for anyone.

The sense of threat in Edwardian Britain was more than military, however. As Rosebery warned, traditional defences like the Navy could not protect Britain in the future 'from the peaceful attacks of trained and scientific rivalry in the arts of peace'.[19] At the turn of the century the growing international economic competition set off waves of panic among journalists and pundits. E.E. Williams's 1896 bestseller *Made in Germany* was emulated by Frederick Mackenzie's book *The American Invaders* in 1902. Both featured the penetration of British markets at home and abroad by superior foreign goods.

In confronting the foreign economic challenge contemporaries were divided in diagnosis and prescription. Some argued that what already was being called 'the English disease'[20] was largely caused by the inefficiencies of Britain's economy and society. Employers, workers, technology and unions were all scrutinised, but most observers agreed that the crucial defect was the neglect of scientific and technical skills. Haldane, a close student of the problem, argued that a middle-class depending on the virtues of 'courage, energy and enterprise' was as out of date in the scientific age as 'the splendid fighting of the Dervishes against the shrapnel and Maxims at Omdurman'.[21] 1902 saw passage of an Education Act that established secondary schooling on a nation-wide basis, run by local education authorities. Some junior technical schools on the German model were set up in the 1900s, as were several civic universities – science-oriented and often closely linked to local industries such as steel in Sheffield or mining in Newcastle. Chamberlain was the inspiration behind Birmingham University, while Haldane and Balfour helped found London's Imperial College of Science and Technology (1907), modelled on Germany's renowned technical university at Charlottenburg.[22]

Others believed that the cause of Britain's economic problems was largely external. Germany and America had built up their industries behind protectionist walls and, it was argued, Britain should respond in kind. This was the cry from many manufacturers, including those in chemicals, glass, iron and steel. But some big industries, notably coal, shipbuilding and sectors of the cotton trade, were still competitive in export markets and their support for continued free trade was matched by that of the City for whom an open international economy was the source of wealth. Nor did protectionism attract much support from landed interests.[23]

Weakening the case further was the fact that the movement for 'fair trade' was highjacked by Joseph Chamberlain as a crusade for imperial integration. Resigning from Balfour's Cabinet over the issue in September 1903, Chamberlain called for protective tariffs but with special preferences for grain and food imports from the white settler colonies. This would be the basis for eventual commercial union of the Empire in which Britain could be assured of secure markets and sources of supply. 'You must call in the new world, the Colonies, to redress the balance of the old. . . . What Washington did for the United States, what Bismarck did for Germany, it is our business and duty to do for the British Empire'.[24] In addition, tariff reform had a fiscal dimension. The Boer War was financed by government borrowing, adding 25 per cent to the principal of the National Debt, and by nearly doubling the income tax. At the same time normal spending had grown between 1895 and 1901 by 40 per cent because of the steady growth of social and educational expenditure.[25] With further increases in direct taxation ruled out by orthodox fiscal policy, Chamberlain's call for protective duties on food imports offered a way out of the budget crisis.

Tariff Reform was therefore a complex programme, involving commercial, imperial and fiscal calculations, as well as constituting Chamberlain's bid for political power. Yet his crusade of 1903–5 split the bipartisan movement for imperial reform. Liberal Imperialists like Asquith and Grey refused to abandon the principles of free trade, concentrating their diagnosis of Britain's economic ills on the lack of businesslike efficiency. Conservatives like Balfour, the Prime Minister, favoured retaliatory tariffs against unfair foreign competition but not duties on food imports. The likely consequence, dearer food, meant that, in Balfour's words, Chamberlain's programme was *'not within the spheres of practical politics'*.[26] Tariff reform divided the Conservative party, contributing significantly to the collapse of Balfour's government in December 1905 and the Liberal election landslide the following month. Moreover, Chamberlain's ill-prepared proposals had diverted attention from selective protectionism against foreign manufactures and from the need for technological innovation and educational reform. By the time the furore over tariff reform died down, the impetus for 'efficiency' had lost momentum – not least because Britain's international position had been transformed since 'Black Week' of December 1899.

DIPLOMATIC REALIGNMENTS

The early months of the Boer war had exposed not merely the inefficiencies of Britain's war effort but also the country's diplomatic isolation. The continental press in 1899–1900 was full of lurid stories of the intrepid Boer farmer defending family and homestead against the gold-grabbing, bloodthirsty English imperialists. 'The favourite theme' of French newspapers, reported the British Ambassador in Paris in October 1899, was 'the prospect of a combination of the European Powers in favour of the Boers'.[27] In the early months of 1900 the Russian Foreign Ministry made two attempts to create a coalition with France and Germany to press Britain to end the war. This crisis came soon after the Anglo–French rivalry for northeast Africa had come close to armed confrontation at Fashoda in 1898. It also coincided with serious international tension over German efforts to gain influence in southern Africa and China. When in January 1901 the Russians forced the weak Chinese government to cede virtual control of Manchuria, it seemed that a partition of China was about to follow the scramble for Africa – with Britain over-extended and already at war.

Talk of Britain's 'isolation' had become commonplace at the end of the century, though some chose to claim it as a virtue. Chamberlain in 1902 defiantly described Britain as being 'in a splendid isolation, surrounded and supported by our kinsfolk'.[28] But in private he and some younger members of the Conservative Cabinet were not so sanguine. Their anxieties were exacerbated by the failing health and grip of Lord Salisbury, despite his seventy years still holding both the offices of Prime Minister and Foreign Secretary. Eventually Salisbury was persuaded to resign the FO, and in October 1900 he was succeeded there by Lord Lansdowne, whose previous posts as Viceroy of India and Secretary of State for War had given him a keen insight into Britain's strategic problems.

Lansdowne favoured a more activist style of diplomacy than Salisbury and he made much more use of advice from civil servants, in his own department and in the War Office and Admiralty. He also presided over a major reform of the FO, designed to make it more efficient in the face of the growing volume of work. Responding to pressure from disaffected officials, Lansdowne agreed that 'there is more room for devolution all through the office. Too much of the work seems to find its way to the top. Papers and drafts not infrequently come to me which I have no time to look at'.[29] The creation of a Central Registry in January 1906 freed the 'first-division' FO officials from most of the routine clerical tasks with which they had previously been burdened. In consequence their role 'was transformed. From being clerks they became advisers engaged in the policy-making process'[30] – free to minute their opinions on incoming papers and offer informed guidance to their more receptive new minister.

Sensitive to Britain's over-extension, in touch with military as well as diplomatic advice, Lansdowne was determined to concentrate Britain's resources to face what seemed to him the most dangerous threat, a war with Russia. In his five years at the FO Lansdowne presided over a major realignment of British relations with three other powers – the United States, Japan and France. This paved the way for an agreement with Russia under the Liberals in 1907.

The Spanish–American war of 1898–1900 prompted America to start translating its new economic strength into international power. Not merely did it acquire the Philippines, Hawaii, Cuba and other territories in the Pacific and Caribbean, but the war precipitated a major naval building programme which by 1908 left the USA second only to Britain in first-class battleships. At a time when the French and

Russian navies were already rivalling Britain's and when Germany and Japan were embarking on their own programmes, it was impossible to imagine keeping up with America as well. The challenge of US sea-power was enhanced by Washington's decision to build a canal through the isthmus of Panama. Construction was not completed until 1914 but the essential diplomatic groundwork was done in 1900–1.

In a treaty signed in 1850 Britain and America had agreed to con-struct such a canal jointly. By the end of the century the British Gov-ernment recognised that in practice the USA could not be prevented from going ahead alone, but British policy was to tie a formal waiver of British rights to a satisfactory settlement by the USA of the disputed Alaskan border – an issue to which the Canadians attached particular importance. In the mood of 1900–1, however, the British abandoned that linkage between the Canal and Alaskan issues. The McKinley Ad-ministration in America, despite considerable public sympathy for the Boers, had done nothing to embarrass the British over South Africa and Britain was able to obtain essential supplies and loans in the USA. Unwilling to imperil these relations at a time of general isolation, Salisbury's Cabinet conceded US demands in two treaties, in February 1900 and November 1901. This left the Americans free to build and fortify a canal and thus to move their growing fleet expeditiously be-tween the Atlantic and the Pacific, instead of having to circumnavigate Cape Horn.

In effect, the treaties 'committed Great Britain to naval inferiority in American waters and therefore to friendship with the United States'.[31] This called in question the two-power naval standard – that the Royal Navy should at least equal the size of the next two fleets combined. In January 1901, making explicit what had already been acknowledged in private, the First Lord, Selborne, proposed simply 'to consider our position almost exclusively from its relative strength to that of France and Russia combined'.[32] Over the next few years the British withdrew nearly all their naval and military forces from North America and the Caribbean, and by 1908 official CID and FO doc-trine assumed that the possibility of war with the USA was so remote that it need not be considered as part of serious defence planning.

While removing America from the list of potential enemies, in the autumn of 1901 Lansdowne also took up overtures from Japan for an alliance directed at Russia. The Admiralty lent strong support. The First Sea Lord observed that 'foreign navies grow by leaps and bounds; we must look to diplomacy or alliances to help us out'.[33] Japan had much to offer in Chinese waters where Britain, with four battleships and sixteen cruisers, faced a Franco–Russian alliance of two more battleships and the same number of cruisers. Japan, however, had six battleships and no less than 31 cruisers to redress the balance.[34] The Treasury was also enthusiastic. Anxious about the costs of the Boer war and therefore implacably opposed to additional naval spending, it saw an alliance with Japan as a way to reduce the naval threat at no extra charge.

Salisbury was more cautious. He warned against a blind pledge which would 'give to Japan the right of committing us to war',[35] but Lansdowne overcame Cabinet doubts and signed a five-year treaty of alliance on 30 January 1902. Under the treaty each power repudiated 'any aggressive tendencies' in China or Korea, and pledged itself to 'strict neutrality' if the other was involved in a defensive war with one other state. In the event that such a war drew in two or more powers, Britain and Japan promised to come to the other's assistance.[36] On the face of it Japan gained more than Britain from the treaty and there was criticism, in the words of *The Times*, that it represented 'a departure from the policy of isolation that England has so long pursued'.[37] This was, however, 'a limited and temporary alliance', confined to the Far East and due to run for only five years, and the lack of general public discussion suggested that it was not widely believed that Britain was making a major departure in foreign policy.[38]

Nevertheless, the diplomatic effects of the Anglo–Japanese alliance were significant. France now faced the possibility of entanglement in a war with Britain, if its ally, Russia, fought Japan.[39] This gave Paris increased incentive to resolve its colonial differences with London. During 1902–3 the French foreign minister, Theophile Delcassé, explored the outlines of agreement, and negotiations were given further impetus when the long-feared war between Russia and Japan broke out in February 1904. The Anglo–French Entente was signed two months later. It was essentially a colonial agreement, covering various disputed issues around the world, but centring on a quid pro quo in North Africa: France would abandon its remaining claims over Egypt, the root cause of Anglo–French animosity since Gladstone's invasion in 1882, and in return the British accepted France's demands in Morocco. Whereas the Egyptian clauses were public, the Moroccan clauses were secret, not least because there were still the rival claims of Germany to be settled, and in mid-1905 the Germans pressed these to the point of a serious international crisis. But, with regard to relations with France, the 'Entente Cordiale' substantially reduced British over-extension and the danger of a Mediterranean war.

Russia still remained the most perplexing problem, however. The fear of a partition of China had abated but old anxieties about the

Russian threat to India remained, preoccupying the CID and Balfour himself. In the early years of the century they were under sustained pressure from Lord Curzon, Viceroy of India from 1898 to 1905. The imperial priorities of Curzon and other 'Indianists' were strikingly different from those of Chamberlain and his ilk who dwelt on the potential of the white Dominions. Curzon's refrain was simple: 'As long as we rule India we are the greatest power in the world. If we lose it we shall drop straight away to a third rate power'.[40] In the early months of the Boer war, when British forces were diverted to South Africa, Curzon and his staff believed that Russia might advance anew on Afghanistan and India's vulnerable northwest frontier. They demanded plans for reinforcements in the event of war. By 1905 figures of 500,000 additional troops for a two-year war were being bandied about.[41] Much of the work of the CID was taken up with debates about how India could be defended if war with Russia broke out – a possibility that seemed appallingly close for a time in October 1904 when some British fishing-boats were sunk in the North Sea by Russian warships, supposedly having been mistaken for Japanese torpedo-boats!

Military reinforcement on the scale that Curzon and Kitchener demanded was inconceivable, raising as it did the politically untouchable issue of conscription. Instead, Balfour and Lansdowne turned once more to diplomacy. In the spring of 1905 the Cabinet agreed to renew and extend the Anglo–Japanese alliance, two years before it was due to expire. The alliance would now be invoked if either side was attacked even by one power, and, in return for recognition of her claims in Korea, Japan agreed to provide Britain with military assistance in the defence of India against Russia.

By the time that this new treaty had been signed, however, in August 1905, the international situation had been transformed by Japan's destruction of the Russian fleet in the Tsushima straits at the end of May and its defeat of the Russian army at Mukden two weeks later. These battles ended the war. The moderation of Japan's terms when peace was signed in September 1905 did not disguise the fact that a minor power had defeated a major power, and, even more striking given the racist assumptions of the age, an Asian state had overcome a western one. The Russian revolution of December 1905, though abortive, was a further blow to the image of Tsarist power.

The consequences for British foreign policy were far-reaching. Tsushima made possible a further reduction of British naval forces in the Pacific, accelerating Admiral Fisher's concentration of the fleet in the Mediterranean and home waters. With the French entente, the

Russian defeat and the exclusion of the United States, the old two-power naval standard lost its traditional meaning. By the time Balfour's government resigned in December 1905 Britain's far-flung empire seemed immeasurably safer than during the early months of the Boer War. And under Sir Edward Grey, Lansdowne's Liberal successor as Foreign Secretary (1905–16), Britain proceeded to settle its differences with Russia as well. Fourteen months of difficult negotiations finally resulted in the Anglo–Russian convention signed on 31 August 1907. Under it disputed territorial issues were resolved – at least on paper. Tibet was neutralised, the Russians acknowledged that Afghanistan was a British sphere of influence, and Persia was divided into three with a neutral zone separating a Russian sphere to the north and a British sphere to the south.

The years 1900–7 had seen a remarkable transformation of Britain's international situation. From near-isolation in 1900 the British had secured agreements with America, Japan, France and finally Russia that blunted challenges to their global position by the sacrifice of peripheral interests. That policy was made possible, firstly, by a large measure of departmental agreement, especially between the FO and the Admiralty (though the War Office remained difficult over India) and, secondly, by the fact that, despite the incipient bureaucratisation of Whitehall, canny ministers like Lansdowne and Grey could still have their way without long battles with entrenched civil servants. In both these respects the appeasement policy of the 1900s differed from that of the 1930s.

A further feature of the period was the broad consensus between the two party leaderships. Asquith, Grey and other 'Liberal Imperialists' believed in the centrality of Britain's imperial position and did not share the opposition of Radical members of their party like Lloyd George to the Boer war or the naval programme. Likewise, the anger of Tory diehards about Grey's Russian détente – 'the efforts of a century sacrificed and nothing or next to nothing in return', in Curzon's words[42] – was not echoed by most party leaders. At root that was because policymakers largely agreed that the looming danger was not Russia but Germany, whose bellicose diplomacy and vigorous naval building were unsettling most of Europe.

Indeed by the time the historian reaches 1907 it is tempting to see the road to 1914 already stretching out ahead – the 'triple entente' with France and Russia clearing the way for war with Germany. Yet that is a misperception based on the simplifications of hindsight. Whatever the eventual outcome, appeasement was intended to include Germany in a new Concert of peace rather than isolate it in readiness for war. Similarly, the ententes proved fragile and were certainly not intended as embryonic military alliances. We therefore need to look more closely at the Anglo–German rivalry of the 1900s.

THE GERMAN CHALLENGE

When Lansdowne became Foreign Secretary in October 1900 he confessed to having only one 'preconceived idea', namely 'that we should use every effort to maintain, and if we can to strengthen the good relations which at present exist between the Queen's Government and that of the [German] Emperor'.[43] Like Joseph Chamberlain he wanted to build on Salisbury's earlier policy in the 1880s of cooperation with the Triple Entente of Austria, Italy and Germany and saw this as a way of containing the Russian threat. In March 1901 Lansdowne proposed a secret alliance with Germany. This envisaged that in the event of 'any Power joining Russia in hostilities against Japan, the British and German Governments will give naval assistance to Japan to defend herself against such an attack'.[44] Confused backstage negotiations ensued over the next few months, but these mainly involved German diplomats in London, whose enthusiasm for an understanding was not shared by the Chancellor, Hans von Bülow. The essential German condition for any alliance was British support on the continent against France and Russia, which was completely unacceptable in London. In any case, Lansdowne's enthusiasm was tempered by criticism from many senior FO officials and from Salisbury himself, both about German ambitions and about the principle of alliance. By the end of 1901 Anglo–German negotiations had withered and Lansdowne turned instead to alliance with Japan as a way of checking Russia.

The search for alliance with Germany in 1900–1 revealed Lansdowne's priorities. But its failure also demonstrated the intractability of the 'German problem'. This was a compound of that country's strengths and weaknesses. In 1870 Germany did not exist as a nation state; thirty years later it was the continent's greatest economic and military power. By 1913 France had only two-thirds the population of Germany and half the GNP, and it produced only one-sixth of the steel.[45] Russia, only just beginning to industrialise, also felt threatened and from 1894 the Franco–Russian alliance against possible German attack was a basic axis of continental diplomacy. Yet Germany suffered internationally from two great disadvantages. The first was geography. A new power in the centre of Europe, 'Germany was born encircled'.[46] Even with the assistance of its ally Austria–Hungary, Berlin faced the danger of having to fight a war on two fronts, especially after 1894. Germany's other deficiency, in an era when all the talk was of struggle among 'worldpowers', was felt to be its late entry into the colonial race. Unlike its main rivals, it had virtually no colonies, apart from a few Bismarckian pickings in Africa and the Pacific. By 1914 the German overseas empire amounted to one million square miles and fifteen million people. Britain's empire was thirteen times larger and had thirty-three times the population. For Kaiser Wilhelm II and for many German statesmen and intellectuals a 'world policy' (*Weltpolitik*) was vital to make Germany a great power.

For a decade from 1897 the decisive voice was that of Admiral Alfred von Tirpitz. His Navy Laws of 1898 and 1900 laid down a twenty-year schedule of naval building to create a fleet of sixty capital ships (battleships and battlecruisers) concentrated in the North Sea. Tirpitz warned the Kaiser in 1897: 'For Germany the most dangerous naval enemy at the present time is England. It is also the enemy against which we most urgently require a certain measure of naval force as a political power factor'.[47] The new navy, in other words, would give Germany the leverage, by diplomacy or if necessary by force, to achieve 'fair play' from Britain.[48] This naval policy also offered some prospect of stabilising German politics by directing class and social tensions outward into aggressive patriotism. Such a risky strategy assumed that Britain would not be able to match Germany because of its preoccupation with naval threats elsewhere. The British diplomatic realignments of 1900–7 were therefore disastrous shocks for Berlin.

Despite the secrecy surrounding German naval building, British policymakers and press had woken up to the challenge by 1901–2. Indeed that was a major obstacle to Lansdowne's bid for an alliance. In October 1902 Lord Selborne, First Lord of the Admiralty, warned the Cabinet: 'The more the composition of the new German fleet is examined the clearer it becomes that it is designed for a possible conflict with the British fleet'.[49] Although the 'Fisher revolution' was initially intended to meet the demands for economy and efficiency at a time of global challenge, the First Sea Lord himself was vehemently anti-German and his concentration of the fleet in home waters obviously strengthened its position against Tirpitz's new navy. At the Foreign Office a consensus about the German danger had also taken root by 1906, facilitated by the recent reforms that gave senior officials greater influence. The new Permanent Under-Secretary Charles Hardinge was particularly concerned, and he did his best to influence the incoming Liberal Foreign Secretary, Sir Edward Grey, not least through the appointment of the like-minded Louis Mallet and William Tyrrell as Grey's private secretaries (1905–7, 1907–15).

The restructuring of the Foreign Office definitely allowed its permanent staff a greater say in the formulation of British policy. Indeed thanks to the efficiency reforms there and elsewhere, particularly in the CID and General Staff, henceforth British foreign policy always reflected a degree of 'bureaucratic politics' unknown to Palmerston or even Salisbury. But although Grey seemed to outsiders a mild and malleable Foreign Secretary – happier fishing or birdwatching than ruining his eyesight reading diplomatic papers – he remained very much his own man. That was not simply because he developed vast experience over his eleven years as Foreign Secretary (1905–16) – a tenure unrivalled in the twentieth century – but also because he was a shrewd political infighter with clear diplomatic priorities. In particular, he came into office convinced, as he had said in 1903, 'that Germany is our worst enemy and our greatest danger'.[50] Although that was not the sum total of his foreign policy, it remained a basic assumption.

Grey's fears of Germany were sharpened by the diplomatic events of 1905–6 as he took over the Foreign Office. The Moroccan crisis caused by Germany's refusal to accept the Anglo–French bargain of 1904 was particularly alarming. Just how secure was the Entente, it was asked, when German pressure could force Delcassé's resignation as French Foreign Minister in June 1905? Such were French anxieties in January 1906 that Grey felt obliged to offer reassurance. He sanctioned contingency planning by the British and French military staffs for co-operation in the event of war with Germany – a significant precedent.

In this atmosphere, the collapse of Russia in defeat and revolution in 1905 took on a different aspect. What had initially seemed a welcome strengthening of Britain's global position began to look like a worrying tilt in the European balance of power. 'I am impatient to see Russia re-established as a factor in European politics', Grey wrote in February 1906.[51] That same month he also noted privately: 'An *entente* between Russia, France and ourselves would be absolutely secure. If it is necessary to check Germany it could then be done'.[52] This reinforced the long-standing, purely imperial, reasons for trying to reduce the Russian threat to India, and thus the burdens on Britain's armed forces, and it intensified Grey's desire for the agreement eventually reached in 1907.

As the ententes with France and Russia were consolidated, so the naval race with Germany entered a more menacing phase with the launching of the *Dreadnought* and of even faster battlecruisers of the

Invincible class. These had not been intended as specifically anti-German but Tirpitz immediately responded, taking advantage of an easier domestic political situation following heavy socialist reverses in the 1907 elections. The 1908 *Novelle*, or amendment to the Navy Law, pushed up the rate of capital-ship building from three to four per year and also established the principle of automatic replacement after twenty years. How far Britain should respond to this prospect of a large, permanently-modernised German navy split the Liberal Cabinet for the next few years.

After 1905 Liberal Imperialists occupied key positions in the new government, with Grey at the FO, the energetic Haldane at the War Office and the sympathetic Asquith first as Chancellor and then premier. But they had always been a minority, and the bulk of the Cabinet and much of the party remained broadly faithful to traditional Gladstonian precepts of peace, non-entanglement and retrenchment. The naval race enlarged the 'foreign policy public' – those engaged by foreign affairs – and led to a series of bitter political rows between 1908 and 1912. In February 1908 the Cabinet forced a cut in the naval estimates and that summer Lloyd George and Churchill, at this time vocal critics of the naval race and the animosity it engendered, campaigned for a naval agreement with Germany. The following year the crisis over naval spending was sharper, coming as it did on the eve of Lloyd George's 'people's budget' with its agenda of high social spending. The Admiralty demanded six new capital ships; the Radicals opposed more than four. And when the issue was debated in Parliament Asquith found himself attacked from the other side by the Conservatives for doing too little. 'We want eight and we won't wait', became the navalists' battlecry. It took a typical Asquith compromise – four now, four later, if the situation demanded – to defuse the crisis.

The worst Cabinet clash came two years later, in 1911. That summer, new German agitation about the growing French control over Morocco led to fears of war and further Anglo–French staff conversations. When news of these leaked out in the autumn, the Cabinet reined Grey in. In November 1911 they voted, fifteen to five, that further staff conversations should be entirely without commitment and should take place only with Cabinet approval.[53] Grey had been firmly rapped over the knuckles.

There was, however, a major benefit for Grey from the Moroccan crisis, namely the defection from the 'pro-German' camp of Lloyd George and Churchill – previously its leading spokesmen but now convinced of the menace from Berlin. The energetic Churchill was given the Admiralty in October 1911. He was soon withdrawing the bulk of the navy from the Mediterranean to concentrate on the German challenge. And in fact that autumn proved to be the Radicals' high water-mark. Divided in views and less concerned with foreign affairs than with domestic reform and the issue of Irish Home Rule, they were never again a serious problem. In effect 'they had reached a *modus vivendi* with Grey. He did not attempt to turn the Ententes into alliances', despite considerable pressure from parts of the FO, including the new Permanent Under-Secretary, Sir Arthur Nicolson (1910–16). For their part, the Radical critics 'did not force him to spell out the exact nature of Britain's relations with her friends'.[54] Thus the bulk of the Liberal party had only a negative influence on Grey's foreign policy, setting its limits but not determining its content. Moreover, in terms of power, Tirpitz's naval challenge was being met and mastered. By 1914 Britain was 'winning' the naval race, 22 to 13 in Dreadnoughts, 9 to 4 in battlecruisers.[55]

THE ELUSIVE BALANCE

With hindsight, the 'triple entente' with France and Russia and the growing rivalry with Germany can easily take on deterministic qualities. The ententes can seem like preparation for the rivalry – 'a policy of "appeasement"' whose 'success in the five years between 1902 and 1907 enabled Britain to wage a war' in 1914.[56] Likewise, to say that by 1906 'the Anglo–German antagonism . . . had been well and truly established' and 'had now become a permanent feature in international politics'[57] can suggest an air of inevitability about the events of 1907–14. Such an impression is unfortunate. It makes it harder to understand not merely the reasons for Britain's involvement in war in 1914 but also the complexity of its foreign policy after the apparent end of the Anglo–German antagonism in 1918.

In fact, it is arguable that, in 1912–14, this antagonism was on the wane. It had largely centred on the naval problem. As we know in the nuclear age, it is possible to have an arms race without that degenerating into war. Indeed what Rosebery in 1909 called 'a silent warfare' in naval building between Britain and Germany[58] has many similarities with the later Cold War between America and Russia.* Battleships

---

* As early as 1893 the German socialist Eduard Bernstein used the term 'cold war' to describe 'this continual arming, compelling the others to keep up with Germany' (Joll 1984: 67).

were the 1900s equivalent of modern strategic missiles – *the* international symbols of power and status. Both sides were playing a 'numbers game' and also, with *Dreadnought*, trying to respond to the 'innovation imperative'[59] of constantly-improved military technology. By 1912 the British were winning this first cold war of the industrial age.

The Anglo–German rivalry had also involved economics but here too the situation was looking more favourable for Britain. The panic about foreign competition abated with renewed prosperity after 1903. Instead of simple rivalry, Britain and Germany were developing a symbiotic trading relationship as spreading industrialisation created a global division of labour. For instance, dumped German steel was ruining British steel mills, but it also enabled British shipbuilders to undercut their German competitors who had to buy their steel in the high-priced home market.[60] Between 1904 and 1914 Britain became Germany's major customer but Germany also became Britain's second-best market.[61] It was true that Britain's growth rate was particularly sluggish between 1899 and 1913 – at 0.5 per cent per man-year against America's 1.3 per cent and Germany's 1.5 per cent (table 1.3), but this was symptomatic of the catch-up phenomenon as newer industrial powers pulled back on Britain's pioneering lead. There *were* underlying problems – slowness in automation, backward technical education, small industrial units, lack of innovative investment – but some of these, such as technical education,[62] were being addressed in the pre-war era, and it is going too far to dismiss Edwardian manufacturing as largely 'a working museum of industrial archaeology'.[63] The picture, more exactly, is that of a country whose early lead had now disappeared and which was beginning to grapple with the inadequacies of its pioneering industrialisation. Serious problems were apparent, but failure to solve them was by no means certain in 1914.[64] What would prove disastrous was the interaction of these problems with the complex impact of two world wars.

Moreover, the outcome of the arms race reminds us that crude manufacturing output alone does not determine military capability. Between 1899 and 1913 Germany just overtook Britain as the world's second largest manufacturer, with nearly 15 per cent of world industrial production, while the leader, America, increased its share from nearly a quarter to just under one-third (table 1.1). Yet the USA chose not to translate its wealth into *military* power. Germany tried, but its mechanism for doing so – its taxation system – was much less efficient than Britain's. Chamberlain's proposed solution for the fiscal problem of growing military *and* social spending was increased indirect taxation

– tariff reform. Asquith's Liberal government took the opposite course. It made the graduated income tax a permanent part of the peacetime fiscal system. Between 1904 and 1914 the top rate rose from 3.75 per cent to 13.33 per cent, and by the onset of war 60 per cent of central government income came from direct taxes as opposed to only 44 per cent in 1888.[65] The old Gladstonian verities about the limits of the country's taxable capacity had been transcended. In consequence Britain had a more stable and efficient fiscal system than many of its rivals. In France and America income tax was introduced only on the eve of the First World War, while in Germany it was used by the states but not by the Imperial Government.[66]

In fact, the political and budgetary problems caused in Britain by the 'cold war' seem trivial in comparison with the crises that Tirpitz's failed naval policy had engendered in Germany. Attempts to impose an imperial income tax brought down Chancellor von Bülow in 1909 and after 1911 German imperial politics were disrupted by a large Socialist bloc in the Reichstag. At the same time, the Army, relatively quiescent for years, began to demand increased spending to cope with the growing military strength of Russia and France. The extension of the Russian railway network, largely financed by French loans, promised to halve to fifteen days the time required for mobilisation. Meanwhile, the increase in the term of French military service in 1913 from two to three years made the French army a far harder nut to crack quickly. Thus Germany's Schlieffen Plan for two-front war – quick victory over France before Russia had time to mobilise – now looked dangerously flawed. At sea and by land Germany was losing out and talk of 'encirclement' became commonplace in Berlin. With growing tension in the Balkans, Germany's now rather desperate emphasis was on a continental rather than a world policy.

The German army's concern was an indication that by 1912 the international balance of power seemed to have shifted, particularly with the military resurgence of Russia. British policy consequently changed in emphasis. Grey's aim, it must be stressed, had never been to confront Germany but merely to contain it. 'Real isolation of Germany would mean war: so would the domination of Germany in Europe', he noted in February 1909. 'There is a fairly wide course between the two extremes in which European politics should steer'.[67] This provides a good summation of his balancing act – from a position of strength provided by the Ententes and the naval build-up, Britain might now hope for a detente with Germany, particularly since Grey identified the new Chancellor, Theobold von Bethmann Hollweg, as a 'moderate'. After the shock of near-war over Morocco in 1911 secret discussions began for an Anglo–German colonial deal should Portugal's rickety African empire collapse. In February 1912 Haldane was sent to Berlin to explore, albeit unsuccessfully, the chances of a naval agreement. These demarches and the refusal to turn the ententes into formal alliances were not merely sops to the Radicals. They also reflected Grey's own desire for improved relations with Germany. He envisaged the Ententes not as a basis for war but as the foundation of a new European Concert.

Grey therefore did not view Anglo–German antagonism as insoluble. Nor was it the case that the Triple Entente with France and Russia was absolutely secure. While the French Ambassador in London, Paul Cambon, was repeatedly pressing Grey for a full-scale alliance, his brother Jules, Ambassador in Berlin, was working for a Franco–German rapprochement. Those efforts had the sympathy of French socialists and radicals, repelled by alliance with Tsarist Russia, and by the many Frenchmen of all political stripes who had little faith in their traditional enemy, perfidious Albion. Even more problematic for Grey was the revival of Russian power. The 1907 agreement had not held in Persia, where the growth of nationalist unrest had given the Russians the excuse to take complete control of the northern zone. The Indian border with Tibet also became an issue again. These developments reopened the whole problem of Indian security, apparently settled by the events of 1905–7. So concerned was Nicolson that, backed by the Indian Government, he urged Grey to make a new effort to appease Russia through a more generous agreement and even a military alliance. But Tyrrell and others in the FO believed, in contrast, that the reduction of the German threat meant that Britain could now afford to call Russia's bluff and take a tougher line.[68] Grey sympathised with this latter assessment and resisted pressures to turn the entente into an alliance right up to the coming of war.[69]

Thus the fixity of British diplomacy after 1907 should not be exaggerated. Germany was not seen as a permanent enemy, nor Russia as an abiding ally. It is not necessary to go to the opposite extreme of claiming that British policymakers 'regarded themselves on the whole as being less threatened by Germany than by Russia'[70] to acknowledge that the German question was only one, albeit currently the most pressing, aspect of a continuing global puzzle of squaring responsibilities, rivals and resources. Neither the Antagonism nor the Entente were everlasting. Palmerston's rhetoric of 1848 was still valid: 'We have no eternal allies, and we have no perpetual enemies. Our interests are eternal and perpetual, and those interests it is our duty to follow'.[71]

Arguably, there is more continuity in British foreign policy in the decades before 1914 than is sometimes acknowledged. In the 1880s Salisbury had tilted towards the Triple Alliance of Italy, Austria and Germany to offset Franco–Russian hostility. In 1901–2 Chamberlain and Lansdowne, feeling even more isolated, had sought to go further and create an Anglo–German alliance. Then, frustrated by German *Weltpolitik*, Lansdowne shifted tack and broke out of isolation by understandings with Japan, America and France – a trend which Grey consolidated by the Anglo–Russian agreement. By 1912 the balance was shifting again, and, without sacrificing the Entente with France and Russia, Grey was working for detente with Germany and worrying over new tensions with Russia. For Sir Edward, like his predecessors, diplomacy was a search for the elusive balance.

REFERENCES

1.   Kennedy 1980
2.   Amery 1969: iv, 421
3.   Beloff 1969: ch. 3; Friedberg 1988
4.   M. Howard 1974: 11
5.   Searle 1971: 39
6.   A.N. Porter 1980: 144
7.   Grenville 1970: 237
8.   P. Warwick (ed.) 1980: 59
9.   Eldridge 1978: 209
10.   Wormell 1979: 154–5
11.   Judd 1968: 38
12.   Bond 1972: 228
13.   Semmel 1960: 62
14.   Adams and Poirier 1987: 16–17
15.   Friedberg 1988: 256
16.   Hyam 1976: 133
17.   Marder 1961: i, 6
18.   Ibid., 39, 55
19.   Martel 1986: 158
20.   Cuniff 1903: 310
21.   Matthew 1973: 228
22.   Pollard 1989: ch. 3
23.   Ibid., 238–44
24.   Amery 1969: vi, 484, 505
25.   Sykes 1979: 25
26.   MacKay 1985: 149–50

27. BD i: no. 285
28. C. Howard 1967: 19
29. R. Jones 1971: 117
30. Steiner 1969: 79
31. Bourne 1967: 350
32. Friedberg 1988: 173
33. Nish 1966: 184
34. Friedberg 1988: 177
35. Bourne 1970: 478
36. C.J. Lowe 1967: ii, doc. 139
37. C. Howard 1967: 93
38. Nish 1966: 229, 244
39. Kennedy 1980: 249–50
40. Dilks 1969: i, 113
41. Friedberg 1988: 248
42. Robbins 1971: 162
43. Rolo 1987: 159
44. Grenville 1970: 340
45. Kennedy 1988: 199, 222
46. Calleo 1978: 206
47. Steinberg 1966: 209
48. Berghahn 1973: 36
49. Marder 1961: i, 107
50. Robbins 1971: 131
51. Steiner 1977: 82
52. BD iii: no. 299
53. K. Wilson 1985: 27–8
54. Steiner 1977: 148
55. Steinberg 1977: 213
56. M. Howard 1974: 30
57. Kennedy 1980: 287–8, 544
58. K. Wilson 1985: 12
59. Mandelbaum 1981: 95
60. Kennedy 1980: 300
61. Steiner 1977: 62
62. Sanderson 1988
63. Barnett 1972: 88; cf. Floud and McCloskey (eds) 1981: chs 1–5
64. Sked 1987: 21; Pollard 1989: 271
65. Emy 1972: 129–30
66. Matthew 1979: 642–3
67. Sweet 1977: 226
68. Steiner 1977: 114–15
69. French 1986: 7
70. K. Wilson 1985: 2
71. Bourne 1970: 293

CHAPTER FOUR

Great War, 1914–22

If war with Germany was not a foregone conclusion, why did it break out in August 1914? The answer offered in the first section of this chapter points particularly to the escalating Balkan crisis, which threatened the stability of all Europe. Even that, however, did not have an automatic effect on Britain but was mediated through calculations of policy and politics. Contrary to most expectations, this proved a protracted conflict, which revealed some of the limitations of British power – in particular its slowness in getting a large army into the field and its growing reliance on American resources. Without allies, Britain could not have defeated Germany. And, as section three shows, allies also formed an important constraint on British diplomacy. Together with the constraints imposed by strategic debate and political argument they helped frustrate any attempt to end the war by negotiation. But perhaps the most significant obstacle to a negotiated peace was the British view of Germany. By analysing that we are better able to understand not only why Britain fought on for so long but also why, apparently paradoxically, the British were so indifferent to Germany in the 1920s and early 1930s.

It is customary to treat the Great War as an unmitigated disaster for Britain. This is understandable. In terms of human and material resources, and of imperial and international relations, British power was severely shaken. Yet, as the last section shows, 1918 brought gains as well as losses for Britain's global position. It was the war's complex legacy of new responsibilities, enhanced power *and* incipient weaknesses which left Britain ill-equipped to cope with the new challenges of the 1930s.

THE JULY CRISIS AND THE OUTBREAK OF WAR

In May 1914 Sir Arthur Nicolson, the Permanent Under-Secretary, observed: 'Since I have been at the Foreign Office, I have not seen such calm waters'.[1] With Ireland in turmoil over Home Rule, Belfast seemed a greater threat to peace than Berlin. If international tension had eased by the spring of 1914, why then did Britain go to war with Germany in August?

Much of the answer lies in the Balkans. Earlier European rivalries, in Africa or China, had occurred because of the collapse of an existing power structure. Britain was sucked into the vacuum – reluctantly yet fearful that otherwise its rivals would benefit. 1914 saw another crisis of empire, this time not on the periphery of Europe but near its heart – the complete collapse of Ottoman rule in the Balkans and the related threat from Slavic nationalism to the polyglot Austro–Hungarian empire of the Habsburgs. Serbia was the principal Slavic agitator. When the heir to the Habsburg throne was assassinated by Serbian terrorists on 28 June 1914, the Austrians decided that only a punitive strike at Serbia could save the empire from disintegration. The German government, for whom the Habsburgs were now its only reliable ally, promised full support – perhaps hoping that the Russians would be deterred from intervening, as happened in the Bosnian crisis of 1908, but in any case increasingly fatalistic that war with France and Russia was coming sooner or later. Once Russia began to mobilise, Germany implemented the Schlieffen Plan to try to knock France out of the war before turning back on the gathering Russian strength. One need not go so far as to claim that '1914–18 . . . was the Third Balkan War'[2] to recognise that, without the crisis in southeastern Europe, the first modern cold war might have remained cold. For all the voices in the 1900s predicting a great war – voices that now we naturally find deafening – there were many others who believed that the tension could be contained. It was the implosion of a whole corner of Europe, with all that this seemed to portend for Vienna and Berlin, which was decisive.

Throughout July Grey had quietly tried to cool this crisis, as he had done in Morocco, the Balkans and elsewhere – and on 29 July the Cabinet decided to maintain the delicate balance. The French and Germans were to be told 'that at this stage we were unable to pledge ourselves in advance either under all circumstances to stand aside or in any condition to go in'.[3] Why, then, did Britain come off the fence and declare war on 4 August?

It did so, in part, because the secret military contacts with France had become compromisingly entangling. In 1911 Eyre Crowe of the FO observed that 'the Entente is not an alliance',[4] but something close to commitments had in fact been undertaken. In the summer of 1912 the French Navy had decided to concentrate all its battleships in the Mediterranean, to confront the growing Austrian and Italian build-up. At the same time the British Admiralty, under Churchill, was trying to pull back from the Mediterranean. He continued the Fisher policy of concentrating British capital ships in home waters, despite considerable opposition from much of the FO where it was viewed as a serious diminution of British influence. The French and British decisions were strictly unrelated, but French Ambassador Paul Cambon, alert as ever to ways of strengthening the Entente, proposed that here was a convenient division of labour and that naval staff conversations should draw up contingency plans in the event of war.

On 1 August 1914 Cambon raised the implications of those 1912 conversations with Grey, arguing that Britain now had a moral obligation to protect France's Channel coast from German attack because France was looking after the Mediterranean to help Britain. Although it was a tendentious reading of what happened in 1912, Grey used this argument to convince all but four members of the Cabinet on the morning of 2 August that Britain did have an obligation to defend France at sea, if not by land.

The confusion about the secret staff talks was indicative of the growing problem of bureaucratic politics in the making of British foreign policy. The growth of professional staffs in the FO, CID, War Office and Admiralty was a response to the demands for more efficient administration and more authoritative analysis to aid hard-pressed and ill-informed ministers. But a bureaucracy inevitably develops a mind of its own and policies that help sanctify its own existence. Significantly the new General Staff in 1905 quickly produced strategic appraisals to justify sending an army to France in the event of war, instead of relying on the naval blockade and coastal raiding, as the Admiralty, equally unsurprisingly, suggested. The Moroccan crisis of January 1906, coinciding as it did with the collapse of Balfour's government over tariff reform and a bitter election campaign, 'offered a unique opportunity to permanent officials of the War Office and Cabinet to influence the course of strategic policy without regard to the wishes of the government of the day'.[5] Cumulatively, the two Moroccan crises, of 1906 and 1911, plus the fleet redeployment of 1912, allowed military and naval staffs to create a web of contingency plans for possible Anglo–French cooperation in time of war. Officially these were purely hypothetical – to be invoked only *if* the British government decided to ally with France – but the sense of moral obligation was hard to avoid, as the Cabinet found in August 1914.

Yet it would be wrong to imply that Britain was entangled unwittingly in war. Grey, too, had stuck out his neck to the French. On 1 August 1914 Nicolson reminded him: 'you have over and over again promised M. Cambon that if Germany was the aggressor you would stand by France.' 'Yes,' Grey replied, 'but he has nothing in writing'.[6] The staff talks, like Grey's promises, were the British response to recurrent French panics about imminent German pressure or even attack. Such fears also arose whenever the British made overtures to Germany: Cambon's call for naval talks in 1912 was an expression of French shock over the Haldane mission to Berlin. As Sir Francis Betrie, the Ambassador in Paris, aptly noted in 1906, the French 'have an instinctive dread of Germany and an hereditary distrust of England, and with these characteristics they are easily led to believe that they may be deserted by England and fallen upon by Germany'.[7] For British policymakers, then, the Entente with France was not a military alliance but a form of political reassurance – symptomatic of the British approach to Anglo–French relations for half a century.

But why was it important to reassure France? And why was it essential to conciliate Russia? In part, as recent friction over North Africa and India had shown, to quote Nicolson in 1913, 'an unfriendly France and Russia would give us infinite trouble, especially the former, in localities where we should find it extremely difficult to maintain our own'.[8] This would be especially true if Germany was also exploiting Britain's problems. And in the event of war with Germany, Britain, lacking a large standing army, would rely, at least initially, on the manpower of Russia and especially France. War by proxy required the diplomacy of reassurance.

But war might not have occurred. Ultimately, the policy of the Entente comes back to the problem of Germany. Although it was not inevitable that Germany would start a war in Europe, if it did, then Britain could not stand aside. During the Moroccan crisis of July 1911 Grey talked to the CID about what would happen 'if a European conflict, not of our making, arose, in which it was quite clear that the struggle was one for the supremacy of Europe, in fact . . . a situation something like that in the old Napoleonic days.' In that case, he said, 'our concern in seeing that there did not arise a supremacy in Europe which entailed a combination that would deprive us of the command of the sea would be such that we might have to take part in that European war'.[9] In other words, despite the security offered by the

Channel, a hostile power controlling much of the Continent, particularly the Channel coast, could render British seapower ineffective. And, conversely, if Germany lost and Britain had kept out, then the relations with the victors, France and Russia – Britain's betrayed friends and erstwhile foes – would be impossible. This, at root, was why the Haldane mission to Berlin failed in 1912. Germany would only give up its naval programme in return for a British guarantee of neutrality in a European war. And that, Asquith observed, was 'a promise we cannot give'.[10] As Grey concluded during the Moroccan crisis of 1906, Britain could not stand aside from a Franco–German war 'without losing our good name and our friends and wrecking our policy and position in the world'.[11] Sir Eyre Crowe of the FO put the point more generally in July 1914: 'The theory that England cannot engage in a big war means her abdication as an independent state'.[12]

The Cold War might have remained cold, but, once the Balkan crisis encouraged Germany to risk a hot war, Britain could not be unaffected. Encircled by France and Russia, Germany aimed to win by a rapid strike through Belgium to defeat France before turning to confront the more slowly mobilising Russians. It was the brutal invasion of Belgium, whose neutrality Britain was officially bound by treaty to protect, which salved the consciences of all but two of the Cabinet and silenced most Liberal and Labour opposition in the Commons. But, even if the Schlieffen Plan had not set the route to Paris through Liège, most British policymakers were by then prepared, however reluctantly, to go to war if Germany attacked France because of the implications for the European and global balance.

One further point must be made in order to understand the insouciance and bungling that surrounded Britain's slide into war in 1914. Stated simply: no one thought they were helping start 'the First World War' – a four-year struggle in which ten million died and the old Europe committed suicide. The paradox is that in Britain, as elsewhere, contemporaries expected a conflict with momentous consequences that would, nevertheless, be over quickly. Kitchener, predicting armies of millions of men kept in the field for years, was almost alone in doubting 'the short-war illusion'.[13]

This helps to explain the shambles of the military planning. The CID had been emasculated under the Liberals and was unable to prevent the army and navy quite simply proceeding with competing contingency plans for war. The Navy proposed assisting France through blockade and raids on the German coast, while the military insisted that six British divisions in France or Belgium could make all the difference in defeating the Germans. In 1911 Asquith dismissed the

Admiralty's ideas as 'puerile',[14] thereby strengthening the Army's position, but the General Staff still had little knowledge of the French army's strategy or of how Britain would help. So Britain had a vast navy that was irrelevant to continental land war, and an army with a continental strategy but no means of making an impact. Both War Office and Admiralty planning was 'riddled with elements of wishful thinking'.[15] Or, more exactly, the strategic irrelevance of the plans highlights the fact that they were intended more as political reassurance to the French than as serious preparation for a long war. Few thought that the muddle would matter.

In politics, too, the motto was 'business as usual'. A factor reconciling the Cabinet to war on 2 August was the desire to stay in office. With the Conservatives announcing their readiness to form a war ministry and with Grey threatening resignation unless France was supported, it seemed better to hang together rather than give way to what one waverer, Sir John Simon, called 'a Coalition Government which would assuredly be the grave of Liberalism'.[16] Again the expectation of a short conflict, akin to Bismarck's victories of 1866 and 1870, helps explain the Cabinet's action.

The war *was* very nearly 'over by Christmas'. Von Moltke's armies almost broke through to Paris in August 1914. Had they done so, forcing France, as in 1870 and 1940, to seek an armistice, the consequences for twentieth-century history could have been far-reaching. But the Germans failed, as much through their own mistakes as because of French or British skill. Meanwhile the Germans held the Russians in bloody battles in East Prussia. Once stalemate ensued on the Western Front and in the East, the war entered a new phase for which no belligerent, certainly not Britain, was prepared.

THE DEEPENING CONFLICT: STRATEGY AND SUPPLY

In retrospect, the Germans' bid for European hegemony seems doomed to failure. They 'had sufficient strength to try but not enough to succeed'.[17] Britain's support for the Franco–Russian alliance tipped the balance of warmaking potential against the Central Powers. On 1913 figures the Allies commanded 28 per cent of the world's manufacturing output, Germany and Austria–Hungary 20 per cent. But British potential was not yet fully realised – the country had no conscript army, the empire's resources had not been mobilised, and the naval blockade, Britain's main instrument of immediate power, was of limited use given the Central Powers' advantage of interior lines on the European continent.[18] Moreover, German development of the U-boat presaged a grave challenge to Britannia's rule of the waves, which culminated in the Atlantic crisis of 1917. The crucial question was whether Germany and its allies could defeat France and/or Russia before the British potential was fully mobilised. In 1915 the Central Powers tried to eliminate Russia; in 1916 they concentrated on bleeding France out of the war at Verdun. By the time British potential was a reality in 1917, France was enervated, Russia was crumbling and Britain itself faced an unrestricted U-boat campaign to starve it into negotiation. It took the support of the United States finally to shift the balance against the Central Powers.

Britain mobilised in a piecemeal and ill-considered fashion.[19] This was hardly surprising given the lack of recent precedent, but the consequences for Britain's war effort and for its post-war position were significant. It would not be much of an exaggeration to say that in the first winter of the war the Asquith Cabinet believed that an increased British effort was simply a matter of more men and more money. There was little logistic and economic planning and the motto remained 'business as usual'. On 4 August 1914 the BEF amounted to six divisions, of which only four were initially sent to France. But the new Secretary of State for War, Lord Kitchener, anticipating a long struggle, persuaded the Cabinet that it must raise a large army. Conscription remained politically taboo and the army lacked the necessary equipment for such an influx. In any case, the supply of volunteers when Kitchener insisted that 'Your Country Needs You' took everyone by surprise, not least the army's enlistment facilities. More than a million had signed up by Christmas 1914.

The effect of this flood of volunteers on the war effort was initially far from beneficial. Not only did it take months to train the raw recruits – Kitchener's 'New Armies' did not make an impact until 1916 – but the uncontrolled voluntary recruitment had siphoned off skilled manpower from British industry. This exacerbated the munitions crisis that hit the BEF in the spring of 1915. There had been no pre-war stockpiling of supplies and no plans for rapid wartime increase in production by government ordnance factories or by private contractors. The 'shells scandal' that broke in May 1915 was therefore hardly the responsibility of Kitchener and Asquith's wartime Cabinet. But it provided a convenient opportunity to settle old scores and this was one strand in the political crisis that forced a coalition government in May 1915.

The other strand was the failure of the Dardanelles campaign. Kitchener, like most of the generals, believed that the war would be decided on the Western Front. But the Admiralty – represented by Churchill as First Lord and Fisher, recalled as First Sea Lord – naturally inclined to a maritime strategy, and this gained support from politicians concerned at the public reaction to the carnage and stalemate in Flanders. Lloyd George, the Chancellor, argued in January 1915 that only a 'clear definite victory' with heavy and visible enemy losses in men, material and territory, would 'satisfy the public that tangible results are being achieved by the great sacrifices they are making, and decide neutrals that it is at last safe for them to throw in their lot with us'.[20] There was protracted debate about where to strike. The Baltic, Greece, even the Levant, were among the options canvassed. But the entry of the Ottoman empire into the war on the German side in November 1914 soon became the focus of British thinking.

The Turkish danger to British interests was far greater than that posed by Austria–Hungary. Egypt, under British occupation since 1882, was still formally an Ottoman possession and the British promptly declared a protectorate in order to avoid a crisis of authority. The Turks posed a real military threat and the British were obliged to open new fronts on the Suez Canal to protect Egypt and in Mesopotamia to guard the route to India. Constantinople's authority as a spiritual centre of Islam also raised the danger of subversion among the Islamic peoples of the British Empire. An attack on the Dardanelles therefore became the preferred option for a second front. This, it was confidently expected, would secure communications with southern Russia and quickly knock the Ottomans out of the war. Moreover – and this brought Kitchener into line with Churchill – it was envisaged as mainly a naval action, requiring no serious diversion of troops from France. In the event, the whole campaign was as ineptly managed as the raising of the New Armies. The commander, Sir Ian Hamilton, lacked maps, staff and ammunition. Naval bombardment alone failed to take the Straits and in April 1915 a hastily-arranged landing at Gallipoli by Australian, New Zealand and British troops soon got bogged down amid heavy casualties in another war of attrition. After further abortive landings in August the British finally cut their losses and withdrew at the end of the year. Probably the best organised part of the campaign was the evacuation.

In May 1915 the 'shell scandal' and the Gallipoli disaster brought to a head disaffection with the Liberal Government, abetted by a strident press campaign. But Asquith rode the storm adroitly, enlarging his Cabinet with Conservative and token Labour representation while keeping most of the principal offices in Liberal hands. The main casualty was Churchill, forced out of the Admiralty as the scapegoat for Gallipoli; the most significant change was Lloyd George's appointment to head the new Ministry of Munitions. For months LG had been a bitter critic of the supply crisis, seeing it as symptomatic of underlying complacency about the war effort as a whole. 'An alliance of war cannot be conducted on limited liability principles' he told the Commons in February 1915.[21] Britain needed to mobilise all its men and wealth and to organise them systematically in order to avoid self-defeating competition of the sort caused by Kitchener's recruitment policy. As Minister of Munitions LG presided over the conversion of much of the engineering industry to war production and arrogated to himself new powers over labour and raw materials. The Ministry's Munitions Board in the USA also took over most of Britain's growing American purchases, hitherto contracted out to the Wall Street bankers, J.P. Morgan's. And during the autumn of 1915 the Cabinet, pressed by Lloyd George, gradually came round to the principle of conscription.

By now the moral and political objections were secondary. Sceptics, such as the new Chancellor, Reginald McKenna, were mostly concerned that enlargement of the army would further damage Britain's economy.[22] But the military reverses of winter 1915–16 – Serbia's collapse, Bulgaria's entry into the war against the Allies, and the German assault on Verdun – convinced the Cabinet that Britain had to do more to sustain the French. The results were conscription for 18 to 41 year-old single males in January 1916 (extended to married men in May) and a major British offensive on the Western Front that summer. Neither was efficacious. The conscripts took months to train and in the meantime Kitchener's New Armies had been destroyed on the Somme, sustaining 400,000 casualties between July and November 1916. By the end of the campaign the mood in London was grim. A frustrated Lloyd George demanded that Asquith put him in charge of a war council of three with full powers to run the war. After dithering, Asquith resigned, confident that LG could not win Conservative support to form a ministry.[23] He was wrong. On 7 December 1916 Lloyd George became Prime Minister, with A.J. Balfour replacing Grey as Foreign Secretary.

Britain's crisis was more than one of leadership, however. By late 1916 there was no longer enough money to prosecute the war. In part this was a consequence of relative economic decline – as an industrial power Germany was in many respects Britain's equal and the war effort was inevitably going to strain British resources. British defence spending rose from £91 million in 1913 to nearly £2 billion in 1918, by which time it represented 80 per cent of total government spending and over half the GNP.[24] Compounding the problem was Britain's role as the Entente's principal banker. It loaned the equivalent of $11.1 billion during the war, largely to Russia, France and Italy.* This was a further strain on the country's resources, but it was necessary, both as compensation for the initial lack of British military activity and, increasingly, to keep the weaker allies in the war.

But policy decisions exacerbated these deficiencies of power. Treasury orthodoxy, shaped by the legacies of the wars against France in the eighteenth and early nineteenth centuries, was to meet war costs as much as possible through the income tax and to avoid heavy loans which would then burden the national debt for years to come. In the Crimean War 46 per cent was raised through loans.[25] But as Chancellor in 1914–15, Lloyd George wished to avoid the social hardship caused by sharp tax increases and preferred to raise much of the extra funds through borrowing, particularly War Loans. These earned generous interest and their holders were allowed to convert to later, ever more attractive issues, and increasingly to short-term Treasury bills. Yet these costly instruments failed to absorb purchasing power.[26] Meanwhile, at Munitions and as premier, Lloyd George helped to release the spending departments from Treasury control, further fuelling inflation. Of course, all the belligerents had to raise most of their war spending from borrowing – Britain's proportion of 80 per cent compares very favourably with the 98 per cent recorded by France and Germany[27] – but the overall scale of Britain's financial effort in funding its own war effort and that of its allies was far greater. The National Debt rose to £7.5 billion by 1919, ten times its 1914 level.[28] Even so, Britain's own financial resources proved insufficient. By 1916 the country was dependent on the USA.

Before the war American money markets had been largely geared to supplying domestic capital needs. There was relatively little foreign lending and scant expertise in that area of finance. It was British, and to a lesser extent French, demand for US private loans which helped convert America into a major international financial power.[29] Britain needed to raise funds in the USA, not merely to fund its own purchases and to refinance its credits to the Allies, but also to support the pound. For the heavy spending on war imports had enlarged the trade gap, while diminished income from shipping and financial services plus

* This was not far short of the US figure of $11.9 billion (Kindleberger 1973: 40).

the loans to the Allies meant that invisible earnings failed to compensate. The strain on the balance of payments was met initially by exports of gold, but this could not continue indefinitely and in 1915 the pound began to slip against the dollar from its normal exchange rate of $4.86. By August 1915 it had fallen to $4.61 and that autumn the British and French governments were forced to float a $500 million loan on the US market. Two others, each for $250 million and at higher rates of interest, followed in August 1916 and January 1917. By October 1916 the Treasury warned that Britain was spending some £5 million a day on the war, of which £2 million had to be raised in the USA – 40 per cent from loans, the rest from gold and the sale of securities – and it warned that virtually all the US funds would have to be borrowed by the spring of 1917.[30]

The crisis was eventually solved only by US entry into the war in April 1917 – a decision taken reluctantly by President Woodrow Wilson in response to unrestricted U-boat warfare in the Atlantic. But the early months of 1917 were perhaps the grimmest of the war to date. The U-boat campaign caused devastating losses to British merchant shipping, until effective convoying and escort measures were introduced. The US government was also slow to organise its own war finance and to offer direct support to Britain in funding US purchases and assisting the exchange rate. Only in July 1917, when Britain's available gold reserves for supporting the pound were down to £10 million, was an arrangement formalised for monthly advances from the US government.[31] For the British government it was unprecedented and deeply humiliating to be 'down on our knees to the Americans', in the words of press baron Lord Northcliffe.[32]

Moreover, British and US war aims were not identical and thus Britain's need for American support could be used as leverage by the United States. This had already been evident in the era of US neutrality. Wilson had sought a negotiated peace – 'peace without victory' as he put it in January 1917 – and by 1916 he believed the British were as much of an obstacle to this as the Germans. In November 1916 he had cast doubt on British solvency, thereby damaging their prospects for a US loan, in the hope of softening up Britain for his peace effort. This tension did not end with US entry into the war. Wilson, now intent on creating a League of Nations, made it clear that America was not an 'ally' of Britain, France and Russia but an 'associate' – indicating that their shared aim of defeating Germany did not betoken agreed objectives for the future peace.[33]

Potentially American entry into the war tipped the economic balance decisively in favour of the Allies. But America, like Britain earlier, needed time to mobilise its resources and initiate conscription, and it was not until mid-1918 that its hastily-raised armies made any real impact in France. By then the military balance had shifted heavily against the Allies with the elimination of Russia from the war.[34]

The March 1917 revolution did not end the Russian war effort completely – there was a renewed offensive in July – but after the Bolshevik takeover in November Lenin immediately sought an armistice. The treaties of Brest–Litovsk in March 1918, and of Bucharest (May) which ended Romanian involvement in the war, opened up vast areas of Eastern Europe all around the Black Sea to German control or influence, even posing a new threat to India.[35] In London and Paris the Bolsheviks were seen as traitors to the Allied cause and, as Russia collapsed into the anarchy of civil war, their opponents were given military support in an effort to revive an eastern front. For Britain, this was not, initially at least, a matter of ideology so much as a logical consequence of its historic policy of war by proxy. Lord Robert Cecil told the Commons in May 1918: 'We wish to see Russia preserved as an Allied country, or, if that is impossible, a non-German one. That is the great foundation stone of our policy'.[36]

Allied intervention in Russia was therefore one consequence of the Bolshevik revolution. The other was the new German onslaught in the spring of 1918. Peace with Russia enabled the Germans, for the first time in the war, to shift the bulk of their troops to the western front. Ludendorff mounted five great offensives from March 1918 – the first nearly splitting the British and French armies, the third stopping barely forty miles from Paris. Only when these were exhausted, in July, did the Allies attack, aided by growing numbers of American combat troops. Even so, the sudden collapse of the Central Powers that autumn came as a general surprise.

NO PEACE, NO VICTORY: ALLIANCE DIPLOMACY

So much for the expectation of a short war. Instead, Britain had become embroiled in a struggle that strained almost to exhaustion its resources and those of its allies. The question therefore arises, given the length and the cost of the conflict, why did Britain not seek a negotiated peace?

Such an idea was certainly canvassed. In November 1916, when British casualties were over one million, Lord Lansdowne, erstwhile appeaser of the 1900s, now a Tory elder statesman and member of the coalition Cabinet, warned his colleagues: 'We are slowly but surely killing off the best of the male population of these islands. . . . Generations will have to come and go before the country recovers from the loss which it has sustained in human beings, and from the financial ruin and the destruction of the means of production which are taking place'. Lansdowne asked whether 'the sacrifice will have its reward' and whether, instead of talking, as Lloyd George had done, about 'knock-out blows' and dictating terms to Germany, it might be better 'to accept less than 20s[hillings] in the £ in consideration of prompt payment'.[37]

Lansdowne's call for a compromise peace got short shrift in Cabinet, but in reality there were many who shared his doubts. Even Lloyd George moaned 'we are losing this war', in a moment of acute despondency that autumn.[38] Likewise, the generals were less optimistic in private than subsequent blimpish caricatures might suggest. Why, then, did Britain fight on? The central reasons for continuing the struggle were the policy divisions within the Government, the extremity of Britain's war aims against Germany, and the complications of fighting with allies.

The tensions among British leaders were pronounced. At the strategic level there was the divide between 'Westerners' and 'Easterners' – those who insisted that the decisive struggle, or at least Britain's vital contribution, must come on the battlefields of France and Belgium, and those who, to quote Churchill, believed that there must be 'other alternatives than sending our armies to chew barbed wire in Flanders'.[39] This was the rationale behind Churchill's and Lloyd George's advocacy of the disastrous Dardanelles campaign of 1915. Likewise in early 1917 Lloyd George repeatedly urged developing the Italian front in the hope of eliminating Austria. Thus British resources were never fully concentrated on one theatre of operations.

Political differences were also significant. Once the Liberals had reluctantly accepted the need for a coalition Cabinet, they constantly had to keep their Conservative partners sweet, or at least not publicly sour. The peace issue was a sensitive point. Curzon observed in August 1916 that he and his friends 'had made sacrifice of many of their views so as to remain in the Cabinet and there oppose an undesirable peace'.[40] Given the influence on the Tory leader, Bonar Law, of Curzon and of diehards like Sir Edward Carson outside the Cabinet, the issue of a negotiated peace was never properly explored within the coalition. Furthermore, many Conservatives were ardent 'Westerners', which added a political dimension to the strategic arguments.

A further division was that of 'Frocks' and 'Brasshats'. Mindful as we are of the aftermath of the carnage, when the aphorism that war is too important to be left to the generals became axiomatic, it is easy now to forget the awe in which military leaders were held in 1914.[41] They knew about war; virtually all the politicians did not. Lord Kitchener, for instance, the victor of Omdurman and the Boer war, was, to quote Asquith's daughter, 'more than a national hero. He was a national institution'.[42] His appointment as Secretary of State for War in August 1914 seemed inevitable, as did the recall of Fisher as First Sea Lord. Only slowly did the prestige of the military decline, only slowly were disillusioned politicians able to exert their own influence. The creation of first a War Committee and finally, in the autumn of 1916, a proper War Cabinet were both attempts to wrest control of grand strategy from the military. Even so the latter were deeply entrenched. The team of Sir William Robertson as Chief of the Imperial General Staff (CIGS) and Sir Douglas Haig as commander of British forces in France, which dated from the end of 1915, proved both influential and durable. In the summer of 1917 they were still strong enough, with support from the Conservatives and the Northcliffe press, to override Lloyd George's objections and mount a new offensive that led to the mud and blood of Passchendaele. It was only in February 1918 that Lloyd George felt strong enough to replace Robertson as CIGS with the somewhat more tractable Sir Henry Wilson.

Arguments between 'Westerners' and 'Easterners', Liberals and Conservatives, 'Frocks' and 'Brasshats' made it harder to develop a single strategy either for winning the war or else concluding a negotiated peace. But none of these rifts should be exaggerated. Equally important was the extremity of British demands on Germany.

As we have seen, the Anglo–German antagonism was a relatively recent development. Most British leaders, coming to maturity in the 1880s, were habituated as a generation to thinking of France and Russia as the traditional enemies.[43] Struggling to understand how relations with Germany had deteriorated so rapidly and completely, they developed what became a durable image of moderates versus extremists. Thus Grey told the American Ambassador on 4 August 1914, the day Britain declared war: 'we must remember that there are two Germanys. There is the Germany of men like ourselves. . . . Then there is the Germany of men of the war party. The war party has got the upper hand'.[44] Building on this 'two Germanys' theory, and on his keen sense of having been betrayed, he concluded that 'it is against German militarism that we must fight' because 'it is not the German people, but Prussian militarism which has driven Germany and Europe into this war'.[45] This became the standard British line, vindicated by the vivid reports of German atrocities in Belgium and reinforced by Germany's vast gains in East and Southeast Europe when it imposed the Treaty of Brest-Litovsk on Russia. Lloyd George insisted in February 1917: 'If we destroy the prestige of the Prussian military idol, that cannot be set up again'.[46] The following month he told the Imperial War Cabinet that 'the democratisation of Europe' was 'the only sure guarantee of peaceful progress . . . If Germany had been a democracy . . . like ourselves . . . we should not have had this trouble'.[47]

So, although the British were slow to specify their war aims, their objective was in fact very radical – nothing less than the complete military defeat of Germany, the toppling of its leadership and the establishment of a representative government. Hence Asquith's observation in February 1916 that 'to the Allies a draw was much the same as a defeat'.[48] It may seem ironic that Lloyd George, leading exponent of the 'knock-out blow', opposed major offensives on the Western front and preferred an indirect strategy to eliminate Germany's allies in the Balkans and Middle East.[49] Yet this points to the bankruptcy of British strategy: the Government lacked the means to achieve its far-reaching aims.

This leads us to another, international, aspect of the question of why the British did not accept a negotiated settlement. Quite simply, Britain was not a free agent, either to make war or to make peace. It is easy to assume, extending the image of Britannia as a nineteenth-century superpower, that the Allies simply did Britain's bidding. In fact, it was only at sea that Britain was demonstrably superior. The initial lack of a large army weakened the country's influence on the battlefield and in allied counsels. Its economic strength, as supplier and banker of the Allies, was considerable, but McKenna and his like were right to warn that this would be sapped by the decision to turn Britain into a major land power as well. The growing economic dependence on the USA demonstrated the truth of their admonitions. In short, there were marked limits to British power. Britain never enjoyed the dominance within the alliance which would have allowed it to ignore its Allies' wishes or to force them to accept its will.[50] Repeatedly British strategy and diplomacy reflected the compromises demanded by alliance politics.

Thus, Britain often embarked on military offensives in order to reassure its Allies. Kitchener's strategy, assuming a three-year war, was to leave the French and Russians to bear the brunt while Britain gradually raised and trained a large army that would prove decisive in 1917, when all the other belligerents, friends and foes, were exhausted.

But a policy of fighting to the last Frenchman or Russian was naturally unappealing in Paris and St Petersburg. To maintain the Allies' will to fight Britain was therefore compelled to fight on a large scale earlier than intended. Loos in 1915 was to a significant degree 'a political offensive',[51] likewise the Somme in 1916 and Passchendaele in 1917.

Diplomatically, too, the Allies exerted powerful influence. Although reluctant to define Britain's own war aims, its leaders acquiesced in Russian demands for Constantinople in 1914 to keep them fighting against Germany.[52] They made far-reaching promises to Italy in April 1915 over territory around the Adriatic in order to draw it into the war. They came out in favour of independent Polish and Czech states in order to encourage new national armies to keep an Eastern front going in 1917–18 after the Russian collapse.[53] While these allies drew Britain into tangled territorial commitments, America, both as a neutral and, from April 1917, as a wartime 'associate', pressed for a liberal peace, characterised by arms reduction, open trade and decolonisation under the aegis of the League of Nations. In January 1918 the danger of President Wilson unilaterally defining the peace terms helped push Lloyd George into the fullest statement to date of British war aims.[54]

The complex repercussions of alliance politics were most acute in the Middle East. The British, while sympathetic about Germany's place among the powers and long reluctant to break up the Habsburg empire, felt no such circumspection about the Ottomans. Their empire was clearly collapsing, it covered an area of strategic British interest astride the routes to India, and it had long been regarded, particularly by British Liberals, as vicious and corrupt. Lloyd George in November 1914 denounced it as 'a human cancer, a creeping agony in the flesh of the lands which they govern, rotting every fibre of life'.[55] Yet there were many would-be claimants to Ottoman territory. To encourage a rising against the Turks the British made promises about Arab independence (the Hussein–McMahon correspondence of 1915–16). To satisfy the French they agreed to divide the Arab territories of the Near East into British and French spheres of influence (the Sykes–Picot agreement of 1916). To rally the Russian Jews in 1917, in the hope that they would help keep their country in the war against Germany despite the growing revolution, Britain promised a Jewish homeland in Palestine (the Balfour Declaration of November 1917). These agreements conflicted at many points. They had been made for reasons of wartime expediency, yet they were to plague Britain in the interwar period and they set the framework for the later Arab–Jewish conflict.[56]

By 1918 Britain had expansive ambitions of its own in the area.

Jerusalem fell in December 1917 and Baghdad the following March. The successful British (largely Indian) armies under General Allenby were given the freedom to advance 'to the maximum extent possible'.[57] Lloyd George now envisaged this as the main theatre of British interest, while waiting for the growing American armies to have a decisive effect on the Western front in 1919 or even 1920. Even after the great German offensives of the spring of 1918 had been repulsed, few believed that the war would be over that year.

Why, then, did the British accept the Armistice that came into effect on 11 November 1918? The conventional answer is that Germany and its allies abruptly collapsed in the autumn and sued for peace. But an armistice is only a cessation of hostilities, not a peace treaty, and the Germans had not been defeated or occupied in November 1918 – facts that would prove of great moment in the post-war period. For the British, part of the explanation lies in the German revolution of October and November. Its positive side was that the Kaiser abdicated and a republic was proclaimed – apparent evidence that the Prussian autocracy had finally lost its hold on Germany. The negative aspect was the growing support for Bolshevism in Central Europe. The CIGS Sir Henry Wilson noted in his diary: 'Our real danger now is not the Boch[e] but Bolshevism'.[58]

Complementing the German situation was the Allied side of the equation. The armistice was negotiated between the new German government and President Wilson, over the heads of the European allies. When they protested at the terms, the President's emissary, Colonel Edward House, effectively told them that if they wished to fight on, they would have to do so alone – a threat which the British and French could not ignore, given their dependence on American supplies, finance and above all manpower. General Jan Smuts, the South African premier and an active member of the Imperial War Cabinet in London in the summer of 1918, had been insisting for months that Lloyd George's aim of total military victory over Germany would simply undermine Britain's international position. He returned to the charge in October, as the Cabinet debated the armistice: 'If peace comes now, it will be a British peace . . . given to the world by the same Empire that settled the Napoleonic wars a century ago'. By fighting on for another year, however, 'the peace which will then be imposed on an utterly exhausted Europe will be an American peace' because by then the USA 'will have taken our place as the first military, diplomatic and financial power of the world'.[59] Such arguments played their part in resigning the British to something less than total victory.

THE BALANCE SHEET

The Great War was detrimental in many respects to Britain's wealth, empire and international position. The first part of this section draws up some of the debits. Yet to take stock in 1918 or 1919 is to foreshorten the historical accounting. By continuing the story up to 1922, the second part offers a more positive audit of war.

The gravest losses were, quite simply, human. The conflict of 1939–45 lasted longer, and was truly global in scope, but only 270,000 British service personnel were killed,[60] whereas in 1914–18 the figure was 723,000, or 6.3 per cent of the male population aged 15–49.* As significant was the effect on the social elite, source of Britain's future leaders. Nearly 28 per cent of the young men going up to Oxford and Cambridge in 1910–14 died in the war.[61] What difference it might have made to British policy in the 1950s if the generation of Harold Macmillan and Anthony Eden had survived intact is an interesting if insoluble problem.

The economic effects were also considerable. While British industry and shipping concentrated on the war, commercial rivals seized British markets – the USA in Latin America, the Japanese in India and East Asia. Japan's share of the China market, for instance, rose from 20 per cent to 36 per cent between 1913 and 1929, while Britain's fell from 16.5 to 9.5 per cent.[62] The war mobilisation also promoted the industrialisation of parts of the British Empire, particularly India and Australia, contributing to the peacetime world over-capacity in textiles, shipping and steel which underlay the slump of the 1920s. In this situation the uncompetitiveness of British exports became increasingly problematic. The loss of nearly 15 per cent of the country's assets reduced its invisible earnings and complicated the balance of payments. At the same time the war converted the USA from a net debtor to a net creditor nation and, through its war lending, into a major new actor in international finance. Henceforth, the world monetary system had two poles – London and New York – with Paris a third force by the mid-1920s.

A further casualty of the war was the old 'gold standard' economy, by which most major currencies were mutually convertible at a fixed price in gold. This had emerged in the last third of the nineteenth century and, like other fabled features of the Victorian era, such as the

---

* On the other hand, civilian deaths were lower in 1914–18 than in 1939–45: 15,000 merchant seamen as against 35,000, and 1,100 killed in air raids compared with 60,000 (Pelling 1970: 273)

Pax Britannica, had rested on ephemeral British advantages. Specifically it depended on the City of London's pre-eminence in the world commodity, money and insurance markets – which meant that most international payments were made in sterling via London – and on Britain's willingness and ability to export capital in vast quantities in the forty years before 1914.[63] More fundamental still, the gold standard had rested on confidence as much as wealth – international trust that, if called upon, the Bank of England would honour its promise to convert sterling into a set amount of gold. Had there been any large demand to do so the Bank would have been unable to respond: its international liabilities greatly exceeded its gold reserves, which also had to function as guarantor for the domestic convertibility of the pound. But in 1870–1914 few doubted that sterling was literally 'as good as gold'.

After the First World War this was no longer the case. With the changes in the world economy, both international confidence and British wealth had diminished. Yet, although forced off gold in 1919, Britain returned to it in 1925. This was partly the result of financial dogma which viewed the gold standard as an automatic regulator rather than a function of British financial power. 'The Gold Standard is the best "Governor" that can be devised for a world that is still human, rather than divine', pontificated Montagu Norman from the Bank of England.[64] It also suited the City, for whom a return to the gold standard at the old rate was deemed vital to restore Britain's credibility as an international financial centre.[65] By the time the Bank was able to achieve this, in 1925, many of Britain's trading partners had already done so. Churchill, then Chancellor of the Exchequer, observed that 'if we had not taken this action, the whole of the rest of the British Empire would have taken it without us, and it would have come to a gold standard, not on the basis of the pound sterling but of the dollar'.[66] To reach this position the Bank had kept interest rates high and, by returning to gold at the old exchange rate of $4.86, it had probably overvalued the currency by 10 per cent.[67] These deflationary policies gave no help to domestic industry as it struggled to compete internationally under less favourable conditions.

The ties of empire were tightened by wartime mobilisation. Nearly a third of British military manpower came from outside Britain and the economies of India and the Dominions were successfully galvanised for war. Yet there was a price to pay. Food shortages, pervasive inflation and firmer British control – all the results of the wartime demand for labour and raw materials – fuelled discontent, and the summer of 1919 saw large-scale newly-organised nationalist challenges

106

in India, Egypt and Mesopotamia which were put down only with considerable violence and expense. Throughout the empire political concessions seemed prudent. In Egypt the protectorate, imposed in 1914, was abandoned and a new constitution granted. In India the Montagu Declaration of August 1917 committed Britain to 'the gradual development of self-governing institutions with a view to the progressive realisation of responsible government in India as an integral part of the British Empire'.[68] Legislation in 1919 transferred some governmental powers, for instance over agriculture and education, to new provincial administrations run by Indian ministers responsible to elected legislatures. And the costs of the war – some two billion rupees in new debt – could only be covered by more than doubling tariff rates, at the expense of British cotton exporters. A clear precedent was set: by 1931 the general tariff rate was 25 per cent, compared with 5 per cent in 1914.[69]

The gravest crisis of all was in Ireland where three attempts by the Liberals to grant Home Rule (1886, 1894 and 1914) had failed either through the opposition of Irish Protestants and their English Conservative allies, or, in the last case, through the onset of the Great War. Following the abortive Easter Rising of 1916, an independent Irish republic was declared at the end of the war and the Government became engaged in a bitter guerrilla struggle.[70] British troops backed by a militarised constabulary imposed martial law and a policy of 'counter-terrorism' in the winter of 1920–1. Then suddenly in July 1921 Lloyd George's coalition reversed its position and opened talks with the Irish nationalists. American protests, the costs of the army presence – over 25,000-strong despite the end of conscription – and revulsion at home at the unavailing policy of repression had all taken their toll.[71] The treaty of December 1921 conceded Dominion status to most of the country, while six largely Protestant counties in Ulster gained regional home rule within the United Kingdom.

As for an integrated federal Empire – envisioned by Joseph Chamberlain, mapped out by the *Round Table* group of Milner's disciples[72] – that ran against the realities of Dominion centrifugalism. The Imperial War Cabinet, operating in 1917–19, was only a crisis innovation and efforts to draw the Dominions into permanent naval cooperation were unavailing.[73] 'What was emerging was a decentralised Commonwealth of white self-governing communities who would cooperate, rather gingerly, in certain agreed areas'.[74] The 1931 Statute of Westminster confirmed what had long been a reality, that, although the British monarch was still head of state, Parliament in London had no right to legislate for the Dominions.[75] In Australia, New Zealand and, more equivocally, Canada the ties of kinship remained strong, but that was not true elsewhere. Henceforth the Irish remained within the Empire only under duress and were neutral in the next war. In southern Africa the Boer war had only checked the growing Afrikaner influence over the region, which was embodied in the new Union of South Africa established in 1910. During the Great War the Union was guided by the pro-British leadership of Louis Botha and Jan Smuts but they were pulling against a growing trend of Afrikaner anglophobia.

Great-power relations also entered a new phase with the Russian revolution and the emergence of the USA as a great power. The fact that the old Tsarist empire did not collapse between 1917 and 1922, unlike its Ottoman and Habsburg rivals, was of profound significance. The old concern for the borders of India remained intense for much of the 1920s. Worse still for Britain, Russia was now led by pro-claimed revolutionaries. 'No force on earth', declared Lenin in March 1919, could 'hold back the progress of the world communist revolution towards the world Soviet republic'.[76] Hungary and Bavaria seemed to prove his point. Churchill urged the Cabinet repeatedly to use the Allied armies in Russia to eliminate 'the foul baboonery of Bolshevism' and even talked of reviving Germany against Russia: 'Kill the Bolshie, kiss the Hun'.[77] As for America, the armistice negotiations had shown that it was now a real international force and Sir William Wiseman, an influential British diplomat in Washington, warned London of the growing sense there of rivalry with Britain. 'Which is going to be the greater, politically and commercially?'[78] The diplomatic consequences of America's wealth and new assertiveness were demonstrated at the Washington naval conference in 1921–2, when Britain accepted the principle of naval parity with the USA in capital ships because it could not afford an all-out arms race.

The growing problems of wealth, empire and rivals can all be seen as part of a long-term trend of diminishing British power. And up to a point that is right. But one should not exaggerate the debilitating consequences of the Great War for Britain. If we regard the upheavals of 1918–19 as part of an inevitable period of post-war instability and look on to, say, 1922, we can see that the empire and the international system gradually became more stable and less threatening. In consequence, Britain's economic problems, though real in the 1920s, were of less moment for its general international position than was the case at a time of global tension.

Thus, the post-war crisis of empire should be understood as the rise and fall of war imperialism rather than the early stages of decolonisation.[79] The war presented new dangers and opportunities as a result of the disintegration of the Ottoman and Tsarist empires and the successive fears that the vacuum would be filled by Germans, Bolsheviks or French.[80] It seemed that the late nineteenth-century 'scramble for Africa' was being repeated in the Near and Middle East, with the British forced to embark on a new bout of formal imperialism to prevent wholesale partition by other powers at their expense. In 1918 the Eastern Committee of the War Cabinet, chaired by Curzon, was making vast demands – the occupation of northwest Persia and large areas of Russia around the Caspian Sea – while Lloyd George favoured the reduction of Turkey to a rump state without Constantinople or control of the Straits.

The underlying struggle in the Middle East was with France. In the final stages of the war the British tried to finesse the earlier Sykes–Picot agreement to minimise the French influence in Syria while maximising their own position in Mesopotamia and Palestine. Eventually an arrangement similar to the 1904 compromise over North Africa was achieved. Under the treaty of San Remo the British gained Iraq and Palestine as mandates from the League of Nations while France acquired what became Syria and the Lebanon on similar terms. But the struggle had revived bitter Anglo–French imperial rivalries, only temporarily allayed by the Great War, which drew on underlying national stereotypes. In 1921 Curzon contrasted 'the British habit of endeavouring to deal with the current problems of diplomacy, as they arise, on the merits of the particular case, and the French practice of subordinating even the most trival issues to general considerations of expediency, based on far-reaching plans for the relentless promotion of French prestige and the gratification of private, generally monetary and often sordid, interests and ambitions'.[81] Coming from one of the most calculating imperialists of the age, that was a bit rich, but the significance of his remark lies not in its accuracy but in its expression of pervasive British sentiments.

The modus vivendi with the French was one reason for the abandonment of the grandiose plans for empire-building outlined in 1918. Equally important was the fact that, internally, the post-war Middle East proved both more stable and also less malleable than the British thought at the height of the war crisis. As the Bolsheviks consolidated power Britain pulled back from most Russian territory in 1919. In Persia and in Turkey, Reza Khan and Kemal Ataturk formed surprisingly stable governments, while Iraq was gradually secured with a client Arab king, Feisal, and the use of the RAF to control tribal insurgency – far cheaper than a large army presence. It became formally independent in 1932, though with close British supervision over its army and oil. The renewed acceptance of informal techniques of imperialism was best demonstrated in Egypt. The protectorate had been a temporary war device and the new treaty gave Britain control over foreign policy and complete freedom of movement for British troops without the headache of having to run the country and cope with its social and economic problems. 'Why worry about the rind, if we can obtain the fruit?', Curzon asked.[82] Thus, by 1922–3 a relatively orderly, post-Ottoman Near and Middle East had emerged and the region was largely insulated from great-power rivalries for the rest of the 1920s and 1930s.[83] And within the region, Britain and France had achieved a modus vivendi under which Britain, for all its problems, was clearly the dominant foreign power in the Middle East. The policy of clientage, apparently successful in Iraq and Egypt, seemed a promising tool for cut-price influence in the future.

The revival of Britain and France was one reflection of the reduced international influence of America and Russia after the crisis of 1917–19. In 1919–20 the US Senate rejected American membership of the League of Nations. Admittedly, this did not signal complete isolationism. Wall Street finance, for instance, helped stabilise Europe in the mid-1920s. But henceforth the USA avoided political and military commitments in Europe and its financial involvement waned with the Crash of 1929 and the deep depression that followed, when the 'American Dream' turned to nightmare amid chronic bank failures, 25 per cent unemployment and a collapse of business confidence. In the 1930s US leaders were not indifferent to Europe but their willingness and ability to exert themselves was severely constrained by the economic and political situation at home. Although the British still hoped for close transatlantic cooperation, they learned not to base their foreign policy upon it. In 1932 Stanley Baldwin summed up the collective wisdom of a generation of British leaders: 'you will get nothing from Americans but words, big words but only words'.[84]

As for Russia, Churchill's calls for an anti-Bolshevik crusade fizzled out, although the half-baked Allied involvement in the Russian civil war left lasting bitterness among the Bolshevik leadership. Lloyd George made it clear that an 'expensive war of aggression against Russia is a way to strengthen Bolshevism in Russia and create it at home'.[85] He wanted to revive trade with Russia, both to promote economic recovery and to dissipate revolutionary fervour – 'commerce has a sobering effect in its operations'.[86] In March 1921 an Anglo–Soviet trade agreement was signed and in February 1924 the new Labour government extended diplomatic recognition. What followed was hardly normal relations – Comintern propaganda continued, there was renewed anxiety about India in 1926–7 and the Tories severed links in 1927–9. Fear of Bolshevism ran deep in British thinking and it soured relations with the Soviet Union throughout the interwar years. At best Russia was kept on the margins of international society, at worst it was regarded as a potential threat. Nevertheless, all this was a far cry from the British panic about world revolution in 1919. By the end of the decade Russia, like America, was more concerned about its own economy than about European politics.

To sum up: between 1915–18 the British had been obliged to mobilise their resources to a degree not seen for a century. The costs had been considerable, and it is tempting to dwell on the harbingers of 'decline'. Yet it must be emphasised that Britain emerged victorious and that its empire reached its largest extent as a result of the war. After the war was over British policy remained assertive, with Lloyd George taking the lead in wooing Russia or reshaping the Middle East. To some extent that reflected his activist personality but the interventionist British policy was also a response to the times. With the world in disorder and the USA aloof, Britain felt obliged to take a more systematic role in directing affairs than was ever the case in the mythical days of the Pax Britannica, when world order largely took care of itself.

On 7 October 1922, Bonar Law, the Tory leader, warned in *The Times* that Britain could not act alone 'as policeman of the world'.[87] The collapse of the Lloyd George coalition that same month signalled the waning of an interventionist foreign policy. The change in personalities was part of the reason, but international realities were more important. The post-war world had assumed a firmer shape – less easy to mould but less fluid than originally feared – and the new British reticence was more an abandonment of war imperialism than a wholesale retreat from world power. From lack of both need and opportunity British leaders thereafter lapsed into passivity. Yet one major issue remained unresolved in 1922, as in 1918 – the one that had caused the war, the problem of Germany.

REFERENCES

1.   Steiner 1977: 215
2.   Remak 1971: 365
3.   Ekstein and Steiner 1977: 404
4.   Hamilton 1977: 324

5. Gooch 1974: 280–1
6. K. Wilson 1987: 191
7. Keiger 1983: 102
8. Hamilton 1977: 341
9. Kennedy 1980: 428–9
10. Koss 1985: 149
11. K. Wilson 1985: 95
12. Steiner 1977: 228
13. Joll 1984: 88–9
14. K. Wilson 1985: 127
15. French 1982: 30
16. K. Wilson 1985: 141
17. Farrar 1978: 125
18. Kennedy 1988: 256–60
19. French 1982: chs 7–8
20. Hazelhurst 1971: 189–90
21. French 1982: 153
22. Neilson 1984: 107
23. Koss 1985: 220–1
24. Kennedy 1988: 267
25. O. Anderson 1967: 201
26. Hardach 1977: 165–6
27. Aldcroft 1977: 31
28. Mitchell and Deane 1962: 403
29. Burk 1985
30. FO 371/2795, 197644, PRO
31. Burk 1985: ch. 9
32. Burk 1979: 228
33. Dimbleby and Reynolds 1988: chs 3–4
34. Kennedy 1988: 271–2
35. Darwin 1981: 149
36. Ullman 1961: i, 186
37. CAB 37/159, 32
38. Hankey 1961: ii, 557
39. Gilbert 1971: iii, 226
40. Jaffe 1985: 31
41. Robbins 1985: 127–32
42. Adams and Poirier 1987: 53
43. French 1986: 6, 211
44. Hendrick 1927: i, 315
45. Calder 1976: 12–13
46. Jaffe 1985: 36
47. CAB 23/43, IWC 1
48. Fry 1977: 228
49. Woodward 1983: 329
50. Neilson 1984: vii–viii; French 1986: xi
51. French 1986: xiii

52. Neilson 1984: 44
53. Calder 1976
54. Kernek 1975: 72–3
55. Fry 1977: 257
56. Ovendale 1984: ch. 2
57. Woodward 1983: 283
58. Jaffe 1985: 107
59. CAB 24/67, GT 6091
60. Pelling 1970: 273
61. Winter 1985: 75, 93
62. Aldcroft 1977: 38
63. Drummond 1987
64. P. Clarke 1988: 36
65. S. Clarke 1967: 20
66. Churchill 1974: iv, 3742
67. Moggridge 1972: 228
68. Moore 1974: 1
69. Tomlinson 1979: 62, 110
70. Lawlor 1983
71. K. Morgan 1979: 125–32
72. Kendle 1975
73. Holland 1981: 10–11
74. Judd and Slinn 1982: 22
75. Mansergh 1982: ii, 31
76. S. White 1979: 114
77. Gilbert 1975: iv, 257, 278
78. Fowler 1969: 292
79. Gallagher 1982: 86–94
80. Monroe 1981: chs 1–3
81. Andrew and Kanya-Forstner 1981: 240–1
82. Darwin 1981: 115
83. Monroe 1981: 74
84. Middlemas and Barnes 1969: 729
85. Ullman 1968: ii, 126
86. S. White 1979: 5
87. Morgan 1979: 329

CHAPTER FIVE

No War, 1919–40

On 24 March 1938 Winston Churchill admonished the House of Commons:

> . . . if mortal catastrophe should overtake the British Nation and the British Empire, historians a thousand years hence will still be baffled by the mystery of our affairs. They will never understand how it was that a victorious nation, with everything in hand, suffered themselves to be brought low, and to cast away all that they had gained by measureless sacrifice and absolute victory – gone with the wind!
>
> Now the victors are the vanquished, and those who threw down their arms in the field and sued for an armistice are striding on to world mastery . . .[1]

Why this happened, why Germany was allowed to revive and bring Britain to the edge of disaster in 1940, is the key question for British foreign policy in the 1920s and 1930s. For the world war that followed revolutionised Britain's economic, international and imperial circumstances far more profoundly than that of 1914–18.

Contemporaries blamed the 'appeasers', particularly the prime ministers of the 1930s – Ramsay MacDonald (1929–35), Stanley Baldwin (1935–7) and Neville Chamberlain (1937–40). In the words of one 1940 polemic these were the 'guilty men' who 'took over a great empire, supreme in arms and secure in liberty' and 'conducted it to the edge of national annihilation'.[2] Since the British archives were opened in the late 1960s, a more sympathetic picture has emerged – of policymakers hobbled by the erosion of Britain's economic, imperial and international power. Yet appeasement was not simply the function of long-term British decline. Contributing were underlying misperceptions of Nazi Germany and its airpower, Britain's failure to win the arms race of the 1930s, and its inability to make fundamental choices about rivals and allies because of the less manageable international situation and the growth of bureaucratic politics in Whitehall. In each case important contrasts with the appeasement of the 1900s are apparent. These policies on Germany, rearmament and global diplomacy will be examined in the next three sections, before looking at their denouement in the Czech crisis of 1938. The final section details the belated British U-turn towards deterrence in 1939 – too late to avoid the debacle of 1940.

THE QUEST FOR AGREEMENT WITH GERMANY

In 1919 Georges Clemenceau told David Lloyd George that 'within an hour after the Armistice I had the impression that you had once again become the enemies of France'. Lloyd George responded: 'Has that not always been the traditional policy of my country?'[3]

Basic to any understanding of what we now call the 'inter-war years' is the fact that most British leaders saw the Anglo–German antagonism of 1904–18 as an aberration. For much of the period, in fact, they were more suspicious of France than of Germany. To grasp this, we need to go back to 1919, to the Treaty of Versailles, which the British quickly came to see not as a definitive settlement, akin to that of 1815, but as an unworkable imposition, which got in the way of a lasting peace that would bring a reformed Germany back into a concert of Europe.

The Paris peace conference lasted from January to June 1919. Germany was not a participant – peace was simply imposed on it under threat of renewed war. Nor was Russia invited, on the grounds that it had already made a treacherous peace with Germany in 1918. The essential decisions were made by the 'big three' – Woodrow Wilson, Georges Clemenceau and David Lloyd George. Wilson's influence was now much reduced. With the fighting at an end, the British and French were less dependent materially on the USA, and the President was politically weak because his Republican opponents now controlled the Senate and did not accept his grandiose war aims centred on a League of Nations. There was therefore a basic equality between the big three, with shifting alignments on various issues.

The British had certain fundamental demands of Germany. They wished to eliminate the German fleet as a threat to British security. The Dominion governments of Australia, New Zealand and South

Africa also coveted the old German colonies in the south Pacific and southern Africa, while Britain, as we have seen, sought control over some of the old Ottoman lands in the Middle East. The 1918 election campaign had also vented popular demands for substantial reparations from Germany – a claim backed vociferously by the Conservative members of Lloyd George's coalition. On all these issues – seapower, colonies and reparations – the British tended to side with the French against the Americans. In general, they got their way, although the enemy colonies were largely allocated not as outright annexations but as mandates from the new League of Nations. In return for American acquiescence the British went along with Wilson's plans for the new international organisation. Their expectations were summed up by the Australian premier, Billy Hughes: 'Give him a League of Nations and he will give us all the rest'.[4]

When it came to the treatment of Germany itself, however, the British usually sided with the Americans against the French. Paris wanted a punitive peace. Militarily, Germany was to be totally disarmed and the French envisaged the League of Nations mainly as an alliance of victors, with an army and general staff to help keep Germany down. They demanded Alsace and Lorraine, lost in 1871, the Saar and the Rhineland – cumulatively the sinews of German industrial power. Territory right up to the Rhine would also give France a more defensible strategic frontier. But Lloyd George and most British policymakers joined with Wilson to block almost all these demands, except for Alsace-Lorraine. On the crucial issue of the Rhineland, only a temporary Allied occupation was permitted, for fifteen years. Though stripped of most of her navy and banned from having an air force, Germany was allowed an army of 100,000 men for internal security. The League was given no peacekeeping functions and an Anglo–American guarantee of French security, offered as an alternative to annexation of the Rhineland, lapsed when the US Senate failed to ratify the Treaty.[5]

Part of the explanation for these Anglo–French differences was that British priorities remained imperial rather than continental. With Germany defeated, re-establishing Britain's global position was more important than commitments across the Channel. Here geography was fundamental: France had only a land border with Germany – a country with 50 per cent more people and four times France's heavy industry. For island Britain, by contrast, once the German fleet had been eliminated, Germany posed very little threat. But there was also a more fundamental disagreement about Germany's place in post-war Europe. Basically the British accepted Bismarck's Germany, *providing* it was democratised; the French did not – hence their demands for dismemberment and permanent demilitarisation. The British eventually acquiesced in the complex bundle of compromises that was the Treaty of Versailles, not least because they feared that further argument would retard post-war reconstruction and enhance the appeal of Bolshevism in a shattered Central Europe. But they did not regard Versailles as definitive. The French, *faute de mieux*, did. This dispute was central to Anglo–French relations until well into the 1930s, for the main aim of British policy became the renegotiation of Versailles. For Whitehall 1919 was the beginning and not the end of peacemaking.

Economically, Lloyd George wanted to bring Germany (and Russia) back into a European trading system, to help restore British trade, finance and prosperity. This policy climaxed at the abortive Genoa conference of April 1922.[6] Even then, however, the British, with the Americans, persistently tried to mitigate the financial penalties of the peace settlement, reducing the reparations demanded from Germany in the Dawes and Young plans of 1924 and 1929, amid British hopes of a general amnesty on war debts that would ease international payments problems. Britain also remained adamantly opposed to France's territorial demands on Germany, forcing the French to end the Ruhr occupation of 1923 and blocking their bid for independent Rhineland states.[7] Recurrent French pressure for a formal Anglo–French military alliance was firmly rebuffed. Nor would Britain commit itself to the network of French alliances in Eastern Europe, concluded as a surrogate for the Franco–Russian alliance that encircled Germany before 1914. The British regarded such treaties with Poland, Czechoslovakia and Yugoslavia as potential entanglements in an area of minimal British interest. And there was a growing feeling that Germany should be allowed a moderate degree of rearmament, commensurate with its dignity and interests as a major power, within the framework of general arms reduction. Again the French were the main obstacle, both to German rearmament and to arms reduction – on grounds of their own national security.

Not all British policymakers were indifferent to French anxieties. Austen Chamberlain, the Tory Foreign Secretary from 1924 to 1929, believed that 'we should make the maintenance of the Entente with France the cardinal object of our policy'.[8] He was ready to offer a British guarantee of the existing borders of France and Belgium. But in early 1925 most of the Cabinet believed that this was dangerous without a Franco–German rapprochement. 'When France has made a real peace with Germany, Britain will seal the bond with all her strength', promised the Chancellor, Winston Churchill.[9] Thus 1925 saw intensive negotiations that culminated in the Locarno agreements of October whereby France, Belgium and Germany committed themselves to respect their existing Rhineland borders, with Britain and Italy acting as guarantors.[10] But again the British made clear that they would not guarantee the French alliances in *Eastern* Europe. Even the francophile Chamberlain was emphatic that the Polish Corridor was something 'for which no British Government ever will or ever can risk the bones of a British grenadier'.[11]

Although some historians now see 1924–5 as the real, de facto peace settlement – with the Dawes Plan and Locarno[12] – British leaders of the 1920s considered it only a step towards a comprehensive pacification of Europe. Their efforts intensified with the economic collapse of 1931, which forced Britain off gold. France was blamed for failing to help the pound as the Central European banks collapsed. Also infuriating was the sustained French opposition to arms control, which was a major obstacle to British efforts at the Geneva Disarmament Conference of 1932–4. Even the francophile Permament Under-Secretary at the Foreign Office, Sir Robert Vansittart, commented in January 1932 that France 'has of late virtually attained the very thing that we have traditionally sought to avoid in Europe, hegemony, if not dictatorship, political and financial'.[13] The British aim was still, to quote Alexander Cadogan of the FO in May 1932, 'to bring to an end the "post war period"' and 'allow Germany to resume her place and rights as a great power on equal footing with the others . . . French policy plainly cannot be maintained for ever'.[14]

Hitler's appointment to the German chancellorship in January 1933 was not generally seen in London as necessitating a re-orientation of British policy. Admittedly Nazi anti-semitism and militaristic displays soon evoked distaste. Austen Chamberlain told the Commons in April 1933 that 'this new spirit of German Nationalism' represented 'the worst of the All-Prussian Imperialism, with an added savagery, a racial pride'.[15] But even Vansittart, already fearful of what Nazism portended, shared the prevailing view in Whitehall in 1933 that Germany was engaged in another battle between 'moderates' and 'extremists' with Nazism the stooge of the old Prussian Junker class.[16] Although Vansittart had altered his view of Hitler by 1935, much of Whitehall was slower to change, and the old Great-War polarity of moderates versus extremists remained the main framework within which British policymakers interpreted German politics. Their aim now became the strengthening of the moderates and the isolation of extremism – all of which gave added urgency to British attempts to revise what they regarded as an unjust and untenable peace settlement.

By the end of 1933 Germany had walked out of the Geneva Disarmament conference and secret reports made clear that it was now covertly rearming. British leaders accordingly abandoned international conferences as a means of European appeasement and hoped that agreement among the leading powers could revise the impositions of Versailles before Germany overthrew them by force. Initially they hoped to use the legitimisation of German rearmament as the main inducement. This ploy failed when Hitler simply announced unilaterally in the spring of 1935 that Germany was imposing conscription and already had an air force equivalent to the RAF. An alternative bait was to give Germany back the Rhineland, but Hitler took it himself in March 1936. Versailles and Locarno were now in ruins.

By the end of 1936 the senior FO experts on Germany doubted that any meaningful agreement was possible. Negotiations were seen largely as a delaying tactic until British rearmament had created a position of strength. 'To the Foreign Office', noted Vansittart, 'therefore falls the task of holding the situation till at least 1939'. By the middle of 1937 Anthony Eden, the Foreign Secretary, may also have been coming round to a similar attitude of 'cunctation'.[17] But he and his advisers had no clear alternative policy to offer, only mounting disillusion with the prospects for negotiation.[18] And from May 1937 the new Prime Minister, Neville Chamberlain, pursued Germany with new energy and determination.

Now that Germany had freed itself from Versailles unilaterally, Britain had to find alternative inducements. Under Chamberlain the main baits became the return of Germany's African colonies, seized after the war, and an international trade agreement to relieve Germany's shortage of raw materials and foreign exchange. This policy of 'economic appeasement' was given focus by the fact that the leading 'moderate' that Britain tried to cultivate was Hjalmar Schacht, President of the Reichsbank and also Nazi economics minister until the autumn of 1937.[19] Despite the crises of 1938–9 this remained the aim of British diplomacy right up to the beginning of war, advocated by Chamberlain, supported by the Treasury and endorsed by at least the economics section of the FO.

Why did the search for agreement with Germany go on for so long? In part, because the British consistently misperceived Nazism. Hitler was nobody's stooge and his grandiose ambitions encompassed an Aryan empire in Central and Eastern Europe and shadowy dreams of world dominion. War was an essential means of expansion and his plans assumed a general European conflict in the early 1940s. He saw Britain as initially friendly, or at least acquiescent – postulating a racial unity among the Anglo–Saxons and arguing that the Kaiserreich had made a fundamental error in 1914 in taking on Britain by sea while facing France and Russia on land. He carefully gave the impression that his intentions lay in eastern and not western Europe and it was not until 1938–9 that he approved his admirals' plans for rapid naval rearmament against Britain. Nevertheless, there is little doubt that ultimately Britain would have been an obstacle to his expansion, albeit at a stage when, with Germany dominant over all Europe, the British and their empire would have had little choice but to succumb.[20]

Thus, at a basic level, Britain misunderstood Nazi Germany. Hitler's aims were far greater than the renegotiation of Versailles or the return of Germany's colonies. Moreover, the moderate versus extremist image of German politics underestimated the ambitions of the moderates while grossly exaggerating their influence. But, as we have seen, by 1936 influential FO officials were doubtful that Hitler was appeasable. To understand why their reservations had so little effect, why there seemed no alternative to negotiation, we also have to look at Britain's failure in the arms race of the 1930s.

ARMS AND THE MEN

In defence, as in diplomacy, Britain's problems in the 1930s were shaped by the policies of the 1920s. In 1918 government expenditure in real terms was ten times the figure for 1900, even though GNP had hardly increased, and 80 per cent of that expenditure, which totalled £2.5 billion, went on defence. As the Treasury sought to regain control of the budget, massive defence cuts were inevitable and by 1924 military spending had been stabilised at around £130 million per annum. Yet total spending was still running at more than £1 billion, which meant that a significant shift in government outlays had occurred. Defence, traditionally accounting for a quarter of the total, now took only about one-eighth. Social spending, less than a fifth of government expenditure in 1900, and only a quarter in 1920, had soared by the end of the decade to a steady 40 per cent. Equally pressing was the national debt, vastly increased to help pay for the war, which consumed nearly 30 per cent of government spending for most of the 1920s compared with only 7 per cent in 1900. In the late 1920s Britain, despite greatly enlarged responsibilities, was spending a somewhat smaller proportion of GNP (2.7 per cent) on defence than it had in the peacetime years of the 1900s.[21]

Apart from finance, the other fundamental defence decision after the war was the end of conscription. We have seen that ever since the 1870s the absence of conscription had been identified by British military Cassandras as a major source of national weakness and that from 1914 the British had been obliged to raise a large army to help combat Germany. In the election of December 1918 the retention of conscription became a salient issue. The War Office, backed by many Conservatives, argued that conscription or at least some form of 'national service' was essential in view of Britain's worldwide military responsibilities. On the other hand, popular feelings ran high, culminating in widespread mutinies in January 1919 and national 'No-Conscription Sunday' on 2 March. Asquithian Liberals, Labour and other government critics exploited it against the Coalition.

To escape this dilemma Lloyd George adroitly made the disarmament of Germany, previously little discussed, into a major British peace aim. 'The real guarantee against conscription in this country', he told voters in Bristol on 11 December 1918, 'is to put an end by the terms of the Peace Conference to these great conscript Armies'.[22] Thus, the reduction at Paris of the German army to a small, professional force was deemed essential to justify the phasing out of British conscription from March 1920. But German disarmament was also seen as a first step in a policy for Europe as a whole. If we grasp that, for the British, the alternative to international arms control was ultimately conscription, then we can better appreciate why they persisted for so long with their efforts at disarmament.

What made these decisions about defence cuts and conscription acceptable in the 1920s was the lack of evident enemies. On 15 August 1919 the War Cabinet instructed the services to operate on the assumption 'that the British Empire will not be engaged in any great war during the next ten years, and that no Expeditionary Force is required for this purpose'.[23] The Treasury made use of this guideline in its battles to restrict expenditure, particularly at sea.[24] In 1925–6 the Cabinet gave it control over all service estimates and in July 1928 Churchill as Chancellor had the 'ten year rule' placed on a continuous basis. The Cabinet agreed 'that it should now be assumed, for the purpose of framing the estimates of the Fighting Services, that at any given date there will be no major war for ten years'.[25] Although a Treasury initiative, it was backed by the FO, who saw an essentially peaceful world, and the Chiefs of Staff offered little opposition.

This 'rolling' ten-year rule set the framework for British defence policy. Hankey, as Secretary of the CID, began to agitate against it in January 1931, concerned at evidence of covert German rearmament, but it was not until March 1932, after the Japanese attack on China, that it was effectively cancelled.[26] Even then – such was the British concern not to jeopardise the Geneva disarmament conference by any apparent provocation – it was not until after Germany left the conference in October 1933 that a Defence Requirements Committee was set up by the CID to assess Service deficiencies. Decisions on its report were delayed until July 1934, eighteen months after Hitler gained power and several years since evidence of German rearmament had become apparent.

To a large extent this delay in overturning the ten-year rule explains what follows. Germany had a head-start in rearming; throughout the 1930s Britain was always struggling to catch up. But the problem of time-lag was aggravated by the implications of the airpower revolution. In the naval race of the 1900s Britain enjoyed crucial advantages over Germany. Its fleet was well-established and it had a strong industrial base in the British shipbuilding industry, the world's leader. Military aviation, by contrast, was a novelty in the 1920s. The minimal post-war programme for a 52-squadron RAF was retarded by spending constraints and was still only four-fifths complete when the Geneva Disarmament Conference began in 1932. Moreover, Britain had no large domestic aircraft industry as a base for rapid rearmament, unlike Germany, Russia or the USA, where air transport played a much larger role in the economy.[27] By 1927 German civil airlines flew greater distances with more passengers than their British, French and Italian competitors combined.[28]

Yet Britain's defence weakness in the 1930s was not totally predetermined. Retention of the ten-year rule reflected the consistent British optimism about Germany and the search for alternatives to renewed arms race, conscription and war. Similarly, the commitment to disarmament testified to the strength of public feeling that there must be no more war and the conviction that the arms race of the 1900s was itself a cause of the conflict that followed. This reached its apogee in the crucial period 1933–5, with a series of remarkable 25 per cent swings against the Government in by-elections and the celebrated if confused 'Peace Ballot' of 1934–5, signed by 11.6 million people, which recorded 90 per cent support for international agreement on arms reduction and for a ban on the production of arms for private profit. These manifestations of 'public opinion' were taken very seriously by MacDonald and Baldwin.[29]

Even when rearmament began, from mid-1934, public fears decisively shaped its character. The grand obsession of the 1930s was the bomber. Films such as Alexander Korda's production of H.G. Wells's

'Things to Come' and newsreel reports of the bombings of Guernica and Barcelona in the Spanish Civil War suggested appalling casualties. The philosopher and peace campaigner Bertrand Russell predicted in 1936 that after a single air raid London 'will be one vast raving bedlam, the hospitals will be stormed, traffic will cease, the homeless will shriek for help' and the Government 'will be swept away by an avalanche of terror. Then the enemy will dictate its terms'.[30] Nor was this obsession confined to the general public. The COS Joint Planning Committee warned in October 1936 that 'it is clear that in a war against us the concentration from the first day of the war of the whole of the German air offensive ruthlessly against Great Britain would be possible. It would be the most promising way of trying to knock this country out.' Extrapolating from some uncontested German air raids in 1917, the JPC predicted a horrifying 150,000 casualties in London in the first week of such an aerial bombardment.[31] To gain some perspective it should be remembered that Britain suffered in total less than 147,000 casualties from all forms of bombing and long-range bombardment in the *whole* of the Second World War.[32]

Public and official fears about the 'knock-out blow' explain British efforts for most of the 1930s to achieve an international agreement either eliminating the bomber or at least controlling its effects.[33] But as these hopes faded and Germany rearmed, some military response was also essential. In the early 1930s, with radar not yet invented and the fighter aircraft still in its infancy as a slow, ill-armed biplane, there seemed no chance of effective defence. In Baldwin's famous speech of 10 November 1932, warning that 'the bomber will always get through', he insisted chillingly that 'the only defence is in offence, which means that you have to kill more women and children more quickly than the enemy if you want to save yourselves'.[34] This had been the line taken in the 1920s by proponents of airpower, notably Sir Hugh Trenchard in his efforts to justify the independent existence of the RAF. After Germany left the Disarmament Conference and Britain began to rearm it was adopted emphatically by the British Cabinet.

The Defence Requirements Committee (DRC) of 1933–4 had advocated a programme of balanced rearmament, remedying the deficiencies in the existing programmes of all three services. But in mid-1934 the politicians pushed through a revised plan at two-thirds the cost, centred on the rapid creation of a bomber force to match Germany. Led by Neville Chamberlain, Chancellor from 1931 to 1937, the Cabinet adopted an air programme in excess of what even the Air Ministry wanted.[35] Their motives were not primarily military, but political and diplomatic – to dispel what Baldwin in July 1934 called 'semi-panic conditions' among the public about the bomber[36] and to act as reinforcement for British diplomacy. British policy in 1934–6 can be described as 'the search for an Anglo–German entente backed by the use of an efficient bomber air force capable of acting as a deterrent'.[37]

The Navy suffered considerably from this skewed rearmament programme, but the principal casualty was the Army's contingency plans for another British Expeditionary Force (BEF) in the Low Countries, should war break out anew.[38] The DRC budget for the Army, the largest item in their original report, was halved and the equipment of such a force postponed until after 1939. Chamberlain and the politicians believed that a rearmament programme concentrating on the army would be politically unacceptable. Not only would it fail to assuage public fears about the bomber, but it would also revive potent memories of the Somme, Passchendaele and the carnage of the Great War. So sensitive was the Cabinet on this matter that it instructed that the term 'Expeditionary Force' not be used even in secret official papers, because the term conjured up 'unpleasant inferences in the public mind'.[39] For the same reason, staff conversations with the French, akin to those from 1906, were sedulously avoided and of course the idea of conscription remained unthinkable. Thus British defence policy in the 1930s assumed that any wartime obligations to continental allies could be honoured without committing a BEF from the start. British economic strength, now supplemented by airpower, would be an adequate alternative. Protests from some senior officers about this 'limited liability' approach proved unavailing.

Thus public attitudes significantly shaped British rearmament from 1934, helping to boost the RAF bomber force at the expense of the other services, especially the army. The other fundamental constraint on rearmament was that quite simply Britain spent much less than Germany on defence – in the crucial years 1933–8 perhaps only a third. In 1933 both countries devoted about 3 per cent of their roughly equal GNPs to defence. Over the next five years, as Britain's proportion grew to 8 per cent, Germany's was at least twice as large. Only in 1939 was there a rough parity: Britain – 21.4 per cent; Germany – 23 per cent.[40] As noted in chapter two, low defence spending reflected the Treasury's 'pre-Keynesian' approach to public finance and its remarkable success in the 1930s, under the auspices of Chamberlain and Sir Warren Fisher, in imposing its views on Whitehall.

Official policy in this area, as in others, was also limited to a significant degree by Britain's larger economic circumstances. The arms race of the 1900s had occurred during relative prosperity. In the 1920s Britain was facing increasing competition from new and more efficient industrial rivals, at a time when the international economy centred on London had been unhinged by the war. In September 1931 that economy collapsed completely amid the Central European banking crisis and MacDonald's Labour Cabinet was forced off gold and into a coalition National Government. Labour backbenchers blamed US bankers for failing to support the pound unless substantial cuts in welfare spending were made, but in reality this was the consensus among British and French bankers as well and it reflected Britain's inability, in changing economic circumstances, to protect an over-valued currency with inadequate reserves.[41] With Britain's closest trading partners following it off gold an embryonic sterling area, pegged to the value of the pound, was beginning to emerge.[42]

Throughout the 1930s the Treasury and the Bank were haunted by 1931. Sterling was no longer as good as gold. Restoring London's credibility as a financial centre was the Bank's primary concern. Reinforcing this was the revolution in Britain's balance of payments position. Over the previous century there had never been a payments deficit in peacetime except for the aberrant years of 1919 (residual commitments) and 1926 (the General Strike). But in 1931 the deficit was £104 million and, for the rest of the 1930s, only 1935 saw an unequivocal surplus.[43] Stagnant exports and diminished invisible earnings were to blame – underlying problems of relative economic decline aggravated by the world depression. For the Treasury the payments position was its prime economic concern for most of the 1930s. Its slogan, stated in 1932 and reiterated thereafter, was that 'today financial and economic risks are by far the most serious that the country has to face'.[44]

The Treasury case was double-barrelled, applying to both peace and war. In peacetime, it argued, rapid rearmament would divert resources away from economic recovery. Increased taxation seemed politically impossible in the Depression and the Labour government's fall in 1931 showed the danger of further cuts in social programmes. The Treasury resisted borrowing until 1937, for fear of its effect on inflation, foreign confidence in the pound and thus the balance of payments. These arguments also applied to Britain's position in the event of war. The Treasury liked to call the economy 'the fourth arm' – as important as the three services in Britain's defence. It insisted that the Empire's commercial and financial strength would again be the main means of victory in another long war and that Germany lacked this economic stamina. Thus it was essential not to dissipate Britain's strength by hasty rearmament, which would upset foreign confidence and draw heavily on imports of machinery and raw materials – in both cases diminishing the precious reserves.[45] Imported raw materials, for instance, accounted for 25 to 30 per cent of the cost of armaments produced in Britain.[46]

Were alternative policies available? It is true that even Keynes agreed as late as 1937 that there were clear limits on the amount the government could borrow without dangerous inflation. Furthermore, many of the bottlenecks as rearmament got going from 1937 were industrial rather than financial – restrictive practices by labour and management which led to shortages of skilled labour in key industries such as construction and engineering.[47] But that is ultimately to say that Hitler was more Keynesian than Keynes. The unorthodoxy of Nazi loan-financed defence spending was used by Whitehall as further evidence for its *idée fixe* about the fragility of Germany's economy.[48] Moreover, the government's failure to direct economic resources was testimony to the prevalence of laissez-faire, or at least corporatist, attitudes. It was left to business and unions to sort out their differences. And the priority given to the balance of payments testifies to the enduring importance attributed by the Treasury-City axis to the stability of the currency above all other economic goals.

In any case, British leaders never concentrated on the German question in isolation. For them it had become part of a global crisis.

THE GLOBAL DIMENSION: BETWEEN APPEASEMENT AND CONFRONTATION

In principle, of course, there was general agreement in Whitehall, to quote the DRC in 1934, that Germany was Britain's 'ultimate potential enemy'.[49] The problem was that there were other rivals, notably Japan and Italy, who might become actual enemies in the meantime. Such a diversity of threats was hardly novel. It had been felt acutely at the start of the century. But in the 1900s, as we saw in chapter three, diplomacy had reduced Britain's isolation; in the 1930s it did not.[50] How far were British policymakers responsible for the 'failure' of global appeasement?

As with defence, British policy in Asia in the 1930s was constrained by decisions taken in the aftermath of the Great War.[51] The first was the acceptance of the principle of equality between the Royal Navy and that of the USA. This was adopted because of American pressure and the British inability, given post-war budgetary problems, to sustain an arms race against an economically stronger state. The principle was accepted for capital ships (battleships and battlecruisers) at the Washington Conference of 1921–2 and extended to cruisers, destroyers and other surface vessels at London in 1930. Japan, now the third largest naval power, agreed to keep its navy at 60 per cent of British or American strength.[52] The second background factor was the abandonment of the Anglo–Japanese alliance when it expired in 1921. On balance the Lloyd George coalition would have preferred to renew it: although no longer of importance against Russia, it did provide some check on Japan and absolved Britain from keeping large forces in Asia. But the USA, now viewing Japan as its main potential enemy, made abrogation of the alliance a condition for a naval agreement at Washington and Britain acquiesced.[53]

By themselves the naval agreement and the end of the Anglo–Japanese alliance were of limited significance. The British did not build even to the limits that the naval treaties allowed in the 1920s, and Anglo–Japanese relations remained good for most of the decade. But in the early 1930s Japan's economy collapsed in the Depression, the military took ever firmer hold over the government and a mood of anti-Western expansionism intensified. Japan broke loose from the naval treaties of the 1920s, building towards parity with America and Britain. It also embarked on a bid for its own sphere of influence in East Asia with the conquest of Manchuria in 1931–2 and the fighting in Shanghai in the first half of 1932. The latter posed a particular threat for British interests – 6 per cent of British foreign investment was in China, three-fifths of this in Shanghai, Asia's greatest port.[54]

It was the Shanghai crisis which prompted revocation of the ten-year rule, and, when the Defence Requirements Committee began its deliberations in the autumn of 1933, Hankey and the Admiralty urged that the Far East posed the most urgent problem. The latter claimed that the growth of Japan's navy had rendered untenable the policies of the 1920s and that 'real security for this country could be achieved only by a two-power naval standard', by which Britain was at least equal to Japan and the greatest European navy.[55] But from the DRC's various demands for modernising ships and equipment, increasing the Fleet Air Arm in Asia and completing the Singapore base, only the latter survived the Treasury axe. As we have seen, the rearmament programme of July 1934 was slanted towards a bomber deterrent against Germany.

Treasury influence was not purely negative, however. Guided by

Warren Fisher, Chamberlain argued that diplomacy should be brought in line with defence realities. Given his assumption that rearming against Germany was the priority and that Britain could not afford at the same time to rebuild the navy, it followed that London should seek an agreement with Tokyo. He felt that there was room for both Britain and Japan commercially in China and that, in a friendlier economic atmosphere, a new naval understanding might then be reached. Chamberlain and the vehemently anti-American Fisher dismissed the anxieties of the FO and Admiralty that this would irritate the USA. 'We ought to know by now', Chamberlain wrote on 28 July 1934, 'that the U.S.A. will give us no undertaking to resist by force any action by Japan short of an attack on Hawaii or Honolulu. She will give us plenty of assurances of goodwill especially if we will promise to do all the fighting, but the moment she is asked to contribute something she invariably takes refuge behind Congress'.[56]

This proposal for a security agreement with Japan, supplemented by economic appeasement, paralleled Chamberlain's approach to Germany. He pressed his case in preparations for the 1935 naval conference and through a Treasury mission in 1935–6 to try to resolve China's economic difficulties in conjunction with Japan. Neither was successful – by the end of 1934 Japan had formally renounced the Washington treaty limits on its navy and the recommendations of the Treasury mission were overshadowed by new tensions culminating in the renewal of the Sino–Japanese war in July 1937.[57] In any case, despite Chamberlain's determination, British efforts at appeasement had always been half-hearted. The reservations of the Foreign Office had seen to that. Repeatedly it warned of the danger of alienating the USA and cast growing doubt on the chances of a real accommodation given Japan's evident 'will to power'.[58]

On the other hand, the alternative to appeasement – deterrence or even confrontation – was also not adopted. Between 1934 and the end of 1937 naval modernisation ranked lower on the list of British rearmament priorities than even the army, despite the continued protests of the Admiralty and the empire-oriented Hankey. In the absence of effective naval strength the British remained reliant on the USA, yet the Americans, while against appeasement, were unwilling and politically unable, in view of isolationist and anglophobe sentiment, to take a firm line with Britain against Japan. The British predicament was dramatised at the turn of 1937–8 when Japanese attacks on British and US vessels in the Yangtse river prompted a debate about sanctions against Japan. Although the Foreign Office, under Eden, wanted to keep in step with any American action, they and Chamberlain agreed that, to quote one FO memo of October 1937, 'sanctions would almost certainly mean war and the USA. is not now prepared to fight, even with the British Empire as an ally. Therefore there will be no sanctions'.[59]

Thus British policy towards Japan drifted between containment and appeasement. Trapped in unresolved conflict between the Foreign Office and the Treasury, Whitehall wandered along 'a middle course of benevolent neutrality that favoured China by giving moral support and limited material aid but nonetheless aimed to prevent a breakdown in Anglo–Japanese relations'.[60] Sir Robert Craigie, the Ambassador in Tokyo, warned that Britain was falling fatally between two stools – 'alienating one party to this conflict without assisting the other'.[61] But even Chamberlain, exponent of appeasing Japan in 1934, who tried to harmonise diplomacy and defence in Europe when premier in 1937–8, did little at that time to resolve the confusion in Asia. Ultimately the drift in British policy is probably due to an underlying, racist complacency about the extent of the damage that a war with Japan could inflict[62] – an error dramatically demonstrated by the Pacific onslaught in the winter of 1941–2. But the lack of sustained attention given by Britain to Asia after 1934 is also attributable to the emergence of a new threat much nearer home – fascist Italy.

This blew up in October 1935 when Mussolini attacked the East African kingdom of Abyssinia – long coveted by Italy. As in Asia, British policy was caught between competing pressures. Although we tend, in retrospect, to think of 'the dictators' as a bloc, that was by no means clear in the mid-1930s. Mussolini particularly feared a German absorption of Austria (Anschluss), which would give Hitler dominance over Central Europe and a border adjacent to Italy, and his prompt movement of Italian troops had proved the main deterrent to an Anschluss in 1934. British policy throughout the 1930s was to prevent or at least weaken a Rome–Berlin axis. Thus Vansittart, one of the toughest FO officials towards Germany, was keen to appease Mussolini. 'We cannot afford to quarrel with Italy and drive her back into German embraces', he minuted in February 1935.[63]

On the other hand, the blatant Italian aggression in Abyssinia caused an outcry in Britain and in the League of Nations. As the Peace Ballot showed, the British public, although reluctant to contemplate war, believed abstractly in the concept of collective security. The Government was therefore obliged to go along with demands for League sanctions, but it tried to minimise these for fear of provoking a war which might leave it unable to respond to aggression by Japan. Secretly the Foreign Secretary, Sir Samuel Hoare, was sent to Paris in

December 1935 to conclude an Anglo–French deal with Italy, but when details leaked out the public outrage led the Government to make him a scapegoat. Further negotiations were inconceivable – in the words of a contemporary joke, 'no more coals to Newcastle, no more Hoares to Paris'.[64] Thus Britain ended up antagonising Italy while failing to deter its aggression. This pattern, reminiscent of Britain's Japanese dilemma, was repeated throughout the 1930s, for instance over Italian involvement in the Spanish Civil War (1936–9).

Unlike the 1900s, therefore, Britain's rivals were not appeased. It is possible that they were unappeasable, but no coherent effort was made in the period before 1937. Complicating the position further was the position of the Dominions.[65] Their manpower would once again be essential in any future war yet their growing independence meant that Britain could no longer take their support for granted. Successive European crises – Abyssinia, the Rhineland and the Anschluss – sharpened Dominion isolationism. In 1936 Canada's premier, W.L. Mackenzie King, stressed that only the Canadian Parliament could decide 'to what extent, if at all' Canada would participate in conflicts involving other Commonwealth countries.[66] The Imperial Conference of 1937 strongly supported the policy of appeasement in Europe, with only New Zealand inclined to a tougher line backed by closer imperial defence coordination. Dominion opinion was also an important contributory factor in the failure to appease Japan – Canada had strongly backed America in 1921 against renewal of the Anglo–Japanese alliance and the Australasian Dominions in the 1930s warned repeatedly of the Japanese military threat. As Robert Menzies, the Australian premier, observed in 1939, 'what Britain calls the Far East is to us the near north'.[67]

Yet, despite this growing *diplomatic* independence, Britain was still responsible for the defence of the Dominions because their own peacetime forces, particularly naval, were negligible. For instance, the British policy of sending a fleet to Singapore in the event of war with Japan was Australia's and New Zealand's only real defence. It was the growth of a global naval threat to Britain – from Italy and particularly Japan – which set the 1930s in contrast with the 1900s, when appeasement and alliance had defused all but the German challenge. And it was in these circumstances that the net costs of imperial defence became, for the first time, significant. In 1937–8 Britain was spending 5.6 per cent of national income on defence spending compared with 1 per cent for Australia and 0.8 per cent for New Zealand (£265.2 million, against £6 million and £1.6 million). Had these two Dominions spent the same proportion of national incomes on defence as

Britain did, 'the *extra* sums available would have totalled about £37 million', more than one-third of the Royal Navy's total budget (£102 million) and sufficient over a number of years to create a significant Pacific fleet.[68] And in the crisis of 1940–2, unlike 1914–18, having a Pacific fleet really mattered.

The sense of global threat, coupled with the lack of ready support from the USA and the Dominions, became part of the worldview of British policymakers by the late 1930s – essential background to their unwillingness to risk confrontation with Germany. The result was policy paralysis which Neville Chamberlain was determined to end when he became premier in May 1937. After the drift of the Baldwin years, the energetic and opinionated Chamberlain set out to make his own foreign policy. He removed the obstinate Vansittart in January 1938 while the highly-strung Eden resigned the following month. The new FO 'team' of Lord Halifax and Sir Alexander Cadogan proved much more sympathetic and tractable. But diplomacy was only part of the story. Chamberlain wanted to bring economics, defence and diplomacy into a new policy synthesis, drawing heavily on the view of his former Treasury advisers.

In December 1937 the Cabinet accepted the findings of a major review of defence policy by Sir Thomas Inskip, who had the title (but not the powers) of 'Minister for the Co-ordination of Defence'. This review had been commissioned by Chamberlain before leaving the Treasury with the task, quite explicitly, of 'correlating the rising burden of Defence liabilities to the whole of our available resources'.[69] In Inskip's review, equipping a BEF for the continent now dropped to lowest priority, to be fulfilled only when the situation elsewhere permitted. The policy of 'limited liability' on the Continent had 'shrunk to one of no liability at all'.[70] Instead, the protection of Britain's colonies and trade moved up to second place, behind the defence of the UK. This reflected persistent warnings from Hankey and the Admiralty about the growing naval crisis in the Mediterranean and Pacific. But it was also a direct consequence of accepting the Treasury axiom that 'economic stability' was 'an essential element in our defensive strength: one which can properly be regarded as a fourth arm in defence'.[71] Defending Britain's formal and informal empire was deemed vital for long-term survival in war.

Yet Inskip went so far as to tell the Cabinet bleakly in February 1938: 'the plain fact which cannot be obscured is that it is beyond the resources of this country to make proper provision in peace for defence of the British Empire against three major Powers in three different theatres of war'. While confident that, in the event of war,

Britain would prevail in the end, he accepted the Treasury argument that *in peacetime* the necessary degree of rearmament would be economically and politically intolerable, as well as undermining Britain's potential staying power in war. The only way out in peacetime, said Inskip, was by 'reducing the scale of our commitments and the number of our potential enemies'.[72]

This was the rationale for Chamberlain's major effort in early 1938 to reach agreement with Italy. He was backed enthusiastically by the Chiefs of Staff. With Germany and Japan deemed the main dangers, Hankey argued, 'we simply cannot afford to be on bad terms with a nation which has a stranglehold on our shortest line of communications between the two possible theatres of war'.[73] But Italy's precondition of any settlement was *de jure* recognition of its conquest of Abyssinia. Chamberlain regarded this as inevitable, but Eden, the Foreign Secretary, believed that such a concession would have no effect on Mussolini and would only damage Britain's international reputation, especially in the USA. On Italy, he took a much firmer line than most of the FO and indeed than Cabinet sceptics about appeasing Germany such as Duff Cooper, the First Lord of the Admiralty – all of whom sought Italian amity as a deterrent against an Austrian Anschluss. This rift with Eden delayed Chamberlain's demarche in the winter of 1937–8 and Eden's eventual resignation on 20 February 1938 came only three weeks before the long-feared Anschluss took place.[74]

Reinforcing Eden's anger about Italy was a row over the USA. In January 1938 London received a sudden, secret proposal by Roosevelt for steps leading to an international peace conference. Chamberlain, operating on the principle that 'it was always best and safest to count on *nothing* from the Americans except words',[75] reacted coolly. He believed that this 'bombshell' could destroy chances of Italian appeasement. Eden believed that any US overture, however naive, should not be snubbed and that 'Anglo–American co-operation in an attempt to ensure world peace' was preferable to 'a piece-meal settlement approached by way of problematical agreement with Mussolini'.[76] This dispute contributed to Eden's resignation, as did his larger frustration at Chamberlain's repeated exercises in secret personal diplomacy.

Whether either an earlier Chamberlain demarche towards Italy or, on the other hand, as the Edenites claimed, endorsement for Roosevelt's initiative could have averted the Anschluss is a moot point.[77] Nevertheless, Eden's stance is worthy of closer examination, suggesting as it does alternatives to Chamberlain's policy. The differences between the two men, though ones of emphasis, were at times substantial. Eden agreed in principle that 'we should make every possible effort to come to terms with each or all of our potential enemies, but not', he insisted, 'by conduct which would lose us our friends, both actual and potential'.[78] He believed that Chamberlain was too fearful of Italy and too cynical about America: the former could perhaps be defied, the latter must be cultivated. He was less willing than the Chiefs of Staff or the Treasury to take the triple threat and the sense of economic constraint as overriding. In other words, in 1938 he disputed the need for Britain to reduce its enemies at all costs and believed that the unheroic tactic of 'cunctation' – of delay until Britain and its friends were stronger – was probably the best policy.

Ultimately he and other critics outside the Cabinet, notably Churchill, accepted that Britain's position in 1938 was not good, but they believed that there was more room for bluff than Chamberlain allowed. The Prime Minister was very clear on this point, re-iterating his belief 'that you should never menace unless you are in a position to carry out your threats'.[79] Chamberlain and his colleagues had convinced themselves that, if their bluff were called, the result would be world war against Britain's empire and airborne destruction of Britain itself. These fears guided them as the Czech crisis unfolded in 1938.

'MUNICH'

British policy in the Czech crisis in fact represents the culmination of the themes examined in the first three sections of this chapter. Czechoslovakia, a polyglot creation of the Versailles settlement but also the most advanced industrial state in eastern Europe, was next on Hitler's list. As before he couched his demands in terms of support for the claims of local German-speakers, in this case the Sudetens, for incorporation in the Reich. But by September 1938 he had pushed matters to the brink of war.

Chamberlain was sure that Czechoslovakia was not a matter of fundamental British interest. As he said on the radio at the height of the September crisis: 'How horrible, fantastic, incredible, it is that we should be digging trenches and trying on gas-masks here because of a quarrel in a far-away country between people of whom we know nothing'.[80] His position was in line with consistent British interwar policy that eastern Europe was an unsettled mess left over from 1919 and that Britain should certainly not be drawn into guaranteeing the position of France's allies in the region. Chamberlain, still working on a moderates–extremists view of German politics, also remained convinced that appeasement of Germany was possible and that Czechoslovakia was an obstacle in the way. Guided by the British ambassador in Berlin, Sir Nevile Henderson, he believed that Hitler genuinely wanted a Czech settlement but might be provoked into war by British intransigence.[81] Almost the opposite was really the case. And in the escalating crisis Chamberlain adopted his own brand of summit diplomacy – making three trips to Germany (his first time in the air) to secure agreement.

Chamberlain therefore believed that Britain had no reason to fight for Czechoslovakia. Military advice confirmed that line by suggesting that war would be suicidal. A Chiefs of Staff report on 21 March 1938, which guided all subsequent assessments of the situation, wildly exaggerated the military balance, predicting that Germany could put 90 divisions into the field against barely 50 from France, Czechoslovakia and Britain combined. (The British contribution would be only two divisions.) Hitler could therefore not be stopped from overrunning Czechoslovakia, the COS argued, and Britain and France would be committing themselves to a 'prolonged struggle' to defeat Germany. Moreover, the Chiefs summoned up the spectre of three-front war. They warned that it was likely that 'Italy and Japan would seize the opportunity to further their own ends and that in consequence the problem we have to envisage is not that of a limited European war only, but of a World War'. This, they had already advised in the Inskip report, would be unsustainable in Britain's present position. 'We cannot foresee the time when our defence forces will be strong enough to safeguard our territory, trade and vital interests against Germany, Italy and Japan simultaneously'.[82]

Of particular concern to the Chiefs and to the Cabinet were the fears of a 'knock-out blow' from the Luftwaffe. This was the result of two years of pessimistic appraisals of German air strength, encouraged by the barrage of propaganda from Berlin and by a failure to realise just how far the Luftwaffe was a 'shop-window' airforce, lacking reserves, spares and modern equipment. In late September the Air Ministry's assessment of front-line aircraft was 2909 (Germany) to 1550 (Britain). In fact, if one measures *serviceable* frontline aircraft Germany had only 1669. Compounding this error were gross over-estimations of the number of aircraft the Luftwaffe could divert from the Czech front, of the range and capacity of the German bombers and of the likely damage from every ton of bombs. The Air Ministry was reckoning on 50,000 casualties in the first twenty-four hours.[83] Mindful of this, Chamberlain told his Cabinet colleagues how he had looked down on London as he flew home from his second visit to Hitler, 'asked himself what degree of protection they could afford to the thousands of homes' spread out below and concluded 'that we were in no position to justify waging a war to-day in order to prevent a war hereafter'.[84]

Yet, ironically, Britain very nearly went to war in September 1938. That it failed to do so was because of Hitler, not Chamberlain. At their second meeting, at Godesberg on 23 September, Hitler increased his demands to immediate control of the Sudetenland. On the 25th two-fifths of the British Cabinet, led by Halifax, the Foreign Secretary, rebelled. Bolstered by (briefly) more optimistic military evaluations and talks with the French, the British announced on the 26th that they were mobilising the fleet and would join France in war against Germany if Hitler attacked Czechoslovakia. Chamberlain still did his best to avoid such an outcome, but trenches were being dug in London, gas-masks issued and war plans in train when, on 28 September, Hitler surprisingly agreed to further negotiations. For months he had been bent on taking Czechoslovakia by force, but the doubts of his own military, Italian reluctance to enter a war and the firm line from London combined to cause a brief loss of nerve.[85] What followed is well-known: when Hitler backed off, Chamberlain pursued him with open arms. At Munich on 30 September Hitler gained the substance of his demands on a slightly longer timetable. At Chamberlain's insistence he also signed a slip of paper affirming 'the desire of their two countries never to go to war with each other again'.[86] Munich, henceforth the synonym for cowardice, was actually made possible because Hitler flinched momentarily at the threat of force.

It is tragically ironic that Europe was spared war in September 1938 because of Hitler. For it is now clear that although Britain was in no position to fight in 1938, the same was true of Germany. The familiar justification – that the extra year gave time for British opinion to solidify – ignores the fact that by late September 1938 the country was, reluctantly, prepared to go to war. And, against the argument that Munich gave Britain longer to improve its air defences, one should note that in 1938 the Luftwaffe had neither the plans nor the capacity to bomb London and that the French enjoyed a five-to-one superiority on Germany's vulnerable western front. In 1938, unlike 1939, Russia might have intervened – Munich helped to convince Stalin that the Western powers would not offer any support in eastern Europe. Even if Russia had remained aloof, and, as in 1939, the Anglo–French forces had not taken the offensive, the German attack in the West, when it came, would probably not have achieved the devastating success it did in 1940.[87] And if France had not been eliminated, the war would have turned out very differently.

THE FAILURE OF CONTAINMENT

The only real change in British policy in the weeks after Munich was a new emphasis on air defence instead of deterrence. The old strategy of bomber parity with Germany had clearly failed by 1937 and the Treasury's recognition of this was reflected in Inskip's defence review at the end of the year, with its new stress on fighters, but it was not until after Munich that the Air Ministry began to take note.[88] By then technological advances had made a policy of air defence conceivable. The development of fast, monoplane fighters – the Hurricane and particularly the Spitfire – and Britain's unique advantage as the pioneer of radar made it feasible for the first time that the bomber might *not* 'get through'. The September 1938 crisis had also revealed the weakness of Britain's air defences – only 100 Hurricanes and two Spitfires in operation, only five of the eighteen radar stations built, no proper 'phone communication between RAF Fighter Command and the airfields.[89] The new air programme approved in November laid the weight firmly on remedying these deficiencies. This is not to negate the basic point that the Luftwaffe was in no position to bomb Britain in 1938, but simply to say that, when it tried, in 1940, the British had made better use of the intervening time.

But the air defence programme still developed within tight financial limits. Indeed the attraction of the new policy for the Treasury was the promise of 'more bang for your buck' more quickly, because four fighters cost roughly the same as one heavy bomber. Moreover, foreign policy as a whole still rested on old assumptions. Chamberlain certainly did not see Munich as signalling the need for a change of course. With the threat of war lifted, he began a new effort to reach agreement with Germany and Italy, including a visit to Rome in mid-January 1939. Many in the FO had been critical of Chamberlain's personal diplomacy in September – 'if at first you can't concede, fly, fly, fly again', as one irreverent verse had it.[90] But when the FO embarked on a major review of British policy in the wake of Munich, it had little new to offer. The consensus was that Britain should now accept German dominance of Central and Eastern Europe, continue to build up Anglo–French strength in the West and try again to detach Mussolini from the Axis. Among senior officials, only Laurence Collier, head of the Northern Department since 1934, consistently opposed appeasement towards both Germany *and* Italy.[91]

The fundamental change in British policy came not after Munich but in the early months of 1939.[92] Between mid-December 1938 and mid-April 1939 Whitehall received no less than twenty warnings from various secret sources about imminent German aggression in the West, many of them predicting a sudden air strike on London. The most authoritative, in mid-January, warned of an invasion of Holland. None of these reports was true and, ironically, many of them emanated from German 'moderates' anxious to stiffen British resistance,[93] but cumulatively they had a profound effect on thinking in Whitehall. By February, Sir Alexander Cadogan, Permanent Under-Secretary at the FO, who in October had still been talking about another peace conference to remedy the deficiencies of Versailles, was writing: 'I have the profoundest suspicions of Hitler's intentions . . . I believe that what he would like best, if he could do it, would be to smash the British Empire'.[94]

This growing conviction in Whitehall that Hitler's objectives lay in Western and not Eastern Europe, with Britain top of the list, was strengthened by his take-over of the rest of the Czech lands on 15 March 1939. His claim simply to be bringing Germans within the Reich was now exploded, and he had also broken a signed agreement with Chamberlain – a matter of some significance for the Prime Minister in view of his repeated assertion that Hitler, though 'half-mad', could be trusted to keep his word. By now, too, a growing reaction against appeasement among the public, and particularly within the Tory party, was beginning to assert itself. Prague let loose these feelings of humiliation, shame and anger. The crucial figure in the policy re-appraisal was the Foreign Secretary, Lord Halifax, originally a compliant Chamberlainite but after the Godesberg revolt increasingly his own man, swayed by the new mood in the FO and sensitive to the shift within the Tory party. It has been claimed that 'the dominating fact as Hitler occupied Prague was Halifax's belief that the policy would have to be changed if the party was to be saved'.[95] This is to exaggerate the primacy of domestic politics. Nevertheless, it is clear that March 1939 was the culmination of a political as well as a bureaucratic U-turn. Chamberlain could not forget that 1940 would be an election year.

Convinced now that Hitler was a 'Westerner' not an 'Easterner' and that he was bidding for European hegemony, the British Government viewed diplomacy, finance and defence in a new light. After the Holland scare in January, the Cabinet agreed to guarantee Dutch security and to enter into staff talks with France – major reversals of the 'limited liability' policy towards the Continent practised throughout the 1930s. New criteria also applied to defence policy. The Secretary of State for War, Leslie Hore-Belisha, appointed by Chamberlain in 1937 to push through the downgrading of the continental commitment, had, like Halifax, turned around by 1939. He now called for substantial immediate spending to ensure that six well-equipped divisions could be on the Continent within two weeks of the start of a war. On 22 February, despite a Treasury rearguard action, these proposals were approved, the Chancellor, Sir John Simon, frankly admitting that now 'other aspects in this matter outweigh finance'.[96]

In the panicky atmosphere after Prague – pervaded once again with rumours of imminent German aggression, this time on Poland and Romania – further action was taken. On 29 March the Government announced that the Territorial Army (TA) would be doubled and a month later a bill authorising conscription was introduced into the Commons. Above all, in the wake of Prague and Mussolini's copycat invasion of Albania on 7 April, the British for the first time committed themselves to the security of Eastern Europe. This (*pace* Newman 1976) was a major shift in policy. In concert with the French, who were in even greater panic, the Cabinet offered guarantees to Poland (31 March) and to Greece and Romania (13 April).

The British Government was now acknowledging the real danger of war. By guaranteeing Poland, it had been shocked into doing what Chamberlain had firmly refused to do over Czechoslovakia, namely to leave Britain's decision for peace or war effectively in Hitler's hands. Nevertheless, it is important to note 'that these new guarantees were almost entirely political in scope and in immediate purpose'.[97] No assessments were made of their military implications; no staff talks ensued with the countries involved; indeed the Chiefs of Staff had been against offering the guarantees. Likewise with the defence measures: the doubling of the TA was announced without taking military advice, and conscription was regarded by the military as an impediment to the quick creation of an efficient BEF. Both of these defence measures were attempts to reassure France, because of Halifax's concern about warnings that if Britain did not make 'un effort du sang' French opinion could turn increasingly defeatist.[98] In other words, the guarantees and the defence measures lacked substance: they were intended, rather desperately, to deter Hitler, bolster France and impress world opinion. As Simon observed, 'we are not preparing for war, we are constructing a peace front'.[99]

Not peace with Hitler, it should be noted. Even Chamberlain now had little hope from that quarter. 'No reliance could be placed on the assurances given by the Nazi leaders', he told the Cabinet on 18 March. But, he also noted, 'this did not mean that negotiations with the German people were impossible'.[100] He particularly hoped that the firm deterrent policy now adopted could bring about a change in leaders in Germany and a more tractable regime. The assumptions about German moderates and about the weakness of the Nazi economy that had animated appeasement still motivated the new policy of containment.

With this in mind, we can better understand the failure to reach agreement with the Soviet Union. There were, of course, deep underlying difficulties. Tory politicians, particularly Chamberlain, had always been morbidly suspicious of Bolshevism and, after Stalin's purges, they were sceptical about the military value of the Red Army. There was also the fundamental problem of the Poles – bitter enemies of the Russians in a bloody war against them in 1920 – who had no intention of again allowing the Red Army on Polish soil, even as 'allies' against Germany. The British lurch into guaranteeing Poland effectively ruled out military cooperation with Russia. Nevertheless, there was a growing British recognition that Russia was an essential part of any attempt to contain Hitler. Pressure from parliamentary opinion and gradually more insistent advice from the Chiefs of Staff pushed a reluctant Chamberlain into negotiations with Russia in the summer of 1939.[101] But the British mission to Moscow acted, under instructions, half-heartedly. For Britain the value of the talks was diplomatic rather than strategic – part of the shopwindow display of strength that was supposed to make Germany think again. In line with their general policy in Eastern Europe, the Cabinet was unwilling to make firm military commitments and it was on this matter that the talks broke down in August 1939. Basically the British were more interested in being seen to talk to the Russians than in reaching an agreement.

All this assumed that the Russians had nowhere else to turn. The news of the Nazi–Soviet pact on 22 August therefore came as a bombshell in London. The FO tried to blame the suppliers of intelligence, but, once again, the failure lay at the level of basic assumptions. Whitehall had received reports of Russo–German talks, but dismissed as unthinkable the idea that the great ideological enemies, Nazism and communism, could come to terms.[102] Given the history of the 1930s, it was fitting that the demarche that left Hitler free to attack Poland with impunity was in part the result of another intel-

ligence failure in Whitehall. Although the Cabinet dithered momentarily, it honoured the Polish guarantee and Britain and France entered
the war on 3 September.

Even then, however, the old attitudes died hard. Three and a half
million people fled London in early September 1939, fearful of the
imminent knock-out blow. But it did not come: the Luftwaffe was
pre-occupied with Poland and Hitler still had no plans to bomb London. Officially the British were now beginning the long struggle for
which the Treasury had been trying to prepare them throughout the
1930s. Three years was the time-span often mentioned. But the Treasury now warned that this was very likely 'much too optimistic'. Compared with 1914 Britain had smaller reserves, and American loans were
ruled out under current isolationist legislation. Without US aid 'the
prospects for a long war are exceedingly grim'.[103] By February 1940
the Treasury doubted that Britain could fund a war unaided for more
than two years.[104]

Yet Chamberlain, Halifax and close colleagues remained hopeful of
a quicker solution. The premier insisted privately in the autumn of
1939 that 'the difficulty is with Hitler himself. Until he disappears and
his system collapses there can be no peace. But what I hope for is not
a military victory – I very much doubt the feasibility of that – but a
collapse of the German home front. For that it is necessary to convince the Germans that they cannot win.' His policy was therefore
one of passive firmness: 'Hold on tight, keep up the economic pressure, push on with munitions production and military preparations with
the utmost energy, take no offensive until Hitler begins it. I reckon
that if we are allowed to carry on this policy we shall have won the
War by the Spring'.[105]

Behind such ideas lay assumptions that by now are familiar. First
was the distinction between German moderates and extremists. Although unready to respond to official Nazi 'peace offensives', the British kept open contacts with the German opposition during the winter
of 1939–40.[106] Secondly, there was the belief that the German economy was fundamentally unsound. Economic intelligence predicted
that, given the shortage of raw materials and foreign exchange, the
Nazi war effort would start to contract seriously after twelve to eighteen months.[107] Given these optimistic assumptions and the balancing
fear of starting a devastating air war, one can better understand the
passivity of British strategy in the winter of 1939–40. In Chamberlain's
view, time seemed to be on Britain's side.

The events of May–June 1940 exposed that fallacy. In six weeks
from 10 May Hitler defeated the Low Countries and France, forcing

the French to sign a humiliating armistice on 17 June. The Germans did not enjoy clear-cut material superiority, except in the air, but they did make better use of their resources through a modernised command structure and a strategy of mobile, armoured warfare backed by air support to which the French and the British had no answer. Even so, as in August–September 1914, it was a close-run thing, depending crucially on the surprise and speed of the German armoured attack across the Meuse and round the back of the Allied front in Belgium. Hitler's slowness in eliminating the Dunkirk salient and stopping the evacuation of the BEF was largely due to the concern of German army commanders that their tank units needed time to refit before the main attack on Paris.[108] To this battle the British contributed very little, considering that they had a larger population than France and double its manufacturing output. In May 1940 there were only 10 British divisions on the Western Front, none of them armoured, compared with 104 French, 22 Belgian and 8 Dutch.[109] It is arguable that if the British had given higher priority to a modernised BEF right from the beginning of rearmament in 1934, this might have made a real difference.[110]

Be that as it may, the Germans succeeded in June 1940 where they had failed in September 1914. Denmark, Norway, the Low Countries and half of France fell, the rest of France came under a puppet government and Hitler's influence extended into Spain, Sweden and the Balkans. Germany now dominated Europe as it had never done in 1914–18. There were global implications, too. Italy entered the war, ready to exploit Britain's weakness in North Africa, and Japan felt freer to intensify the war in China and to press the European colonial powers for economic concessions. Moreover, as early as July 1940 Hitler was already making plans for the invasion of Russia – a project that had seemed years away only a few months before. The events of mid-1940 were decisive in turning a European conflict into a global war.[111]

1940 was also the nemesis of appeasement. Throughout the 1930s most British leaders had combined a 'worst case' analysis of Britain's military predicament with a 'best case' analysis of the motives of its opponents.[112] The misperceptions of Hitler, the exaggeration of German air strength, the preoccupation with economic stability, the lack of concerted policies towards Italy and Japan – all these contributed to Whitehall's failure to call Hitler's bluff until it was too late. But 1940 finally exposed the most basic British assumption of all. As Sir Orme Sargent of the FO admitted in October 1938, 'we have used France as a shield, behind which we have maintained ourselves in Europe since our disarmament'.[113] This had been the basis of appeasement; it was also, in Halifax's shocked words in May 1940, 'the one firm rock' on which the belated policy of containment had rested since early 1939.[114] The French were more blunt: the British, they said, would always fight to the last Frenchman. British policy in the years before 1939, as in the run-up to 1914, had assumed that if war broke out the defensive strength of the French army would give Britain time to rearm and to mobilise the resources of empire (both so difficult in the atmosphere and priorities of peacetime). Hence the low priority given to the BEF before both wars. This strategy worked, just, in 1914. It failed, just, in 1940. The result was world war.

REFERENCES

1. Gilbert 1976: v, 927
2. 'Cato' 1940: 19
3. Waites (ed.) 1971: 67
4. Dockrill and Goold 1981: 59
5. Néré 1975; Stevenson 1982
6. Fink 1984
7. McDougall 1978
8. Dutton 1985: 238–9
9. Gilbert 1976: v, 124
10. Orde 1978: 71–154
11. Dutton 1985: 250
12. Jacobson 1983
13. CP 4 (32), CAB 24/227
14. Bialer 1980: 10
15. Bennett 1979: 378
16. Rose 1978: 95
17. Peters 1986: 223–5, 248–9
18. Medlicott 1981: 99
19. Wendt 1971; MacDonald 1972
20. Hildebrand 1973; Hillgruber 1974; Weinberg 1970, 1980; Hauner 1978; Overy 1982
21. Peacock and Wiseman 1967: tables A–5 and A–15
22. Jaffe 1985: 139
23. Gibbs 1975: 3
24. Ferris 1987
25. Gibbs 1975: 58
26. Roskill 1972: ii, 535–8
27. M. Smith 1984: 311–12

28. Murray 1988: 21
29. Middlemas and Barnes 1969: 744–7, 791–2
30. Bialer 1980: 47
31. Ibid., 130
32. Collier 1957: 528
33. Bialer 1980
34. Middlemas and Barnes 1969: 735
35. M. Smith 1984: 121–39
36. Bialer 1980: 51
37. Middlemas 1972: 1
38. Bond 1980: ch. 7
39. Bond 1977: 85
40. Peden 1979b: 8; Peden 1984a: 25; cf. Bairoch 1976: 303
41. Williamson 1984; Kunz 1987
42. Drummond 1981
43. Peden 1979b: 62–3, 208
44. Shay 1977: 24
45. Coghlan 1972; Parker 1975; Shay 1977; Peden 1979b
46. Peden 1984a: 24
47. Parker 1981; Peden 1983a
48. Peden 1984a: 18–19
49. Wark 1986: 17
50. M. Howard 1974: 30
51. Callahan 1974
52. Dingman 1976; McKercher 1984; Hall 1987
53. Nish 1972
54. Thorne 1973: 49–50
55. Gibbs 1975: 120
56. NC 18/1/881
57. Trotter 1975
58. Lee 1973: 213–17
59. Ovendale 1975: 77
60. Lee 1973: 212
61. Louis 1971: 256
62. Lee 1973: 128–9, 217–18
63. Parker 1974: 296
64. Avon 1962: 317
65. Ovendale 1975
66. R. Holland 1981: 190
67. A. Watt 1965: 24–5
68. Peden 1984b: 416
69. Pratt 1975: 77
70. M. Howard 1974: 118
71. Gibbs 1975: 284
72. Ibid., 293
73. Roskill 1974: iii, 270–1
74. Douglas 1977: 6–16, 130–1

75. NC 18/1/1032
76. Reynolds 1981: 19–23
77. Rock 1988: 89
78. FO 371/20702, C8704/205/62, CID, 2 Dec. 1937
79. NC 18/1/1068; cf. Murray 1984: 189
80. Feiling 1946: 372
81. Wark 1986: 207
82. Murray 1984: 157–9
83. Wark 1986: 66–9
84. CAB 23/95, f. 180
85. Weinberg 1980: 452–62; Murray 1984: 214–15
86. Thorne 1967: 83
87. Murray 1984: ch. 7
88. Peden 1979b: 128–34
89. M. Smith 1984: 214–17
90. Rose 1978: 231
91. Lammers 1973
92. D.C. Watt 1989: ch. 6
93. Andrew 1985: 412–15
94. Dilks (ed.) 1971: 120, 152
95. Cowling 1975: 291
96. Peden 1979b: 148
97. Gibbs 1975: 713
98. Bond 1980: 289–310
99. Colvin 1971: 216
100. Aster 1973: 50
101. Manne 1974
102. Andrew 1985: 422–7
103. CAB 24/287, CP 149 (39)
104. T 177/52
105. NC 18/1/1116 and/1124
106. Ludlow 1977; MacDonald 1978
107. Hinsley 1979: 71–2, 232
108. Bond 1975: ch. 5
109. Carr 1985: 93
110. Bond 1980: 337–8
111. Reynolds 1990a
112. Murray 1984: 92, 177
113. R. Young 1978: 214
114. Reynolds 1981: 103

CHAPTER SIX

World War, 1940–7

The total collapse of the European balance of power in 1940 revolutionised Britain's international position. Its chances of defeating Germany now depended heavily on America and, after Hitler turned east in June 1941, the Soviet Union. This would have significant repercussions for the post-war world. At the same time Italian and Japanese exploitation of the international power vacuum helped broaden the struggle by 1942 into global war, with Mussolini's botched opportunism opening up a North African theatre and Japan's more serious bid for power transforming East Asia and the Pacific in the early months of 1942.

The ultimate resolution of this three-front war was surprisingly favourable to Britain, given its grave predicament in 1940–2, for the Axis was totally defeated and all Britain's lost colonies regained. But the post-war crisis of 1945–7 was far graver than that following 1918, with Britain's economic, international and imperial positions seriously undermined by the war. By 1947 it seemed to some that the country's days as a world power must surely be over. The way in which that crisis was resolved and those expectations apparently falsified shaped British policy for the next quarter-century.

All this lay in the future, however, in June 1940, when Britain's very survival was in doubt. America was still neutral and, despite Churchill's blandishments, Roosevelt's support for Britain evolved slowly in 1940–1, constrained by isolationist opinion. Only Japan's attack on Pearl Harbor in December 1941 pitchforked America into formal war. As for the USSR: Stalin was Hitler's ally in 1940 and, even after the Nazi onslaught began in June 1941, it was far from clear that Russia would survive. In 1940–1 Britain stood alone.

BLUFF

In 1940 the British were almost totally unprepared to fight alone against Nazi Germany, let alone take on Italy and perhaps Japan at the same time. 1940–1 made real the nightmare of global overstretch that had haunted British leaders recurrently since the turn of the century. In the 1900s appeasement had staved off disaster; in the 1930s it had helped bring it closer. In 1940, as Cadogan of the FO gloomily acknowledged, Britain had to fall back completely on bluff – already the basis of its policy in Europe for much of the 1930s and in Asia for half a century.[1] In Winston Churchill they had a new prime minister who was adept at the art.

Although Britain's finest hour in 1940 is now an indelible feature of national mythology, it was not a foregone conclusion at the time that the country would fight on. During the early days of the Dunkirk evacuation, it seemed that only 50,000 troops (and not the eventual 330,000) could be saved and the War Cabinet pondered the question of peace in a series of meetings on 26–28 May 1940.[2] Halifax, backed at first by Chamberlain, suggested that Mussolini should be used to ascertain Hitler's peace terms, in case an offer guaranteeing the independence and integrity of the British Isles could be extracted. Churchill did not oppose such an arrangement in principle. 'If we could get out of this jam by giving up Malta and Gibraltar and some African colonies, he would jump at it', recorded Chamberlain.[3] But he believed that the time had passed when Hitler would, if ever, be satisfied with as little as Central Europe and the return of Germany's lost colonies. And he had no doubt that even to inquire about terms would be counter-productive until Hitler had been shown that Britain could not be defeated: 'We should get no worse terms if we went on fighting, even if we were beaten, than were open to us now'.[4] Churchill's argument convinced Chamberlain, Halifax became isolated, and Britain fought on. But even Churchill had not ruled out an eventual negotiated peace with Germany, and in private there were times that summer when he was gloomy about Britain's prospects of survival alone. Learning on 12 June of the French decision to surrender, he grunted to one of his advisers: 'You and I will be dead in three months time'.[5]

As in the era of appeasement, Churchill was willing to call Hitler's bluff, convinced that a resolute defence would, at the very least, elicit better terms than immediate capitulation. Publicly, he adopted a stance of pugnacious confidence, talking of 'victory at all costs' and invoking the darkest hours of British history as inspiration. But Halifax's fears were understandable. In line with British policy throughout the 1930s, it was assumed that the Luftwaffe had the capability and plans for a massive assault on British cities. And, continuing British thought since early 1939, it was accepted that the elimination of Britain was Hitler's prime objective.[6] Both these assumptions were erroneous. After his surprise victory over France, Hitler believed that the British would see sense and talk peace. Only on 2 July did he order the services to draw up contingency plans for an invasion of Britain and only two weeks later did he decide to go ahead. The Luftwaffe had not built up a heavy bomber fleet suitable for the destruction of British cities, and its diversion to this task from its much more successful onslaught on Fighter Command airfields was a crucial error. Without air supremacy over southeast England, no invasion could be mounted.[7]

German unpreparedness was the essential reason why Britain was not invaded in 1940. But the success of the RAF was a contributory factor. By 1940 the shift in air rearmament policy from deterrence to defence, made in 1937–8, had taken effect. The radar early-warning system had been improved and extended, and the fast modern fighters, the Hurricanes and Spitfires, had been properly incorporated into Fighter Command. (French fighter modernisation occurred about a year after Britain's and they were still working up the new machines at the time of the German attack, with the result that some squadrons were functioning at under half-strength).[8] The RAF was operating against slow German medium bombers, often beyond range of Luftwaffe fighter escorts, and its losses were roughly half those of the Luftwaffe between July and October 1940. The policy of air defence, which Britain had developed far more than any other power after 1938, had been vindicated, but ironically the enemy against which it was aimed, the Luftwaffe, never had the devastating capacity for strategic bombing with which it was credited.

In 1940 Churchill successfully called Hitler's bluff. But bluff did not work in the Pacific in 1941. There British policy remained an attempt 'to reconcile the irreconcilable'.[9] Paralysed between appeasement and containment, the British had tried to bolster China and promote cooperation with the USA, without allowing relations with Japan to deteriorate to the point of war. This latter consideration was even more pressing from mid-1940. With Germany and Italy rampant in Europe and North Africa, Britain was in no position to fight Japan as well – the three-front nightmare of Inskip and the Chiefs of Staff in 1938 was coming near to reality. With the French fleet out of the reckoning, Britain had to contain the Italian navy in the whole Mediterranean alone, or risk the two Axis navies combining in the Atlantic against Britain.

Under these circumstances, the shocked Australian and New Zealand governments were told on 28 June 1940 that Britain could not send a fleet to the Far East in the present crisis and that their only possible naval help must be the USA, whose main fleet had been based at Hawaii since the spring. However, given Britain's invasion crisis, antipodean troops were now vital for the defence of the Middle East, and the Australian and New Zealand governments were becoming understandably agitated at the prospect of Japanese attack while in such a defenceless position. To reassure them, Churchill sent a telegram in August 1940, against the advice of the Chiefs of Staff, promising that if Japan started to invade their countries 'I have explicit authority of Cabinet to assure you that we should then cut our losses in the Mediterranean and proceed to your aid sacrificing every interest except only [the] defence position of this island on which all else depends'.[10] That reassured the antipodeans for the moment and their troops continued to reinforce Egypt.

Yet Churchill's assurance was disingenuous, for the Far East was always low on his list of priorities. In May 1941 the War Office, unaware that Hitler was ready to attack Russia, still feared an invasion of Britain and felt that 'we must cut our losses in places that are not vital before it is too late'. It opposed the continued build-up of troops in Egypt, arguing that after the defence of the UK 'it has been an accepted principle in our strategy that in the last resort the security of Singapore comes before that of Egypt'. Churchill had no time for such arguments. If faced with a choice he put Egypt above Singapore, but, he added, 'I do not think the alternative is likely to present itself'.[11]

Just as the War Office's desire to determine defence priorities echoed the debates of the 1930s, so Churchill's confidence about the Far East reflected long-standing convictions. Essentially, these were twofold. First, he was sure that in the event of any Far Eastern crisis the Americans would be allied with Britain. In that he was eventually proved right, but throughout 1940–1 the US Government remained both unwilling and politically unable to make firm commitments. In particular, given American suspicions of British imperialism, no promises were given to help defend Britain's empire in Southeast Asia by moving part of the US fleet to Singapore. Not until the autumn of 1941, with growing US activity in the Atlantic, were the British able to send even a token fleet of capital ships to the China Seas.[12] Secondly, Churchill still thought in terms of seapower. He assumed that Singapore was a vast fortress and that it could easily hold out until such time as a British fleet was sent out. He failed to grasp what the Chiefs of Staff had emphasised from June 1940, namely that the strategic situation had been transformed. Japan's steady expansion into Southeast Asia, made possible by the impotence of the colonial powers and the growing range of aircraft, meant that the prime threat was no longer naval. Britain now had to defend much of Malaya by land and particularly by air if it wanted to maintain the Singapore base for an eventual British Pacific Fleet.[13]

Even more critically, no British leader fully grasped the extent of the Japanese danger. Churchill again was particularly at fault. He assumed that the arrival in Singapore from November 1941 of the token British force of two capital ships – the *Prince of Wales* and the *Repulse* – would deter the Japanese. Unsuccessfully, the Admiralty tried to delay its despatch until a stronger, more balanced force could be prepared. Even if the Japanese did start a war Churchill assumed their effect would be small – the loss of Hong Kong, some trade raiding, but not much more from what he revealingly called the 'Wops of the Pacific'.[14] The elimination of Britain's token fleet and the devastating success of the Japanese attacks on British, Dutch and American territory in December–January came as a total surprise. On 27 January 1942, with Singapore about to fall, Churchill defended himself in a vote of confidence debate in the Commons using language reminiscent of the Cabinet in 1937–8:

> There never has been a moment, there never could have been a moment, when Great Britain or the British Empire, single-handed, could fight Germany and Italy, could wage the Battle of Britain, the Battle of the Atlantic and the Battle of the Middle East – and at the same time stand thoroughly prepared in Burma, the Malay Peninsula, and generally in the Far East.[15]

Neville Chamberlain could not have put it better!

It was not merely that Japan had called Britain's bluff but that it had done so with such astonishing ease. In the Malayan campaign the Japanese lost less than 10,000 troops, the British 138,700, of which 130,000 surrendered, mostly at Singapore.[16] Few in Asia were unaffected. The panic-stricken Australian premier, John Curtin, fearful of Japanese invasion, announced that 'Australia looks to America, free of any pangs as to our traditional links or kinship with the United Kingdom'.[17] 1942 saw increasing US influence in Australia as the country became a major American base for the Pacific war. India also seemed in danger, with all that this implied for Britain's manpower and resources. Churchill, a diehard supporter of the Raj, was forced to shift ground under pressure from the increasingly influential Labour members of his Cabinet. Concerned at the lack of Indian support for the war, at a time when Japanese invasion seemed imminent, Clement

Attlee, the Labour leader, told Churchill that 'now is the time for an act of statesmanship. To mark time is to lose India'.[18] In March the Labour politician Sir Stafford Cripps was sent to India to offer participation in the wartime government and some form of independence when the war was over. His mission failed, unable to square both Churchill and the Congress party, but Britain had now committed itself in principle to a rapid post-war transfer of power.

From 1942 to 1945 Britain gradually extricated itself from the global crisis that developed in 1940 and 1941. The fact of ultimate victory was of vast historical significance, for had Nazi Germany or militarist Japan survived, even in truncated form, the future of world history would have been very different. Yet the way victory was won was almost as important, for Britain's global bluff had been called. Its growing reliance on America and Russia and the shifting balance of its imperial relationships were to shape British foreign policy decisively after the war was over.

FIGHTING WITH ALLIES

'There is only one thing worse than fighting with allies', Churchill observed in April 1945, 'and that is fighting without them'.[19] His dictum encapsulated Britain's position in 1942–5. Out of necessity, British policy had to accommodate itself to the demands of America and Russia, yet as the war neared its conclusion Britain was engaged in a constant struggle to advance its interests against those of its two increasingly powerful partners.

Of the two, of course, the USSR was far more disturbing. The historic friction over the borders of India in the Near East and South Asia had been reinforced since 1917 by the ideological challenge of Bolshevism.[20] Constant if often crude Comintern attempts to subvert British trades unions and soldiers and to promote agitation in India and other parts of the empire led the Tories to sever diplomatic relations with the USSR in 1927–9. Despite enthusiasm on the intellectual left for Stalin's economic modernisation, official distaste was intensified in the late 1930s by reports of his brutal purges and by his pact with Hitler. The mood changed only after Hitler had turned on his erstwhile friend. Thus wartime alliance was one of convenience, held together by common animosity towards Nazi Germany. In Churchill's words in 1941, 'if Hitler invaded Hell, I would at least make a favourable reference to the Devil in the House of Commons'.[21]

By contrast, the wartime Anglo–American alliance was rooted in culture and history. The ties of a common language, in particular, made contact, though not always comprehension, much easier than in the case of Anglo–Russian relations. Once America's vast economic power had been mobilised in the war of 1914–18 it became widely accepted among British leaders that Anglo–American cooperation was in future essential. Lord Robert Cecil told the Cabinet in 1917 that, given its 'vast power', if 'America accepts our point of view' in foreign policy, 'it will mean the dominance of that point of view in all international affairs.' He was sure that the USA could be so persuaded because, despite the diverse ethnic background of the American people, 'their rulers are almost exclusively Anglo–Saxons, and share our political ideals'.[22] Though largely unfulfilled in the interwar era, these hopes were given new substance by the alliance of 1941–5, which involved close contact at all levels of government and public, unlike the remote connection with Russia. For the half-American Churchill the core of his policy was what he called in 1943 'the natural Anglo–American special relationship',[23] based on his rapport with Roosevelt.

But Churchill's hopes did not represent the whole reality of Anglo–American relations. British desire for close cooperation with the USA had long co-existed with an underlying rivalry between the world's two leading economic powers over the wealth and very existence of the British empire. In the 1930s and 1940s this took the form of a bitter argument over Britain's protected economic system of imperial preferences and the sterling area, which had been created in the Depression. To the Americans these were barriers to world trade, particularly the sale of their own agricultural surpluses; to the British they were an essential means of maintaining commerce and finance after the collapse of the multilateral world economy in the Depression. America took a smaller proportion of British exports than South Africa – it was a highly self-sufficient country with little dependence on foreign trade. Moreover, its own tariff barriers were generally far higher than Britain's. On average 50 per cent duty was charged on foreign imports in the early 1930s.[24] An Anglo–American trade agreement in 1938 elicited few significant concessions on either side and tension was exacerbated in the war when the British concentrated even more on trade within the sterling area to save scarce foreign exchange.

Overseas finance was Britain's wartime Achilles heel. In 1914–18 the British war effort had quickly become dependent on US production financed by credit; this happened even more dramatically in 1940–1. After the fall of France the British, out of necessity, had to abandon all attempts to conserve foreign exchange in order to purchase what they needed for survival, trusting, in Churchill's words, that 'if we were unable to pay, America would nevertheless continue to deliver'.[25] At this stage US loans were banned under Acts of Congress and by the end of 1940 British gold and dollar reserves were virtually exhausted. Britain was only able to carry on buying from the USA because of Lend–Lease, which from its inception in March 1941 amounted to $27 billion. Even allowing for reciprocal aid from Britain to the value of nearly $6 billion, Lend–Lease covered 54 per cent of the country's total payments deficit during the war.[26]

Unlike the US assistance of 1914–17, these were government credits not private loans. Roosevelt was determined not to repeat the mistake of the Great War by piling up huge international debts that could not be repaid and only served to dislocate the world economy. So, instead of monetary recompense, the Americans demanded repayment in kind – with the elimination of imperial preference and sterling controls at the top of the list. This, they argued, would benefit not only US exports but also world trade and prepare the way for a new multilateral economy. Negotiations dragged on for the whole of the war. On imperial preference the British remained adamant – pro-Commonwealth sentiment had increased and the goal of an imperial trading bloc remained strong on the right of the Tory party. On currency matters, however, guided by Keynes, they were willing to envisage a new international monetary system, *provided* the USA, as the world's leading creditor, was willing to make a far greater contribution to international liquidity than in the 1930s. American moves in this direction were not as pronounced as Britain wished, but in July 1944 the Bretton Woods conference agreed in principle on a post-war system of fixed exchange rates, with an International Monetary Fund (36 per cent subscribed by the USA) to help countries overcome balance of payments problems. Still unhappy, the British Government was slow to ratify this agreement and in 1945–6 it was to become a major issue in transatlantic relations.[27]

This nexus – British financial reliance on America, consequential US leverage over British economic policy – was in fact to be a theme of most of the 1940s. Equally durable were the moral arguments about empire, which to Americans remained a dirty word from their own colonial experience. The British complained that the Americans were economic imperialists on the quiet, but nevertheless, the scale of the USA's formal empire was tiny compared to Britain's and the ideology of empire had never taken root. In 1942 Roosevelt pushed Churchill so hard on Indian independence that the Prime Minister had to employ dark threats of resignation to make him desist.[28] In 1943–4 there were bitter arguments about the Southeast Asian theatre, where Churchill's desire to concentrate on the recovery of Burma and Malaya rather than assistance to China was frustrated by America's control of the essential logistic support – planes and landing craft – for Mountbatten's forces. His South East Asia Command (SEAC) was quickly retitled by the Americans 'Save England's Asiatic Colonies'.[29] And throughout the war, the President pressed his opinion that in future Britain's Asian territories, particularly Hong Kong, should be held as 'trusteeships' from the United Nations, in preparation for early independence.[30] The American critique of imperialism was to plague British foreign policy for the next two decades.

The most urgent Anglo–American dispute of the war was over strategy. In principle both governments agreed in January 1942 that 'once Germany is defeated, the collapse of Italy and the defeat of Japan must follow'.[31] But in practice they found it hard to agree on how Germany should be overcome.

British strategy stood squarely on traditional foundations. In both wars the use of large conscript armies was a last resort. Their preference was for a war of attrition based on blockade and economic pressure. After 1940 that strategy was more difficult, with the fall of France and the inefficacy of the blockade against Hitler's now vast European empire. On the other hand, the new British faith in the bomber offered the hope that Germany might be smashed from the air rather than strangled by sea. 'Bombers alone provide the means of victory', Churchill told the Cabinet in September 1940[32] and the next two years saw a sustained build-up of the RAF for its campaign of strategic bombing. Moreover, the memories of the Somme and Passchendaele strengthened Churchill's determination to avoid bloody land battles. And 1940 meant that Britain had not merely to push a western front from Paris to Berlin, which took four bloody years in 1914–18, but also to establish such a front in the first place by a hazardous crossing of the Channel. Churchill and the Chiefs of Staff were not against such an invasion eventually, but they envisaged it taking place late in the war, with Germany near collapse, and saw it as part of a strategy of 'closing the ring' on the Axis by various smaller landings at vulnerable points around Hitler's Europe. As Churchill told the Russian Foreign Minister in May 1942 Britain and the USA aimed

> to build up overwhelming air superiority, which in the course of the next eighteen months or two years would enable us to put down a devastating weight of air attack on the German cities and industries. We should moreover maintain the blockade and make landings on the Continent against an increasingly enfeebled opposition.[33]

Of these potential landing points, the most attractive was Italy. Ever since 1939 British military planners had identified this as the easiest place to begin operations against the Axis.[34] And once Mussolini took advantage of Britain's plight in 1940 to extend his empire in North Africa, this strategy had the additional rationale of protecting important British interests in Egypt, the Suez Canal and the Middle Eastern oil-fields. In 1941 Churchill had rated Egypt more highly than Singapore, but the Americans did not share his concern for the Middle East. They had no vital interests in the region, drawing most of their oil from the Americas, and US military planners pressed repeatedly in 1942 for an early cross-Channel invasion, in miniature perhaps that year but certainly in strength in 1943 (Operation 'Round-up'). At this stage, however, the British held the dominant position in strategic debates. With the US Army still being trained, Britain would provide most of the manpower for any invasion in 1942 and Churchill had no intention of permitting a 'useless massacre of British troops on the Channel beaches'.[35] With President Roosevelt anxious to get US soldiers into action against Germany quickly, to head off pressure at home to concentrate on Japan, the Americans therefore went along with Britain's Mediterranean thrust in 1942, mounting landings in Morocco and Algeria (Operation 'Torch') that November. Italian and German forces were driven out of North Africa by May 1943.

Contrary to American suspicions, Churchill and his advisers never consistently tried to place British interests in the Middle East before the defeat of Germany itself.[36] There were times in mid-1943 and mid-1944 (like the spring of 1918) when British leaders were tempted by success to envisage a full-blown Mediterranean strategy, but basically they saw the struggle against Italy as the most expeditious way of advancing the war against the Axis. And in 1942 Churchill remained convinced that France could still be invaded in 1943. Despite warnings from the Americans and his own Chiefs of Staff he failed to understand that 'Torch' in 1942 precluded 'Round-Up' in 1943.[37] This was partly because of logistics. There simply was not enough equipment, trained manpower and above all shipping for two major European theatres, particularly when it was obviously sensible to capitalise on the conquest of North Africa by an early invasion of Sicily and then Italy (July and September 1943). But Churchill also underestimated the effect of fighting a truly global war, in harness with an ally who had different strategic priorities and domestic pressures. Once the decision for 'Torch' was made, the US Joint Chiefs of Staff, especially the Navy, treated continental Europe as a minor theatre for 1943, and secured a large diversion of men, supplies and crucial landing craft to the war in the Pacific. For many Americans, seeking revenge for the humiliating Japanese attack on Pearl Harbor, this was the 'real war'. It was therefore the combination of Britain's Mediterranean bias and America's tilt to the Pacific, in the context of a truly *world* war, that postponed an invasion of France until June 1944.[38]

Had the invasion occurred in 1943, its success would have been by no means assured, and the debate on 1943 versus 1944 will perhaps never be settled.[39] But undoubtedly postponement until June 1944 had serious consequences for Anglo–Soviet relations. It left the Red Army with the main burden of fighting the Germans in the three years from mid-1941. It also meant that invasion occurred a full year after the turning point on the Eastern Front at Kursk in July 1943. Consequently, it did not relieve the Soviet forces in their hour of need – the original expectation and the reason for Stalin's insistent pleas – but instead hit the Germans in the back at a time when the Red Army was already deep into Poland, thereby facilitating its rapid advance into Eastern and South-Eastern Europe. So Anglo–American strategy had the effect of both exacerbating Stalin's suspicions and also facilitating his conquests.

British military planners were already concerned about a possible post-war threat from Russia in 1944,[40] but among the politicians, as might be expected given his previous attitudes, it was Churchill who was particularly alarmed. In November 1943 he was already brooding gloomily on the implications of the Red Army's victories. Yet his moods were erratic. For more than two years the British press had extolled the heroism of 'our Russian allies' and in January 1944 Churchill himself could write to the Foreign Secretary, Anthony Eden, of 'the new confidence which has grown in our hearts towards Stalin'.[41] He still had no doubt that, as he told US Congressmen in May 1943, 'the first preoccupation must be to prevent further aggression in the future by Germany and Japan. To this end he contemplated an association of the United States, Great Britain and Russia'.[42]

Churchill's hope in 1944–5 was to reach agreement on a Soviet sphere of influence in Europe. In October 1944 his 'percentages' deal in Moscow tried to do this for the Balkans, with Stalin conceding British predominance in Greece and Churchill acknowledging Soviet primacy in Romania and Bulgaria. He took essentially the same line over Poland and Eastern Europe at the Yalta conference in February 1945. After two devastating German attacks, the Russians, he agreed, had a right to a secure buffer zone. What he and Roosevelt sought was to prevent a legitimate sphere of influence from becoming a closed Stalinist bloc. Hence the insistence at Yalta on free elections in eastern Europe.

In the afterglow of the conference Churchill was rash enough to tell his ministers: 'Poor Nevile [sic] Chamberlain believed he could trust Hitler. He was wrong. But I don't think I'm wrong about Stalin'.[43] His hopes dimmed in the spring and some of his telegrams to Washington became almost apocalyptic in tone, but his object remained negotiation from strength rather than direct confrontation. Warning Roosevelt's successor, Harry S. Truman, on 12 May 1945 that an 'iron curtain is drawn down upon their front' he urged: 'Surely it is vital now to come to an understanding with Russia, or see where we are with her, before we weaken our armies mortally or retire to the zones of occupation'.[44] By now, however, his influence at home and abroad was waning. In July 1945 the long-delayed general election swept Churchill and the Tories from power, with the war against Japan still unfinished and relations with Russia increasingly strained and uncertain.

THE COLLAPSE OF THE WARTIME ALLIANCE

At first sight, the election of a Labour government in July 1945 portended a shift in British foreign policy. The war had seen a 'swing to the left' in domestic politics, encouraged in part by the widespread admiration for the struggle of the Soviet Union against Nazism.[45] Labour came to power committed to the creation of a welfare state and a wide-ranging programme of nationalisation and many backbenchers also wanted a 'socialist foreign policy'. Labour had taken the lead in recognising the USSR in 1924 and in 1945 the slogan 'Left understands Left – and Right doesn't' was bandied about in party debate on future diplomacy. Within the FO, Sir Orme Sargent, soon to replace Cadogan as Permanent Under-Secretary, feared 'a Communist avalanche over Europe, a weak foreign policy, a private revolution at home and the reduction of England to a 2nd-class power'.[46]

Such anxieties were unfounded. Clement Attlee, the new Prime Minister, and Ernest Bevin, the bluff, shrewd former union leader who was his Foreign Secretary, both had a deep detestation of communism, born of their long struggles to exclude it from the Labour party and union movement. Moreover, the Labour leaders had developed an informed sense of Britain's international position through their years of service in the wartime coalition. Attlee in particular had chaired the key Cabinet committees on post-war planning and broadly shared Churchill's conception of an Anglo–American–Soviet condominium.[47] It was widely recognised among British leaders that the UK was not entirely in the same league as America and Russia but in May 1947 Bevin spoke for most British policymakers, Labour and Tory, when he vehemently rejected the claim that Britain had 'ceased to be a great Power' and insisted that 'we regard ourselves as one of the Powers most vital to the peace of the world'.[48]

It was from this perspective in 1945–6 that British leaders addressed the growing number of disputes with the Soviet Union. In Eastern Europe the USSR was not honouring the British understanding of the Yalta agreements – democratically-elected governments that were friendly to the Soviet Union – and the communist domination of Poland, Bulgaria and Romania was a fundamental issue in 1945. In Germany, the Allies – Britain, America, Russia and France – were administering zones of occupation (at considerable cost) prior to an eventual peace settlement, but progress on the latter was delayed by the Soviet insistence on massive reparations from Germany. In Western Europe, particularly France and Italy, the new appeal of communism was a source of anxiety at a time when most western communist parties were closely controlled by Moscow. Outside Europe there was also alarm about Soviet expansion in the Mediterranean, a sensitive area for British imperial power. The Russians wanted a new agreement with Turkey over control of the Dardanelles – access point for the Red Navy into the Mediterranean – and also matched British claims for a share of Italy's North African colonies. Particularly worrying was their failure in early 1946 to withdraw troops, as agreed, from the neighbouring state of Iran, a traditional area of Anglo–Russian rivalry.

What did all this signify? The Chiefs of Staff and their post-war planners had warned since 1944 that the Soviet Union was the emerging threat, but the Foreign Office was less ready to give up the aim of a post-war Big Three framework. Although anxieties increased in 1945, the FO was inclined to see the USSR as exhibiting a brutal obsession with its own security rather than as harbouring sinister expansionist goals.[49] In late 1945, 'on balance, the Foreign Office outlook was distinctly more anti-German than anti-Russian'[50] and Bevin was hesitant about forcing an open breach with Moscow. As late as December 1947 he said in private that 'he doubted whether Russia was as great a danger as a resurgent Germany might become'.[51]

During 1946, however, the FO gradually came round to the Chiefs of Staff's pessimistic view of Soviet intentions, primed by Frank

Roberts, the influential British Minister in Moscow. At his suggestion a special 'Russia Committee' was created in the FO, to review weekly Soviet conduct and also Moscow's new and vituperative campaign of Marxist propaganda. The latter helped convince Bevin's private secretary, Pierson Dixon, that there was 'hardly any doubt any longer that Russia is intent on the destruction of the British Empire'.[52] Henceforth this committee provided the focus for a hardline FO analysis of Russia.[53] Its head, Christopher Warner, concluded in an influential memo of April 1946 that 'the Soviet Government, both in their recent pronouncements and in their actions have made it clear that they have decided upon an aggressive policy, based upon militant Communism and Russian chauvinism'.[54] Although the FO did not believe that the USSR wanted war, it assumed that the Russians would extend their influence by all means possible, taking advantage of the chaos in postwar Europe and the new appeal of communism, and it accepted the COS view that war was more likely as the Soviets built up their military strength in the 1950s.

The enhanced position of the Soviet Union in Europe became the principal concern of British policymakers – understandably since it was the most marked difference between the situation in 1945 and that of 1918. Yet Soviet actions were still susceptible of various interpretations.[55] For instance, Stalin had honoured his spheres of influence agreement of 1944 with Churchill – keeping out of the Greek civil war – and he restrained communist revolutionaries in France and Italy. Even in Germany the picture was not clear-cut. The French were causing as much trouble as the Russians, with their demands, as after 1918, for amputating the Ruhr and the Saar. But these nuances – and their significance remains debatable – were neglected because British policy-makers drew on the 'lessons of appeasement', which encouraged a worse case interpretation of Stalin's policy. Chamberlain had been fatally wrong about Hitler in the 1930s, and his successors were understandably wary of giving Stalin the benefit of the doubt. Bevin put the point explicitly to Attlee when the latter suggested trying to negotiate with Russia over Greece, Turkey and Iran: 'If we speak to Stalin as you propose, he is as likely to respect their independence as Hitler was to respect Czechoslovakia's and we shall get as much of Stalin's goodwill as we got of Hitler's after Munich'.[56]

While assessments of Russia were growing increasingly grim, links with the USA were also weakening in 1945–6. Although a special relationship had been the lynch-pin of British post-war planning, Whitehall privately feared that the 'erratic' Americans would repeat their post-1918 pattern and, in the words of FO Minister Richard

Law in January 1945, 'swing back to . . . an expansionist isolationism of a highly inconvenient character'.[57] In the summer of 1945 such fears seemed well-founded. Roosevelt's successor as president, Harry S. Truman, was pre-occupied with domestic demands for 'bringing the boys home' and getting the country back to normal. US troops in Europe were run down from 3.5 million in June 1945 to 200,000 two years later[58] and Washington concentrated its post-war energies on the democratisation of Japan, wary of getting dragged into what it saw as old-style Anglo–Russian power politics in Europe. By the end of 1945 Truman and his Secretary of State, James Byrnes, had settled the composition of governments in Poland, Romania and Bulgaria on essentially Soviet terms, without reference to the British, much to Bevin's irritation.

This lack of US support was particularly worrying in two areas – the bomb and finance. The atomic bomb had been developed during the war as an Anglo–American project in which preliminary British research had been invaluable in 1940–1. As the project advanced the USA rapidly became the dominant partner but in 1943–4 Churchill had secured from Roosevelt agreements that required British approval before the bomb could be used and committed the USA to 'full collaboration' in atomic matters after the war.[59] In November 1945 Truman pledged himself to 'full and effective co-operation in the field of atomic energy' between the US, UK and Canada,[60] but during 1946 he restricted the implications of that pledge under pressure from a nationalist and spy-scared Congress. That August he approved the McMahon Act, terminating all meaningful atomic cooperation between the two governments.[61] Attlee and his colleagues were left angry and resentful.

More public was the row about a post-war American loan. Lend–Lease ended abruptly with victory over Japan in August 1945. These wartime US credits had enabled Britain to concentrate on war production and essential imports, without having to sustain normal exports to help the balance of payments. Consequently exports had been allowed to fall by 1944 to 30 per cent of their 1938 level and it would clearly be several years before manpower and resources could be reallocated to restore the position. Moreover, Britain had accumulated wartime debts of some £4.7 billion and had sold off £1.1 billion of overseas assets – all of which would affect the flow of 'invisibles' on which for more than a century Britain's ability to balance its trade deficit had depended. Also problematic was the extent of Britain's military commitments in the wake of the war – a drain both on finances and on manpower that otherwise could be demobilised for industry.[62] The mounting tension with Russia was reflected in the failure to agree on peace settlements in Europe and Asia, which meant that British troops had to remain in occupation duties that the country could ill afford.

In these circumstances, American financial help was deemed essential to help Britain overcome the immediate problems of post-war adjustment. Keynes, the Treasury's negotiator, was confident of securing an $8 million dollar grant, interest-free, on the grounds of Britain's wartime sacrifices. Such hopes proved utopian.[63] Hard bargaining that autumn eventually produced an American offer to write off Britain's Lend–Lease debts, worth some $21 billion net, for $650 million, and to provide a loan of $3.75 billion at 2 per cent interest. In return, following their wartime policy of payment in kind rather than cash, the USA demanded that Britain ratify the 1944 Bretton Woods agreements on the international monetary system and make the pound convertible into dollars.

Compared with the war debt tangle after 1918, these were enlightened, indeed generous, gestures. But MPs and the public, insufficiently aware of Britain's balance of payments problems since 1931, bitterly resented them. In Cabinet Emanuel Shinwell warned that the effective break-up of the sterling area by the Americans would leave Britain 'entirely at their mercy in world trade'[64] and when the agreement was pushed through Parliament in December 1945 it was denounced as 'an economic Munich' by Tory MP Robert Boothby. The final Commons vote was 343 to 100, with Churchill and most of the Tories among the 169 abstentions[65] – a remarkable degree of opposition on a major foreign-policy issue. To add insult to injury, the US Congress then failed to ratify the loan agreement until July 1946.

The problems of atomic cooperation and the loan demonstrate the British dilemma in 1945–6. They needed US help to maintain their international position, yet that help was not forthcoming to the degree desired. In short, relations among the Big Three seemed in 1945–6 to be slipping into a state of general estrangement. Bevin depicted Britain as 'the last bastion of social democracy . . . as against the red tooth and claw of American capitalism and the Communist dictatorship of Soviet Russia'.[66] In November 1945 he considered that 'instead of world co-operation we are rapidly drifting into spheres of influence or what can be better described as three great Monroes' – a reference to the American Monroe Doctrine of 1824 claiming hegemony over Latin America. The USA seemed mainly interested in the Western Hemisphere plus China and Japan, Russia was consolidating its hold from Lubeck to Port Arthur, and Britain was left with its empire and the leadership of western Europe.[67]

Bevin's emphasis on the British Empire was familiar official doctrine but the talk of Western European cooperation testified to a new outlook in the Foreign Office. In October 1945 Sargent urged the need 'to strengthen our world position vis-à-vis of our two great rivals by building up ourselves as *the* great European Power'.[68] The idea of a British-led Western European bloc centred on France had been broached during the war[69] but had progressed little because of Churchill's opposition and de Gaulle's anglophobia. Bevin, however, was more sympathetic and the (brief) appearance in Paris of an anglophile Socialist government in early 1947 facilitated the signing of an Anglo–French treaty of alliance in March at Dunkirk, symbol of the two countries' bitter parting of the ways in 1940. In the absence of great power agreement, this treaty was to provide a basis for French security against a resurgent Germany and against the possible threat from Russia.[70] Bevin also wanted to move beyond mere military cooperation. Persistently from the summer of 1946 he and the FO urged the economics ministries in Whitehall to explore the idea of a Western European customs union including Britain.[71]

Anxious about Russia, uncertain about America, inclined to take the lead in organising western Europe – this was the mood of British policymakers in 1945–6. From this perspective we can better understand crucial British strategic decisions in 1947, sometimes dismissed as signs of dated imperial hubris.

In April 1947 Parliament approved the maintenance of conscription – a marked contrast with its attitude in 1919. The period of twelve months national service was later extended to eighteen months in 1948 and two years in 1950 because of the mounting Cold War crisis.[72] Peacetime conscription was unprecedented in British history, except for a few months in the pre-war summer of 1939.

Even more significant was the decision to develop Britain's own atomic bomb, which received the formal go-ahead in January 1947. Status considerations played a part. Bevin swung a crucial meeting in October 1946 by insisting that in future no British Foreign Secretary should be talked to in the way he had been recently by Secretary of State Byrnes. 'We have got to have this thing over here whatever it costs. . . . We've got to have the bloody Union Jack flying on top of it'.[73] Nevertheless it is misleading to say that Britain developed the bomb simply 'to retain its claims to an independent say in global power-politics and thus avoid being regarded merely as an American satrapy'.[74] Given the international situation of 1945–6 – Russian pressure and American neo-isolationism – there was clearly a strategic rationale for a British bomb.[75] Unlike America, Britain lay well within range of Soviet bombers. It was also a small, highly-urbanised island (42 per cent of the British population lived in cities of over 100,000, compared with 14 per cent in Russia). The Chiefs of Staff's technical advisers estimated in April 1946 that thirty Soviet atomic bombs might be enough to 'produce collapse in this country' and that the USSR would have such a stockpile by 1952–6.[76]

The atomic bomb decision remained a closely-guarded secret, but the general build-up of British peacetime power became the subject of intense debate in London in 1946–7. Although the Tory and Labour leaderships shared broadly the same foreign-policy orientation, there was growing disaffection on the Labour backbenches. In April 1947 72 Labour MPs opposed the introduction of eighteen-month peacetime conscription and another 76 abstained – judged by commentators the most important backbench revolt against the Labour governments of 1945–51.[77] And in May 1947 the 'Keep Left' group published an in-fluential pamphlet asserting that 'the world wants neither Russian nor American domination' and urging the government to 'seize the opportunity for leadership in the United Nations which Socialist Britain is offered'.[78] Such 'third-force' ideas had considerable appeal at this time.

The strongest case against Britain's extensive postwar responsibilities came from the Treasury and Board of Trade, represented in Cabinet respectively by Hugh Dalton and Sir Stafford Cripps. They insisted that Britain's balance of payments crisis had only been eased and not solved by the belated US loan. In order to achieve equilibrium, they argued, costly overseas military commitments must be reduced and in-dustrial exports increased as quickly as possible. These two issues were closely linked, particularly in the manpower question, because more men in the armed forces meant less for domestic industry. Thus Cripps opposed the decision on peacetime conscription and Dalton tried to maintain a ceiling of £600 million in defence expenditure during 1946.

One target for cuts was Britain's role in Greece, where the aim of establishing an independent, democratic government had been frus-trated by the polarisation of Greek politics between the royalist right and communist insurgents in bloody civil war. Since 1944 the British had been trying to hold the ring, supplying troops, equipment, and gold reserves to bolster the Greek currency – fearful that a communist takeover would extend Soviet influence into the Mediterranean. Pressed by the FO, the Cabinet agreed in mid-1946 to carry on paying the Greek army up to £15 million to cover its sterling costs, but Dalton demanded that all aid must end on 31 March 1947.[79]

The worst financial drain, however, was Germany. International failure to agree on a peace settlement meant that the occupation troops remained and the German economy was kept close to subsistence level, with basic needs supplied by the occupying power in each zone. Britain controlled northwest Germany, including the Ruhr – the most heavily damaged area in the war – and in 1946 it provided 70 per cent of the zone's food needs, out of British taxpayers' pockets. Dalton complained publicly that, in ironic contrast to the aftermath of the 1914–18 war, Britain was paying reparations to Germany. His predicted figure of £80 million for 1946 proved to be only two-thirds of the eventual total. In July 1946 the Cabinet imposed bread rationing in Britain, an expedient avoided even in the darkest days of the war, in order to maintain the flow of US wheat to feed Germany, paid for in scarce dollars from the US loan.[80] Such a situation could not continue indefinitely. In July the British and Americans agreed to fuse their zones, regardless of Russian or French objections, and to start increasing German industrial production to encourage self-sufficiency. Germany's exports could then pay for its imports. But the 'bizone', which came into existence in January 1947, did not solve the financial crisis and it only exacerbated relations with Moscow, fearful of renewed aggression from a revived Germany.

Thus, Britain was in a desperate predicament by 1947. The growing confrontation with Russia, at a time of limited US help, necessitated military and political commitments that the economy, struggling with a huge post-war balance of payments deficit, could not sustain. Compounding the problem of the deepening Cold War, moreover, the British Empire was facing the worst peacetime crisis in its history, created by the strains of war and centred on the heart of empire, India.

CRISIS OF EMPIRE

In the early months of 1942 the British Empire had seemed on the verge of destruction. Malaya, Singapore, Burma and Hong Kong were lost and India and Australia seemed in jeopardy. By the autumn of 1945, however, Britain's fortunes had been remarkably transformed. Had the struggle with Japan dragged on, as expected, for a full year after victory in Europe in May 1945, the outcome might have been different, for the British Government had neither the resources nor the public support for a major campaign in Asia. But the sudden Japanese surrender in August 1945, following the dropping of the atomic bombs on Hiroshima and Nagasaki, enabled the small British forces in Southeast Asia to regain colonial territories quickly rather than waiting for US forces to help recover them by force and then impose American desiderata, such as international trusteeships. Thus, by the end of 1945, it could be proudly claimed that 'no British colonies had been permanently lost as a *direct result* of foreign conquest'[81] – a fact of some importance since, to the untutored eye, it confirmed the general impression of Britannia victrix.

Moreover, the war had seen Britain mobilise the empire's resources to an unprecedented degree. The sterling area was tightly regimented. Colonial economies were regulated by government controls over output, prices and marketing, and labour was conscripted, in some cases forcibly. Political rights, often extended in the 1930s as part of controlled devolution, were suppressed. The Indian National Congress mounted a 'Quit India' campaign of civil disobedience after the failure of the Cripps Mission, prompting the Government to ban the party and lock up its leaders for the duration of the war.[82] In Egypt, nominally independent but where the British retained control over defence, the emergence of an anti-British government in February 1942 at a time when the Germans were menacing Cairo led to even more autocratic action. The Ambassador, Sir Miles Lampson, drove to the royal palace at the head of an armed convoy, entered the king's chamber and obliged him to form a new government friendly to Britain. Among those incensed at such 'surrender and servility' was a young army lieutenant, Gamal Abdel Nasser.[83] Thus, in conditions of world war 'Britain was acting more imperialistically than ever before. In a sense this was the heyday of empire'.[84]

Yet, as feared in 1942, the war had undermined the foundations of British power in some of its leading dependencies. In India the shifting calculus of burdens and benefits had now tipped the balance against formal British rule. Even in 1939 India was fiscally autonomous, with its own tariffs against British goods, and the Indianisation of the army and civil service was proceeding apace. It was agreed in 1939 that Britain must pay all costs of the Indian army that exceeded normal peacetime defence expenditure and of war measures undertaken purely to protect Indian interests. By 1945 the result was a £1.3 billion bill which turned the Anglo–Indian financial relationship from creditor to debtor.[85] During the war the Labour party had pressed Churchill for an early concession of Indian independence, and the mounting costs of the Raj reinforced the Attlee government's anti-colonial principles in 1945.

But the British had not given up all interest in India. They assumed that Britain would remain the 'natural guardian of India'[86] – with British personnel continuing to guide the armed forces and civil service – and, in view of Britain's post-war responsibilities, the Chiefs of Staff stressed in March 1946 that 'we shall have to rely to an even greater extent upon reservoirs of manpower such as India can provide'.[87] With the new concern about Soviet airpower, the Chiefs also identified air bases in northwest India as of major importance for retaliation against Soviet cities.[88] All these strategic aims were to be achieved, it was hoped, by a defence treaty with the new Indian government – a condition of granting independence – and through Indian membership of the Commonwealth.

The war, however, had made these objectives less easy to attain. By 1945 the British had lost control of the process of devolution. Congress – by 1939 the main party of provincial government in India – was antagonised by its incarceration from 1942. This left the political field open to M.A. Jinnah's Muslim League, which grew over the next three years from a minority movement into the voice of most Muslims, becoming a major political force in several north Indian states and an important new collaborator for the British. Britain had committed itself in 1942 to post-war independence for India, but the prospects of an orderly transfer of power to a friendly government had deteriorated with the alienation of the Hindu Congress leaders and the rise of the Muslim League – the former wanting a united India, the latter a separate Pakistan. Despite the efforts of Lord Wavell, the Viceroy, and a special Cabinet mission, no constitutional settlement could be achieved in 1945-6. League and Congress were ultimately irreconcilable, and the British did not want partition or a centralised 'Congress Raj' (either of which would exacerbate communal violence and imperil their defence aims). Britain had now also lost its always tenuous capacity to maintain order. Jinnah's 'Direct Action' campaign in Calcutta in August 1946 sparked off riots across most of North India. Hundreds of thousands died and by the end of the year Wavell was planning what he called Operation Madhouse – 'withdrawal of the British province by province, beginning with women and children, then civilians, then the army'.[89]

Much the same process also occurred in 1945–6 in Palestine, where Britain's contradictory pledges to Arabs and Jews, made in the heat of Great War diplomacy, had come to haunt British policy. The Balfour declaration of a Jewish homeland in Palestine had never been accepted by the Arab population, and their resentment increased in the 1930s as migrants escaping Nazi persecution increased the size of the Jewish minority to nearly 30 per cent.[90] Growing communal violence and consciousness of the importance of Arab goodwill in a future war led the British to announce in May 1939 that henceforth Jewish migration would be restricted and subject to Arab consent. Their goal was an independent Palestine, containing Arabs and Jews, but with a permanent Arab majority.[91]

After the war the Arab–Israeli struggle intensified, with the embattled British unable to keep order or to promote an agreed transfer of power. At the same time the Chiefs of Staff insisted that Britain's strategic need for bases in Palestine must be secured. In these respects the Palestinian and Indian problems were very similar. Yet there were also important contrasts, because Palestine was much more of an international issue. Unlike India, a British dependency, Palestine was held as a mandate from the United Nations. Moreover, world interest was intense. Pictures of Belsen, Dachau and other extermination camps gave powerful moral impetus to the Zionist case for an independent Jewish homeland and there was outrage when the British turned back refugee ships by force. Feelings ran particularly high in America, where President Truman, courting the Jewish vote, demanded continued immigration and an independent Jewish state, while refusing to assume any responsibilities for law and order in the mandate. The British Government became progressively angrier with the Americans who, Attlee commented, 'forever lay heavy burdens on us without lifting a little finger to help'.[92]

Denied Arab and Israeli agreement or US support, entangled by moral constraints on the use of force, British efforts were doomed to fail. In Palestine, as in India, in 1946–7 policy was overwhelmed by events. Attacks on British personnel and installations by Jewish terrorist groups had forced the government into protected security zones, dubbed 'Bevingrads' by the Zionists, and obliged Britons to go around only in armed groups. One-tenth of Britain's armed forces, 100,000 men, now occupied a territory the size of Wales – the equivalent of one soldier for every eighteen inhabitants – at an annual cost of £40 million. Even Churchill, militant on the folly of abandoning India which he still regarded as an essential possession, could see no merit in hanging on in Palestine. Conscripts there 'might well be at home strengthening our depleted industry', he told the Commons. 'What are they doing there? What good are we getting out of it?'.[93]

Churchill was now leader of the opposition. More potent was the critique of empire emanating from number 10 Downing Street itself. For 1946 saw a remarkable backstage conflict between Attlee and the Chiefs of Staff over British strategy – perhaps the most sustained attack by a peacetime premier on his military advisers.[94] Attlee was slower than Bevin to abandon hopes of reaching agreement with Russia within the UN framework. And he was relentlessly critical of the COS demands for high defence spending, supporting the formulation of a '5 + 5' rule which anticipated virtually no danger of war until 1950 and then gradually increasing danger in the next five years. This implied a restricted defence posture at least until Britain had overcome its immediate postwar economic problems. Attlee told the Cabinet's Defence Committee bluntly in January 1946 that it 'was not necessary in present circumstances to have a large fleet ready for instant action as there was no one to fight'.[95]

Attlee's most persistent target was the British presence in the Eastern Mediterranean, of which Greece and Palestine were part. The wartime Foreign Secretary Anthony Eden had insisted in April 1945 that the defence of this area was 'a matter of life and death to the British Empire' because, as both wars had proved, 'it is there that the Empire can be cut in half'.[96] Attlee took a different view, repeatedly opposing the COS demand for a North African mandate in Cyrenaica and also questioning the value of hanging on in Greece. His case was partly diplomatic – what the British saw as defence the Russians might regard as preparations for attack – but he also argued that in the era of airpower and Indian independence the obsession with Mediterranean sealanes was outmoded. 'We must not, for sentimental reasons based on the past, give hostages to fortune'.[97] In vain the COS advanced a new rationale for their strategy. 'The threat of attack by air or long-range weapons will be our one effective military deterrent to Russian aggression', they argued in March 1946. Given the vulnerability of the British Isles to atomic attack, other air bases were essential, and 'the Middle East is nearest to the important Russian industrial and oil-producing areas'.[98] Attlee remained unpersuaded and he renewed his criticism in January 1947, much to the fury of the military. It was only when the Chiefs of Staff, led by Montgomery, threatened to resign that he desisted.[99] But he used the Labour opposition to conscription in April 1947 to reduce the term of service from eighteen months to one year, against COS wishes, thereby making it harder to maintain substantial forces outside Europe.[100]

DENOUEMENT: 1947

By early 1947, therefore, the Labour Government was in turmoil. The conjunction of Cold War and anti-colonial nationalism presented it with major challenges in continental Europe, the Near East and South Asia. Yet, unlike the similar 'triple crisis' of 1940–2, this occurred in peacetime not during war, with US help limited and intense domestic pressure to reduce the costs of overseas commitments. The final straw was the grim winter of early 1947 – worse than any since 1881.[101] Freezing cold and heavy blizzards brought transport, industry and the coal mines to a virtual halt for several weeks. Manufacturing output in February was 25 per cent down on January, itself far worse than the previous autumn.[102] In these circumstances the payments deficit widened alarmingly. Dalton warned the Cabinet that 'we were racing through our United States dollar credit at a reckless, and ever-accelerating, speed' and predicted 'a looming shadow of catastrophe'.[103]

Between 14 and 20 February an exhausted Cabinet made a series of fateful decisions.[104] First Bevin announced that Britain would refer the Palestine problem back to the United Nations. The FO still hoped that the pro-Arab majority in the UN might facilitate a settlement favourable to Britain,[105] but undoubtedly this was 'a gamble that would not have been taken by a power able and determined to retain control'.[106] Secondly, the Cabinet confirmed its earlier decision that British aid to Greece and Turkey would end on 31 March – Dalton's financial arguments and Attlee's strategic scepticism carrying the day over continued objections from Bevin and the COS.[107] Finally, Attlee announced that Britain would leave India, come what may, no later than June 1948. Announcement of this deadline, to which the Cabinet had been reluctantly moving during the winter, was demanded by the new Viceroy, Lord Mountbatten, as a condition of his appointment to succeed the discredited Wavell.[108]

Over the next few months these decisions – made in a mood of panic akin to that of March 1939 – took effect. Forewarned of the British pull-out from Greece and Turkey, the Americans hastily took up the burden, as proclaimed in the Truman Doctrine. In India Mountbatten quickly concluded that partition was the only answer and, against the odds, he pushed it through by August 1947, abandoning in the process all hopes of a new defence treaty. And when the UN special committee on Palestine reported in September 1947 in favour of partition there, the British Government announced that it would not be responsible for implementing such a solution and that preparations were being made for unilateral evacuation. Arabs and Jews were left to decide the issue by bloody war.

Given these developments, it is not surprising, perhaps, that, then and later, 1947 has been portrayed as a symbolic hinge of history. 'It is with deep grief I watch the clattering down of the British Empire with all its glories', Churchill told the Commons in March 1947. '"Scuttle", everywhere, is the order of the day'.[109] Likewise, the February 1947 British decision to abandon Greece and Turkey was seen as marking the moment when 'world power was . . . changing hands' as Britain made 'an irrevocable admission of impotence' and left America to assume the role of world balancer.[110] One recent historian depicts 1947 as signalling 'the end of Britain's role as one of the major determinants of world events'.[111]

Undoubtedly the crisis of 1947, particularly the abandonment of India, dramatically indicated the diminution of Britain's relative power. But, rather than seeing these events as accelerators of long-term decline, they have been depicted here as part of a crisis of post-war adjustment – graver than that of 1918–22 but nevertheless to be understood in analogous terms, as retrenchment after wartime overstretch. The atmosphere of panic in which the decisions were taken also illustrates the fact that they were not a considered judgement on British power but a hasty attempt amid sudden economic crisis to ease Britain's predicament. Thus, the withdrawals from India and the *Near* East (Greece, Turkey and Palestine) in 1947 represented a cutting of losses in areas where the balance of burdens and benefits had tilted disastrously against Britain. The Government did not pull out of *Middle* Eastern countries such as Iraq or Egypt, which henceforth became the new foci for British power. Nor did it abandon the search for more informal means of global influence in Africa and Southeast Asia.[112] What made this new strategy of informal empire possible was the revolution in US policy heralded by the Truman Doctrine. Over the next four years the United States committed itself to a North Atlantic alliance that relieved Britain of the burdens of Western European security which it had previously assumed alone.

Henceforth the 'special relationship' and the Commonwealth connection became the foundations of British diplomacy for a generation. In consequence the interest in Western European cooperation, emerging in 1945–6, faded away. The consolidation of these policies towards America, the Commonwealth and Europe in the late 1940s and early 1950s is the theme of the next chapter. The failure of all of them by the 1960s left problems with which Britain is still wrestling today.

REFERENCES

1. Reynolds 1981: 264
2. P. Bell 1974: 38–48; Gates 1981: 143–52
3. NC 2/24A, 26 May 1940
4. CAB 65/13, f. 187
5. Reynolds 1985b: 154
6. Hinsley et al. 1979: i, 164–90
7. Overy 1980: 30–7
8. Murray 1988: 71
9. P. Lowe 1977: 134–5
10. Day 1988: 75
11. Churchill 1950: iii, 373–6
12. Reynolds 1981: ch. 9
13. Haggie 1981: 178–9
14. Reynolds 1981: 249
15. Commons 377: 601
16. Thorne 1978: 202
17. Barclay 1977: 252
18. Moore 1979: 56
19. Bryant 1957: 445
20. Northedge and Wells 1982
21. Colville 1968: 89
22. CAB 24/26, GT 2074
23. FO 954/22A, f. 197
24. Drummond and Hillmer 1989: 11, 158
25. Reynolds 1981: 98
26. Sayers 1958: 498, 522
27. Gardner 1980; Dobson 1986
28. Reynolds 1986: 28
29. Thorne 1978: 337
30. Louis 1977
31. CAB 80/33, COS (42) 75
32. CAB 66/11, WP (40) 352
33. Gilbert 1986: vii, 111
34. Gibbs 1975: 668
35. Gilbert 1986: vii, 432
36. M. Howard 1968
37. M. Howard 1972: ch. 11
38. Reynolds 1986: 23–7 icf. Stoler 1980
39. cf. Sainsbury 1976: 171–2; Grigg 1980
40. Lewis 1988: 107–35
41. PREM 3/399/6, f. 81
42. CAB 66/37, WP (43) 233
43. Reynolds 1985a: 503
44. Churchill 1954: vi, 498–9

45. Addison 1975: 134, 140
46. Morgan 1985: 42
47. Burridge 1976: 94–6
48. Commons 437: 1965
49. Kitchen 1986: 262
50. Morgan 1985: 235
51. Bullock 1983: 269, cf. 138, 358
52. Rothwell 1982: 252
53. Merrick 1985
54. Lewis 1988: 363
55. Reynolds 1990b: 113–16
56. Smith and Zametica 1985: 251
57. Thorne 1978: 502
58. T. Anderson 1981: 152
59. Gowing 1964: 447
60. Gowing 1974: i, 76
61. Gormly 1984
62. Cairncross 1985: ch. 1
63. Ibid., ch. 5
64. Barker 1983: 26
65. Gardner 1980: 226, 235
66. Edmonds 1986: 28
67. FO 800/478, MIS/45/14
68. FO 371/44557, AN 2560
69. Baylis 1983
70. Zeeman 1986: 357–8
71. J.W. Young 1984: 38–42, 67–9
72. Darby 1973: 38–9
73. Bullock 1983: 352
74. Kennedy 1981: 334
75. Clark and Wheeler 1989: 4–5, 38–40
76. Lewis 1988: 232–5
77. Myers 1984: 55
78. Bing et al. 1947: 47
79. Alexander 1982: 197
80. Rothwell 1982: 316, 321
81. Darwin 1988: 43
82. Moore 1979: 135–6
83. Lapping 1985: 242–3
84. Pearce 1982: 209
85. Moore 1983: 21–9
86. Singh 1982: 573
87. Tomlinson 1979: 147
88. Aldrich and Coleman 1989b
89. Ziegler 1986: 353
90. Monroe 1981: 86
91. Ovendale 1984: 69–70

92. Louis 1984: 419
93. Ibid., 467
94. cf. Myers 1984; Smith and Zametica 1985
95. Grove 1987: 20
96. Smith and Zametica 1985: 240
97. CAB 131/2, DO (46) 27
98. Ibid., DO (46) 47
99. Smith and Zametica 1985: 251
100. Myers 1984
101. Pelling 1984: 185–6
102. Robertson 1987: 251
103. R. Clarke 1982: 156
104. Bullock 1983: 362
105. Louis 1984: 459–60
106. Cohen 1982: 392
107. Alexander 1982: 240–3
108. Ziegler 1986: 355
109. Gilbert 1988: viii, 301–2
110. Quoted in Hathaway 1981: 302
111. Douglas 1986: 187
112. Frazier 1984: 726–7; Louis 1984: 97–9

CHAPTER SEVEN
Superpowers, 1947–55

The term 'superpowers' was coined by the American scholar William
Fox in 1944, to describe states with 'great power plus great mobility of
power'. He included Britain with America and Russia in that cat-
egory.[1] Today that seems strange. Conventional wisdom suggests that
after 1945 Britain, 'nearly bankrupt, dependent, and unable to police
its empire, was reduced to a resentful second-rate power',[2] 'a warrior
satellite of the United States'.[3] But if we view the mid-1940s from the
perspective of a crisis of post-war adjustment, we can see that 1947 did
not mark the finale for Britain as a great power. Cutting one's losses in
India, Palestine and Greece did not mean abandoning empire as a
whole. Likewise, the payments crisis of 1946–7 reflected the immediate legacies of war – vast overseas commitments burdening an economy not yet re-converted from warmaking to wealth creation. At this
time the underlying problem of industrial uncompetitiveness was
masked by the wartime devastation and post-war instability of all
Britain's European rivals. By the early 1950s Britain was producing
nearly a third of the industrial output of non-communist Europe and
more weapons than all the other European NATO partners combined.[4] For much of the decade Britain was America's principal ally, in
Europe and globally, at a time when the twin challenges of communism and anti-colonialism were contorting world politics. The idea of
'the big three' – or at least the big '2½' as Cadogan of the FO put it
in 1945[5] – still seemed credible. If it eventually proved a myth, we
should remember that myths derive their power from their plausibility.

CREATING THE ATLANTIC ALLIANCE

The bedrock of British policy was NATO. This emerged from the European crisis of 1947–50 largely as the result of rapid and radical changes in US diplomacy. The British were major beneficiaries of these changes rather than their instigators. Nevertheless, the American initiatives were significantly shaped by British policymakers, notably Ernest Bevin.

Behind the scenes in 1945–6 the British and American military, anxious about Soviet policy, had maintained clandestine contacts under cover of the continued existence of the wartime Combined Chiefs of Staff. Secretly in mid-1946, Air Chief Marshal Tedder and General Carl Spaatz identified and prepared four East Anglian air bases for use by American strategic bombers in the event of an emergency.[6] During 1946, as in Britain, US diplomats and politicians came round to views held by their military colleagues for some time – about the Soviet threat and the need for a coordinated Anglo–American response. In the case of Greece and Turkey, the State Department had been concerned throughout the winter of 1946–7 about the deteriorating position and accepted the need for American support,[7] but the US political situation was unfavourable and no firm action had been taken.

The British were aware of this trend, and their notes to Washington on 21 February 1947, dramatically announcing the decision to terminate aid to Greece and Turkey by the end of March, forced the Americans to act immediately. To overwhelm Congressional and public doubts, the 'Truman Doctrine' speech of 21 March portrayed the proposed aid programmes in apocalyptic terms as part of a global struggle between 'democracy' and 'totalitarianism'. Some in the Foreign Office feared that such hyperbole would be counter-productive[8] – but in general the British reaction was positive. At last, it seemed, the USA was ready to offer public and concrete support in the stabilisation of Europe.

Even more welcome was Secretary of State George C. Marshall's offer of US financial aid if the Europeans formulated a joint recovery plan. Marshall's speech, on 5 June 1947, was a response to the impasse among the Big Four over a peace settlement with Germany, which delayed German economic recovery, and to the economic crisis caused by the winter of early 1947 which seemed to threaten the stability of the whole of Western Europe. As the US zonal commander in Germany, General Lucius Clay, observed, 'there is no choice between becoming a Communist on 1500 calories [per day] and a believer in democracy on 1000 calories'.[9] Bevin reacted with alacrity to Marshall's speech, orchestrating a concerted West European response while adroitly excluding the Russians from what was assumed would be further obstructionism.[10] Under his aegis the western Europeans put forward a joint plan which, in modified form, was approved by Congress. In 1948–50 America provided some $12 billion for European economic recovery, of which Britain received the largest share – $2.7 billion.[11]

But even before the Marshall Plan became law, in April 1948, it seemed that US economic aid alone would be insufficient. Marshall's speech and the Soviet veto on East European participation in the Plan accelerated the partition of Europe. The Stalinisation of eastern Europe gathered pace and Moscow called communist workers out on strike in France and Italy. In December 1947 the Council of Foreign Ministers broke down in Moscow, completely deadlocked over Germany, and in February 1948 the communists seized power in Czechoslovakia. The 'lessons' of appeasement seemed ever more pertinent. The FO told the Cabinet in March: 'physical control of the Eurasian land mass and eventual control of the whole World Island is what the Politburo is aiming at – no less. . . . It has really become a matter of the defence of Western civilisation'.[12]

This crisis atmosphere helped silence the critics of Bevin's policy. Attlee's doubts about Soviet hostility and extended defence were subdued by events. In January 1948 he told the nation in a radio broadcast that 'Soviet Communism pursues a policy of imperialism in a new form – ideological, economic, and strategic – which threatens the welfare and way of life of the other nations of Europe'.[13] The 'Keep Left' group of Labour MPs also changed its tone. Richard Crossman admitted in January 1948 that 'my own views about America have changed a great deal in the last six months. Many Members have had a similar experience'.[14]

Bevin's attitude also hardened. He was now convinced by the FO that a divided Europe was inevitable and it seemed essential to consolidate the western half or risk economic and political collapse, abetted by the resurgent communist parties. From January 1948 he pressed on the Americans the need for 'some form of union, formal or informal . . . in Western Europe backed by the United States and the Dominions'.[15] Bevin's calls for 'Western Union' exhibited what was still a genuine interest in closer Western European cooperation.[16] But his overriding priority was now to draw in the newly-receptive Americans, for they alone had the wealth and power to shore up western Europe. The State Department had made it clear that any US commitments would depend on evidence that the Europeans were ready to help themselves, and it was in deference to the USA that Bevin abandoned his original idea of bilateral British treaties with other European countries and negotiated the multilateral Brussels Pact between Britain, France and the Benelux countries in March 1948.[17] This was to be the 'sprat' to catch the American 'mackerel'.

The deteriorating international situation again forced the pace. At the end of June, the Russians began to blockade Berlin – under four-power occupation but deep within the Soviet zone of Germany. Their aim was probably to head off the creation of a West German state, which was now being promoted by the western Allies as the next-best alternative to a unified and peaceful Germany. British officials in Berlin proposed an airlift to keep the Western zones of the city supplied. Bevin took this up with enthusiasm, swinging the Americans away from earlier talk of sending an Army convoy up the autobahn – a strategy with far greater risk of war.[18] The joint Anglo–American airlift kept Berlin supplied for eleven months, until the Soviets abandoned the blockade.

The crisis also provided the occasion for US strategic bombers to return to Britain, as anticipated in the secret Spaatz–Tedder agreement of 1946. Three groups of B-29s arrived in July and August. This proved the start of a growing US presence, including atomic-capable aircraft from 1949. Given the magnitude of the Berlin crisis, a Cabinet Committee quickly gave approval, leaving vague the duration of the presence or the degree of British control – issues of growing concern after the 1948 crisis abated.[19]

Above all, the Berlin crisis expedited the evolution of the Brussels Pact into an Atlantic Treaty. By the summer of 1948 support from the Truman Administration and on Capitol Hill permitted serious negotiations to start and the North Atlantic Treaty was signed in April 1949. This pledged America, Britain and ten other nations to treat an attack on one as an attack on all. This was America's first peacetime alliance – a breach with George Washington's hallowed tradition of no foreign entanglements – which has been described as 'a latter-day American Revolution'.[20]

In negotiating the pact the British took the view that 'the form of such an arrangement was of secondary importance; the main thing was to secure US participation'. Nevertheless, they did wish to ensure that the obligations in the pact were drawn as tightly as the US Senate would permit.[21] Thus, Bevin rejected as 'inadequate' the idea, canvassed by George Kennan of the State Department, for a presidential guarantee of European security instead of a full alliance. That might leave Europe, as in the 1930s, at the mercy of an unsympathetic Congress.[22] As Bevin often observed, in the era of jet bombers and impending Soviet nuclear weaponry, Britain would not be able to repeat the holding action it performed in 1914–17 and 1939–41 while the Americans were 'slowly girding themselves for the fray'.[23]

Nevertheless, because of isolationist sentiment in the US Senate, the crucial article five of the treaty was deficient from the British point of view. In the event of armed attack each party would take 'such action as it deems necessary, including the use of armed force, to restore and maintain the security of the North Atlantic area'.[24] That left the USA in principle free to choose whether to go to war or not. It took the Korean war, in Averell Harriman's words, to 'put the 'O' in NATO'[25] – turning a loose mutual defence pact into a tight military alliance. It was assumed that the North Korean invasion of the South in June 1950 had been sanctioned by Stalin and, less justifiably, that it presaged possible Soviet aggression in Europe in the next few years. In the crisis atmosphere of late 1950, the USA committed four divisions to Europe – the first ground combat troops sent since the war – and established an integrated NATO command under US direction. The first Supreme Commander was General Eisenhower.

The revolution in US foreign policy that occurred in 1947–50 proved both profound and durable – so much so that it has been seen as totally transforming world politics. Thus, it is claimed that the Marshall Plan 'saved Europeans from imminent economic ruin'[26] and that by mid-century the international situation had been 'reduced to the primitive spectacle of two giants eying each other with watchful suspicion'.[27] Yet such statements exaggerate. Recent research has described Marshall Aid as the 'lubricant' rather than the 'fuel' of Europe's industrial engine – 'allowing the machine to run that would otherwise buckle or bind' for immediate want of dollar goods.[28] And even after 1950, the permanence of the US commitment to NATO remained an open question in Washington. In late 1951, when Eisenhower was asked how long US troops would stay in Europe, he replied 'six to seven years'.[29]

For British policymakers at the time, 1947–50 certainly seemed an incomplete revolution. Britain's position was eased not transformed. The Soviet 'threat' was now widely acknowledged at home, reducing criticism of defence spending, while at the same time the new US commitments offered a way to reduce British overstretch. Although in crucial respects now reliant on the USA, British leaders believed that this did not preclude a great-power role but, on the contrary, made it easier, by relieving them of prime responsibility for European security.

The next few years saw an extended effort by Britain to harness the new American internationalism to help maintain its own global position, or, as the FO put it in 1944, 'to make use of American power for purposes which we regard as good'.[30] The policy of power by proxy reached its apogee in this concept of a special relationship.

GREAT POWER BY INTERDEPENDENCE

This process, with its potentialities and problems, can be explored in three crucial areas in the late 1940s and early 1950s – international economics, military security and Cold War diplomacy. Together they illustrate the broad party-political continuity of British policy towards America under Attlee (1945–51) and Churchill (1951–5). Britain's reliance on the USA was evident in each case, but that did not preclude an independent line and, given the differences between London and Washington, what were deemed to be British interests could often only be protected by British actions.

Taking economics first: the mid-1940s saw a sustained British attempt to rebuild the country's position in international finance. Britain had some £3.5 billion in sterling debts accumulated from the war. Unlike the dollar debts these were regarded by the Treasury and Bank of England as assets and were allowed to increase in the immediate post-war period, as European countries such as Belgium and Sweden were drawn into the sterling area. The rationale for such a policy was that Britain not only obtained imports on credit through these sterling debts but also used them to help recreate Britain's financial role as banker for much of the non-communist world outside the Western Hemisphere.[31]

This policy overestimated the strength of the pound, as became clear in the sterling crises of 1947 and 1949. The convertibility of sterling into dollars, set for 15 July 1947, was a condition of the US loan agreed in 1945. But although in origin a US imposition – part of Washington's continuing effort to dismantle the sterling area – by 1946–7 the Treasury and Bank of England were inclined to welcome convertibility as a sign of the strength of sterling, further bolstering foreign confidence.[32] Yet Britain lacked the reserves to manage such a policy and was dependent on the US loan for its international liquidity. Of the $3.75 billion granted in July 1946, two-thirds was used up within a year through military spending and growing convertibility. After 15 July 1947 the dollar drain became a haemorrhage, with $650 million being lost in the first twenty days of August.[33] At that rate the remainder of the loan would have been used up by the end of September. Consequently convertibility was suspended on 20 August.

The devaluation of sterling in 1949 also revealed the element of hubris in British policy. By 1949 the problems of the sterling debts, foreign speculation against the pound and the exaggerated exchange cost of British export prices all made a devaluation of the pound widely predicted. Washington pressed strenuously for such a move. But devaluation was resisted by the Bank as a blow to foreign confidence in sterling, and Treasury opinion was divided. Confusion and delay in Whitehall exacerbated the run on the pound and in the end the issue was forced by a few junior economics ministers, led by Hugh Gaitskell. The massive 30 per cent devaluation – from $4.03 to $2.80 – was taken without prior consultation in Europe, although it required compensatory moves in most continental capitals, and the French in particular were incensed.[34]

Both these crises indicated British overestimation of their financial strength. In direct competition with the US dollar the pound was now much weaker. Yet one should not, in consequence, undervalue sterling's importance in the post-war world – it was still the vehicle for half the world's trade[35] – and the worst pressures on Britain's balance of payments were relieved by the withdrawals from India and the Near East in 1947 and by the growing US assistance. Moreover, by 1948 Britain's current account was once again in balance, thanks not least to a remarkable surge in exports, and the main problem was the continued deficit with the dollar area. The 1949 devaluations put the pound and other European currencies in a more realistic balance with the dollar and enhanced Britain's competitive position. By 1952–3, despite the economic problems caused by rapid rearmament during the Korean war, UK trade with the dollar area was roughly in balance.[36]

Moreover, September 1949 also marked a new modus vivendi in the long American campaign to demolish the sterling area and Britain's trading bloc. Enforcing the 1945 commitment to full convertibility had been one attempt to achieve this goal. In 1947–9 the USA tried to use Marshall Aid as another lever. Aside from bridging Europe's dollar gap, Marshall Aid was also intended to promote the State Department's longer-term remedy for Europe – namely increased production through integrating as much of Europe as possible into a single economic unit forming part of an American-led open world economy. Britain was envisaged as the potential leader of this tariff-free United States of Europe.[37]

The British disagreed fundamentally. They believed that the dollar shortage was worldwide not merely European, reflecting what the Treasury called a 'post-war supply crisis' which required a revival of the third-world's production as well as Europe's to offset global dependence on the Western Hemisphere. Here the sterling area could play a special role, for Britain's trade and currency network constituted the principal 'bridge between the Western and Eastern hemisphere'. This should be strengthened, rather than imprisoning Britain within Washington's 'continental' strategy, centred on European integration.[38]

The years 1947–9 saw a spirited Anglo–American battle to shape the Organization of European Economic Co-operation (OEEC), which oversaw Marshall Aid. The Americans wanted it to become a supranational body promoting European integration, while the British successfully steered it towards a looser, intergovernmental structure.[39] And by September 1949 the frustrated Americans had acquiesced in Britain's position on the special role of the sterling area. Henceforth most US policymakers would 'exempt Great Britain from their plans for an integrated Western Europe', looking instead to France for leadership in that regard.[40]

By 1950, then, the British had overcome the immediate post-war crisis and had achieved a modus vivendi with the USA on economic policy. They were able to play a semi–independent international role, with the sterling area operating as an arena for reviving world trade, although they ultimately remained reliant on the USA for maintaining international liquidity.

Establishing a similar special relationship in defence policy proved more difficult, for here the crux was America's most valued advantage over the USSR – nuclear weaponry. Despite intense British efforts, there was no easing of the almost total embargo on access to US nuclear secrets imposed by the 1946 McMahon Act. In January 1948 the British surrendered their right of veto over the US use of the atomic bomb, in the hope – unfulfilled – of greater access to American nuclear information. What made nuclear ostracism worse for Britain was the fact that by 1950 the country had become America's leading European base.[41] The arrival of B-29s to use RAF airfields in the Berlin airlift had been followed in 1949 by plans to build proper US bases around Oxford and by further expansion after the onset of the Korean war. By then the B-29s were operating with atomic bombs. Parliament was never consulted, even though the Ministry of Defence recognised that these developments would probably mean acceptance of the USAF 'remaining in this country indefinitely'.[42] The FO insisted in January 1950 that the bases were essential: 'the primary aim of our foreign policy must be to keep the United States firmly committed in Europe. . . . We must face the fact that this island is strategically well placed as an advanced air base and that we must accept this role'.[43]

The underlying problem was that, without US atomic bombers, the British still had no possible deterrent against Soviet attack. Although work on a British A-bomb was going ahead, it was years away from completion and, despite the RAF now getting the lion's share of defence expenditure, a British long-range atomic bomber force would not be ready until the mid-1950s. By this time, it was believed, the Russians would have the capability to mount a nuclear attack on Britain. In the interim the British were reliant on the US nuclear deterrent against possible Soviet conventional attack, both from the air and across Europe. Their predicament was increased by the Soviet atomic test in August 1949, which British intelligence had not expected until perhaps 1954.[44] Yet the British Government still had no access either to US nuclear material or to Pentagon war plans and targeting.[45] Essentially, its expectation of American nuclear support in time of war remained an act of faith.

Thus, by the early 1950s the British were totally dependent on the USA for their nuclear deterrent policy, yet they had no influence over American use of the bomb. Moreover, the development of US atomic bases in Britain meant, in Churchill's words, that the country had probably become 'the bull's eye of a Soviet attack'.[46] When Churchill returned to power as Tory Prime Minister in October 1951, he did his best to revive the wartime nuclear alliance. But the best he could obtain from Truman was a promise in January 1952 that the use of US bases in Britain 'in an emergency would be a matter for joint decision' between the US and British governments, 'in the light of the circumstances prevailing at the time'.[47] Dwight D. Eisenhower, Truman's successor as president in 1953, was sympathetic to British pleas, believing that they had been unfairly treated after the war and that closer cooperation would be of benefit to the USA, but he was only able to secure minor amendments to the McMahon Act in 1954–5.

Given this impasse, the bipartisan commitment to an independent British nuclear deterrent was understandable. Britain became the third nuclear power in the world, testing its own atomic bomb in October 1952. But by then the thermonuclear age was dawning, with American and Russian tests of an H-bomb in 1952 and 1953. This was a weapon of vastly greater power. Churchill observed 'that we were now as far from the atomic bomb as the atomic bomb itself [was] from the bow and arrow'.[48] In July 1954 the Cabinet decided that Britain

must match the superpowers. Considerations of status were one motive. Churchill insisted that 'we could not expect to maintain our influence as a world power unless we possessed the most up-to-date
nuclear weapons'. Also evident was the hope that a British H-bomb
might somehow compensate for the lack of a formal veto over America's use of nuclear weapons, by ensuring 'more respect for our
views'.[49] How this would happen was unclear, but the concern reflected deep anxieties at American utterances during the Korean War
about possible use of the bomb. Above all, as in 1947, there seemed
compelling strategic arguments. Because Britain had no firm commitments from the United States, it was judged essential to have its own
modern deterrent against Russia. The limits of interdependence made
independence seem essential.

Thus, Britain's A-bomb and H-bomb decisions exhibited a certain
strategic rationality and were not merely the product of great-power
nostalgia. By the mid-1950s Britain had its own nuclear strike force as
the long-range V-bombers began to come into service. And in May
1957 it became the world's third thermonuclear power. The previous
year Tory MP Julian Amery had predicted that the H-bomb 'will
make us a world power again. The atom bomb rather put us out of
the race', he observed, because Britain's small, densely populated territory was far more vulnerable to attack than the vast open spaces of
America and Russia. But the H-bomb, with its vastly-enhanced
power, was 'a great leveller. . . . It would be just as dangerous for the
Soviet Union, or the United States, to incur thermonuclear bombardment as it would be for us'.[50] Such talk was not mere nationalist
delusion; it had a basis in strategic realities.

The postwar Anglo–American alliance was forged from common
anxiety about Soviet policy and, more generally, the challenge of
communism. For many Americans the 'red menace' became an obsession by the early 1950s, fostered by the Republican right for its own
political ends. The new US policy of containment was viewed ambi-
valently in Whitehall: 'it provided an answer to Britain's security problem but only at the cost of hardening the East–West conflict into the
cold war'.[51] In the early 1950s the two governments disagreed about
how far international communism was an unyielding monolith. Was
China merely a tool of Moscow? Did Stalin's death open up opportunities for detente with Russia itself?

Differences over China surfaced immediately after Mao's communist
victory in October 1949.[52] The Truman Administration opposed early
diplomatic recognition, being under heavy political pressure from the
'China lobby' in Congress, which still supported Chiang Kai-shek's

Nationalist regime – now confined to the offshore island of Taiwan. Bevin and the FO disagreed. A hostile regime in Beijing could make life impossible in the British colony of Hong Kong and might also damage British business interests in China, which far exceeded America's. As for Washington's fears of a communist monolith, Bevin believed that 'the only counter to Russian influence is that China should have contacts with the West'.[53] In January 1950 Britain duly recognised the People's Republic of China (PRC). It assumed that Mao would in due course take Taiwan and that the PRC would be given the Nationalists' seat at the United Nations.

The strain between London and Washington intensified after North Korea crossed the 38th Parallel and invaded South Korea in June 1950. The FO had no doubt that the Russians 'had connived at, if they have not instigated, the aggression'[54] or that a firm deterrent response was essential. The Government endorsed the American-led UN action and, after pressure from Washington, agreed to contribute a token force. But it was anxious lest Washington be diverted away from Europe into a major land war in Asia and it deprecated the growing US support for the Nationalist regime in Taiwan which imperilled hopes of normalising relations with the PRC.[55] When MacArthur's UN forces turned the tide and pushed north towards the PRC border to reunify Korea, Chinese forces entered the war at the end of November, driving MacArthur back in disarray. Truman's incautious talk about possible use of the atomic bomb ushered in one of the tensest periods in Anglo–American relations at the turn of 1950–1.

The crisis was both diplomatic and economic, causing deep rifts in the Labour party. Truman's comments prompted an outcry in the Commons and Attlee quickly invited himself to Washington in early December to play a restraining role.[56] Although only vague American promises resulted, the US Government had been reminded of Allied concerns and the visit seemed to symbolise, in the words of the British Ambassador, that Britain was 'out of the queue' of European countries and 'one of the two world powers outside Russia'.[57] Meanwhile, the USA demanded increased Allied defence spending, particularly in Britain. The Cabinet agreed in principle – hopeful of compensatory US aid and fearful that Korea was the harbinger of Soviet aggression in Europe. It boosted the defence budget for 1951–3 from £2.3 billion to £3.6 billion and then, in January 1951, to £4.7 billion. This meant that defence spending would rise from 8 per cent of GNP to 14 per cent.[58] The consequent cuts in normal production for export and, even more, the sharp increase in British import costs as world raw material prices soared because of NATO rearmament, conspired to create a new payments crisis for Britain's recently stabilised economy.[59] Among the Treasury's domestic economies was the imposition of charges on National Health Service (NHS) prescriptions. This prompted the resignation from the Cabinet of Aneurin Bevan, the flamboyant leftwinger and architect of the NHS, who charged that 'we have allowed ourselves to be dragged too far behind the wheels of American diplomacy'.[60] Bevan became the focal point of growing Labour opposition to the US alliance for the next decade.

Nor did these strains over the Asian Cold War abate after the Tories returned to power. Churchill was the leading exponent of the 'special relationship' – 'my hope for the future is founded on the increasing unity of the English-speaking world', he told Eisenhower on 5 April 1953[61] – but his Foreign Secretary, Anthony Eden, believed that Britain could and should take a more independent line from the United States and this caused further tension in Anglo–American relations in 1954.

The new setting was Indochina, where the long French struggle against communist forces reached its climax in the siege of Dien Bien Phu that spring. In Washington there were demands for a US air strike to assist the beleaguered French, but one of Eisenhower's conditions for such a move was Allied support and Eden was adamantly opposed. After the French duly collapsed, Eden took the lead in the international peace conference in Geneva, while John Foster Dulles, his US counterpart, sulked on the sidelines, refusing even to shake hands with the Chinese Foreign Minister. The Geneva accords on Indochina included the partition of Vietnam – long the preferred British option in a country which they, unlike the Americans, deemed of little overall importance in world politics.[62] US intransigence over non-recognition of the PRC, coupled with bellicose support of the Nationalists in Taiwan, was seen in London as a serious obstacle to exploiting Sino–Soviet tensions and easing the Cold War.

By now Churchill believed that detente was possible with Moscow itself, offending the Eisenhower Administration in his efforts to achieve this by personal diplomacy. The ageing Churchill became obsessed with the idea when, after Stalin's death in March 1953, the new leader, Georgii Malenkov, made conciliatory noises to the West.[63] On 11 May Churchill called publicly for an informal summit conference to capitalise on the new mood in Moscow, arguing that 'the security of Russia' and 'the freedom and safety of Western Europe' were not incompatible.[64] He spoke against the advice of the FO and Eisenhower, all of whom believed that such a move would only unsettle the process of West German integration into the Atlantic Alliance.[65]

Churchill's stroke that summer ruled out further action, but he returned to the charge in mid-1954, appalled at new reports of the destructive power of the H-bomb. A unilateral cable to the Russians in July, sounding them out on a personal visit by Churchill, elicited threats of resignation from several Cabinet members.

As Foreign Secretary, Eden had deprecated Churchill's passion for summitry, but he changed his tune once he became Prime Minister in April 1955. German inclusion in NATO was now complete, thus eliminating one major obstacle to a summit, but Churchill may also have been right when he observed: 'How much more attractive a top-level meeting seems when one has reached the top'.[66] A great-power summit in Geneva was arranged for July 1955, its announcement helpfully timed by Washington to boost Eden's election campaign.[67] Although Eden was upstaged at Geneva by Eisenhower, he remained determined to take a lead in disarmament proposals. Against the FO he argued in August 1955 'that we should be unwise to wait too long upon the Americans in this matter: it might be some considerable time before they produced any views of their own. We should not hesitate . . . to bring forward suggestions of our own as soon as we were ready'.[68]

Thus British leaders of the late 1940s and early 1950s took a far from sentimental view of their 'special relationship' with America. The two governments did not have identical views, especially outside Europe, and, while generally preserving unanimity in public, Britain tried to manipulate American policy behind the scenes. In that relationship, of course, the British were the junior partner, but their influence remained significant. This was because Britain, despite 1947, remained a global empire and the resources of that empire became increasingly important to America in the containment of communism. The empire, now largely transmuted into Commonwealth, was the basis of Britain's claims to continued world-power status.

DEVELOPING THE COMMONWEALTH

The creation of India and Pakistan in August 1947 was followed by the granting of independence to Burma in January 1948 – not so much a 'transfer of power' as a 'capitulation of power'.[69] The following May the British evacuated Palestine and left the Jews and Arabs to fight it out – 'an act of abdication for which there was no imperial precedent'.[70] In all these areas Britain was no longer able to maintain order and the advantages gained from formal empire were far out-weighed by the costs. Strategic arguments for hanging on, once de-claimed by the Chiefs of Staff, now seemed irrelevant. As Hugh Dalton, the Chancellor of the Exchequer, observed of Palestine in August 1947, 'you cannot . . . have a secure base on top of a wasps' nest'.[71]

Elsewhere, however, circumstances seemed more propitious for maintaining Britain's global interests. And the Labour government, though committed to promoting self-government where possible, had no doubt that Britain should remain a world power by more informal means. Despite his battles with the Chiefs of Staff in 1946–7, Attlee was not a crude Little Englander.[72] Right from August 1945 he was sure, for instance, that Britain should possess its own atomic bomb. His strategic radicalism had abated by 1948 with the deepening Cold War and the elimination of Britain's most expensive over-commit-ments. Bevin, for his part, was a convinced advocate of modernised empire. In January 1948 he expressed a basic assumption of British policy: 'Provided we can organize a Western European system . . . it should be possible to develop our own power and influence equal to that of the United States of America and the USSR. We have the material resources in the Colonial Empire, if we develop them'.[73]

One stratagem for doing this was through the Commonwealth, en-visaged as a more enlightened and informal version of the British Em-pire. As early as 1884 Lord Rosebery had insisted that 'the Empire is a commonwealth of nations' and the concept of the 'British Common-wealth' was popularised by Smuts during the Great War.[74] But in the interwar period it was applied exclusively to the 'white dominions' of Canada, Australia, South Africa, New Zealand and the Irish Free State, and immediately after the war it seemed in danger of dissolution, with Ireland breaking away and Burma refusing to join. One of the sticking points was 'common allegiance to the Crown', posited by the Balfour report of 1926 as the main bond between Britain and the now auton-omous Dominions.[75] In 1947–8 India, Burma and also Ireland, whose neutrality during the war had been bitterly resented in London, de-clared themselves republics. Burma and Ireland left the Common-wealth, but India wished to remain a member and, because the stakes were so high, special arrangements were considered.

In the debacle of 1947 the original British aim of retaining some residual control of India's bases and armed forces had to be abandoned. But the strategic utility of India was not in doubt and, amid the Berlin crisis of 1948 and the imminent communist victory in China, fears of the country falling into the Soviet orbit were strong. The FO urged sympathetic consideration to the Indian request – the Commonwealth could 'influence the young Indian State during it[s] adolescence' – and the Cabinet agreed that in this way Britain could present 'a solid front against communist domination in the East'.[76] A conference of Commonwealth prime ministers took the same view in April 1949 and agreed to allow republican India to be a member of the Commonwealth on the basis of its acceptance of the King as 'Head of the Commonwealth'.[77]

The new formula, subsequently applied to other countries, gave the Commonwealth flexibility to transcend barriers of polity and race. The title 'British' was dropped and the Dominions Office renamed 'Commonweath Relations Office'. A 'Commonwealth Division' fought in the Korean War, comprising British, Canadian, Australian and New Zealand troops, an Indian ambulance unit, and an integrated staff, including South Africans.[78] In particular, British strategists worked hard to devise a coordinated defence policy. Australia and New Zealand were less willing than in the crisis of 1940–1 to deploy their troops in the Middle East: the expansion of communism in Asia was now their main concern[79] and since 1942 they had looked increasingly to the USA for security. These new priorities were symbolised in the ANZUS treaty of mutual protection signed in September 1951 between the USA, Australia and New Zealand. The USA intended this as the basis of a larger Southeast Asian pact and Britain was deliberately excluded, to Churchill's fury, on the grounds that its membership would attach a colonialist stigma.[80] On the other hand, South Africa seemed more promising. The Nationalists' victory over the pro-British Smuts in 1948 had suggested a weakening of ties, but this was counterbalanced by obsessive Afrikaner fears of communism. Although Britain was unable to fit South Africa into a Middle East defence pact, the Simonstown naval base remained vital and South Africa was a major source of uranium and gold, extracted with British capital. Because of this strategic and economic nexus, the Labour Government toned down its criticism of the Nationalists' apartheid policy.[81]

Apart from the Commonwealth, a second instrument for continued British global influence was colonial economic development. For the Colonial Office and its Labour minister, Arthur Creech-Jones, altruism was genuinely a factor here. As reluctant practitioners of formal empire, the British had previously tried to keep their responsibilities in dependent territories to a minimum. As long as order was maintained, little was done to promote social reform or ameliorate poverty. This mood of 'complacent trusteeship' was shaken, however, by a damning official report into riots in the West Indies in 1935–8, which provoked outrage at conditions in what Lloyd George called this 'slummy empire'.[82] A small Colonial Development and Welfare Act was passed in 1940 and another in 1945, allocating £120 million over ten years. Within the Colonial Office, Lord Hailey's report of 1941 identified economic development as the crucial precondition for progress to self-government. Under Creech-Jones, this became a central theme of colonial policy.

Noblesse oblige aside, a further incentive for colonial development was the wartime American critique of imperialism,[83] which made it important to give empire a kinder, gentler face. This ideological imperative was reinforced by the Soviet attacks on Western imperialism during the Cold War. But the overriding motive for development, especially outside the Colonial Office, was to strengthen Britain's economic position against that of the United States. For most of the Labour government, 'spanning the gap between Bevin and Bevan', that was the lesson of the payments crisis of 1945–7.[84] Sterling substitutes for dollar imports were encouraged, such as East Africa vegetable oils or Southern Rhodesia tobacco; likewise the dollar-earning potential of West African cocoa was assiduously promoted.

The most valuable dependency of all was Malaya, which provides a striking example of what the British were willing to do where empire remained worthwhile. Faced with communist terrorism exploiting the Chinese community's disaffection, Britain imposed a state of emergency from June 1948. It took some five years to break the guerrillas, requiring substantial commitments of troops and money as well as a major rural resettlement programme which evoked memories of the Boer War. There was no question of withdrawal. Malaya was the most profitable part of the Sterling Area. In 1948 its *net* dollar earnings amounted to $170 million and it provided over half the USA's imports of rubber and nearly all its imports of tin.[85]

The mechanism for controlling this process of development to Britain's benefit was the Sterling Area – hence the intensity with which London battled (successfully) against Washington's efforts to dissolve it. Under the Area's wartime rules Britain bought all the hard currency earned by its members at a fixed price and then credited them against sterling balances in London. This meant that net dollar earners such as Malaya or the Gold Coast could not use the dollars they earned to buy goods outside the Sterling Area and had to tie up their earnings in (low-interest) loans to Britain. Britain also imposed physical controls on trade and investment. Colonial imports and exports were licensed and shipping space rationed, while government monopoly buying of key commodities kept prices below world levels. Meanwhile private British investment in the colonies was strictly rationed and British exports concentrated on dollar-earning areas. In the colonies, consumer discontent intensified. 'Between 1945 and 1951 Britain exploited those dependencies that were politically unable to defend their own interests in more ways and with more serious consequences than at any time since overseas colonies were established'.[86]

Although development was officially envisaged as a preparation for eventual independence, a third strand of British policy was the belief that the process of devolution could still be planned and controlled. This was particularly evident in Africa, previously assumed to be incapable of self-government for decades to come. Attitudes had begun to change in the Colonial Office during the war, but it was not until 1947 that a new policy was clearly enunciated.[87] Creech-Jones's altruistic philosophy was a major influence but equally important was the debacle in India and the belief that in future Britain should shape colonial nationalism rather than be overwhelmed by it. The 'Cohen report' of May 1947 assumed that much of the colonial empire might be self-governing 'within a generation' and that Britain should now start to build up an educated middle-class elite and a proper system of local government, replacing the tribal chiefs. The new collaborators would be given increasing responsibility in the legislative and executive councils as these were gradually transmuted into parliaments and cabinets. In this way Britain might show itself a progressive imperial ruler *and* also ensure an orderly transfer of power to stable, pro-British governments.[88]

'Nation-building' was therefore a British strategy for informal empire and not simply the result of anti-colonial pressures. Not that British administrators believed that the embryonic new states always had the capacity to survive alone. A related policy objective was the idea of federations – long favoured by the British as a framework for unstable parts of the world such as the Balkans. Thus, a union of the Malayan states and Singapore was a cherished aim in Southeast Asia after 1945.[89] The Central African Federation, formed in 1953 from Southern and Northern Rhodesia and Nyasaland, was intended 'to erect a counterpoise to the expansion of South Africa' and prevent Southern Rhodesia in particular from being swamped by Afrikaner capital and migrants.[90] And, after suppressing the Mau Mau rebellion in Kenya – with its vital base at Mombasa commanding the Indian Ocean – Britain then tried to build an East African Federation. In this ambitious strategy, new black elites in Tanganyika and Uganda would be harnessed and subordinated to the now-stable, multiracial but white-led Kenya.[91]

Controlled devolution of power might be appropriate for Britain's dependencies, but different methods were required for its informal empire, particularly in the Middle East. Here Bevin was the leading exponent of a new mutuality, resting on 'a common basis of partnership'[92] whereby Britain would offer investment, development aid and technical assistance in return for new treaties guaranteeing its essential interests. It was the old ploy of empire by treaty, dressed up in socialist garb. In 1946 Bevin negotiated a treaty with Transjordan, modified in 1948, guaranteeing British bases in return for continuing subsidies for the Jordanian army, the Arab Legion, which was under British command. A similar treaty with Iraq in 1948 was repudiated after rioting in Baghdad, but in this case and that of Egypt Bevin strove throughout his foreign secretaryship to build a new relationship benefiting, as he liked to put it, 'peasants and not pashas'.[93]

Despite the language of social imperialism, however, Whitehall's imperatives were still power-political. At the beginning of the century Britain's formal and informal empire in the Middle East had been seen mainly as protection for the routes to India, particularly via the Suez Canal – mere 'tollgates and barbicans' of the Indian fortress, in Curzon's famous image.[94] Yet, after India had been abandoned in 1947, the barbicans of empire became its new strongpoint. For one thing, the air age offered a new strategic rationale. The Middle East linked the two great concentrations of power in the non-communist world – the North Atlantic area and the Pacific rim of Asia from India round to Japan. As the British COS reiterated, bases there could threaten much of the USSR. And although the merits of Palestine, Iraq and even Kenya were canvassed at times, the primary military centre was Egypt where the Suez Canal Zone formed a complex of air and naval bases, support installations and training areas the size of Wales, in which nearly 40,000 troops were located in 1951.[95]

There was now also an urgent economic argument for Britain's position in the Middle East, resting on the post-war revolution in energy supplies. In 1950 coal and other solid fuels accounted for 83 per cent of Western Europe's energy consumption and oil only 8.5 per cent. Twenty years later the proportions were 29 per cent against 60 per cent.[96] Sources of supply also shifted dramatically. In 1945 65 per cent of the world's crude oil came from North America and only 7 per cent from the Middle East. By 1973 the respective shares were 21 per cent and 38 per cent.[97] And Britain's dependence on the region was acute – in 1949 the FO estimated that by 1951 82 per cent of Britain's oil supplies would come from the Middle East, compared with 23 per cent in 1937 – figures roughly comparable with the pattern for Western Europe as a whole.[98] But where Britain scored over its continental neighbours was that British companies controlled a significant part of Middle Eastern oil production in 1950, being dominant in Iran and having a half-share with the USA in Kuwait, respectively the region's top and third-largest producers.[99] These supplies were vital for Britain's industrial growth and its sterling earnings, and their protection was an additional justification for a strong military presence in the region, not least astride the Suez Canal – the prime artery for oil traffic to Europe.

Retaining this position was the biggest challenge of all for the new partnership policy. In 1951 the Iranian government nationalised the oil refineries and then forced the British staff out of Abadan. Without the Indian army, the British lacked ready manpower to intervene and in any case the Truman Administration opposed the use of force. The Labour Cabinet agreed that 'we could not afford to break with the United States on an issue of this kind'.[100] But the Eisenhower Administration was more forthcoming. A 1953 counter-coup (secretly backed by US and British intelligence) toppled the Iranian premier, Mossadeq, and restored British oil interests. Admittedly the new oil arrangement involved 40 per cent British and US shares rather than the erstwhile Anglo–Iranian monopoly, and in consequence the US proportion of Middle Eastern oil rose from 44 per cent to 58 per cent, while Britain's dropped from 53 per cent to 24 per cent.[101] Nevertheless, the humiliation of 1951 had been revenged and Britain's prestige largely restored in cooperation with the USA.

A new partnership with Egypt proved harder to arrange. Despite the importance of the Canal Zone, Bevin had been unable to reach an agreement and the problem was exacerbated by the officers' coup in 1952 from which Gamal Abdel Nasser soon emerged as leader. This destroyed the whole network of clientage elaborately built up since the Great War. For Nasser, foreign bases were the touchstone of Western imperialism and British evacuation of the Canal Zone became his primary goal. As Foreign Secretary Eden persisted in the search for a new base agreement, arguing against vocal Tory critics that 'in the middle of the twentieth century we must deal with Egypt as an independent nation. . . . It is a case of "new times, new methods"'.[102] His keenest opponent was Churchill himself, who continued to denounce 'this policy of scuttle',[103] and the latter was only reconciled by his growing conviction that the thermonuclear age had made vast permanent bases vulnerable and obsolete.[104] The eventual October 1954 agreement required withdrawal of all British forces from Egypt within twenty months, but the Suez base would be maintained in peacetime and Britain had the right of re-entry in wartime for seven years.[105]

A new relationship with Egypt apparently established, the British renewed their efforts to form a regional security organisation. Its nucleus was Turkey, a recent member of NATO, and Iraq, Britain's main Middle Eastern ally, who created the Baghdad Pact in February 1955. Britain joined in April, followed by Pakistan and Iran. For the British this promised a pro-Western grouping in the northern tier of the Middle East and a way of using Iraqi bases under an alliance framework that would be more popular than a bilateral agreement with Britain.[106] In 1955 British hoped to draw Nasser into the pact, using the offer of Western funding for the Aswan High Dam as an enticement, and the FO also worked energetically behind the scenes for a settlement of the Arab–Israeli dispute at Israeli expense – codenamed Alpha'.[107] Both these facets of the 'partnership' policy involved close cooperation with the Americans – a further instance of Britain trying to maintain its great-power role through transatlantic interdependence.

EUROPEAN INTEGRATION AND THE GERMAN QUESTION

It was from this globalist perspective that British governments viewed the idea of Western European integration in the late 1940s and early 1950s. Their economic priorities centred on the Commonwealth and the Sterling Area; their real but limited interest in integration was mainly diplomatic, as a framework for Franco–German rapprochement.

At times in the 1940s the British had evinced genuine interest in close cooperation with France and its neighbours. But these had been at times of extreme insecurity – 1939–40 and 1946–7 – and in both cases the enthusiasm proved ephemeral. In 1940 France collapsed and Britain turned towards the USA. Much the same transference of affections occurred from 1947 with the revolutionary US commitments to Europe at a time when France and its neighbours remained mired in economic depression, social strife and political instability. France had no less than eight coalition governments between May 1947 and June 1951, some punctuated by gaps of several weeks. Thus, trust in America waxed while faith in France waned. At the same time the new policies for making the Commonwealth and Sterling Area more effective instruments of British global power seemed to be bearing fruit. As Lord Garner, then a senior official at the Commonwealth

Relations Office recalled, 'we were, if you like, euphoric about the Commonwealth and its possibilities and significance for us, we were most pessimistic about Europe'.[108]

In January 1949 an interdepartmental meeting of FO, Treasury and other officials summed up the essentials of British policy:

> . . . Our policy should be to assist Europe to recover as far as we can . . . But the concept must be one of limited liability. In no circumstances must we assist them beyond the point at which the assistance leaves us too weak to be a worth-while ally for U.S.A. if Europe collapses – i.e. beyond the point at which our own viability was impaired.[109]

'Limited liability' was the catchphrase of the 1930s, minimising a continental military commitment. It also echoed the equivocations of British policy towards France in the decade before 1914. Now the emerging American alliance gave such ideas added force and during the next few months they were confirmed as Cabinet policy. The creation of NATO and the devaluation crisis seemed, in different ways, to prove, as Bevin and Cripps told the Cabinet in a joint paper, that America and the Commonwealth 'take priority over our relations with Europe'.[110] When the French bureaucrat Jean Monnet came to London in the spring of 1949 to sound out British officials on an Anglo–French economic union, he received a polite brush-off. The Sterling Area took half Britain's exports, continental Western Europe only a quarter. In 1947 British exports equalled those of France, Germany, Italy, Benelux, Norway and Denmark combined.[111] Commercial logic seemed clear: Britain's future lay with the Sterling Area, not in a European customs union.

Monnet had been the architect of a last-ditch proposal for Anglo–French union after Dunkirk. His main motive in 1949, as in 1940, was to counterbalance German power now that a Federal German state had been created out of the three western occupation zones. Rebuffed by Britain in 1949, Monnet turned in 1950 to Germany itself. In May 1950 French foreign minister Robert Schuman launched Monnet's new plan for a European coal and steel community centred on France and Germany. 'If you can't beat them, join them', was in effect the philosophy: German recovery would be accelerated, benefiting its neighbours, but the Germans would surrender control over their heavy industry, the sinews of war, to a 'higher authority'. Thus, French sovereignty would be eroded but its security, and Europe's prosperity, enhanced – that was Monnet's objective.

The Schuman Plan of 9 May 1950 came as a rude shock to White-hall.[112] To prevent British obstruction Monnet gave them no advance warning. There were some genuine British enthusiasts. Sir Oliver Harvey, Ambassador in Paris, who had supported the 1940 plans for union, insisted that 'this is a never-to-be-repeated opportunity of getting a real move on in Europe',[113] but the newly-nationalised coal industry was opposed to joining and steel producers, only 5 per cent of whose exports went to Western Europe, were more interested in defending their global markets.[114] In Whitehall there was a tendency to see the plan as mainly a device to 'dispel the traditional enmity and suspicion between France and Germany'. That, the COS observed, 'cannot fail to have long term strategic advantages',[115] but it was not a reason for British involvement. Ideally, the Cabinet and its advisers would have preferred to be loosely involved in the talks, without prior commitment, but the French demanded an advance commitment to the principle of a supranational authority by 1 June as the essential precondition for entering into negotiations.

This issue of national sovereignty became central. In all previous talk of cooperation with continental Europe, including Bevin's ideas for 'Western Union', the philosophy was confederal not federal – intergovernmental links between separate states rather than a surrender of sovereignty to a higher authority. The objections to federalism were rooted and bipartisan – in Bevin's inimitable phrase, 'if you open that Pandora's Box you never know what Trojan 'orses will jump out'.[116] Taken in conjunction with the divergent commercial orientations of Britain and France, they seemed compelling. Reminding his superiors of the 'limited liability' formula 'that we should not be involved in Europe in the economic sphere, beyond the point of no return', Sir William Strang, the Permanent Under-Secretary at the FO, observed that acceptance of the French proposals would imply readiness to make 'a surrender of sovereignty in a matter of vital national interest which would carry us well beyond that point'. Thereby 'we shall have tipped the balance against the two other elements in our world-situation, the Atlantic Community and the Commonwealth'.[117] Although the final decision was taken by a 'rump' Cabinet on 2 June, with Bevin, Attlee and Cripps ill or on holiday, it was fully in line with the tenor of official and ministerial thinking since 1947. Britain stood aside, anticipating that the talks would fail and that it could offer a counter-proposal, but the opportunity did not arise and the European Coal and Steel Community (ECSC) came into existence in April 1952, with France, West Germany, Italy, Belgium, Luxembourg and the Netherlands its six founder members.

Similar considerations dictated Britain's initially brusque reaction to the Pleven plan of October 1950, which called for an integrated, multi-national European army responsible to a European assembly and defence minister. This European Defence Community (EDC) was an extension of Monnet's supranationalist principles from economics to security, in hasty response to US demands for German rearmament. Bevin considered the plan 'a manoeuvre in French domestic politics' and Attlee dismissed it in Cabinet as 'unworkable and unsound'. By the autumn of 1951 the Labour government's attitude had modified because of US support for the plan and because it seemed the best way to placate backbench opposition to German rearmament, but, despite its new tone of welcome for the Schuman and Pleven plans as contributions to European unity, the Government still made clear that Britain itself would not be involved: 'while we cannot join the "European Community" we nevertheless wish to be closely associated with it'.[118]

The bipartisan character of this policy became clear when the Tories regained power in October.[119] In the late 1940s Churchill had spoken out for European unity and had been one of the founders of the unelected assembly, the Council of Europe, created in 1949. But the expectations aroused by his return to power were misplaced. Churchill believed in Europe 'for them, but not for us',[120] as a means of bringing France and Germany together. In November 1951 he told the Cabinet:

> I never thought that Britain or the British Commonwealth should, either individually or collectively, become an integral part of a European federation. . . . Our first object is the unity and consolidation of the British Commonwealth and what is left of the former British Empire. Our second, the 'fraternal association' of the English-speaking world; and third, United Europe, to which we are a separate, closely- and specially-related ally and friend.[121]

In line with this policy, Eden, his Foreign Secretary, slowly negotiated treaties of British association with the EDC (May 1952 and April 1954) and the ECSC (December 1954).[122] But both agreements involved a process of piecemeal and grudging British concession, and the EDC arrangement failed to satisfy the increasingly nationalist tenor of French politics in the early 1950s. The ensuing NATO crisis forced a major restatement of British defence policy.

Britain had been almost as reluctant in defence as in commerce to make firm commitments to the continentals. The Anglo–French treaty of Dunkirk (1947) and the Brussels Pact of March 1948 stood in a long tradition of British gestures of reassurance to France. They were not binding military alliances. Until 1948 the basic British war plan in the event of a Red Army offensive was to evacuate British troops from the continent, assuming a 1940–5 scenario of retreat to the island fortress prior to eventual recapture of the continent with American help. In May 1948, to give substance to the Brussels Pact, the Cabinet agreed that the existing two British divisions would stay and fight 'unless and until they were pushed out', but, despite the North Atlantic treaty, it was not until March 1950 that the Defence Committee agreed to promise reinforcements in the event of war.[123] The European war scare sparked off by the crisis in Korea accelerated the abandonment of the Dunkirk/D-Day scenario in favour of defending West Germany, but the architect of this shift, Air Chief Marshal Sir John Slessor, saw it mainly as justifying a greater role for the RAF – particularly through the nuclear V–bomber force.

In the EDC negotiations of 1950–4 the French therefore tried to extract more precise British troop commitments. The April 1954 agreement was clinched by a promise to place one British division in an EDC corps[124], but then the whole EDC project was rejected by the French Assembly in August. The British failure to participate was a major factor. From America Dulles had already warned of an 'agonizing reappraisal' of US policy towards Europe if the EDC collapsed: for nearly four years the EDC had been the projected framework for German rearmament, on which the Americans were adamant to avoid having to carry Europe's burdens alone. Eden and the FO now feared that the Atlantic alliance itself was in jeopardy, and with it the whole delicate fabric of British global policy laboriously stitched together after 1947. Fears of an American relapse into isolationism seemed to require a decisive British response.

Shuttling between European capitals in September 1954 Eden proposed that West Germany should be admitted into NATO, but that it should renounce the right to nuclear weapons and incorporate its forces totally in the Alliance. In addition, French fears of German aggression and American isolationism, plus British objections to the EDC, could all be reconciled by including Germany in the existing European mutual defence arrangements of the Brussels Pact. What decided matters for the French was Eden's readiness to make a further concession, held in reserve since early in the year, of a precise, permanent British troop commitment. In London on 29 September he stated that Britain would not unilaterally withdraw the existing four divisions and tactical air force then assigned to NATO forces in Germany. The French ambassador wept openly, saying that 'for fifty years – ever since 1905 – French public opinion has waited for this announcement; and at last we have it!'[125] The agreements signed on this basis in Paris in November 1954 satisfied the French Assembly. The following May

West Germany entered NATO and the process of West German rearmament began.

The Paris accords seemed to vindicate British policy of limited intergovernmental cooperation in Western Europe. German rearmament
had been accomplished through the Atlantic alliance and not European
integration.[126] Moreover, with the collapse of the EDC, enthusiasm
for supranationalism seemed to have waned, even in France – in 1950
the champion of such ideas. The British were therefore ill-prepared for
their renaissance in 1955. A meeting of the Six's Foreign Ministers at
Messina in Sicily resulted in an invitation to Britain to join in detailed
discussions in Brussels on further European integration. At this stage
the proposals were vague and the dread concept of 'supra-nationalism'
had not been broached, in contrast with 1950. The Treasury felt that

> we cannot stop the six countries doing what they want, but if we accept
> their invitation we can seek to ensure that their actions are as little
> prejudicial to our interests as possible. And it may be possible to guide
> their thoughts towards suggestions for forms of co-operation in which we
> would be willing to join.[127]

Though Harold Macmillan, a keen European and at that time Foreign
Secretary, argued that Britain could exert 'a greater influence' on the
talks if it were a full participant 'and not an observer',[128] it was eventually agreed that a senior Board of Trade official, Russell Bretherton,
would attend as a British representative 'without commitment'.

While the Brussels talks developed during the autumn, a working
party of officials examined the issues in detail.[129] The Board of Trade
was now sympathetic to the idea of a common market but the bulk of
Treasury opinion, backed by the Bank of England and the Commonwealth Relations Office, was not, and this carried the day. The official
report, at the end of October, emphasised the importance of Britain's
extra-European economic interests, the dangers of a protectionist European bloc and the likely tendency towards political federation. It
concluded that Britain could not join a common market and that the
latter's very establishment would 'on the whole' be bad for Britain and
should be frustrated.[130] These conclusions were endorsed by the
Cabinet. As in 1950, ministers concurred with officials and there was
remarkably little discussion in Cabinet or Parliament.[131] Eden, the
Prime Minister, had even less time for such ideas than Churchill –
joining a continental federation was 'something which we know, in
our bones, we cannot do' he had stated in 1952[132] – and Macmillan
and the FO took little detailed interest, confident that the French ambivalence would undermine this initiative as it had the EDC. In short,

most British leaders did not think they were making a momentous decision. The Chancellor, R.A. Butler, dismissed Messina as 'archaeological excavations'[133] – an attempt to dig up discredited ideas like federalism, not laying the foundations for Europe's future.

Despite the disasters of 1947, therefore, British policymakers still envisaged a world role for themselves in mid-century. Indeed Britain was exerting itself as a power more energetically than at any time outside the world wars, certainly far more than in its supposed Victorian heyday. Conscription, the continental commitment, the sterling area and intensive Commonwealth development were all peacetime novelties, not to mention the unprecedented nuclear programme. In 1953, with only a fraction of its forces committed to hot war in Korea, Britain spent nearly 10 per cent of GNP on defence and kept 865,000 men under arms.[134] It had the leading economy of Europe, manufacturing as much in 1951 as France and West Germany combined,[135] and it was about to become the only other nuclear power apart from the USA and USSR. Britain was less than a superpower, perhaps, but greater than the 'queue' of Europeans – all of whom had been defeated and occupied in the war – hence the visceral refusal to be lumped in with them. Ernest Bevin summed up the mood well in 1950 when he exploded to American advocates of European integration that 'Great Britain was not part of Europe; she was not simply a Luxembourg'.[136]

REFERENCES

1.   Fox 1944: 21
2.   Paterson 1979: 23
3.   Barnett 1972: 592–3
4.   Baylis 1984b: 60
5.   Dilks (ed.) 1971: 778
6.   Duke 1987: 20–5
7.   T. Anderson 1981: 150–1, 161–5
8.   Boyle 1982: 377–8
9.   Reynolds 1990b: 126
10. Bullock 1983: ch. 10
11. Boyle 1987: 525
12. CAB 129/25, CP (48) 72
13. Warner 1986: 28
14. Commons 446: 566
15. Wiebes and Zeeman 1983: 353

16. J. Young 1984: ch. 9
17. Baylis 1984a
18. Bullock 1983: 576
19. Duke 1987: chs 2–3
20. Kaplan 1988: 1
21. Henderson 1982: 39, 51
22. Ireland 1981: 88
23. Barker 1983: 130
24. Kaplan 1988: 219
25. Dimbleby and Reynolds 1988: 190
26. Mayne 1973: 132
27. Morgenthau 1954: 339
28. Maier 1981: 342; Milward 1984: ch. 3
29. Henrikson 1980: 38, 103 n.
30. FO 371/38523, AN 1538
31. Cairncross 1985: 123–30
32. Ibid., 123–30
33. Gardner 1980: 315, 317
34. Cairncross 1985: ch. 7
35. Edmonds 1986: 106
36. Cairncross 1985: 44, 87, 503
37. Hogan 1987: chs 1–2
38. Newton 1984: 396
39. Milward 1984: ch. 5
40. Hogan 1987: 271; cf. Newton 1985b
41. Duke 1987
42. Dimbleby and Reynolds 1988: 186–7
43. PRO, DEFE 7/516
44. Aldrich and Coleman 1989a: 538
45. Clark and Wheeler 1989: 135
46. Commons 484: 630
47. FO 371/97592, AU 151/12
48. Colville 1985: 676
49. Clark and Wheeler 1989: 214–15
50. Pierre 1972: 94
51. Frankel 1975: 198
52. Ovendale 1985: ch. 7
53. Edmonds 1986: 147
54. P. Lowe 1986: 165
55. Dockrill 1986
56. Dingman 1982
57. Dockrill 1986: 476
58. P. Williams 1982: 169
59. Cairncross 1985: ch. 8
60. Foot 1973: ii, 335
61. PREM 11/1074
62. Cable 1986

199

63. J. Young 1988a
64. Gilbert 1988: viii, 831
65. Fish 1986
66. Macmillan 1969: 587
67. Carlton 1981: 372
68. CAB 128/29, CM 28 (55) 10
69. Tinker 1986: 479
70. Darwin 1988: 119
71. Cohen 1982: 268
72. cf. Louis 1977: 557; Pearce 1982: 92
73. Gupta 1983: 108; cf. Kent 1989
74. Mansergh 1982: i, 21–4
75. Judd and Slinn 1982: 62
76. Singh 1985: 475–7
77. Mansergh 1982: ii, 158
78. Judd and Slinn 1982: 89
79. Devereux 1989
80. Ovendale 1985: 231–3
81. Ibid., ch. 9
82. Pearce 1982: 1, 17
83. Louis and Robinson 1982
84. Gupta 1983: 107
85. Stockwell 1984: 78
86. Fieldhouse 1984: 95; cf. Hinds 1987
87. Flint 1983; Pearce 1984
88. Pearce 1982: ch. 7
89. Stockwell 1984: 71–2
90. Hyam 1987: 169
91. Darwin 1988: 184–93
92. Bullock 1983: 114
93. Louis 1984: 17
94. M. Howard 1974: 14
95. Louis 1984: 9–10
96. Brondel 1977: 227
97. Venn 1986: 11
98. Ovendale 1985: 111; Bullock 1983: 36
99. cf. Venn 1986: 172
100. Louis 1984: 666, 688
101. Ovendale 1984: 136
102. PREM 11/636
103. Moran 1968: 504
104. Louis 1989: 62
105. Ovendale 1988; Louis 1989
106. Reid 1988
107. Shuckburgh 1986: chs 9–10
108. Charlton 1983: 62; cf. Würzler 1989
109. R. Clarke 1982: 208–9

110. J. Young 1984: 127
111. Cairncross 1985: 276, 278
112. J. Young 1984: chs 15–16
113. *DBPO* II: i, 75
114. Milward 1984: 401–4
115. *DBPO* II: i, 30
116. Bullock 1983: 659
117. *DBPO* II: i, 134
118. Warner 1984: 74–9
119. J. Young 1985
120. Charlton 1983: 137
121. CAB 129/48, C (51) 32
122. J. Young 1988b, 1988c
123. Barker 1983: 118–19, 196–7
124. J. Young 1988c: 91
125. Fursdon 1980: 321–2
126. S. Dockrill 1989: 168
127. CAB 128/29, CM 19 (55) 9
128. Ibid.
129. Burgess and Edwards 1988; J. Young 1989
130. Burgess and Edwards 1988: 407
131. Moon 1985: ch. 6
132. Carlton 1981: 311
133. Charlton 1983: 194–5
134. M. Dockrill 1988: 151
135. Cairncross 1985: 278
136. FO 800/517, US/50/35

CHAPTER EIGHT

Circles, 1955–70

In the early 1950s Winston Churchill popularised the concept of 'three great circles among the free nations and democracies' – the Commonwealth, the English-speaking world and Europe. 'If you think of the three inter-linked circles', Churchill argued, 'you will see that we are the only country which has a great part in every one of them' – through leadership of the Commonwealth, a 'special relationship' with the United States and close 'association' with the institutions of European security and prosperity. Britain's influence in each one was reinforced by its role in the other two.[1]

Today this geometrical conceit seems far-fetched, but it grew out of international circumstances in mid-century. Britain did have a place in all three arenas. The problem was that those circumstances did not last. In a decade from 1955 Britain's relationship with America became one of dependence, the Commonwealth and Sterling Area crumbled, and Western Europe was transformed by the creation of the EEC without British participation. Underlying all three developments was the country's rapid and catastrophic economic decline.

The Tory governments of Anthony Eden (1955–7), Harold Macmillan (1957–63) and Sir Alec Douglas-Home (1963–4) were slow to come to terms with these changes. Eden exaggerated Britain's power and independence, leading to the Suez debacle, while Macmillan was unable to harmonise his bid for membership of the EEC with Britain's transatlantic and Commonwealth connections. And, for all its apparent modernity, Harold Wilson's Labour government of 1964–70 conducted a highly traditional globalist foreign policy against the background of growing economic weakness – going round in ever-decreasing circles into the vortex of 1967–8.

SUEZ

The limits of post-war British power were dramatised by the Suez debacle of 1956. The main events are now clearly established.[2] On 26 July Nasser nationalised the Suez Canal, in retaliation for Anglo–American cancellation, a week before, of the Aswan dam. Although the USA sought a negotiated settlement, Eden prepared an invasion force and in mid-October a French proposal of collusion with Israel gave him the pretext he needed. When Israeli troops attacked Egypt on 29 October the British and French announced their intention to intervene – ostensibly to protect the Canal. But by the time the invasion force arrived, on 5–6 November, sterling was under pressure and the outcry at home and abroad was overwhelming. On the 6th the British accepted a ceasefire and on 29 November they agreed to withdraw their forces – the condition of US support for sterling.

In part, the crisis revealed the weakness of the new policy of partnership – on both sides. Eden had assumed that, with enlightened handling, Nasser could be made into a tractable client. But, for Nasser, foreign bases and regional pacts were the emblems of imperialism. After the 1954 agreement, the Suez base was in liquidation but the Baghdad Pact, centred on his main regional rival, Iraq, was a major challenge. Threatened by this and by Israeli raids, he turned to the Soviet bloc for weapons in September 1955. Today this appears unremarkable but at the time the West monopolised arms sales to the Middle East and the deal seemed a significant shift in the regional balance of power. Then, in March 1956, King Hussein of Jordan dismissed General Sir John Glubb from his command of the Jordanian army, largely officered and financed by Britain and thus a potent source of British influence. Eden blamed Nasser for this move, doubly angry because he had gone out on a limb politically in 1954 to defy Tory diehards over the Suez agreement. He now saw Nasser not as a potential partner but as a jumped-up dictator. Invoking the 'lessons' of appeasement, with which his reputation had become so closely associated, he compared Nasser with Mussolini, saying that 'his object was to be a Caesar from the Gulf to the Atlantic, and to kick us out of it all . . . '. He was quite emphatic that Nasser must be got rid of. "It is either him or us, don't forget that", he exploded in March 1956.[3]

The failure of 'partnership' revived the old imperialist reflexes. The Aswan funding was cut, the search for an Arab–Israeli settlement abandoned and British and US intelligence began to prepare a coup in Syria (reminiscent of Iran in 1953) to prevent that country uniting with Egypt.[4] The new policy towards Nasser was agreed in Cabinet on 21 March and nationalisation of the Canal only served to provide justification for a full-scale effort to overthrow him.[5] Although much was made publicly of the potential threat to British trade and oil supplies, that was not the real issue. The military planners were told that 'while our ultimate purpose was to place the Canal under international control, our immediate objective was to bring about the downfall of the present Egyptian Government'.[6] But this was not 1882 or even 1942. As the FO legal adviser warned Eden, there had been an 'immense change . . . in the climate of world opinion on the question of the use of force'.[7] Over Palestine in 1946–7 the Attlee government had taken heed. But Eden ignored the warning. Britain's invasion not only consolidated Egypt around Nasser, it also mobilised opinion in the UN, where Britain was almost totally isolated. Of the nine members of the Commonwealth, only Australia and New Zealand supported Britain. In 1956, barely a decade after Britain had helped found the UN, such international ostracism was not only unprecedented but also deeply demoralising.

The biggest British underestimation was of the Americans. The US government agreed that Nasser was a menace and that he should be checked – hence the termination of funding for Aswan. But from the start of the crisis Eisenhower repeatedly warned Eden of 'the unwisdom even of contemplating the use of military force' to recover the Canal as long as an international solution was possible.[8] To the Americans the Canal was a colonial relic. Moreover, Nasser's legal case was a strong one: nationalisation backed by offers of compensation was legal and the derided 'Gypos' showed, much to British surprise, that they could operate the Canal efficiently by themselves. Eisenhower was clear that Suez 'was not the issue upon which to try to downgrade Nasser'.[9] If Eden was deceived about the US attitude, it was by himself and not by Dulles.[10]

Eden had repeatedly shown a greater confidence than Churchill in Britain's ability to function as a great power – independently, if necessary, of the USA. He had told the Cabinet in October 1955 that because Britain's interests and experience in the Middle East exceeded America's, the British should not feel 'restricted overmuch by reluctance to act without full American concurrence and support. We should frame our own policy in the light of our interests in the area and get the Americans to support it to the extent we could induce them to do so'.[11] Thus, when the Treasury made economic contingency plans for an invasion of Egypt it assumed that Britain would either have 'full US, and general UN and Commonwealth support' or else would 'go it alone with France – with only limited US, Commonwealth and other support'.[12] No one seems to have expected American leadership of opposition in the UN, their harassment of the task force in the Mediterranean or Eisenhower's steadfast refusal to assist sterling until the troops were out. Macmillan, the Chancellor, was particularly culpable, having misunderstood Eisenhower's own opinions or misrepresented them to Eden after talking to the President in September.[13]

The consequences of Suez were far-reaching, particularly in public. British policymakers had known for years of their underlying weaknesses, but the public image, accentuated by 1940, 1945 and post-war recovery, was of a country that was still a major power. For an Egyptian ex-colonel to twist the lion's tail, and get away with it, was a palpable and lasting blow to national self-esteem and international prestige. Nasser's successful defiance made him into a Third World hero, encouraging anti-colonial nationalists elsewhere. American and Russian influence increased in the Middle East and no British leader ever again made the mistake of trying to defy the USA on a major issue. For France the lessons of Suez were also far-reaching, but different. Having subsumed its forces under British command – itself a striking concession – it now felt betrayed by Britain and, even more, the USA. 'Europe will be your revenge', the German leader, Konrad Adenauer told the French premier on the day Britain announced it was halting the Suez invasion.[14] France's irritation with NATO and its enthusiasm for a European Community were both greatly accentuated by the crisis.

Nevertheless, the impact of Suez should not be exaggerated. Relations with America were soon restored, Britain remained an important power east of Suez and the crisis itself probably did not prompt a new policy on African decolonisation.[15] In some ways, in fact, Suez was idiosyncratic, revealing oddities of the moment as much as underlying trends in the decline of British power. Thus, the collapse of the operation owed much to the gaping divisions in Whitehall.[16] Almost all the FO officials were excluded from the collusion and most bitterly opposed it. The Minister of Defence (Sir Walter Monckton) and the First Sea Lord (Mountbatten) both had profound doubts about the invasion. When one also bears in mind Labour's overt opposition, it is clear that Suez was one of the most divisive events in twentieth-century British foreign policy. The lack of firm domestic support soon undermined the government's will to fight.

The idiosyncracies of the Suez debacle do not end there. Eden, for all his experience of foreign affairs, was a petulant and unstable man, by 1956 seriously ill from a botched gall bladder operation. His obsessive determination to destroy Nasser and then the snapping of his resolve under pressure in November 1956 both probably owe something to these personal circumstances. Furthermore, the Suez operation was an aberration from key post-war British policies. Collusion with Israel conflicted spectacularly with the search for new partnerships with the Arabs; allying with France and not America was likened by one British diplomat, in a revealing phrase, to visiting 'the whore-house' because it seemed impossible to marry one's true love.[17] For these bizarre U-turns Eden was largely responsible. Even the vulnerability of sterling in the absence of US help was partly self-inflicted, reflecting the Bank of England's refusal to take precautionary measures before November for fear that they would undermine foreign confidence in the pound.[18] Yet this last point does speak to a deeper problem behind the whole crisis – shifts in the world economy that were undermining the basis of Britain's post-war global strategy.

BRITAIN AND THE WORLD ECONOMY

Since the 1930s Britain had gradually retreated from open competition in the world economy and developed its own commercial and financial orbit, centred on the Commonwealth and the sterling area. This had initially been a response to the collapse of a multilateral economy in the Depression; it was consolidated as a strategy for victory in the Second World War and a policy for recovery after 1945. Initial results seemed impressive. Exports quadrupled between 1944 and 1950, the balance of payments was in equilibrium overall from 1948, the dollar gap had been bridged by 1952 and sterling became convertible into dollars – partially in 1954–5, fully at the end of 1958. By then, however, a new international economic system had taken shape. Covering only the non-communist world, it was not as comprehensive as the world economy of the late Victorian era, but it made possible the transcending of economic blocs, of the sort that had prevailed since the 1930s, and allowed world trade to revive. It was based on the security provided by American military alliances and on the willingness of the USA to offset its huge trade surpluses in the 1940s and early 1950s by exporting capital through economic loans and military aid. In these auspicious circumstances, unknown in Europe since before 1914, the economies of Germany and its neighbours began to revive and, in conditions of renewed competition, the underlying weaknesses of British industry became apparent again.

The dominance of Britain in the post-war European economy was artificial, resulting from the destruction of most of its continental rivals in the war. In retrospect, it is clear that Britain should have used this grace period to modernise its industrial structure – a plethora of small plants, backward technology, poor management, fragmented and bitter unions. The war effort had built on these weak foundations, rather than reforming them. Even in shipbuilding, where the £6 million investment programme in 1942–4 was the biggest for half a century, the underlying structure of a Victorian craft industry had not been broken down. The Cabinet's Reconstruction Committee warned in July 1944 that the country had about a decade's leeway in which to modernise the industry – a prescient forecast, since Britain was passed in shipbuilding by Germany in 1954 and by Japan a year later.[19]

In explaining why the opportunity for industrial renewal was missed, it is easy to blame 'the "enlightened" Establishment' for foisting their welfare-state 'New Jerusalem evangelism' on the British people in blithe indifference to economic realities.[20] Even at the time, in 1944, the Treasury warned that 'the time and energy which we are all giving to the Brave New World is wildly disproportionate to what is being given to the Cruel Real World'.[21] Yet the political pressures were intense. The British people had fought two wars in a quarter-century and there was an understandable expectation that the suffering must be proved worthwhile. In March 1942 the Government's morale reports noted 'a general agreement that "things are going to be different after the war"'.[22] Demands for a 'welfare state', which crystallised around the Beveridge plan of 1942, became part of 'an implied contract between Government and people'[23] – sacrifice today, salvation tomorrow. Had Britain lost the war, popular expectations might have been checked. Defeat implies failure, suffering and the need for change. But Britain emerged in 1945 on the winning side. The commitment to a welfare state, no less than renewed faith in national sovereignty, was 'the price of victory'.

In any case, it is arguable whether much could have been done in one decade to reform the industrial practices of two centuries. What is clear is that by the late 1950s the new international competition was beginning to bite. In 1950 the UK generated 25.5 per cent of the total value of world manufacturing exports and West Germany only 7.3 per cent. In 1960 their respective shares were 16.5 per cent and 19.3 per cent. A decade later, while Germany's proportion remained about 20 per cent, Britain's had fallen to 10.8 per cent and Japan's had grown to

11.7 per cent (table 1.2). That collapse, from a quarter to a tenth of world trade in manufactures in only two decades, was devastating.

Although mainly a reflection of the underlying uncompetitiveness of British industry, this disaster was also the result of the false assumptions on which post-war British economic strategy had rested.[24] British leaders had assumed a scenario similar to the post-1918 era – a brief post-war restocking boom, then weak industrial growth or even recession. They anticipated a worldwide shortage of raw materials and believed that Britain's dominance of key commodities would ensure prosperity. Hence the intensive programme to develop colonial resources. During the 1950s these expectations were dashed. After the Korean War boom, commodity prices sagged while the industrial economies saw sustained and unprecedented expansion, lasting in fact until the early 1970s. This growth was concentrated on continental Western Europe, where the Six, in further contrast to British expectations, created a tariff-free common market in the decade after the EEC was founded in 1958. Thus, in 1950 the British expected that the Commonwealth and Sterling Area would give them dominance of world commodity trade – the presumed growth area. By 1960 this strategy had left them outside the real growth area – the industrial economies of the EEC.

The changing world economy affected not only British industry but also the position of sterling.[25] Around 1900 sterling was a 'top currency' – its international use rested on Britain's central position in the flow of world trade and finance. By the late 1920s both the dollar and franc were serious rivals; when open financial markets resumed in the 1950s the Deutschmark and then the yen joined the competition, reflecting their countries' growing importance in world trade. Sterling gradually declined to the status of a 'neutral currency', that is to say one among several in international economic use. Within a part of the world, however, sterling had a special position as a 'master currency' – in countries tied to Britain as part of the Empire or heavily dependent on it commercially – and from the 1930s Britain consolidated this position through the sterling area controls. In due course, however, as the empire became independent and the sterling area broke up, so sterling slipped to being a 'negotiated currency' – one that British clients had to be *persuaded* to use by inducements or penalties.

The problem was that sterling slipped from being a top currency to a neutral currency and from a master currency to a negotiated currency just at the time, around 1960, that the new multilateral Western economy took shape and a further wave of decolonisation broke. Maintaining sterling's international position, still the goal of British policy, became ever more burdensome. To keep it attractive as a neutral currency interest rates were held high, despite the deflationary effects on domestic industry. To keep it attractive to countries no longer formally controlled by Britain required inducements such as military and economic aid to keep new states like Malaysia within the sterling area.

Not only was sterling a growing burden at home, it was also increasingly vulnerable abroad because of convertibility. The Bank argued that full convertibility was essential if the pound were to remain credible as a major international currency,[26] yet that meant additional pressure on the reserves which were not adequate for the task. The trade gap was widening as Britain faced renewed competition in world markets and there were serious balance of payments deficits in 1955, 1960 and 1964 – re-opening a problem that had emerged in the 1930s, only to be temporarily allayed by the distortions of the world economy in the 1940s. By the 1950s invisible earnings were even less able to play their balancing role than in the Depression, because Britain had lost half its overseas assets in the war and the growth of rivals in world financial, insurance and shipping markets had eroded other sources of income. Invisibles had paid for 40 per cent of British imports in 1913, a third in the mid-1930s and only 5 per cent by the 1960s.[27] Moreover, to exert leverage over the sterling area, the Bank had been unwilling to run down the £3 billion that existed in sterling balances. Yet the existence of these debts, largely convertible from 1955, was a source of chronic instability, since the money could be moved around in any crisis – as happened during the Suez operation in 1956.

Thus, in the late 1950s sterling was being maintained as a major reserve and trading currency, both for the sterling area and the new international economy, at cost to the domestic economy and without the necessary reserves. The problem would have been eased had the City not identified its financial position with the stability of the exchange rate, but the latter had become a symbol of national power rather than just 'a price in a market for currencies'.[28] For much of the late 1950s and 1960s, devaluation was the lurking nightmare. When it came close in the Suez crisis, the Chancellor predicted that it could mean that 'sterling might cease to be an international currency . . . which would lead almost inevitably to the dissolution of the sterling area' and thus constitute 'a major blow to the prestige of the United Kingdom and a major victory for the Soviet Union'.[29]

These changing industrial and financial realities became apparent gradually during the late 1950s and 1960s, but the Suez disaster was an early and shocking intimation. It provided a stimulus for the major shifts in British power and policy that occurred under Harold Macmillan, who succeeded the ailing Eden in January 1957. These began to transform Britain's relationships within its three circles of power – the Atlantic alliance, Europe and the Commonwealth.

DEFENCE AND TRANSATLANTIC INTERDEPENDENCE

The pressure of defence spending on the economy had been an issue since 1945. Attlee's attempts in 1945–7 to achieve radical cuts in spending and commitments had been frustrated by the deepening Cold War. Rearmament during the Korean War cut the export drive, aggravated the balance of payments problem and left Britain with a heavier defence burden than its major economic rivals.[30] In 1955 Germany was spending 4.1 per cent of national income on defence, Japan 1.8 per cent and Britain 8.2 per cent.[31] The Treasury repeatedly called for cuts on the grounds that defence spending aggravated the payments deficit and weakened foreign confidence, both of which increased the pressure on the reserves. On 23 March 1956 Macmillan, then Chancellor, told Eden: 'it is defence expenditure which has broken our backs....The only way I can see by which we could restore our economy is by really getting down to the defence problem'.[32]

The Services were naturally resistant to cuts and fought a highly successful rearguard action after the Korean War. Their major advantage was the lack of a unified defence policymaking structure. The Ministry of Defence, created in 1946, had little effective power. The Chiefs of Staff retained independent access to the Cabinet, separate service ministers represented their interests and the Minister of Defence was in no sense 'their mouthpiece'.[33] Defence budgets were bargained out by the three services separately, backed by powerful RAF and Navy lobbies in Parliament and the arms industry,[34] while the Army clung tenaciously to conscription which provided about half its manpower. National service, increasingly unpopular, was becoming a political liability for the Tories, but the military's resistance frustrated Eden's attempt in 1955 to cut it from two years to eighteen months. The Ministry of Defence claimed that British defence commitments could simply not be met by voluntary recruitment.[35]

Buttressing service politicking was the strategic doctrine of the time. Although British defence policy now centred on the V-bomber nuclear deterrent, strategists had not completely abandoned a 'global war' scenario modelled on 1939–45. In particular, the Navy advanced the concept of 'broken-backed' warfare, claiming that the initial nuclear exchange would not mean the end of civilisation and that the crippled belligerents would then engage in a protracted struggle in which control of the sealanes would again be vital for Britain.[36] On these grounds the Navy justified retaining a large 'reserve fleet', the RAF insisted on fighter defence and the army argued for overseas garrisons supplied by conscription.

Suez provided both justification and opportunity to cut through this impasse. The new Chancellor, Peter Thorneycroft, insisted in January 1957 that 'the most urgent need was to achieve . . . such measures of budget retrenchment as would safeguard the parity of sterling', with some £200 million to come from the £1.6 billion defence budget.[37] To effect the cuts Macmillan appointed a new Minister of Defence, Duncan Sandys – a ruthless political infighter who was given enhanced powers over the individual services. Moreover, the military were deliberately excluded from the essential decisions which were taken by politicians and civil servants in isolation, to reduce service obstruction. The Sandys White Paper of April 1957 announced major changes in Britain's defence posture. Conscription was to be phased out from 1960, reducing the armed forces from 690,000 to 375,000 by the end of 1962. British troops in Germany would be cut from 77,000 to 64,000 in the next year and the RAF component there halved. The White Paper was presented, with some justification, as 'the biggest change in military policy ever made in normal times'.[38]

The primary justification was economic. Defence was consuming 10 per cent of GNP, one-seventh of the population was in the services or supporting them, and one-eighth of the output of metal-producing industries, vital for exports, was devoted to defence. In language reminiscent of the 1930s and indicative that, after two decades, a measure of Treasury control was being re-established, the White Paper insisted that, without a strong economy, 'military power cannot in the long run be supported'.[39] But what made the economic rationale persuasive was that, for the first time, the politicians had exploited the full implications of the new theory of nuclear deterrence.[40] This was used to justify the elimination of two fighter programmes, the Navy's reserve fleet and several overseas garrisons – all on the grounds that another 1939–45 global war was implausible in the nuclear age. As Macmillan himself had observed in a trenchant critique of defence policy in November 1956, 'we cannot hope to emerge from a global war except in ruins'.[41] In future, the central defence tasks would be nuclear deterrence and the ability to fight limited wars against insurgents in the Third World – hence the new emphasis on a 'Central Reserve' with 'the means of rapid mobility'.[42]

In discussing nuclear deterrence, the White Paper also made explicit Britain's reliance on the USA – 'the free world is to-day mainly dependent for its protection upon the nuclear capacity of the United States'.[43] The British nuclear weapons programme had originated in the mid-1940s at a time when the wartime Anglo–American nuclear alliance had collapsed and the USA remained reluctant to undertake European commitments. Its continuance once NATO was established reflected both military and political considerations – the need to respond immediately against targets of specific interest to the UK and the conviction that the possession of nuclear weapons gave Britain international status and also special influence in Washington. Moreover, the case for independence remained strong as long as US nuclear ostracism of Britain continued. Macmillan's goal as premier was to create a true transatlantic nuclear alliance.[44] Like Churchill, Macmillan's feelings were affected by the fact that he was half-American by birth. Yet his concept of 'interdependence' was not mere nostalgia, but, in his mind, a response to the new realities of the nuclear age. He believed ardently 'that the old concept of national self-sufficiency is out of date and that the countries of the free world can maintain their security only by combining their resources and sharing their tasks'.[45]

A personal meeting with Eisenhower, a wartime colleague from North African days, was an early priority. This took place in March 1957 and helped to dispel post-Suez bitterness. More substantially, secret agreements expanded intelligence collaboration and began the process of joint targeting – an area of vital British interest.[46] It was also agreed to base up to 60 Thor medium-range ballistic missiles in Britain. This was significant because the V-bomber force was already obsolescent as the missile age dawned and Britain had been slow to respond. The RAF had concentrated on a supersonic bomber, the Avro 730, which Sandys eventually axed in his White Paper, and Britain's own medium-range missile, Blue Streak, would not come into service until 1962–5. Thor would therefore give Britain a missile capacity in the interim.

In October 1957 more momentous agreements were reached in Washington after Russia had launched Sputnik, the first artificial earth satellite. This demonstrated that the USSR had developed a missile of intercontinental range before the USA. Consequently, the Americans were anxious for real allies in the arms race. Eisenhower, long a critic of the McMahon Act of 1946 which had cut Britain out of nuclear collaboration, promised Macmillan that he would press Congress to restore contacts. US legislation in 1958 and 1959 opened up a new flow of information, equipment and materials between the two governments. No other American ally was given similar treatment.

The British did contribute to American programmes, particularly in supplying plutonium, but overall the nuclear special relationship was very one-sided. Its effect was 'to increase British dependence upon the United States without markedly increasing British influence in Washington'.[47] This became more apparent in 1960. In February the Cabinet Defence Committee, on the unusually unanimous advice of the Chiefs of Staff, agreed in principle to abandon Blue Streak. Cost was a major factor: £65 million had already been spent and it was predicted that another £500-600 million would be required. Furthermore, Blue Streak was a liquid-fuelled missile, requiring fifteen minutes to prepare, and therefore hardly ideal for rapid response now that Russia and America were developing solid-fuelled missiles.[48] However, a final decision was not made until Macmillan visited Washington in March 1960. There he secured agreement that Britain could purchase the Skybolt missile, now being developed for the USAF. Skybolt was an air-to-ground missile which would prolong the life of the RAF's V-bombers. The alternative, America's submarine-launched Polaris missile, was not popular with the Royal Navy, whose main concern was to maintain its 'blue-water' role through aircraft carriers. But Macmillan's account states firmly that 'it was certain . . . that we could obtain Polaris, although at heavy cost, in some form or another when we might need it'.[49]

With Skybolt soon available and Polaris a future option, the Cabinet confirmed the decision to abandon Blue Streak. In return Macmillan offered the Americans a base at Holy Loch on the Clyde for their own Polaris fleet. By the spring of 1960, therefore, Britain had become completely dependent on the USA for its strategic nuclear weaponry. Yet, at the same time, the concept of an 'independent' nuclear deterrent was becoming a shibboleth for many Tories, largely as a status symbol in reaction to the loss of national power. In 1960 the Government employed a great deal of casuistry to represent Skybolt as 'independent', on the grounds that, although produced in America, it would be under British control. In the Cuba and Skybolt crises of late 1962 it became politically vital for Macmillan to maintain that interdependence did not mean dependence.

After the close accord with 'Ike', his wartime partner, Macmillan had feared for relations with Eisenhower's successor, John F. Kennedy – over twenty years his junior – but he soon developed a witty and avuncular rapport with the new President. According to White House aide Arthur Schlesinger this became 'Kennedy's closest relationship with a foreign leader'. Macmillan's counsel after Kennedy's trying meeting with Khrushchev in Vienna in June 1961 was particularly welcome and the appointment of an old Kennedy friend, David Ormsby Gore, as Ambassador to Washington, gave the British unique access into the Kennedy circle.[50]

These special personal relations undoubtedly played their part in the Cuban missile crisis of October 1962, when Kennedy imposed a block-ade of the island after learning that Soviet missiles were being erected there.[51] The two leaders spoke frequently over the 'phone during the crisis and Ormsby Gore persuaded Kennedy to take certain significant decisions, notably to restrict the area of the blockade and to publish photographic intelligence to convince British opinion of the existence of the missiles. But although valuable as a sounding-board, Britain was as impotent as the rest of humanity in this Soviet–American confronta-tion. As Russian vessels carrying more missiles steamed towards the blockade zone, the world seemed on the brink of nuclear war. Only Khrushchev's decision to back down and dismantle the missiles, in return for a secret deal to remove US missiles from Turkey, ended matters peacefully. The crisis dramatised as nothing else, even Suez, the international dominance of the superpowers. It mocked the claims of successive British leaders that they were influential interlocutors in the Cold War. Despite repeated efforts, Britain still had no real in-fluence over American use of nuclear weapons, yet US bases in Britain would have been among the first targets of a Soviet nuclear strike. As Labour leftwinger Richard Crossman observed, Cuba 'exploded' the 'myth' that British nuclear weapons 'make sure that the Americans will listen to us more than any other ally'.[52]

Indeed, within weeks the very existence of that British nuclear deterrent was placed in doubt. On 7 November 1962 Kennedy ac-cepted Pentagon advice and agreed to cancel Skybolt on grounds of cost overruns and poor test performance. Some State Department ad-visers wanted to use the opportunity to eliminate Britain as a nuclear power. But, according to the crisis post-mortem by White House in-sider Richard Neustadt, the President 'had never been disposed to withhold an agreement on POLARIS if there were no other way to meet the British problem'.[53] In 1960 Skybolt had been part of a deal over Holy Loch, and Macmillan probably had secured some lien over Polaris at the same time. However, the issue was insensitively handled by the Kennedy Administration, for whom Skybolt was just one wea-pon in America's varied missile arsenal rather than, as in Britain's case, the country's sole remaining claim to be a nuclear power. News of the cancellation had leaked out in Britain by December, before any discussions had been held about an alternative, and a diplomatic problem became a domestic political crisis.

In the post-Cuba mood of shock and impotence in Britain, the so-called 'independent nuclear deterrent had become a symbol of Britain's greatness which the Conservative backbenches refused to do without'.[54] Tory MPs were angry and shocked and the Prime Minister went to the Anglo–American summit at Nassau in the Bahamas in mid-December 1962 afraid that his political future lay in the balance. Henry Brandon, the veteran Washington correspondent, found an atmosphere of 'resentment and suspicion of American intentions such as I have never experienced' in covering two decades of Anglo–American conferences.[55] Kennedy proposed various alternatives to Skybolt, but Macmillan insisted that the only acceptable arrangement was for Britain to be offered Polaris missiles of its own. Eventually convinced that this was 'a political necessity' for Macmillan, Kennedy ignored State Department pressure and gave his agreement.[56]

The Polaris deal, confirmed in April 1963, was at first sight a tribute to the special relationship. Uniquely among America's allies, Britain was allowed to buy the latest submarine-launched missiles on generous terms – cost price, plus only a 5 per cent contribution to the development costs of the programme. Although the British missile force would be normally committed to NATO, the Government could act independently whenever it 'may decide that supreme national interests are at stake'.[57] Thus, Macmillan still claimed proudly that 'interdependence and independence were two sides of a coin'.[58]

Yet, on closer inspection, the agreement underlined Britain's dependence – obliged to take whatever the USA offered, first Skybolt and then Polaris, even though this meant grinding shifts in defence programmes. Throughout the 1950s the Navy and Army had been squeezed to sustain the V-bomber force; then, with the lurch from Skybolt to Polaris, the prime strategic role was transferred from the RAF to the Navy, whose abiding passion remained aircraft carriers and not the generally-despised submarines. Moreover, the crisis atmosphere in December 1962 precluded a proper Cabinet debate about the merits of Britain remaining a nuclear power. Several Cabinet ministers, including Butler, Macleod, Maudling and Heath, were unhappy, while Thorneycroft and Amery had been exploring the possibilities of an 'entente nucléaire' with France.[59] But these options were not properly evaluated. With the Government's survival apparently at stake, politics made policy.

The Polaris deal had far-reaching consequences. It locked Britain into a transatlantic nuclear dependence that has endured to the present day. Moreover, it occurred at precisely the same time as France was embarking on its own genuinely independent nuclear deterrent, manufactured as well as controlled by the French. Their success shows that the lesson drawn by the Cabinet from the failure of Britain's Blue Streak, namely that 'in the age of missiles no middle power would be able to create and maintain an "independent deterrent" of its own', was erroneous.[60] It was not the cost of advanced technology *per se* that defeated the project. More important was the lack of coordination in British defence planning which meant that there were too many competing programmes each with insufficient resources. Furthermore, Britain was a victim of its earlier technological success – not far enough behind the USA to learn from American mistakes and thus, like France, to identify easily the 'winning' systems – solid-fuel and submarine-launched. Above all, the search for an independent deterrent might have continued, but for the availability of the American option. France enjoyed no such special relationship. Indeed Charles de Gaulle, French president from 1958, believed that the whole NATO connection had become a device for unwarranted American domination of Europe.[61]

Thus, Macmillan was trying to transcend old-style nationalism at precisely the time when it was enjoying a successful resurgence in France under de Gaulle. Equally problematic, Macmillan's alternative to nationalism – *transatlantic* interdependence – was being elaborated just as the *Europeanist* alternative to national sovereignty was also taking shape with the rapid development of the EEC. By the time the British woke up to what was happening, a new European circle had been formed without Britain – an uneasy blend of Monnet's supranationalism and de Gaulle's nationalism, with which Macmillan's concept of transatlantic inter-dependence proved impossible to reconcile.

OUTSIDE EUROPE'S MAGIC CIRCLE

When the British decided to pull out of the Brussels talks on European integration in November 1955 they did their best to draw the Germans with them and to mobilise US support. The idea, endorsed even in the FO, was to 'deter the Six from their course – arguably one step away from "sabotage"'.[62] Although that obstructive attitude was abandoned by February 1956, it left lasting bitterness among the Six, whose cohesion the British consistently underestimated. In May 1956 the Six agreed to use the Brussels talks as the basis for formal negotiations to create a common market. The major difficulties were then caused by France, who insisted on a longer transitional period and on including its overseas territories within the internal tariff. These demands were eventually conceded because French membership was crucial to the project and French ministers persuaded their colleagues that only in this way could another EDC-style political crisis be avoided in France. In March 1957 the treaty of Rome was signed and on 1 January 1958 the European Economic Community (EEC) came into existence.

After abandoning its overt blocking policy early in 1956, Whitehall tried to create a counter-balance to the emerging EEC.[63] The leading actors were Macmillan, first as Chancellor and then as premier, and Peter Thorneycroft, Eden's President of the Board of Trade and then Chancellor under Macmillan until January 1958. By late July 1956 they had secured interdepartmental agreement for 'Plan G' – a European free trade area in *industrial* goods, comprising the Six, the UK and any other member of the OEEC that wished to join. Free trade among members rather than a common external tariff would preserve all Commonwealth preferences. The concentration on industry further protected Commonwealth agricultural interests and placated the very powerful farm lobby within the Tory party. The Cabinet agreed to the plan in October 1956 and formal negotiations began early in 1957.

Signature of the treaty of Rome gave the talks real urgency, as far as Britain was concerned. 'What we must at all costs avoid,' Macmillan wrote in April, 'is the Common Market coming into being and the Free Trade Area never following'.[64] If that happened, Thorneycroft told the Cabinet on 2 May, 'we should be liable to suffer severe damage' to British exports, from the discriminatory tariffs imposed by the Six and their 'intensified competition' in markets overseas. The Cabinet also noted real political dangers because the EEC would constitute 'a European "third force"', capable of exerting considerable leverage internationally. 'Our special relationship with the United States would be endangered if the United States believed that our influence was less than that of the European Community'.[65] On both economic and political grounds, therefore, some form of British association with the Community was deemed essential.

Yet these were essentially traditional arguments, adopted before towards the ECSC and EDC – association not membership, on terms designed primarily to safeguard relations with America and the Commonwealth – and advanced for the negative reason that Britain could not afford to stay out. Moreover, as one of the principal British negotiators, Sir Frank Figgures of the Treasury later admitted, 'throughout this period we consistently exaggerated our bargaining position'.[66] Macmillan even talked of threatening 'our European friends that if Little Europe is formed without a parallel development of FTA we shall have to reconsider the whole of our political and economic attitude towards Europe....I doubt if we could remain in NATO....We should take our troops out of Europe'.[67] Such bluster was vain in the face of Franco-German solidarity. The firm British stance on excluding foodstuffs and Commonwealth preferences soon had to be modified and by mid-1958 the British were negotiating piecemeal, sector by sector. They also placed too much faith in German influence over the French, failing to see that the strong free-trade sentiments of German business, championed by Economics Minister Ludwig Erhard, were more than offset in the last analysis by the anxiety of Konrad Adenauer, the German Chancellor, for a new entente with France. In mid-November 1958 the French information minister announced that 'it was not possible to form a free trade area as had been wished by the British'.[68] Although this effective French veto outraged the British press, it simply made explicit the deadlock already acknowledged by the Cabinet.[69]

To some extent the negotiations failed because of divergent commercial interests. Britain's trade was still global – 25 per cent of British exports enjoyed Commonwealth preferences, about the same proportion as was sold to the Six.[70] But the root problem was that the Government would not accept the degree of economic harmonisation that the Six, particularly France, required. 'Had the British at any time been willing to accept a customs union it seems clear enough that they would have had little difficulty, at this period, in negotiating the kind of sweeping exceptions for agriculture and the Commonwealth that, later, it became impossible for them to do'.[71] The French, after all, had done precisely that for their own agriculture and overseas territories within the Treaty of Rome. Thus, the real issue was, again, national sovereignty – or, more exactly, given the trend of Macmillan's defence policy, British unwillingness to erode national sovereignty through *European* rather than *transatlantic* interdependence.

After the French veto, the Government slid, rather uncertainly, into negotiations about an industrial free trade grouping with other European states – Denmark, Norway, Sweden, Austria and Switzerland – who were unhappy about the EEC because of the threat to either their low tariffs or neutrality. These six, together with Portugal, signed an agreement in Stockholm in November 1959 to create the European Free Trade Area (EFTA) by July 1960. The merits of this move were dubious for Britain. Sweden, Switzerland and Denmark all won significant commercial concessions in the British market, and the political intent was primarily defensive – to have something to match the Six's economic bloc. The idea that in some way the creation of EFTA would make it easier to 'build bridges' with the Six was only hazily thought out, as Macmillan himself admitted.[72] In fact, the commitments to EFTA added to Britain's problems when it did seek membership of the Community. This was a further indication that even in 1959 the Macmillan government continued to rule out the idea of joining the EEC.[73]

The creation of EFTA left Europe, in the wisecrack of the times, 'at Sixes and Sevens'. But during 1960 the British attitude shifted as it became clear that the EEC had come into existence and, moreover, was accelerating its progress to economic and political union. By January 1961 internal tariffs had been cut by 40 per cent and the Six were beginning the process of harmonising their tariffs against the rest of the world. Moreover, de Gaulle's ambitious plans for an intergovernmental confederation, with a council of heads of government, a permanent secretariat and a nominated assembly – though unpopular with the supranationalists – was engendering a lively debate. Since 1950 British policymakers had acknowledged that, if an effective European grouping were formed, Britain could not afford to remain outside it, but they assumed that the continentals were not capable of doing so alone. By 1960 their bluff had been called on the economic and political fronts and Macmillan began a slow but profound foreign-policy revolution.

In the spring of 1960, Macmillan asked Whitehall departments to assess in detail the costs of possible British adherence to the Treaty of Rome. But when the Cabinet discussed the issue in July, the divisions were so profound that only a step-by-step approach was possible. That summer Macmillan reshuffled his ministers, putting pro-Europeans like Christopher Soames and Duncan Sandys into sensitive positions at Agriculture and Commonwealth Relations and placing the former Chief Whip, Edward Heath, in charge of European affairs. Heath was made Lord Privy Seal and a Foreign Office Minister – an important contrast with 1957–8 when the FTA talks were handled by Reginald Maudling from outside the FO. Heath's soundings in the autumn satisfied the Cabinet that the Six would not accept 'association' with the EEC – Britain had to adhere to the Treaty of Rome – and by mid-1961 Macmillan secured grudging approval from EFTA and the Commonwealth to embark on negotiations. But because of such reservations abroad and at home, Macmillan's case, when he announced it to the Commons on 31 July 1961, was not that Britain should join the EEC but that it should find out if terms could be secured to make joining acceptable.[74] He stressed the essentially political rationale – the danger of British isolation – dismissed federalist ideas, and made clear that his conception of Europe was similar to de Gaulle's: 'a confederation, a commonwealth if hon. Members would like to call it that – what I think General de Gaulle has called *Europe des patries*'.[75]

Of all the factors influencing Macmillan's decision to apply to join the EEC, 'perhaps the controlling element' was the conviction that this was 'the shortest, and perhaps the only, way to a real Atlantic partnership'.[76] The Eisenhower Administration had made very clear both its support for the EEC and its coolness to EFTA. In 1961 Macmillan was anxious to ascertain Kennedy's position. The new Administration had its own 'grand design' for transatlantic interdependence, based firmly on British membership of the EEC to offset the new nationalism of France and the new wealth of Germany.[77] In Washington in April 1961, Macmillan was given the clear message 'that relations between the United States and the United Kingdom would be strengthened, not weakened, if the UK moved toward membership in the Six'.[78]

In September 1961 Heath and his team accordingly began talks to discover whether acceptable terms could be achieved. The British now made clear that they accepted the basic features of the treaty of Rome – a common external tariff, a common commercial policy and a common agricultural policy – a fundamental change in their position. But they sought special provisions, at least during a transitional period of perhaps twelve to fifteen years, for the Commonwealth, British agriculture and EFTA. By the summer of 1962 outline agreement had been reached on Commonwealth food imports, except for New Zealand, but that autumn the discussions on British agriculture were exceedingly difficult, with the EEC wanting an *immediate* shift to its methods of price support. The farm vote was potent in all these countries but, although the talks were difficult, it was generally expected that January 1963 would see an intense bargaining session, akin to that which established the Common Agricultural Policy a year before, when a final compromise package would emerge.

At this point de Gaulle delivered an effective veto to British entry, thereby killing the negotiations completely.[79] Although opposed to supranationalist integration, the French president saw the Community as an instrument of renewed French hegemony in Europe and had no intention of sharing its leadership with Britain, whom he regarded as an American 'Trojan horse'. In a regal press conference on 14 January 1963 he argued that Britain, with an economic and political orientation very different from that of the Six, was not yet ready to enter the EEC. He also interpreted both the Cuban missile crisis and the Nassau agreement on Polaris as indicating a dangerous British dependence on America which highlighted the need for France to have its own nuclear force. He concluded that British entry could mean 'a colossal Atlantic Community under American dependence and leadership which would soon completely swallow up the European Community'.[80]

In the last analysis it was not supranationalism but nationalism which defeated the British application – not federalism but Gaullism. Britain had moved a long way between 1960 and 1962, but it had moved too late – *after* a viable European Community had been formed with de Gaulle in the driving seat. Moreover, the shift in British policy had occurred for largely negative reasons, above all fear that a powerful EEC would replace Britain as the European pillar of the Atlantic alliance. It was more a tactical than a strategic change. Thus, Macmillan proved unable to square the circles – to strengthen Britain's links with America *and* bring his country within the EEC. Moreover, in both cases his search for interdependence had revealed Britain's growing dependence on the powerful forces embodied by superpower America and the European Community. And, as the acrimony generated by the EEC negotiations indicated, Britain's links with the Commonwealth – the other great circle of interest – were also weakening rapidly during the Macmillan premiership.

THE GLOBAL ROLE: CONTRACTION AND CONTINUANCE

The crises in India and Palestine in 1947–8 did not signal a tidal wave of decolonisation. Between 1948 and 1960 only three British colonies became independent – the Sudan (1956), the Gold Coast and Malaya (1957). In the decade after 1947 recruitment into the colonial service increased by 50 per cent.[81] The Tory governments of Churchill and Eden continued Labour's policy of cutting British losses in unmanageable situations, notably Egypt, but otherwise holding on to empire for strategic and economic reasons. Aware of the forces eroding colonial power, their intent was nevertheless to keep change within bounds, and a junior Colonial Office minister, Henry Hopkinson, gained lasting notoriety for his comment in 1954 that 'there are certain territories in the Commonwealth which, owing to their particular circumstances, can never expect to be fully independent'.[82] A special Cabinet committee on colonial policy concluded in September 1957 that only four colonies apart from Malaya were likely to obtain independence in the next ten years.[83]

In the period 1960–4, however, seventeen British colonies gained independence,[84] many of them African territories previously deemed unready for independence for several generations. The shift of policy by Macmillan's government partly reflected the broad changes in Britain's economic circumstances.[85] Currency convertibility, Europe's industrial boom and Britain's growing interest in the EEC all reordered Britain's patterns of trade and investment. The proportion of British exports going to Commonwealth countries fell from 47.7 per cent in 1950 to 40.2 per cent in 1960 and 24.4 per cent in 1970. Imports from the Commonwealth likewise declined from 41.9 per cent of Britain's total in 1950, to 34.6 per cent in 1960 and 25.9 per cent in 1970. And whereas 60 per cent of British foreign investment went to the sterling area in 1960, the figure was only 38 per cent in 1970.[86] Macmillan was sensitive to these economic realities. As Chancellor under Eden he had tried to cut colonial development aid because it was unproductive for Britain[87] and within weeks of becoming Prime Minister in January 1957 he asked the Cabinet's Colonial Policy Committee for 'something like a profit and loss account for each of our Colonial possessions', in order to calculate 'the balance of advantage . . . of losing or keeping each particular territory'.[88]

Nevertheless, decolonisation 'was not in any direct sense the outcome of economic considerations'. The official report judged that overall 'the economic considerations were fairly evenly matched',[89] with expenditure savings here being offset by reduced commercial or strategic advantages there. Thus, economic benefit was no longer a positive reason for maintaining formal control, as in the heyday of the sterling area in the decade after the War, but it did not dictate decolonisation. Moreover, the really pronounced shift in Britain's commercial patterns occurred in the 1960s, after the crucial decisions on empire had been taken.

More potent than economics was the changing international setting.[90] Here again de Gaulle upset British calculations. His 1958 offer of independence to French Africa resulted in sixteen new African states entering the UN in 1960, almost all of them still closely tied to

France. It also stimulated the precipitate Belgian decision to pull out of the Congo in mid-1960. This left Britain, erstwhile pioneer of devolution, in the embarrassing position of seeming more illiberal than the Continentals. Moreover, it created a highly unstable climate in the rest of Africa, encouraging nationalist pressure in the remaining colonial enclaves and stimulating an alarming cycle of violence. This was not only costly to contain but it also was becoming increasingly vexatious internationally as charges of 'imperialism' and 'racism' became weapons in the Cold War.[91]

Macmillan grasped the colonial nettle not in 1957, after Suez, but following the Tory election victory in October 1959. Earlier that year the 'massacres' at the Hola detention camp in Kenya and the Devlin report on 'police state' conditions in Nyasaland had both been matters of acute sensitivity for Macmillan. He appointed the inexperienced but energetic Iain Macleod as Colonial Secretary, with a brief to 'get a move on', and his own convictions about the strength of colonial nationalism were deepened by his long tour of Africa early the following year. The Sharpeville massacre in March 1960 focused international attention on South African apartheid, but it was the bloody anarchy in the Congo from 1960 to 1962 which was the most alarming development, because the territory bordered on British east and central Africa and the civil war drew in the Superpowers and the UN. In August 1960 Macmillan feared that the Congo might play the role of Serbia in 1914 or Korea in 1950 as catalyst for a great-power conflict.[92] Macleod later claimed that 'there had been a deliberate speeding up of the movement towards independence' because 'any other policy would have led to terrible bloodshed in Africa'.[93]

African decolonisation was a fraught political issue for a Tory premier and on numerous occasions in 1959–61 he feared irreconcilable Cabinet splits. But, unlike the French over Algeria, a major political crisis was averted. The hold of empire over the Tory party had always been complex.[94] The idea of empire as an economic bloc, powerful in the 1930s and 1940s, was by now on the wane, despite lingering support for Commonwealth preferences which complicated the EEC negotiations. The battle over the empire as a source of prestige had been fought and lost over Suez between 1954 and 1956. What was left was emotional and economic ties with the 'empire of kith and kin' in east and central Africa. From 1959 Macmillan and Macleod gradually abandoned the earlier efforts to maintain white leadership through regional federations and acquiesced in the demands for black majority rule and early independence. It was these policies which caused the greatest bitterness among not only the right-wing but also moderate

Tory MPs. But party unity held, the row did not engulf the Tory rank and file and, after the resignation of Lord Salisbury in 1957 over Cyprus, there was no alternative leader of stature. Tory faith in the Commonwealth was severely damaged by its exclusion of South Africa over apartheid in 1961, despite Macmillan's mediatory efforts. That showed the Commonwealth's growing independence of British wishes.

The end of empire did not bring down a government, as in France in 1958. Nevertheless, the problem of Rhodesia proved more intractable than any French colonial crisis and its ultimate resolution took two decades.[95] By 1959 the strains within the Central African Federation (CAF) of Northern and Southern Rhodesia and Nyasaland were reaching breaking point. The Federation was dominated by Southern Rhodesia, where there was 1 white to 13 blacks, compared with ratios of 1:31 in Northern Rhodesia and 1:328 in Nyasaland.[96] The two latter territories had vigorous nationalist movements, with charismatic leaders (Kenneth Kaunda and Hastings Banda respectively), and opposition to the Federation and its leader Roy Welensky was a major unifying force. Macleod and, more slowly, the Cabinet gave way to this from 1959. A black majority legislature was appointed for Nyasaland. But a similar move in copper-rich Northern Rhodesia was more controversial and the Cabinet baulked at this in June 1961, pressed hard by Welensky and some ninety Tory MPs. Macleod, too impetuous for Macmillan and much of the Cabinet, was moved from the Colonial Office. But by March 1962, horrified at the mounting racial violence in the Congo and South Africa, the Cabinet had accepted majority rule in Northern Rhodesia and, once elected, the new black governments in both Nyasaland and Northern Rhodesia demanded secession from the Federation and full independence. This duly followed in 1964. In Southern Rhodesia, however, the whites refused to concede black majority rule and in December 1962 the Rhodesia Front won power on a platform of independence for a white-dominated Rhodesia. Denied this by London, their premier, Ian Smith eventually made a unilateral declaration of independence in November 1965.

The collapse of the Federation might suggest a British Government capitulating before the overwhelming forces of black nationalism. In his famous 'wind of change' speech in Cape Town in February 1960, Macmillan portrayed the growth of 'African national consciousness' as 'a political fact', reflecting the inevitable spread of European nationalist ideas to the wider world.[97] Yet, outside the CAF, African 'nationalism' was often weak and in many places the British withdrawal owed as much to changing judgements about economic and strategic utility.

This was true in both Tanganyika and Uganda in 1961–2. Moreover, the British expected, as elsewhere, that formal empire would be replaced by informal influence, sealed by economic ties and defence treaties. Here the Gold Coast seemed a potential precedent. Its leader, Kwame Nkrumah, had been a model collaborator in the years prior to Ghanaian independence and it was hoped that his example might be emulated elsewhere. Nkrumah's 1960s swing to a virulent anti-Western line came as a painful shock.[98]

All this highlights the fact that the British did not regard African decolonisation as the abrogation of their world role. In fact, the retreat from Africa coincided with a new effort to maintain Britain's influence 'east of Suez'.[99] Aden had become a major British base after the loss of the Canal Zone, and the number of British servicemen stationed there quadrupled between 1957 and 1959. But the colony was threatened by Arab nationalism within and by growing pressure on the neighbouring states from the radical, Nasser-backed Yemeni government. The British created a new Federation of South Arabia in 1963 and over the next year they put down a violent insurrection. In Southeast Asia, too, the British remained deeply committed. Malaya was given independence in 1957, but Britain agreed to assist with internal and external security in return for Malaya remaining within the sterling area and keeping its reserves in London. In Singapore, also independent in 1957, Britain retained control of defence and foreign policy. By 1961, fearful at growing communist influence in Southeast Asia, the British encouraged the demands in Singapore for a larger federation. Malaya was won over to the idea by the inclusion of the British territories in Borneo (where no vigorous nationalist movement yet existed) and by the British promise to continue the defence commitments made in 1957. But Sukarno in Indonesia had designs of his own on Borneo. When the new Malaysian federation was formed in September 1963, he severed diplomatic relations and Britain became engaged in a bloody war of counter-insurgency to preserve Malaysia.

In December 1962 the former US Secretary of State, Dean Acheson, observed that 'Great Britain has lost an Empire and has not yet found a role'.[100] The outcry among Tories, led by Macmillan himself, indicated that Acheson had struck a raw nerve. Yet the 'east of Suez' doctrine shows that even with Britain ready to make considerable sacrifices to enter the EEC, the concept of a global role had not been abandoned. That was partly because the economic realities were still complex. Half Britain's oil came down the Persian Gulf from Kuwait, independent from 1961 but still linked to Britain by a defence treaty.[101] Twenty-five per cent of British exports still went to countries bordering the Indian Ocean and Western Pacific.[102] Given the region's political instability, it was not unreasonable to believe that a British presence of sorts was still essential.

Moreover, geopolitics were reinforced by bureaucratic politics. The Royal Navy had also lost an empire and also sought a role. With global war judged unlikely and the strategic deterrent going to the RAF, the exponents of the 'blue water' navy were struggling in the mid-1950s to justify the existence of the aircraft carrier.[103] In the crucial months before the Sandys White Paper they were fortunate that the First Sea Lord was Mountbatten, a canny and well-connected Whitehall infighter, who successfully established the doctrine that the carrier had a special role as 'a mobile air station',[104] ideal for policing and counter-insurgency around the Indian Ocean.[105] With Europe increasingly stable and Asia in turmoil, all three services in fact began to see advantages for themselves east of Suez. The Chiefs of Staff's 1962 planning study envisaged this as Britain's 'major role in the next decade'.[106]

THE CENTRE CANNOT HOLD, 1964–70

In the election of October 1964 Harold Wilson and the Labour party won a narrow majority, bringing to an end thirteen years of Conservative government. At forty-eight, Wilson was the youngest prime minister of the century to date and he cultivated a Kennedyesque manner – mocking his Tory rival as 'the fourteenth Earl of Home' and calling for a technological revolution to transform Britain's flagging economy. Some of Wilson's initiatives were striking – a new Ministry of Technology, a 'National Plan' for economic growth and a Department of Economic Affairs (DEA) intended to wrest control of 'the real economy' from the financial axis of the Treasury and the Bank. But the economic revolution failed to materialise. Part of the problem was institutional – these were all half-baked proposals, poorly thought-out, and the DEA was quickly and adroitly neutralised by the Treasury. But, more fundamentally, Wilson sacrificed the domestic economy on the altar of his foreign policy. His government saw a last, desperate effort to maintain Britain's global role, or at least the status symbols of that role – the parity of sterling and the commitment East of Suez.[107]

In the 1950s Wilson had been associated with the left-wing critique of British foreign policy, resigning over the rearmament budget of

1951 and demanding an end to Britain's nuclear deterrent. As party leader, however, he stood firmly in the Bevinite tradition. 'We are a world power, and a world influence, or we are nothing', he proclaimed in his first major foreign-policy speech as premier[108] and the following month he told the Commons that 'whatever we may do in the field of cost effectiveness . . . we cannot afford to relinquish our world role – our role which for shorthand purposes is sometimes called our "East of Suez" role'.[109] Equally sacred was the parity of the pound. Inheriting a balance of payments deficit of nearly £800 million in October 1964, the three leading Labour politicians – Wilson, the Chancellor, James Callaghan and the head of DEA, George Brown – considered and immediately rejected the option of devaluation. Thereafter the idea was taboo. It became known among Wilson's entourage as 'the dreaded word'[110] and Wilson proclaimed repeatedly the Government's 'unalterable determination to maintain the value of the pound'.[111]

The new government was equally conservative about the nuclear deterrent. Its election manifesto had proposed 're-negotiation of the Nassau agreement' but Wilson was backing away from anything substantial well before the election. Once he assumed power only one of the projected five Polaris submarines was axed.[112] Officially it was claimed that the project was too far advanced for significant savings, but Whitehall estimates put the current cost at £40 million out of a total £300 million. Indeed it appears that the fifth submarine had no clear military requirement and had been included by the MOD to give Labour 'something visible to cut'.[113] In Washington in December 1964 Wilson resisted a new American attempt to erode the operational independence of the Polaris fleet by making it part of a NATO nuclear force.

For Wilson, the American connection was as axiomatic as it was for Macmillan. In Washington in December 1964 he suggested that the Tory idea of special relationship was redolent of 'past grandeur', but his own claim that 'we regard our relationship with you not as a *special* relationship but as a *close* relationship, governed by the only things that matter, unity of purpose and unity in our objectives'[114] seemed only a casuistic difference. In fact, American documents show that under Wilson Britain's attempt to play a residual world role made it even more dependent on the USA.[115] The Johnson Administration was anxious to maintain the value of sterling as a first line of defence for the dollar. It also wanted Britain to maintain its military commitments, particularly east of Suez. During the summer of 1965 Wilson and Callaghan made a secret deal with the Americans to avoid devaluation and remain east of Suez in return for US financial support for sterling. Washington also sought British military aid in the Vietnam war but, on this, Wilson, aware of the feelings of the Labour left, was immovable.

Why was Wilson so committed to policies that made him dependent on the USA for their implementation? One reason was political. Labour came to power in 1964 with a majority of only five. Wilson had to nurse both government and party along until it seemed opportune to go to the country and seek a clear-cut victory. He felt exceedingly vulnerable to Tory gibes that Labour, the 'party of devaluation' in 1949, could not be trusted to maintain Britain's position in the world. He told one critic of his sterling policy, 'devaluation would sweep us away. We should have to go to the country defeated'.[116] Strategic considerations were also important. 1964–5 was a volatile time in the politics of the Indian Ocean, with Indonesia's insurgency against Britain's ally, the Malaysian federation, spreading from Borneo to Malaya itself. At the peak of the crisis Britain committed 68,000 servicemen and a third of the entire surface fleet to honour its defence treaty with Malaysia – concluded in part to persuade the new federation to keep its foreign earnings in sterling.[117] Moreover, China, now veering into the revolutionary turmoil of the Cultural Revolution, tested its own atomic bomb in October 1964 and Indonesia announced its intention to do so the following July – doubly alarming since the country had the third-largest communist party in the world and this nearly seized power in October 1965. In these circumstances Wilson's claim that 'our frontiers are in the Himalayas' was not so preposterous as it now sounds, when one bears in mind his addendum that the future of Asia depended on the outcome of a struggle between 'the democratic way' exemplified by India and other Commonwealth countries and the communist way 'exemplified by a determined and extrovert China'.[118] And at root, Wilson's policies reflected personal preferences. He believed deeply in the American alliance and the Commonwealth connection, in the commitments east of Suez and in the reserve status of sterling. As with Eden in 1956, Washington may have pulled the rope tight but it was Wilson who put his head in the noose.

Within this self-imposed policy straitjacket on sterling and defence, there was nevertheless some room for manoeuvre. The new Defence Secretary, Denis Healey, claimed that the defence budget was like 'a runaway train'[119] and set about imposing American criteria of 'cost-effectiveness'. In this he was helped by the reforms introduced at the MOD under the aegis of Mountbatten in the last years of the Tory government – resuming the momentum of the Sandys era. These abolished the Admiralty, War Office and Air Ministry, consolidating all three bureaucracies in a unified Ministry of Defence, and began to establish for the first time effective budgetary and planning procedures.[120]

Within a few months of taking office Healey had persuaded the Cabinet to cut three major aircraft programmes – the P1154 fighter, the HS 681 jet transport and, most controversially, the advanced TSR-2 strike aircraft – in each case replacing them with American alternatives at about half the total cost. During 1965 Healey conducted a searching review of the Navy's new CVA 01 aircraft carriers, three of which were on order at a projected price of £1.4 billion.[121] The RAF made out a compelling case that almost all the carrier roles east of Suez could be fulfilled at one-fifth of the cost by land-based F-111s – the American replacement for the TSR-2. Healey's Defence Review in February 1966 cut the CVA 01. It also announced a new policy rationale – 'Britain will not undertake major operations of war except in co-operation with allies'[122] – in other words the United States.

But, as Cabinet critics such as Richard Crossman observed, the thrust of this policy was still traditional – commitments were maintained but the services' capability to honour them emasculated.[123] Even with the cuts, moreover, the balance of payments problem and the pressure on sterling continued. In July 1966 George Brown tried and failed to mobilise Cabinet support for devaluation. In retrospect, many commentators have seen this failure to devalue as a crucial error.[124] By mid-1966 Wilson was politically freer, with a majority of nearly one hundred after the March election, and the country had experienced the pain of the alternative – deflation. Devaluation coupled with a programme of industrial regeneration might have proved significant. But only five Cabinet ministers supported Brown and none was willing to push things to the point of resignation. Instead a new deflationary package was imposed, including a six-month freeze on prices and wages (partly a response to US pressure) – in direct contrast to the DEA's growth strategy. This signalled the end of the National Plan.

Thus in defence and financial policy Wilson was becoming trapped by preference and commitment into putting the status symbols of world power before his goal of economic regeneration. During 1967, however, his attitude shifted. With unemployment higher than at any time since the war, the political cost of further deflationary measures seemed unbearable, particularly with an election coming into view. The Malaysian emergency eased after a counter-coup in Indonesia broke communist power. And there was a growing consensus in the Cabinet that government spending overseas had become a crucial element in the balance of payments problem, because, with the erosion of the sterling area, this spending did not 'come back to Britain' through purchases of British goods and services.[125] In a further defence review in July 1967 Healey finally bit the bullet and announced that British forces in Singapore and Malaysia would be halved in 1970–1 and finally withdrawn 'in the middle 1970s'.[126] It seemed both desirable and possible for Britain to reduce its commitments and thus free itself from deflationary dependence on the USA and the international bankers. In July 1967 Wilson at last mentioned 'the unmentionable' to his closest advisers, but presented it as a policy choice rather than an economic inevitability: it 'must be a political issue when it comes: we devalue to defend our independence'.[127] In the sterling crisis of November 1967 the Cabinet agreed to devalue the pound by some 14 per cent, from \$2.80 to \$2.40. Callaghan, who had repeatedly pledged that its value was secure, moved from the Treasury to the Home Office, swapping posts with Roy Jenkins.

In retrospect it was a major policy failure – the totem of three years of policy, costing some £1 billion net to the reserves, finally surrendered. In November 1967, it seems that the Cabinet hoped that devaluation would eliminate the need for further deflationary measures[128], but the Treasury soon dashed that hope. After bitter debates in January 1968, the Cabinet agreed to total withdrawal from East of Suez (except Hong Kong) by the end of 1971 and the elimination of the F-111 aircraft purchases. Healey at the MOD and Brown at the FO were united against these cuts, but the appointment of Jenkins as Chancellor had finally upset the Bevinite consensus at the heart of the Cabinet.[129] Jenkins was determined that commitments should be cut as well as capabilities, preferably in time for Labour to recover control of the economy before the next election, and he drove the programme through the Cabinet. Also important was the pressure from Crossman and the Left, adamant that the sacrifice of domestic 'sacred cows', such as free medical prescriptions, should be matched by a similar 'slaughter' overseas.[130] Most significant was Wilson's own shift. His casting vote decided the fate of the F-111 and his shrewd management of Cabinet headed off the counter-attack from the FO and MOD, which was encouraged by the horrified Americans and by Britain's erstwhile allies in Singapore and the Persian Gulf. In Crossman's view Wilson was finally 'breaking through the status barrier' – psychologically as painful as going through the sound barrier – and at last abandoning the old symbols of wealth and empire.[131]

In other words, the decisions to devalue and to pull out from east of Suez were political as well as economic – reflecting changes in Cabinet balance and policy calculation, not just sheer economic exigency. It is noteworthy, for instance, that the Gulf states and Saudi Arabia repeatedly offered to fund a continued British presence but 'none of these offers was explored'.[132] Likewise, the Americans had been willing to help fund Britain's continued global role on a semi-permanent basis. In February 1967 Washington proposed a joint sterling-dollar area to protect both currencies and a twenty-five year loan to fund the sterling balances, in return for a long-term commitment to remain east of Suez. This Wilson rejected on the grounds that it would be public and therefore politically unacceptable. Moreover, it would also have made entry into the EEC politically and economically impossible[133] and this was by now an object of Wilson's foreign policy. Significantly, Jenkins, the architect of the defence cuts east of Suez, was an ardent pro-European.

Thus, the revolution in financial and defence priorities in 1967–8 reflected a more fundamental re-orientation of Labour's priorities towards Europe. In 1961–2 Labour had been divided over the EEC, with its then leader, Hugh Gaitskell, finally coming out passionately against Macmillan's terms as a total betrayal of all that Britain stood for. Joining a European political federation would mean 'the end of Britain as an independent nation . . . the end of a thousand years of history . . . the end of the Commonwealth'.[134] De Gaulle's veto saved Labour from a major debate and the issue lapsed until after the March 1966 election. By then the FO, headed after August 1966 by the keenly pro-European George Brown, was anxious to join it and Wilson now agreed that this was necessary – perhaps needing to buy Brown's continued support after the DEA debacle.[135]

His strategy, however, like Macmillan's in 1960–2, was to move circumspectly. He tried to prevent Cabinet resignations by cleverly leaving his own position obscure and by a step-by-step approach which avoided raising major issues of principle. Thus, in November 1966, he secured Cabinet agreement for a declaration of intent to join, if the terms were right, and for a personal 'probe' of continental opinion by himself and Brown. Following this tour, in April 1967, he deftly insinuated that Britain was now obliged to make a decision[136] and then took the Cabinet through five lengthy discussions and a weekend conference which simply wore down the opposition. 'We shall go into Europe on a wave of exhaustion', complained one critic.[137] Behind the scenes the debate was adroitly manipulated. Opponents such as Douglas Jay were unable to get their submissions properly discussed and the official papers were all carefully weighted towards entry.[138] (Ironically the main draftsman, wily Cabinet Secretary Sir Burke Trend, had done a similar job, but to opposite effect, as head of the Whitehall committee assessing the Messina proposals in 1955.)

Some members of the Cabinet now supported entry for economic reasons. Tony Benn, the Minister of Technology, wanted to replace 'imperial Britain' with 'industrial Britain' and saw entry as a way 'to cut Queen Victoria's umbilical cord'.[139] But no one now pretended that entry would be an economic panacea: even Jenkins admitted that 'in the first three or four years we shall lose but not gain'. The real case was political – the globalist framework (sterling area, east of Suez, special relationship) had failed, but not before the effort to maintain it had made the economy too weak to sustain what Crossman called an alternative 'socialist insular offshore island solution'.[140] The whole tenor of the official papers, as packaged by Wilson and Trend, was 'that it would be disastrous if we didn't get in'.[141] On that basis the Cabinet, without any resignations, agreed to apply and, with three-line whips on both major parties, the proposal went through the Commons in May 1967 by 488 votes to 62.

Thus Wilson's Government, even more than Macmillan's, went as suitor to Brussels not out of positive enthusiasm but because there seemed no other option. Yet Wilson's 'voyage into Europe' foundered, like Macmillan's, on the rocks of de Gaulle's intransigence. The General still viewed Britain as not truly European and issued his second veto on 27 November 1967, nine days after devaluation.

So Britain was left betwixt and between, the three-circles metaphysic no longer even a credible conceit. The special relationship had become one of growing dependence, both nuclear and, under Labour, financial as the USA propped up Britain's pretensions of global power. Wilson's attempts to take a middle course on Vietnam, pressed by the Labour Left, had gained him nothing. Neither of the superpowers took any heed of his frenetic efforts at mediation, while the failure to make even a token military commitment (as had been done over Korea in 1950) infuriated Washington. Dean Rusk, the Secretary of State, once growled at a British journalist: 'when the Russians invade Sussex, don't expect us to come and help you'.[142] At the same time, the Commonwealth and sterling area had fallen apart as effective instruments of British influence. From the remnants of empire, only Rhodesian UDI was left to plague a government that could solve it neither through half-hearted sanctions nor periodic negotiations. Particularly striking was the erosion of ties among the old white Dominions, with South African ostracism and the growing shift of Australia into the American orbit, as indicated by its readiness to send troops to Vietnam. The end of Anglocentric Robert Menzies's long tenure as Australian premier (1949–66) symbolised the passing of an era in Australian policy. Finally, Wilson's belated bid for entry into the EEC had come to nothing – highlighting, in retrospect, the error of not being present at the creation of the new Europe, to prevent it becoming a vehicle for French ambitions. As long as de Gaulle remained in power, Britain had lost its empire and its special relationship and was denied a new European role.

To cap it all the Wilson years saw the recurrence of a very old problem – Ulster.[143] Despite expectations in London in the 1920s that partition would be temporary, Northern Ireland congealed into a durable state, with the Protestant Unionists ensuring their dominance over the Catholic minority through the denial of political and civil rights, backed by a paramilitary Protestant police force. In the mid-1960s limited reforms by Terence O'Neill, the Unionist premier, only whetted the appetite of the new Catholic middle class. In 1968–9 demonstrations by their Civil Rights Association led to a series of bloody clashes with the police. But 'it was the crisis within Unionism, as much as the radicalization of Catholic politics, which created the explosion'.[144] O'Neill's concessions alienated working-class Protestants and enabled the fundamentalist demagogue, Ian Paisley, to splinter the Unionist monolith – eventually creating a separate Democratic Unionist party in 1971. At the same time the mounting Catholic discontent had also revived the Irish Republican Army (IRA), whose new Provisional Wing was dedicated to the armed struggle against the old enemy – Britain. With the Unionists unable to keep order, in August 1969 the Wilson government agreed to their request to use British troops. But the troops were soon denounced by both sides – symbols of decaying Unionist autonomy as well as targets for IRA violence. Ulster was becoming Britain's Algeria – a legacy of empire tied into the domestic polity, which constituted a significant defence commitment as well as a growing diplomatic embarrassment. It was to prove less bloody than Algeria, but much more enduring.

Late-sixties Britain, for all the enhanced social freedoms, was pervaded by a sense of 'decline' – a word that was becoming a cliché. Rebuffed by the continentals, dependent on America, shorn of empire except for headaches like Rhodesia and Ulster, with the economy in disarray – all that was left for Britain seemed to be nostalgia. In the defiant words given by novelist John Le Carré to a frustrated British diplomat: 'all power corrupts. The loss of power corrupts even more . . . . However, I would rather fail as a power than survive by impotence. I would rather be vanquished than neutral. I would rather be English than Swiss.'[145]

REFERENCES

1. Frankel 1975: 157–8
2. Rhodes James 1986; Lamb 1987; Carlton 1988
3. Shuckburgh 1986: 327, 346
4. Gorst and Lucas 1989
5. Dooley 1989: 489–92
6. CAB 134/1216, EC (56) 3rd
7. Kyle 1989: 114
8. PREM 11/1177, 31 July
9. Kunz 1989: 221
10. Rhodes James 1986: 512–16; cf. Bowie 1989: 204–5
11. CAB 128/29, CM 34 (55) 8
12. T 236/4188, f. 32
13. Horne 1988: 420–4
14. Vaisse 1989: 336
15. Darwin 1988: 229–30; cf. *CR* summer 1987: 31–3
16. Adamthwaite 1988: 455–63
17. Fry 1989: 312
18. Reynolds 1989a: 80–3
19. Barnett 1986: 123
20. Ibid., 12, 25, 38–51
21. Hancock and Gowing 1949: 542
22. Addison 1975: 163
23. Hancock and Gowing 1949: 541
24. Peden 1986: 256–9
25. Strange 1971a; Strange 1971b
26. Lamb 1987: 41–2
27. L. Williams 1971: 177
28. Scammell 1983: 120
29. CAB 128/30, CM 89 (56) 5
30. Cairncross 1985: 231
31. Chalmers 1985: 113
32. PREM 11/1326
33. M. Howard 1970: 7
34. M. Dockrill 1988: 51
35. Navias 1989
36. Grove 1987: ch. 3
37. CAB 128/31, CC 2 (57) 3
38. Cmd. 124: para. 67

39. Ibid., para. 6
40. Navias 1989: 195; Rees 1989
41. Horne 1989: 47
42. Cmd. 124: para. 35
43. Ibid., para. 15
44. Baylis 1984b: ch. 4
45. CAB 129/90, C (57) 271
46. Simpson 1986: 125–6
47. Botti 1987: 204
48. Pierre 1972: 198
49. Macmillan 1972: 252
50. Dimbleby and Reynolds 1988: 229–31
51. Nunnerley 1972: ch. 7
52. Ibid., 75
53. JFKL, NSF 322: Neustadt report, p. 92
54. *Economist*, 29 Dec. 1962: 1253
55. *Sunday Times*, 8 Dec. 1963: 30
56. Horne 1989: 439
57. Baylis 1984b: 105
58. Horne 1989: 437
59. Private source; Pierre 1972: 222–3
60. Ibid., 321
61. Harrison 1981: chs 2–4
62. J. Young 1989: 215
63. Camps 1964: chs 4–5; Lamb 1987: ch. 4; Schmidt (ed.) 1989: ch. 6
64. Macmillan 1971: 435
65. CAB 128/31, CC 37 (57) 4
66. Charlton 1983: 217
67. Schmidt (ed.) 1989: 176
68. Camps 1964: 164
69. CAB 128/32, CC 79 (58) 2, CC 80 (58) 8
70. CAB 129/92, C (58) 67
71. Camps 1964: 169
72. Macmillan 1972: 58
73. Camps 1964: 216, 230
74. Commons 645: 928–37
75. Ibid., 1491
76. Camps 1964: 336
77. Costigliola 1984
78. JFKL, NSF 170/2, Bundy memo, 7 April 1961
79. Camps 1964: 471–2, 506
80. JFKL, NSF 73
81. Austin 1982: 231
82. Goldsworthy 1990: 100
83. D. Morgan 1980: v, 100–1
84. B. Porter 1984: 335
85. R. Holland 1985: 205–7

86. Darwin 1988: 304–5
87. Goldsworthy 1990: 86
88. D. Morgan 1980: v, 96
89. Quotations from Fieldhouse 1986: 8 and D. Morgan 1980: v, 102
90. Darwin 1988: 243–4, 251–3
91. cf. Low 1988
92. Macmillan 1972: 265–6
93. Lapping 1985: 435
94. Kahler 1984: 129–60
95. Hargreaves 1988: 198–203; Darwin 1988: 269–78; Low 1988: 57–69
96. Kahler 1984: 317
97. Macmillan 1972: 156
98. R. Holland 1985: 219
99. Darwin 1988: 281–8
100. I. McDonald (ed.) 1974: 181–2
101. Grove 1987: 246
102. Darwin 1988: 359
103. Grove 1987: 197–217
104. Cmd. 124: para. 37
105. Ziegler 1986: 548–54
106. Darby 1973: 218
107. Ponting 1989; Schmidt (ed.) 1989: ch. 7
108. *The Times* 17 Nov. 1964: 6
109. Darby 1973: 284
110. M. Williams 1972: 196
111. Browning 1986: 3
112. Pierre 1972: 262–72
113. Ponting 1989: 87–8
114. H. Wilson 1971: 50
115. Ponting 1989: 48–54; Schmidt (ed.) 1989: 272–6; cf. Dobson 1990: 250–7
116. Crossman 1975: i, 71
117. Darwin 1988: 290; Grove 1987: 266
118. C. Hill 1988: 48–9
119. Bartlett 1972: 170
120. Johnson 1980: ch. 7
121. Grove 1987: 270–80
122. Cmd. 2901 ch. 2: para. 19
123. Crossman 1976: ii, 155–6
124. e.g. Brittan 1969: 219; Ponting 1989: 396–7
125. Grove 1987: 283–4
126. Cmd. 3357: 5
127. Castle 1984: 282
128. Ponting 1989: 295
129. Darwin 1988: 293
130. Crossman 1976: ii, 619
131. Ibid., ii, 635, 639

132. Gause 1985: 253
133. Callaghan 1987: 211–12; Ponting 1989: 288–9
134. P. Williams 1982: 404
135. George 1990: 37
136. Castle 1984: 244
137. Ibid., 242
138. Ponting 1989: 210–11
139. Benn 1987: 464, 496
140. Crossman 1976: ii, 335–6
141. Castle 1984: 244
142. Dimbleby and Reynolds 1988: 252
143. Harkness 1983; Boyce 1988
144. Foster 1989: 587
145. Le Carré 1969: 300

CHAPTER NINE
Europe, 1970 – 9

The first half of the 1970s saw perhaps the most profound revolution in British foreign policy in the twentieth century. In January 1973, after intense parliamentary debate, Great Britain joined the European Community. This was the achievement of Tory premier Edward Heath. But the Labour party remained deeply divided and, after its return to power in February 1974, Wilson 'renegotiated' the terms of entry and then submitted them, in June 1975, to an unprecedented national referendum. The two-thirds majority in favour gave Britain's membership of the Community a popular mandate.

From 1973 the orientation of Britain's foreign policy became inexorably more European. This trend, though rarely hitting the headlines, underlies this chapter and the next. Yet Britain was a reluctant European. Its erstwhile globalism continued to shape public attitudes and government policies. It was entering a grouping whose institutions were already formed, and the terms of entry, negotiated from a position of weakness, did not prove advantageous. Moreover, Britain joined just as the long European boom was tailing away, amid the oil crisis of 1973–4, into inflation and recession. Both Heath and Wilson had their own, very different, strategies for trying to mitigate the disadvantages of Britain's ill-timed entry, the first by trying to reshape the EC, the latter by attempted renegotiation. Neither was successful, partly because of the obstacles already outlined but also because the 1970s was the period when Britain's growing economic malaise became acute, endangering not merely the country's prosperity but even its political stability. The United Kingdom ended the decade uncertain not merely about Europe but also about its own identity.

THE CHANGING CONTEXT OF POWER AND POLICY

By the early 1970s there were clear signs that the bipolar world order was in flux. Most striking was the apparent diminution of America's relative power compared with its exaggerated dominance of a devastated postwar world. The defeat in Vietnam seemed the most visible and humiliating indicator, but equally important was the end amid economic crisis in 1971 of the US commitment to convert dollars into gold on demand and the new American desire, under President Richard Nixon and his National Security Adviser, Henry Kissinger, to reduce the tensions of the Cold War. Nixon's visit to China in February 1972 and his signature of arms control agreements in Moscow in May were seen as harbingers of a new 'multipolar' order. 'It would be a safer world and a better world', Nixon observed, 'if we have a strong, healthy United States, Europe, the Soviet Union, China, Japan; each balancing the other'.[1] In 1973 Kissinger called for a 'new Atlantic Charter' to share more equitably the burdens of NATO in the light of Europe's growing wealth and America's relative decline (tables 1.1 and 1.2).

Within the 'new Europe' there could no longer be any doubt about the importance of the Federal Republic of Germany (FRG) as America's most powerful European ally. By 1970 the FRG, with nearly one-fifth of the world's exports of manufactured goods, had outstripped America. Its share was double that of Britain (table 1.2). The growing strength of the German Deutschmark had been one of the main speculative forces driving the dollar off gold and obliging most international currencies, including sterling, to float by 1973. Moreover, German economic muscle was being translated into military might. By 1964 German armed forces exceeded Britain's by 430,000 to 425,000. On the crucial Central Front in Europe Germany's troop contribution of 274,000 outstripped America's and was over five times that of Britain.[2] The Anglo–American relationship remained special in *quality* compared with Washington's links with other allies. Global collaboration in signals intelligence, the unique nuclear alliance and the habit of close consultation between the two diplomatic and defence establishments all stood out. But, unlike the 1950s, the relationship was no longer special in *importance* either to the USA or in international politics.[3] Germany was replacing Britain as America's single most important European partner. Its growing independence was demonstrated by Chancellor Willy Brandt's *Ostpolitik* of detente with the FRG's communist neighbours, particularly East Germany. Fears of possible German reunification intensified, not least in Paris. Most striking of all was the emergence of the European Community as a major force in international politics. For Britain this constituted a new framework of power and policy. An examination of its basic institutions is therefore appropriate.[4]

Strictly speaking, there were three European Communities. One was the Coal and Steel Community (ECSC), formed in 1952. The Treaty of Rome in March 1957 had created two more – one economic, the other (Euratom) dealing with atomic energy. The latter proved of limited importance but the economic community established itself firmly during the 1960s, particularly through a common agricultural policy and a tariff-free common market. In the 1960s there were four principal EEC institutions (see also Appendix 2). The *Court of Justice*, with a permanent member from each state, interpreted the Treaties and used them as criteria to judge the actions of the Community and its members. Its judgements took precedence over national law. The *Commission*, comprising two appointees from the larger states and one from each of the smaller states, was responsible for proposing legislation and implementing Community decisions. Yet the *Council of Ministers* was the formal decision-making body, whose votes turned Commission proposals into Community law, and its composition was clearly intergovernmental. The Council was in reality the group of national ministers relevant to the issue in question, most often foreign ministers, but also those responsible for agriculture, transport, and so on. Finally, there was an *Assembly*, modelled on national parliaments, but distinct in two respects. One was its appointive character, as a group of nominated national MPs, which was eventually rectified from 1979 with direct elections by the voters of the member states. The other, abiding, feature was its largely consultative character. It lacked the power to legislate itself and in most cases could only comment on what the Commission and the Council had done.

The Community was therefore a hybrid political organisation, 'neither wholly federal, confederal nor supranational'.[5] The Assembly was not a proper legislature, the Commission lacked executive powers. The Treaty of Rome had made clear that the Community, though economic in its initial focus, was intended to 'lay the foundations of an ever closer union among the peoples of Europe'.[6] In the 1960s that objective was frustrated by de Gaulle. It was he who prevented the enlargement of the EC through the admission of Britain. And he also obstructed its development into a more supranational community, by blocking the increased use of majority voting in the Council of Ministers

– as provided for in the Treaty of Rome. Instead, the 'Luxembourg compromise' of January 1966 allowed a member government still to exercise a veto on issues that it deemed 'of vital national importance'.[7]

De Gaulle's resignation in April 1969 enabled the momentum for European integration to resume. The Hague Summit of the Six that December proposed a 'relaunch' of the Community. This had three elements. *Completion* of the economic community would be achieved by finally giving it automatic revenues from what were designated as its 'own resources'. Previously the Common Agricultural Policy and the Community budget had been funded by annual contributions from national governments. Secondly, plans were drawn up for *deepening* the Community through Economic and Monetary Union (EMU) by 1980 and through European Political Cooperation (EPC) in foreign policy. Thirdly, *widening* of the Community through new members was now to be encouraged. De Gaulle's successor, Georges Pompidou, indicated that France would no longer exercise a veto if Britain could prove its European credentials.

The early 1970s debate about Britain's membership of the EC therefore took place in a changing international context, with 'Europe' reviving, Germany resurgent and the 'special relationship' on the wane. But the European Community that opened its doors to Britain was also newly committed to enhancing its own supranational character. This dual commitment to widening *and* deepening was to prove to be a fundamental and recurring problem for Britain in the future.

HEATH AND BRITISH ENTRY: THE PRICE OF SUCCESS

In June 1970 the British elected a prime minister who was particularly ready to exploit the new European situation. Edward Heath was unique among post-war British premiers in the depths of his commitment to Europe and of his coolness about the 'special relationship'. On the latter he noted that 'the instinct is no longer so strong in Washington' and predicted that British officials would gradually 'turn more to Paris, Bonn or Rome'. He envisaged a stronger European pillar to NATO and even spoke of a European nuclear deterrent 'based on the existing British and French forces'.[8] In 1961–2 he had been Macmillan's EEC negotiator and, once premier, he conducted the new talks with urgency. Yet he was also conscious that a third failure would be disastrous for British and continental confidence, and the 1970 Tory manifesto adopted the cautious Macmillan–Wilson stance that Community membership would be desirable 'if we can negotiate the right terms....Our sole commitment is to negotiate; no more, no less'.[9]

Negotiations with the Six began on 30 June 1970, but made little progress.[10] In early 1971 there was deadlock on the major issues of New Zealand butter, Commonwealth sugar and Britain's budget contribution. What cleared the way was the summit between Heath and Pompidou in Paris on 20–21 May 1971. Pompidou was no ardent federalist, but he was favourably disposed to British membership, seeing it in part as a counterweight to Germany's new economic strength and diplomatic independence.[11] But Pompidou, like de Gaulle, still had his doubts about Britain's European credentials. These Heath successfully allayed in their meeting, during which the symbolic, but to Pompidou significant, promise was made to scale down the sterling balances – erstwhile token of Britain's attempts to play an independent and, for France, destabilising monetary role. 'I have confidence in the England of Mr Heath', Pompidou affirmed afterwards, and the word went out to the French negotiators to be more accommodating over the remaining obstacles.[12] By the end of June 1971 terms for British entry had been agreed.[13]

Selling the agreement to Parliament and public took a further year. The Government's detailed White Paper in July 1971 stressed the political benefits. In a more multipolar world, 'a Europe united would have the means of recovering the position in the world which Europe divided has lost'. If Britain said 'no', 'in a single generation we should have renounced an Imperial past and rejected a European future'.[14] This was the essentially geopolitical argument that had disposed both the Macmillan and Wilson governments towards membership. Yet, for the general public, the short version of the White Paper played up the likely economic benefits. 'The Government believes that membership of the European Economic Community will enable Britain to achieve a higher standard of living.' While entering caveats that 'membership will not automatically improve our performance', the overwhelming impression from the text and tables was that the EC had been the key to the Six's higher earnings and, once in the club, the magic would work for Britain as well.[15] The cost in increased food prices and contributions to the EC budget was given little space. Indeed the White Paper itself claimed it was impossible to estimate the size of Britain's *net* contribution to the Community after the transitional period 1973–8 expired.[16] Anti-marketeers were less circumspect, and their predictions of £600 to £1.13 billion per annum[17] proved closer to the £1 billion deficit officially admitted by the European Commission in 1980 than the rosy estimates of £200 million or less provided by the pro-Market weekly *The Economist*.[18]

This disingenuousness about the costs of entry was one reason for Labour's opposition. But far more important was the weight of continued anti-Market feeling on the Left and the electoral need for an opposition party to offer clear alternatives to Government policies. For all these reasons, Wilson retreated from his pro-market stance of 1967 and, like Gaitskell in 1962, declared himself unhappy with the Tory terms as a betrayal of the Commonwealth and as 'an intolerable and disproportionate burden on every family in the land'. He reaffirmed the 1970 manifesto commitment that Labour favoured entry 'if the terms were right' but, if they were not, then 'Britain was strong enough to stand alone'.[19] The Labour conference voted five to one against entry and the issue, like nuclear disarmament before, became a battle between right and left for control of the party.

Confident of victory and anxious to minimise the embarrassment caused by 39 diehard Tory anti-Marketeers, Heath conceded a free vote in the Commons, but the Labour Left, as part of its power struggle, forced Wilson to maintain a three-line whip. Even so, 69 Labour MPs voted for entry, led by Roy Jenkins who believed that 'if we rejected Europe we wouldn't have a rugged independence but would be dependent upon America'.[20] On 28 October 1971 the Commons voted 356 to 244 in favour of British entry.* On the basis of this declaration of intent Heath signed the treaty of accession in January 1972. Translating that treaty into English law required the assent of Parliament to a detailed bill, and the reluctance of Labour pro-marketeers to continue helping the government resulted in only eight- and seventeen-vote majorities on the Second and Third Readings.[21] Nevertheless, the bill received the royal assent in October and on 1 January 1973, Britain, together with Denmark and Ireland, joined the European Community. The Six had become the Nine.

Heath now set out to coordinate Britain's foreign policy with its new partners.[22] His response to Kissinger's call in April 1973 for a 'new Atlantic Charter' was particularly striking. Kissinger had envisaged Britain as a useful interlocutor between the USA and Europe, building on the familiar 'consultative relationship' between the American and British bureaucracies. Instead, much to Kissinger's chagrin, Heath

---

* 131 MPs – one-fifth of the Commons – had gone against their party leaderships, the biggest backbench rebellion since the vote against Chamberlain in May 1940 (Kitzinger 1973: 400).

joined Britain in a common negotiating front among the Nine, orchestrated by the French. In July Kissinger indicated to the Cabinet Secretary, Sir Burke Trend, that, if this pattern continued, 'we were at a turning point in Atlantic relations'.[23]

Anglo–American tension increased that autumn over the Arab–Israeli war. In early October 1973 the Americans wanted to use their NATO bases in Britain to airlift supplies to Israel, but they were quietly rebuffed by Whitehall. On 24 October, fearing Soviet intervention to help Egypt, Nixon put US troops around the world on a high state of nuclear alert. Britain, and other allies, were informed soon afterwards but they were not consulted in advance, even though US bases in Britain would be a prime target for Soviet attack in any war. In a stormy House of Commons the Foreign Secretary, Sir Alec Douglas-Home, resorted to the argument that 'if the bases were to be *used* for any purpose, Britain would have been consulted' under the Truman–Churchill agreement of 1952. 'But the Americans must be allowed to *alert* their forces the world over, just as we might in certain circumstances' (emphasis added).[24] In the worst superpower crisis since Cuba in 1962, such casuistry seemed more than a little dubious. By the end of Heath's government in February 1974 transatlantic relations were severely strained.

Yet Heath's Europeanism was more complex than subsequent mythology (and his own affirmations) have implied. This is important because it became clear that the terms of entry were in significant respects very unfavourable to Britain, especially on the question of budget contributions, and the growing evidence of this exacerbated anti-EC feeling in the country for a decade after 1973. The root problem was that the Community had been established for some fifteen years and its central institutions represented a delicate compromise among the original Six.[25]

In key respects their interests were very different from Britain's. Agriculture, for instance, employed nearly 15 per cent of the civilian work force in the Six, compared with only 3 per cent in Britain, where the average farm size was 67 acres against the EC average of 27.[26] The Common Agricultural Policy (CAP) was therefore designed to suit countries, particularly France, where small farmers were still economically and politically very important and where a high degree of agricultural self-sufficiency had been attained. The CAP system of price support, which kept food prices high through levies on outside imports, and did not discourage inefficiency, was directly at odds with the British reliance on agricultural imports – 40 per cent of grain consumption, 30 per cent of meat, 70 per cent of sugar, for instance.[27]

Also problematic was the related method of calculating national contributions to the EC budget. This had been the source of bitter argument during the de Gaulle era and, when Pompidou gave the go-ahead for British negotiations, he was nevertheless insistent that the issue had to be decided by the Six before the EEC was enlarged, without any British participation.[28] It was agreed in 1970 that certain national revenues constituted the Community's 'own resources', accruing automatically to Brussels. These included 90 per cent of all levies on imported food and manufactures, plus up to 1 per cent of VAT revenues. Again this penalised a high-importing country like Britain more than countries less reliant on extra-European foodstuffs and manufactures.

In fact, by the end of the transitional period, in 1978, the British contribution itself was not inequitable. Britain provided about 20 per cent of EC income, roughly equivalent to its share of the Community's total GDP. The problem was that in return Britain received only 8.7 per cent of EC spending in 1980.[29] This was because over two-thirds of EC expenditure was on the CAP, and little of this went to Britain with its small and efficient farm sector. To provide a fifth of the Community's income and receive less than a tenth of its expenditure was hardly acceptable.

This outcome represented a defeat for Heath's strategy for entry. He was well aware of the problems posed by the CAP and budget, but he was negotiating from a very weak position. After two vetos, the Six knew that Britain, 'with nowhere else to go', could 'hardly take "no" for an answer'.[30] Heath therefore believed that some of the Community's fundamentals had to be taken as given. 'However much we should like it, there is no evidence that the Community will change the CAP as such', he warned before negotiations opened.[31] On the budget, the best he could get was a promise that if unacceptable situations should arise 'the very survival of the Community would demand that the [EC] institutions should find equitable solutions'.[32] He was ready to accept the essentials of the CAP and budget but wanted compensatory advantages for Britain. One was the expectation that 'in return British industry would receive the benefit of the Common Market'.[33] Heath also hoped to enlarge the Community's budget to offset its dominance by the CAP. In particular he wanted a European Regional Development Fund (ERDF), from which Britain, with its pockets of uncompetitive heavy industry, would be a particular beneficiary.[34]

Heath's Europeanism was therefore a calculated strategy for national self-advancement. In 1973 he lobbied hard for an ERDF. He was also an enthusiast for closer foreign-policy cooperation in the EPC process. Personally he favoured sterling's membership of the proposed EMU monetary union and even a Central Bank, although the Treasury was sceptical.[35] Yet he would have nothing to do with proposals by the German Social Democratic government for a common social policy, including worker management of firms and harmonisation of social security measures. And in 1973 he backed away from a joint oil policy, persuaded by the Treasury arguments and public outcry about 'our oil' that the North Sea reserves of oil and natural gas, by then beginning to come on stream, would make Britain a special case.

Thus, even Heath's Europeanism was selective. In this, of course, he was no different from any of the other national leaders, each of whom pushed their own projects under the guise of common European interests. The Italians, for instance, shared his desire for a development fund, while the Germans particularly wanted an energy policy. It was over this latter issue that the ERDF came to grief in late 1973. The Germans would have been the main contributors, but they were willing to accept this burden to ease Britain's adjustment into the Community. In return, however, they wanted support for a joint energy policy and Heath's refusal led them to block the ERDF at the Copenhagen summit in December 1973. Before the deadlock could be resolved, Heath was out of power, and with him went the goal of a large regional fund to help offset Britain's budget deficit.[36]

The failure of Heath's strategy was only part of the reason for Britain's problems of adjustment. More fundamental was the impact of the oil crisis of late 1973, sparked off by the October Arab–Israeli war, in which oil prices quadrupled, with knock-on effects on all energy and transport costs. This marked the end of a quarter-century of steady growth in western Europe, lubricated by cheap, secure supplies of energy. Thus Britain joined the European Community at the worst possible moment, when the basic institutions were set to its detriment, and when economic recession minimised both the chances of institutional reform and also the opportunities presented by the enlarged common market.

The oil crisis also finished off the post-war domestic political consensus. Recession was coupled with mounting inflation – a paradox for Keynesian orthodoxy. In the British case it had been fuelled by Tory Chancellor Anthony Barber's ill-judged credit boom of 1972 which increased the money supply by 25 per cent in 1972 and 27 per cent in 1973.[37] Barber's goal, achieved in the short-term, was to reduce the level of unemployment, then nearing one million. But in order to control the inflationary consequences of his expansion, Heath tried to impose a prices and incomes policy. Challenged by the coal miners just as the oil crisis took effect, he was forced into energy-conservation measures, including a 'three-day week', and went to the country in February 1974 on the slogan 'who governs Britain?'. He was defeated, though narrowly, then failed to regain power in the next election in October and finally lost the Tory leadership to Margaret Thatcher the following February. The image of trades union power haunted the Tory party for a decade.

Not only domestic stability but the very unity of the United Kingdom seemed in doubt as well. In Wales and Scotland nationalist parties won unprecedented support. In October 1974 Plaid Cymru picked up 10 per cent of the Welsh vote while the Scottish Nationalist Party (SNP) gained over 30 per cent, and eleven seats – given new appeal by the prospect of control over North Sea oil. But the most intractable problem was Ulster. The introduction of British troops in 1969 had failed to pacify the province and in March 1972 Heath decided that the Unionist Government was incapable of either maintaining order or promoting reform. He took the fateful step of resuming direct rule from London, with a Secretary of State for Northern Ireland. Heath's intent was to enforce an equitable polity from outside, but the 'power sharing' executive established in January 1974, comprising moderate Unionists and Catholics, collapsed within a few months in the face of strikes by Protestant workers. What gradually became clear was that March 1972 had 'marked the final stage in the dismantling of the Anglo–Irish settlements of 1920–21'.[38] In 1969 Healey and Callaghan had told the Labour Cabinet that 'our whole interest was to work through the Protestant government . . . we can't afford to alienate them . . . and find ourselves ruling Northern Ireland as a colony'.[39] But that is what had happened by the mid-1970s. Northern Ireland, a relic of the English empire yet also part of the United Kingdom, had reverted to quasi-colonial rule.

Heath's defeat therefore marked more than the end of the one distinctly 'European' phase in post-war British foreign policy. It also signalled the passing of the conditions of domestic stability on which British foreign policy had consistently been based. In the next decade, under Labour and Tory governments, Britain tried to adapt to its new role within Europe just when the cohesion of the United Kingdom was under greater strain than at any time in living memory. The result was a foreign policy characterised by the rhetoric of insular nationalism just when the realities of European interdependence were becoming ever more demanding.

LABOUR AND 'RENEGOTIATION': DOMESTIC POLITICS AND FOREIGN POLICY

February 1974 saw Britain's first minority government since 1929–31. Labour had 4 seats more than the Tories, but was 34 seats short of an overall majority and depended on third-party support (especially the Liberals and SNP) for its survival. Prime Minister Harold Wilson called another election in October, but only gained an overall majority of 3.[40] Had he been able to count on party unity, things would have been easier, but in the 1970s Labour was more divided than ever – with Tony Benn leading a powerful left-wing movement calling for radical socialist measures and antagonistic to much of government policy.

Consequently, Wilson, and his successor James Callaghan (1976–9), remained reliant on the minor parties whose representation had soared from 9 before the February election to 26 after October. This dependence was dramatised in the formal 'Lib–Lab pact' of 1977–8. But its consequences for policy were most apparent in the offer of devolution for Scotland and Wales. Callaghan was willing to countenance a weakening of the Union, with elected Scottish and Welsh assemblies and devolved executive powers, in order to keep the support of the third-party MPs, most of whom represented the 'Celtic fringe', and to protect Labour seats in Scotland from the SNP tide. Trying to balance these requirements against the 'English backlash' preoccupied him from 1976 to 1979 and it was the loss of SNP support after the failure of the Scottish referendum which was the immediate cause of Callaghan's Commons defeat in March 1979.

British foreign policy has normally been insulated from much of the ebb and flow of domestic politics. On the Continent, where coalitions are frequent under proportional representation, the constant horse-trading required to hold a government together spills over into foreign affairs. In Britain, a tight two-party system sustained by a winner-takes-all system of representation, usually ensured a clear working majority for either Labour or Tories since 1945. External policy, while affected by domestic concerns, was rarely a function of domestic politics. Wilson's approach to the European Community' constitutes a major exception.

Labour opposition to the EC became linked in the early 1970s to the conviction that radical socialism required complete national independence in economic and social policies. Former EC supporters, such as Benn, took this line. In 1971 Wilson committed the party to renegotiating the terms of entry and this he embarked on as soon as Labour regained power. In the early months of the new government Wilson won a crucial battle against his own anti-Marketeers by insisting that the manifesto commitment to 'fundamental renegotiation' meant improving the terms and not trying to amend the 1957 Treaty of Rome.[41] During the winter of 1974–5 he and Callaghan, then Foreign Secretary, won concessions on some concerns, notably access for Commonwealth products. But the CAP proved sacrosanct and on the vexed issue of Britain's budget contribution Wilson and Callaghan were only able to secure a 'correcting mechanism', whereby Britain would receive a rebate of up to £125 million should its share of the EEC budget exceed its proportion of the Community's total GDP. The sum involved was not large but the principle was of significance for the future.

Having done something to honour Labour's manifesto commitment, Wilson felt able to recommend to Parliament in March 1975 that 'continued membership of the Community is in Britain's interest on the basis of the renegotiated terms'.[42] To satisfy the Left, Labour was already committed to the unique expedient of a national referendum on the issue, but, to accommodate the public split within his own Cabinet, Wilson also decided to waive the traditional rules of collective Cabinet responsibility so that 'the minority should be free to campaign in the country on their own point of view'.[43] For the referendum, the pro-Europe forces spent some £1.8 million compared with £133,000 by their opponents.[44] On 5 June 1975 64.5 per cent of the electorate voted, 8.3 per cent less than in the October 1974 general election. The Government's recommendation was endorsed by 67.2 per cent, while 32.8 per cent said 'no'.

Renegotiation and the referendum were largely ploys in domestic politics. But they did serve to give a somewhat stronger base of popular legitimacy to Britain's membership of the Community. Throughout the 1971 debate poll data suggested that no more than 30 to 40 per cent of the public were in favour of entry.[45] Now, by a clear majority of two to one, voters had endorsed British membership. Wilson proclaimed that 'fourteen years of national argument are over' and called on all erstwhile dissenters to 'join wholeheartedly with our partners in Europe' to confront the challenges ahead.[46] But although 'unequivocal', the verdict 'was also unenthusiastic. Support for membership was wide but it did not run deep'.[47] This was a vote for the status quo – staying in – not a commitment to further European integration, and even that was made by only 43 per cent of the total potential electorate.

The deepening economic crisis did nothing to enhance the British public's enthusiasm for the EC. In the wake of the 'Barber boom' and the oil crisis, 'stagflation' set in − stagnant growth (the economy actually contracted in 1974–5), mounting unemployment (6 per cent by 1977) and spiralling inflation, which reached a peak of 26 per cent in 1975.[48] Although by 1978 inflation was restrained and the balance of payments returned to surplus, Labour could do nothing to reverse Britain's relative economic decline internationally (tables 1.1 and 1.2). Given that the popular case for EC entry in 1971 had stressed the material benefits, it was not surprising that the Community became a scapegoat for the economic malaise. By the late 1970s support in the opinion polls was down to 30 per cent and in the first direct elections to the European Parliament in June 1979 only 32.8 per cent of the British electorate bothered to vote − roughly comparable to the percentage usually voting in local elections. The turnout in the Community as a whole averaged 62.3 per cent.[49]

Popular disenchantment was only accentuated by the slowness of the Community to realise the early 1970s vision for it as a major actor in a multipolar world. The much-trumpeted 1969 relaunch soon lost momentum. Progress towards European Monetary Union (EMU), with all Community currencies broadly aligned, did not last − undermined by international monetary instability and the underlying conflict between France's expansionist monetary strategy and the German Bundesbank's obsession with controlling inflation. Britain stayed within the system only a few weeks in the spring of 1972 before letting sterling float. By 1977 only five of the nine EC members kept their currencies aligned − Germany, Denmark and the Benelux states.[50] Nor did European Political Cooperation (EPC) prove as impressive as some had hoped. The initial achievements were procedural rather than substantive: Community foreign ministries were linked through regular meetings and through a direct telex network (COREU) to disseminate information. But until 1974 the French refused to bring the EPC process within the EC framework. It took the Arab–Israeli war and the oil crisis to force the Nine to start developing a common foreign policy and, even then, EPC remained a peripheral concern for most of them.[51]

Domestic politics, reinforced by economic crisis and growing disenchantment with the EC, therefore largely explain the direction of British foreign policy in the 1970s. Nevertheless, Wilson and particularly Callaghan also left their own mark by abandoning Heath's priorities. As Wilson's Foreign Secretary, Callaghan felt that 'Heath's deep and lasting commitment to Europe had weakened our relations with the

United States, and as a strong believer in the Atlantic Alliance, I was determined that these must be strengthened'.[52] In his first major speech as Foreign Secretary he denounced 'anti-American tinges' in European opinion, called for the 'fullest and most intimate' cooperation with the USA, and repudiated 'the view that Europe will emerge only after a process of struggle against America'.[53] This set the pattern for the remaining Labour years – coolness towards Europe matched by a renewed cultivation of the 'special relationship'.

Of particular importance was Labour's surreptitious renewal of the Anglo–American nuclear alliance as Polaris became obsolescent. In 1972 Heath, in line with his previous public statements, had explored the possibilities of Anglo–French nuclear collaboration. France's absence from NATO's integrated command was eventually deemed a major obstacle, but the Government decided not to request a new US system, such as Poseidon or Trident, but to update Polaris.[54] Labour was already pledged not to acquire a new generation of missiles, but, once in power again, it carried on the updating programme, code-named 'Chevaline'. This took account of recent developments in weapons technology, particularly improved Soviet anti-ballistic missile defences and the innovation of multiple warheads. The Chevaline programme, not revealed publicly until 1980 when the cost had reached £1 billion, renewed the nuclear axis between Britain and America, especially in testing, data exchange and fissile materials.[55]

Under Labour, then, British policy had slid back somewhat into the old grooves, compared with the new directions mapped out by Heath. Its sense of affinity with America remained strong, but the power of Germany and the weakness of the British economy rendered relations with Britain much less important to the USA than before. Britain was a member of the European Community, but a reluctant one, critical of the CAP and budget and lacking a sense of European identity. And although the EC did not realise the more grandiose integrationist goals of 1969, its own evolution continued regardless of Britain. From 1974 summits between the heads of government were placed on a thrice-yearly basis, instead of being responses to crises. Known as the *European Council*, these gatherings became an institutionalised feature of Community life. They helped to increase contact among national leaders and tilted the balance of EC policymaking away from the bureaucrats in the European Commission. The Council soon became the key Community decision-making body.

At the heart of this intergovernmental framework was the Franco–German axis. After the friction of the early 1970s, relations between Bonn and Paris achieved a new cordiality under Helmut Schmidt and

Giscard d'Estaing, both of whom came to power in 1974 and survived the rest of the decade. The idea of a dynamic Anglo–French–German triangle at the heart of the Community – touted by Pompidou and conceivable as long as Heath remained premier – had evaporated.[56] It was Schmidt and Giscard who promoted a new and more successful effort to create a European Monetary System (EMS) in 1978. This involved both the pegging of participating currencies in an Exchange Rate Mechanism (ERM) and, novelly, a European Monetary Fund (EMF), comprising 20 per cent of the members' reserves, to help support currencies under pressure.

Schmidt viewed the EMS as a European response to the instability created by America's depreciation of the dollar. True to his Atlanticist bent, Callaghan preferred a solution arranged through the International Monetary Fund in Washington. Of the two rival conceptions, the EMS took off and Callaghan's did not – a pattern reminiscent of Britain's earlier efforts to divert European integration in the 1950s. Callaghan had then to decide whether to join the new monetary system. After some dithering, he eventually stayed out. Pressure from the Labour left in Cabinet and at the October 1978 party conference was probably the decisive reason, but the party's desire for monetary independence was shared, albeit for different reasons, by the Treasury who preferred to work more informally with the IMF. These arguments overcame the political case for membership, pushed with increasing urgency by British embassies on the Continent.[57] When the EMS came into operation in March 1979 Britain contributed its share of the Fund's reserves but refused to link sterling with the other currencies in the ERM. It was the only Community country to reject full membership, thereby reinforcing Britain's image as a reluctant European.

This continued attempt under Wilson and Callaghan to play a mid-Atlantic role might have been more credible if the country had seemed prosperous and strong. Given the problems he inherited from the Tories, Chancellor Denis Healey's overall record was creditable: between 1974 and 1978 a current account payments deficit was transformed into a surplus of £1.2 billion and the rate of growth in wages and salaries came down from 30 per cent to 7.5 per cent in his first two years. But Healey's management of the economy was overshadowed by two politically-disastrous policy failures. One was the sterling crisis of 1976, when the Government vacillated over the exchange rate. International perception that public expenditure was out of control led to sterling's precipitate slide from $2.02 to $1.55. Eventually it was humiliatingly bailed out by IMF loans on tough, deflationary terms. These included credits to help scale down the sterling balances and thus end sterling's role as a reserve currency – actions promised by the Heath Government to the EC in 1971 but frustrated by the Treasury and the Bank. Few images of the period were more durable and embarrassing internationally than that of the usually bullish Healey driving to Heathrow on 28 September 1976 to fly to an IMF meeting and then turning round at the airport and returning to the Treasury on hearing news of a further fall in the value of sterling.[58]

Even more damaging was the collapse of the 'social contract' with the unions – restraint on wage claims in return for government maintenance of real living standards – which was Labour's key weapon in the struggle against inflation. This was severely strained by the fall in sterling in 1976, which drove up import prices and eroded real incomes. The unions' refusal to accept government pay targets in 1978 led to a rash of industrial disputes in the 'winter of discontent' early in 1979. TV pictures of rubbish uncollected, hospitals picketed and the dead unburied contributed to the Tory victory in May 1979. The impression at home and abroad was of Britain in terminal economic decline, held hostage by anarchical unions and teetering on the edge of ungovernability. US economist Milton Friedman had predicted in 1976 that Britain was going the way of Chile: socialist crisis followed by military coup was, he said, 'the only outcome that is conceivable'.[59]

This was hyperbole, but the 1970s was a watershed in British politics, marking the end of an underlying post-war consensus.[60] Since 1945 Chancellors of both parties had tried and generally succeeded, in Harold Macmillan's image of the juggler, in keeping four balls in the air simultaneously – continued growth, full employment, a strong pound and stable prices.[61] And the trades unions – Labour's paymasters – had been enlisted by both parties to help manage the corporatist economy. In the 1970s the juggling act failed: growth stagnated, unemployment rose, sterling sagged and inflation soared. Economic failure threatened the central principle of consensus politics – the welfare state, whose mounting costs were already straining the pre-70s growth economy. And the agents of the breakdown of political consensus were the trades unions, now unable to control their fragmented, grass-roots structure, which made free collective bargain into a recipe for industrial anarchy and increased inflation.

Healey's turnaround from Heathrow in 1976 seemed to dramatise Britain's economic predicament. The 'winter of discontent' likewise symbolised for many abroad the collapse of consensus politics. In the world of diplomacy perceptions matter as much as realities. Few understood this better than Margaret Thatcher.

REFERENCES

1. Dimbleby and Reynolds 1988: 262
2. IISS 1964: 17–18, 21–4
3. Reynolds 1985/6: 10–14
4. Daltrop 1982; Arbuthnott and Edwards 1989
5. Arbuthnott and Edwards 1989: 17–18
6. Daltrop 1982: 14
7. Arbuthnott and Edwards 1989: 9
8. Heath 1970: 67, 73
9. Conservative Central Office 1970: 28
10. Kitzinger 1973
11. Simonian 1985: 80
12. Campbell 1982b: 432–8
13. S. Young 1973; Swann 1981: 35–42
14. Cmd. 4715: paras 61, 64
15. HMG 1971: 8–9
16. Cmd. 4715: para. 93
17. Haack 1972: 139–40
18. *The Economist*, 10 July 1971: 72
19. Commons 823: 2094, 2096
20. Benn 1988: 357
21. Kitzinger 1973
22. Dimbleby and Reynolds 1988: 262–6
23. Kissinger 1982: 191
24. Commons 863: 969
25. Arbuthnott and Edwards 1989: chs 6, 12
26. S. Young 1973: 60–1
27. Ibid., 64
28. George 1990: 52–4
29. P. Taylor 1983: 238
30. Northedge 1983: 26, 30
31. S. Young 1973: 36
32. Cmd. 4715: para. 96
33. P. Taylor 1983: 248–9
34. George 1990: 56
35. Heath 1988: 203; George 1990: 63–4
36. George 1990: 56–70
37. Browning 1986: 50–1
38. Boyce 1988: 111
39. Ibid., 108
40. Butler 1989: 27–32
41. Butler and Kitzinger 1976: 29
42. Cmd. 6003: para. 150
43. Castle 1980: 287
44. H. Wilson 1979: 105

45. Zakheim 1973: 192–5
46. H. Wilson 1979: 108
47. Butler and Kitzinger 1976: 280
48. Peden 1985: 206
49. Reif (ed.) 1985: 1, 16
50. George 1985: 130–6
51. Regelsberger 1988: 5–20
52. Callaghan 1987: 295
53. *New York Times*, 20 March 1974: 1, 6
54. Baylis 1984b: 172–5
55. Simpson 1986: 171–80
56. Simonian 1985: 266, 360
57. Ludlow 1982: esp. 81–2, 109–11, 217–25
58. Browning 1986: ch. 5
59. Nossiter 1978: 13
60. Kavanagh 1987: chs 2, 5; also Beer 1982
61. P. Jenkins 1989: 5

CHAPTER TEN
Thatcher, 1979–90

Margaret Thatcher was a self-proclaimed 'conviction politician', certain of her free-market philosophy and intolerant of opposition. Although primarily a would-be domestic reformer, her impact on British foreign policy and on international affairs in general was considerable. That was due to her re-establishment of political stability, though not consensus, after the upheavals of the 1970s and to the forceful nationalism of her diplomatic style, particularly in dealings with the European Community and the Soviet Union. She gloried in her nickname of 'the Iron Lady'. Internal stability and external assertiveness enhanced Britain's image, if not its popularity, abroad. The somewhat fortuitous Falklands victory in 1982 was adroitly used by her as the leitmotif for her leadership and for a new Britain. Better than any Prime Minister since Macmillan, Thatcher understood that prestige was a form of power. During her premiership, Britain kept a high profile in world politics.

But there is more to power than prestige. Similarly, rhetoric is not the same as reality. Looking more closely at her handling of post-imperial problems, we can see that the Fortress Falklands policy was an aberration, not the norm. Simultaneously, Britain was loosening its hold on most of its other remnants of empire, including Rhodesia, Hong Kong and even Northern Ireland. In European affairs her aggressive and remarkably successful campaign for a rebate on Britain's budget contribution took attention away from the less spectacular but more significant process of further integration. Her attempts to restrict this to a free market, without concomitant harmonisation of economic, monetary and social policies or the development of more efficient central decision-making, succeeded in delaying rather than diverting the tide of events. And although her enthusiastic support of American policy in the new cold war of the early 1980s gave her influence in Washington and, more briefly, Moscow, in the latter part of the decade, Britain was rapidly marginalized by the new superpower detente and the emergence of a united Germany as the principal European actor. Furthermore, at root, the vaunted economic revolution of Thatcherism had failed to solve the historic problems of British industrial uncompetitiveness. Despite attempts to stimulate entrepreneurial values and reduce state control, the country still imported far more than it sold abroad and by the late 1980s serious payments problems had recurred, after an inflationary boom in the middle of the decade.

Thus, the Thatcher premiership saw a revival and then decline of Britain's international role. It did not prove a real deviation from the trends already established in the early 1970s – growing EC cohesion, reluctant British immersion in this, increased German influence and a waning of superpower bipolarity. Thatcher's successes showed just how far a resolute leader could buck the rules of normal diplomacy and get away with it. Yet her career also demonstrated that, in policy, what is said is not always what is done, and that the appearance of power is often not the same as the reality. Thatcher, in short, was a case study in the possibilities and limitations of the diplomacy of bluff.

'BRITAIN IS GREAT AGAIN'

Margaret Thatcher brought to her new task a rooted mistrust of the ways of diplomacy. 'I am not always the world's greatest diplomat', she admitted – adding proudly 'and thank goodness for that'.[1] As veteran ambassador Sir Nicholas Henderson observed: 'She doesn't really believe that there's any such thing as a useful negotiation. She doesn't see foreign policy as it is, which is a lot of give and take'.[2] Thatcher, innately sceptical of all Whitehall bureaucrats, believed that British diplomats instinctively represented foreigners rather than Britain. Moreover, she came to office with virtually no experience of external affairs. Unlike Heath, who travelled widely ever since his student days, she had not set foot outside Britain until her honeymoon in 1951 at the age of 26, and had taken little interest in foreign policy during her earlier political career. She was a quick learner, however – assiduous in mastering her briefs, forceful in stating her opinions, often relishing being in a minority of one. But growing experience of foreign affairs did not alter her fundamental outlook. Her suspicion of foreigners was intense and her contempt for the French and Germans in particular was a matter of common gossip in Whitehall and West-minster.[3] Coming of age in the 1940s, she remained deeply affected by the memories of the World War and Cold War. This left her hostile to Russia, enthusiastic about America, sceptical about the continentals and convinced of the need for a strong defence.

Her impact internationally during the 1980s owed much to her formidable character, her style and also her gender. But her image as an eminent statesperson depended above all on sheer survival. She ruled as prime minister for a tenure unprecedented in Britain in the twentieth century. By doing so, she re-established the domestic political stability whose lack had so undermined Britain's foreign policy and international image in the previous decade.

Thatcher's political longevity was due primarily to the absence of effective opposition for most of the 1980s. After its 1979 defeat, the Labour party swung to the left, and dissident centrists broke away in 1981 to form the Social Democratic Party (SDP). Between them, Labour and the uneasy SDP–Liberal Alliance divided the anti-Tory vote, thereby facilitating Thatcher's victories in 1983 and 1987. On both occasions the Tories took about 42 per cent of the vote, while the two opposition parties split 53 per cent between them. It took Labour all the 1980s to transform itself into a plausible 'social market' party on continental lines, by which time the Alliance and its constituent parties had collapsed and two-party politics were resumed. In the interim, however, Thatcher flourished.

The other main reason for her success was that the Government's handling of the economy paid dividends at crucial political moments. By election-time in June 1983 inflation was running at 4 per cent, compared with 21 per cent in late 1979. 1984–5 saw the miners' strike defeated – a vital contrast with Heath in 1974 – and an accelerating sale of state industries to widen share ownership. By the election of June 1987 the stock market was booming, income tax was down from 33 per cent in 1979 to 27 per cent and growth rates since 1981 were faster than most of Europe. The Tories campaigned and won with posters of a British bulldog dwarfing a German Alsatian and a tiny French poodle, above the slogan 'it's great to be great again'.

In 1983 and 1987 'the government was re-elected because of a divided opposition and a prosperous economy'.[4] Yet neither of these factors was apparent in 1981. Industrial production had fallen 18 per cent in 1979–81. Inflation was still running at over 20 per cent and unemployment at 11 per cent[5], yet Thatcher persisted in her determination to control public expenditure and government borrowing, to the alarm of many of her Cabinet. At the same time, the Alliance had burst on the political stage, winning 50 per cent support in one opinion poll in December 1981. Of considerable importance in establishing the Thatcher premiership and changing Britain's image abroad was the totally unexpected Argentine invasion of the Falklands on 2 April 1982 – which caused Britain's worst foreign-policy crisis since Suez.[6]

These barren islands, 8000 miles away in the South Atlantic, had been occupied by Britain continuously for nearly 150 years and their 1850 inhabitants were determined to remain British. But Argentina also laid claim to the islands and neither government had an unassailable case in international law. Moreover, the islands were economically dependent on Argentina, and Britain's continued responsibility seemed to many in London a post-colonial hangover, damaging relations with Latin America. Accordingly, since the mid-1960s successive British governments had sought a negotiated settlement acceptable to both the islanders and the Argentines.

Blame for the war in 1982 lay primarily with the new Argentine military junta led by General Leopoldo Galtieri. On 26 March it decided to retake the islands by force. Yet policy failures in London contributed to the crisis. Under Thatcher, the continued search for a negotiated settlement had concentrated on a leaseback agreement, whereby Argentina would have sovereignty over the islands while leasing them back to the islanders under conditions of autonomy. Exploration of this option by the FCO fell foul of the islanders' fears and an outcry from the small but effective Falklands lobby in Parliament at the end of 1980. Thereafter Thatcher, always suspicious of an FCO sell-out, blocked further attempts at meaningful negotiation.[7] Yet at the same time, the government did nothing to reinforce the islands' defences. In part this was due to intelligence underestimation of Argentine intentions. But it also reflected deliberate government policy, embodied in the defence cuts of 1981, to concentrate on Britain's nuclear and NATO roles at the expense of the surface navy. One of the casualties was HMS *Endurance*, an ice-patrol ship in the South Atlantic, which, though small and ill-armed, served as a token of Britain's commitment to defend the Falklands. These decisions were taken by Defence Secretary John Nott, but on 9 February 1982, less than two months before the Argentine invasion, the Prime Minister publicly indicated her support for plans to withdraw the *Endurance*.[8] Her failure to send a firm ultimatum to Buenos Aires in the last week, when invasion was clearly imminent, disturbed several of her close advisers.[9]

Thus the Thatcher government, like those of Baldwin and Chamberlain in the 1930s, was caught between appeasement and deterrence. The Buenos Aires junta saw nothing to contradict its impression that, although Britain would not negotiate, it would not resist an Argentine takeover. That was a fundamental error. Although her pre-invasion diplomacy on this apparently peripheral issue had been irresolute, the Prime Minister was now determined to recover the Falklands, come what may. Even before the Commons howled down Nott's blustering defence of the government on 3 April, plans were in train to send a naval task force. At the same time both Nott and Lord Carrington, the Foreign Secretary, tendered their resignations. The former was quickly dissuaded, the latter was not, even though Carrington was far from being solely to blame. He had, for instance, three times warned Nott in writing of the danger of withdrawing the *Endurance*[10] and the Defence Secretary once more poo-pooed the case for *Endurance* in the Commons only three days before the Argentine invasion.[11] Politically, Carrington served as a necessary sacrifice for government failure, protecting his own leader.[12] But as a result of his resignation, and that of his junior ministers, the FCO was made the all-purpose scapegoat for the debacle.

The recovery of the Falklands took two months: the Argentine forces surrendered on 14 June. It cost Britain 255 men killed and 777 injured. Six ships from the task force were sunk, including two destroyers. In retrospect, it was clearly a 'close-run thing'. The Argentine air force and weaponry caused heavier casualties than expected and all the time the operation was working against the imminence of the South Atlantic winter. Without crucial US logistic support the outcome might well have been in doubt. Initially the Reagan Administration had tried to secure a mediated settlement: 'we're friends of both sides,' the President insisted.[13] But even before he came off the fence publicly, the Pentagon was channelling vast quantities of essential supplies to the task force, as well as offering crucial intelligence and use of US facilities on Ascension island.[14]

Close-run or not, in war nothing succeeds like success. The biggest beneficiary of all was the Prime Minister herself. With relish and resolution she assumed the role of a Churchillian war leader. Failure would have ended her premiership – after the Argentine invasion a third of the public believed that she should resign. In early April Tories, Labour and the Alliance were running level in the polls. By the time the war ended, the Tories had 51 per cent support, Labour 29 per cent and the Alliance 17 per cent.[15]

Abroad as well as at home the war had a profound effect. Although most of the world continued to see the issue in dispute as a bizarre post-colonial hangover, Britain's ability to launch and win a risky military operation 8000 miles from home contrasted strikingly with the 1970s image of indecision and decline. It was the source of new respect abroad and, for some at home, renewed national pride. Thatcher made it the motif for her vision of a new Britain: 'We have ceased to be a nation in retreat. We have instead a new-found confidence – born in the economic battles at home and tested and found true 8,000 miles away'.[16] Or, more crisply, 'Great Britain is great again'.[17] Politically it set her on course for re-election in 1983. Undoubtedly other factors contributed to that victory, including an economic upturn and the implausibility of Labour's contender, Michael Foot. But despite dissent from some psephologists,[18] most analysts and politicians judge that the image of Thatcherite resolution and the feelings of pride evoked by the Falklands war were of major importance in paving the way for her crucial election victory in 1983.[19]

After 1982 sovereignty over the Falklands was a non-negotiable issue for Thatcher. To change policy 'would be tantamount to admitting that she had let British troops die in vain' and that was 'politically and personally impossible'.[20] But the 'Fortress Falklands' policy, costing over £5 billion in all,[21] did not portend a global policy of proud neo-imperialism. In fact, it stood in marked and ironic contrast with Thatcher's handling of Britain's other post-colonial headaches. On Rhodesia, Ireland and Hong Kong, the 'Iron Lady' was made of more malleable metal.

By the late 1970s Ian Smith's defiant white minority government in Rhodesia was crumbling.[22] The collapse of the Portuguese empire in Africa, one of his main allies, and the growing strength of the Patriotic Front guerrillas had eroded his position. In April 1979 a black-led government under Bishop Abel Muzorewa had been elected, but Smith remained in control and many Tories wanted their new government to recognise Muzorewa. But Carrington, who as Foreign Secretary treated Rhodesia as a high priority, insisted that any settlement, to be viable, had to win 'the widest possible international recognition'.[23] He and the FCO gradually persuaded Thatcher to ignore the Muzorewa government, organise a conference in London in the autumn of 1979 and impose a new constitution on all the participants. A new British governor, Lord Soames, then oversaw the transition to 'free elections' and Southern Rhodesia finally achieved independence as Zimbabwe in April 1980.[24] Against Thatcher's own instincts and in defiance of the Tory right, who festooned their party conference with 'Hang Carrington' banners, the FCO had brought her to a solution of this long-running colonial problem.

A similar pattern emerged over Ulster. Thatcher believed tenaciously in the Union, and her own brand of Protestantism fostered little
sympathy for Catholicism. Furthermore, her revulsion at terrorism was
intensified by the IRA attempt to blow her up in Brighton in October
1984. Nevertheless, in November 1985 she signed the Hillsborough
agreement with the Irish leader, Garret Fitzgerald. While affirming that
any change in the status of Northern Ireland 'would come about only
with the consent of a majority' of its people, they agreed to set up an
'Intergovernmental Conference', involving ministers and officials in
regular meetings. For the first time the Dublin government was given
a formal say in the political, security and legal affairs of Ulster.[25]
Unionist leaders denounced this as an appalling betrayal. James Moly-
neaux announced: 'We are going to be delivered, bound and trussed
like a turkey ready for the oven, from one nation to another nation'.[26]
Again Thatcher had been persuaded, against her preferences and politi-
cal allegiances, by the FCO, backed this time by Cabinet Secretary
Robert Armstrong and the Northern Ireland Secretary, Douglas
Hurd.[27] The Hillsborough agreement did not solve the problem of
Ulster, far from it, but it transformed the context. For the first time a
British Government had admitted the Irish dimension and acknow-
ledged that Ulster was a problem of foreign as well as domestic policy.

Hong Kong provides a third example of her capacity, albeit reluctant, to be argued out of deeply-felt convictions. The 'New Territories'
were held on 99-year lease from China and this would expire on 30 June
1997. Although the rest of the Crown Colony had been ceded to Britain
in perpetuity in 1842 and 1860, it comprised only 8 per cent of the
total land area and was not viable alone. Moreover, the 5.5 million
population of the Colony depended for food, water and fuel on China
and, in the judgement of the FCO, some form of Chinese rule would
have to be acknowledged after 1997. When negotiations began in
1979, the FCO had hoped for a leaseback arrangement, similar to that
then envisaged for the Falklands. But Beijing demanded untrammelled
sovereignty and the best that could be secured was a Joint Declaration
in September 1984 that Hong Kong would continue as a capitalist
enclave within the PRC. For fifty years from 1997, Hong Kong
would be a 'Special Administrative Region', enjoying 'a high degree
of autonomy'. Its social and economic system would 'remain un-
changed', and civil and property rights would be 'protected by law'.[28]
Thatcher signed a formal agreement in Beijing in December 1984,
calling the one-nation, two-systems concept 'an idea of genius'. One
senior British minister said it had taken 'many long and very bitter
sessions' to abandon her rooted dislike of 'giving in' to China.[29]

In the Commons the agreement was applauded from almost all sides in what Shadow Foreign Secretary Denis Healey called an 'unfamiliar feast of love'. Healey himself dubbed it an 'outstanding achievement of British diplomacy'.[30] And an Assessment Office set up by the Government concluded that 'most of the people of Hong Kong find the draft agreement acceptable'.[31] Foreign Secretary Sir Geoffrey Howe made great play with these words in promoting the agreement.[32] But things soon began to go sour. The Government's 'independent monitors' warned that 'the verdict of acceptance implies neither positive enthusiasm nor passive acquiescence'.[33] As they predicted, the next few years saw the growing politicisation of the Colony[34] – whose lack of any real democratic rights was a damning comment on the claim that the British empire had been intended to prepare its subjects for self-government. The agreement depended for its plausibility on faith that China was moving towards western notions of economic and political liberalism. But the recrudescence of a hardline gerontocratic leadership in Beijing and its vicious repression of the pro-democracy movement in June 1989 made such faith very difficult to sustain. After the Tienaman Square massacre it was hard to believe that the same Chinese government would honour its commitments to social and political freedoms in Hong Kong. Emigration from the colony accelerated and the Thatcher government's offer of passports to some 250,000 of the Hong Kong elite did nothing to assuage discontent there, while antagonising its own right wing.

Thatcher, that indefatigable critic of Marxism, had committed Britain in 1997 to 'the return of more free people to Communist rule than has ever been undertaken before'.[35] Like the 'betrayal' of the whites in Rhodesia and the Orangemen in Ulster, it seemed an incongruous outcome for someone so firm in her opinions and so proud of her reputation as a leader of 'conviction'. 'If I were the odd one out and I were right, that would not matter, would it?', she once asked a hostile interviewer triumphantly.[36] Yet these examples show that the obdurate image could often deceive. Her instincts could be 'subordinated by her to what her intellect came to decide made political sense'.[37] That required hours of persuasion undertaken by those who commanded her intellectual respect. Moreover, she was by nature a doer, a problem-solver – as befitted one trained as a chemist and a lawyer. According to one FCO official, she was inclined to see foreign affairs not as a complex flux, an 'ever-shifting context', but as 'a set of finite, set piece problems, which raise the British interest in a fixed way, which she has to sort out and solve once and for all'.[38] And once convinced of the need to act, her pride and obstinacy then tied her into the policies to which she had publicly committed herself, however distasteful their consequences might be. Rhodesia, Ulster and Hong Kong all fit this pattern. FCO failure in 1980 to persuade her to adopt a leaseback solution for the Falklands may have been because Carrington had used up most of his political capital with her and the Tories over the Rhodesia settlement the previous year.[39]

Thus, the Falklands, for all its importance for Thatcher's image and her political security, was the exception rather than the rule if we look at her 'imperial policy'. Indeed this strident nationalist went further to liquidate what little remained of the British empire than her derided predecessors of the previous decade. Whether the policies were successful or not, this was a striking departure from rhetoric and appearance. And it underlines a basic point – that often in the Thatcher years 'declaratory and operational policies followed rather different paths'.[40] In other words, what Margaret Thatcher said at first was not always what the British Government eventually did. That is crucial for an understanding of her policies on both the European Community and East–West relations.

THE EUROPEAN COMMUNITY AND THE ROAD TO 1992

Thatcher came to power with deep doubts about the EC. She believed in an enlarged market and in the importance of European diplomatic cooperation, but had no time for federalist ideas about a 'United States of Europe'.[41] According to Lord Soames, on Europe 'she is an agnostic who continues to go to church. She won't become an atheist, but on the other hand she certainly won't become a true believer'.[42] And on the Common Agricultural Policy (CAP) and, above all, Britain's budget contribution she was a ferocious heretic. 'I cannot play Sister Bountiful to the Community . . . . We want our money', she insisted.[43]

The first five years of Thatcher's premiership were dominated by the budget issue. In 1979, the transitional period negotiated by Heath had expired and Britain was experiencing the full disparity between budget contributions and receipts. The Treasury estimated that Britain was entitled to a £1 billion rebate and Thatcher began to harangue her European partners on this issue. At the European Council meeting in Dublin in November 1979, incensed at the patronising attitude of

Schmidt and Giscard to 'la fille d'épicier', she turned down an offer of £350 million.[44] At the next Council, in April 1980, the offer was doubled to about £760 million but it was only for two years and she still said 'no'. On 30 May 1980 a new compromise was thrashed out by foreign ministers in Brussels. The rebate involved was marginally better and it would run for three years not two, if no fundamental reform of the budget had been agreed by 1982.[45] But Thatcher was still hostile and it took an implicit threat of resignation by Carrington, backed by at least six Cabinet colleagues, to force her acquiescence – 'one of the quite rare instances during the Thatcher era when the Cabinet collectively gathered sufficient will to divert the prime minister from her favoured course'.[46]

Thatcher's intransigence was deplored by many British diplomats. They did not regard the budget inequities as worthy of such pyrotechnics. The total EC budget in 1983 was only £15 billion – equivalent to 'that of a large UK Department' such as Education.[47] For her there was a principle at stake, but, at root, her calculations were political as much as financial. 'At a time when economic problems were piling up at home, the leader who was seen as struggling to the death against no fewer than eight foreign powers made much of her image of patriotic valour'.[48] Her leverage over the EC was considerable, because its revenue was now proving inadequate for its needs. She was ready to block any increase in EC income until Britain's budget contribution had been resolved.[49] And she was able to do this because so much of EC business was despatched now at European Council meetings of heads of government rather than by the diplomats and foreign ministers. These European summits often degenerated into national virility contests, much to the FCO's regret.[50]

May 1980 did not prove a lasting settlement. Fundamental reform of the EC budget failed to materialise and Francis Pym, Carrington's successor as Foreign Secretary (1982–3), secured another ad hoc rebate, amounting to £850 million for 1982. Pym was sensitive to FCO scruples, but his non-Thatcherite values and his evident lack of enthusiasm for the Falklands war made him an immediate casualty of the post-1983 election reshuffle. In his successor, Sir Geoffrey Howe (1983–9), Thatcher had an assiduous, loyal and unflamboyant lieutenant, whose lawyer's mind gave him a readiness, matched only by his leader, to master the minutiae of the budget issue. In the European Council meetings of 1983–4 they wore down the opposition – François Mitterrand and Helmut Kohl were less experienced than their predecessors, Giscard and Schmidt, and much less ready than Thatcher to do their homework in advance. She was now reaping advantage from the fact that the budget issue was being handled by heads of government.

What also helped was the growing urgency felt by all EC members to restructure the whole budget in order to reduce the wastage of the CAP and to increase EC revenue. This would be part of the new general 'relaunch' proposed by the European Council in Stuttgart in June 1983 'to tackle the most pressing problems facing the Community so as to provide a solid base for the further dynamic development of the Community over the rest of the decade'.[51] In this more favourable atmosphere Britain inched towards a settlement. After acrimonious failure at the European Council meetings at Athens in December 1983 and Brussels the following March, the Fontainebleau summit in June 1984 reached a successful conclusion. Thatcher agreed to an increase in EC VAT revenues from 1 per cent to 1.4 per cent. In return she accepted a formula for an annual rebate of 66 per cent on the difference between Britain's VAT contributions to the budget and its receipts from the EC.

Even the FCO now admitted that Thatcher's obduracy had secured a far larger rebate than they would have expected in 1979 and that it had also helped force EC attention on to the budget and CAP problems. In these respects the 'British budget campaign has to be judged a diplomatic success in the short to medium term'.[52] But the image of Britain as a negative element in the Community had been reinforced by Thatcher's highly public, confrontational style. The budget was the main instance, but there were others, of which the question of South African sanctions was particularly instructive.

This issue came centre-stage from 1984 because of the uprisings in the townships and the Pretoria government's 'state of emergency'.[53] In both the Commonwealth and the European Community Thatcher resolutely opposed sanctions. Britain's historic economic interests in South Africa set it apart from most of its partners in both organisations, few of whom would lose much by cutting off economic links. But what is less often noted is the fact that by the mid-1980s Germany had replaced Britain as South Africa's most important EC trading partner. Of EC exports to South Africa 42 per cent were West German in 1986, compared with Britain's 30 per cent, while each of these countries took about 16 per cent of EC imports from South Africa.[54] When, in 1985–6, the EC debated tighter economic sanctions against South Africa, Thatcher attracted international attention for her outspoken opposition. Meanwhile, behind the scenes, Chancellor Kohl engaged in 'quiet sabotage of the sanctions exercise' to protect German economic interests.[55] Kohl got what he wanted; Thatcher got the blame.

By the mid-1980s the FCO was deeply concerned about the consequences of such intransigence. While others masked their pursuit of
national interest in Euro-rhetoric, Thatcher's forthright criticism of the
EC ensured that Britain was always depicted as the uniquely 'bad European'. To counter this Howe gave a major speech in London in
November 1983, setting out a positive agenda for the future of Europe
to show that 'this government . . . has ideas as good, and as *communau-
taire*, as anyone else's'.[56] And when the budget issue was finally resolved, at Fontainebleau in June 1984, Thatcher tabled a paper entitled
'Europe – the Future' embodying essentially the same themes.[57] The
message was clear: with the major obstacle of the budget contribution
now removed, Britain was ready and able to help shape Europe's future. Put more cynically, Thatcher had been persuaded of the need to
play Europolitics – dressing up her conception of national interest in a
suitably European form. As part of the campaign to improve Britain's
image 'Europe – the Future' was given extensive publicity.

The paper (HMG 1984) touched on various issues, ranging from
pollution to high technology. But it had two central themes, both
presenting positively Thatcher's minimalist view of the EC as a free
market formed by allied but sovereign states. Thus, great stress was laid
on the value of European Political Cooperation (EPC). This had always been an area of genuine British enthusiasm.[58] Carrington was
particularly supportive and took an active role in European attempts to
end the Afghanistan crisis and to promote a Middle Eastern settlement
through recognition of Palestinian rights – an aim embodied in the
Venice Declaration of June 1980. Over the Falklands war the EC partners rapidly imposed a ban on Argentine imports and their solidarity
held until late May 1982, with the escalation of hostilities.[59] Thatcher
wanted to enlarge the EPC to embrace security matters, thereby
strengthening the European 'pillar' of NATO. This was opposed by
Denmark, Ireland and Greece. In the 1984 paper she was reported to
have attached particular importance to the proposal for 'a common
approach to external affairs'.[60]

But the main theme of this paper was a call to complete the single
European market, particularly in the service sector. Formal tariff barriers had been abolished by the Six within its first decade, but many
other obstacles remained – currency regulations, trading standards, restrictions on the mobility of labour and capital. In line with its free
market philosophy, the Thatcher government proclaimed this as the
key to Europe's future and in 1984–5 one of the British Commissio-
ners in Brussels, Lord Cockfield, played a leading role in drawing up a
timetable for the elimination of remaining obstacles, involving some

300 items of legislation to be passed by member governments. In this area, as Thatcher liked to point out, the British were more advanced Europeans than many. The French socialist government, for instance, was slow to abolish exchange controls, which Thatcher had done as soon as she assumed power in 1979.

Even on the single market, however, Thatcher's radicalism was selective: she insisted on continued customs checks (to stop terrorists and rabid dogs) and opposed VAT on children's clothes for domestic electoral reasons. Furthermore, she emphatically rejected the argument that a fully effective free market required concomitant integration among governments – specifically a common monetary policy, leading to eventual currency union, harmonisation of economic policy on such issues as taxation, and coordinated regional and social policies to help disadvantaged areas and groups. That these ideas were advanced with particular fervour by continental socialists did nothing to endear them to 10 Downing Street.

Thus, Thatcher insisted that the single market did not need further governmental integration to work properly. She also stood out against the continental belief in the need for fundamental institutional reforms of the EC. This belief reflected not merely the rooted commitment of continental federalists to political union but, more immediately, growing disquiet about the capacity of the EC to act cohesively and quickly. The paralysis caused by Britain's budget battle dramatised the problem, and the difficulties were only likely to increase with the inclusion of Spain and Portugal in 1986, following Greece in 1981. All these were countries with large and very backward agrarian sectors, even more different in their own way from the original Six than Britain had been. Adjusting to their needs would pose yet more strains on both the budget and the decision-making process. The call at Stuttgart in June 1983 for a 'relaunch' articulated these concerns and in February 1984 the veteran Italian federalist, Altiero Spinelli, pushed a draft treaty for 'European Union' through the European Parliament. Although having no binding force, the political support the treaty won from member governments left the British isolated. Particularly striking was the shift in the French position.[61] Under Mitterrand it was gradually moving from a Gaullist defence of national sovereignty towards greater integration, paralleling its growing cooperation across the board with West Germany.

Thatcher's Fontainebleau paper was partly a response to this isolation,[62] but it failed to divert the debate. The broad interpretation of 1992 and the demand for institutional reform were firmly on the agenda. From 1985, with Britain's budget contribution largely resolved, these became Thatcher's new battlegrounds. But, despite the belligerent rhetoric, she was fighting a delaying action. This pattern can be illustrated by looking briefly in turn at the ensuing rows over the Single European Act, enlarged expenditure, and economic and monetary union.

At the Milan European Council in June 1985 agreement was reached on Cockfield's timetable for implementing the single market by the end of 1992. This was an apparent British victory. Yet, at the same time, on Franco–German initiative, the meeting also agreed to set up an intergovernmental conference to revise the Treaty of Rome with institutional reforms. This was driven through by seven votes to three, with Britain, Denmark and Greece opposed. Thatcher was particularly exercised by proposals for majority voting on most issues and increased decision-making powers for the European Parliament (an issue backed strongly by Italy and the Benelux countries). Like de Gaulle in the 1960s, she wanted to keep the EC an intergovernmental rather than a supranational body and in particular insisted on retaining the national right of veto. She told the Commons angrily that 'some positive improvements in the Community's decision-making could have been decided in Milan and did not require any treaty amendment'.[63] Britain did attend the conference but Thatcher's Cabinet Office adviser on EC affairs, David Williamson, persuaded her to take a back-seat and thereby oblige others, especially France and Germany, to take on the onus and thus the blame for diluting federalist proposals about which they too had reservations.[64]

At the Luxemburg European Council in December 1985 a compromise was reached in the 'Single European Act' (SEA) – as the new treaty was called in English. The British Government chose to highlight two elements – the 1992 timetable for achieving the single market and the formal inclusion of the EPC process within EC affairs.[65] The Minister of State at the FCO, Lynda Chalker, went so far as to claim that 'most of the changes' embodied in the Act 'give expression in juridical form to proposals which we made before Milan'.[66] But it soon became clear that other aspects of the treaty, played down by the Government, had subtly changed the balance of the Community.[67] The principle of majority voting, though limited, was permitted for some items of business in the Council. And a new 'cooperation procedure' gave the Parliament, when backed by the Commission, enhanced powers to amend Council proposals. Taken together these changes made it less easy for a single national government, such as Britain, to block Community business in the Council. In March 1990 the Commons Foreign Affairs Committee concluded that 'the SEA has had much greater institutional impact than anyone predicted' in Britain when its provisions were passed into British law in 1986.[68]

These institutional changes, and the commitment in the SEA to making 'concrete progress towards European unity',[69] served as a rallying point for the proponents of deeper integration. The latter made further progress in 1987–8, when a new EC budget crisis threatened to reopen the question of Britain's contribution. This provides a second indication of the successes and failures of Thatcher's EC policy. As in 1983–4 Thatcher and Howe tried to make increased EC revenue conditional on improved rebates for Britain. At the Council meeting in Brussels in June 1987 Thatcher was in a minority of one in opposing the European Commission's offer. Even the ever-loyal Howe was reportedly left 'shaking with anger' at her failure to accept what he deemed a good deal.[70] An emergency meeting in Brussels in February 1988 resulted, after exhausting argument, in another compromise. Thatcher retained the Fontainebleau rebate mechanism and obtained assurances of tight controls on the CAP. The latter were a major step in addressing the scandal of continental agriculture. In return, she was forced to concede increased EC expenditure, at some cost to Britain, including a doubling of social and regional funds by 1992. This enlargement of EC spending, especially in what she deemed a 'socialist' direction, was decidedly against her preferences. Characteristically, however, she presented the outcome of the summit as a personal triumph and denounced others for their own tactical ploys. 'Only a Frenchman could have done that', she complained at one point.[71]

Thatcher also found it increasingly difficult to maintain her rearguard action against the European Monetary System (EMS). In Opposition she had professed full support and castigated Labour for not joining,[72] but after her election she took the line that Britain would only join the Exchange Rate Mechanism (ERM) 'when the time was ripe' – a phrase that became a synonym for 'over my dead body'. By the mid-1980s the Treasury had joined the FCO in criticising this stance. In 1987–8 the Chancellor, Nigel Lawson, informally allowed sterling to shadow the Deutschmark, to help control inflation and prepare for entry into the ERM. But, by doing this outside the EMS, sterling was denied the protection of the system's reserves, and the signal sent to the exchange dealers was negated by the denials of the strategy trumpeted by Thatcher and her economic adviser, Sir Alan Walters.

Britain's isolation intensified with the intergovernmental proposals for economic and monetary union, issued in April 1989.[73] These considered that the gradual development of a central bank and common currency were essential counterparts of the single market. Thatcher had made clear her abhorrence of such ideas. 'I neither want nor expect to see such a bank in my lifetime,' she told journalists in October 1988, 'nor, if I'm twanging a harp, for quite a long time afterwards'.[74] At the Madrid summit in June 1989, Howe and Lawson combined to insist that total British isolation was becoming untenable. They forced Thatcher to accept the principle of eventual monetary union and the first stage of the Commission's proposals – informal cooperation on exchange management. But Thatcher soon had her revenge,[75] removing Howe from the FCO in July and refusing publicly to back Lawson against Walters, when the Chancellor gave her an ultimatum in October. Despite Lawson's resignation, she continued to insist on many pre-conditions for entry into the ERM, including lower inflation, liberalisation of EC capital markets and further progress on the single market. And when the new Chancellor, John Major, came out with the government's own proposals for monetary union in November 1989, they were couched in an 'evolutionary', market-based form acceptable to Thatcher (HMG 1989).

In 1988 Thatcher's animus towards the EC became personalised in the figure of the Commission's energetic and ambitious President, Jacques Delors: socialist, federalist, intellectual – and French. In July 1988 he predicted that 'in ten years, 80 per cent of economic legislation – and perhaps tax and social legislation – will be directed from the Community'. In September he addressed the TUC conference in Bournemouth on the need for a 'social dimension' to 1992, to benefit workers and not just businessmen.[76] Film of Delors being given a standing ovation to the strains of *Frère Jacques* infuriated Thatcher. Even after the FCO had toned down her language considerably,[77] her speech at Bruges in September 1988 was her frankest exposition to date of her vision of Europe. 'Willing and active cooperation between independent sovereign states is the best way to build a successful European Community', she stated, attacking her opponents for trying 'to suppress nationhood' and to create 'some sort of identikit European personality'. And she warned that 'we have not successfully rolled back the frontiers of the state in Britain, only to see them re-imposed at a European level, with a European super-state exercising a new dominance from Brussels'.[78] She went on to outline the Community she wanted – a free market formed by free governments, who cooperated in foreign policy to strengthen the NATO alliance, while retaining sovereignty over most areas of economic, financial and social policy.

The events surrounding the Bruges speech marked an important shift in British political debate about the European Community.

Hitherto, Labour had been the more reluctant Europeans, reflecting the predilection of much of the left for an insular socialism in defiance of what it deemed a capitalist club. The Tories, though anxious about sovereignty and the loss of national status, as usual kept their doubts to themselves. But Thatcher's speech prompted the formation of 'the Bruges Group', determined to make her vision of a free market formed by sovereign states a live political issue. And this acted as a focus for much more public airing of Tory fears. At the same time, the growing undercurrent of Tory resentment by 1989 at Thatcher's unending tenure of office, though rarely surfacing, did strengthen the leadership pretensions of others, notably Michael Heseltine. He had resigned as Defence Secretary in January 1986 after unsuccessfully backing a European rather than an American-led consortium to rescue Westland Helicopters.[79] The crisis, which revealed Whitehall infighting at its dirtiest and which briefly shook the government to its foundations, was largely a political affair – exacerbated by the tendency of the 'Iron Lady' to dither in the face of rows among her entourage. Heseltine's resignation, like that of Lawson in 1989, exemplified her failure to move quickly and decisively in such situations, thus allowing pressure to reach explosive proportions. Nevertheless, there was an underlying issue at stake. Heseltine had good European credentials and part of his pitch to Tory MPs as doubts about her leadership deepened was a different and more constructive approach to Europe.

While the Tories began to wrangle publicly about the EC, Labour was finding a new, if tenuous, unity on the issue. In February 1986 its foreign affairs spokesman George Robertson had called the Single European Act a 'measure of profound irrelevance to the deep-seated concerns of Europe's peoples' and warned that the EC had 'massive and seemingly insuperable problems'.[80] Privately the word was that British withdrawal from the EC remained an option, albeit a last resort, for a future Labour government. But Delors's speech to the TUC about the 'social dimension' to 1992 offered the party a new gloss on Europe. It seized on the proposed 'social charter' for workers' rights – dismissed by Thatcher as 'outdated Marxist doctrines'[81] – to make the EC more attractive to socialist values. Labour's leader Neil Kinnock claimed that 'we are better Europeans' because Thatcherism merely wanted a market Europe for 'big business' whereas 'we want Britain to take a lead in building social Europe', benefiting all its people.[82] In the European elections of June 1989 Labour secured 46 seats to the Tories' 32 – compared with the 1984 result of 33 to 46.[83] Labour's new image of 'Europeanism' was bolstered by Tory jingoism. One slogan, personally authorised by Thatcher, warned 'Stay at home on June 15th, and you'll live on a diet of Brussels'.[84]

In fact, Labour and Tories shared many attitudes to the EC. Both parties favoured cautious intergovernmental cooperation, rather than rapid monetary and political union, and both insisted on the 'sovereignty' of the Westminster Parliament. To some extent, the British were simply more honest about their pursuit of national self-interest. All their partners were playing the same game beneath the Euro-rhetoric – the Germans over the EMS or South African sanctions; France over the CAP or arms-for-hostages; Denmark, Greece and Ireland in opposing a security dimension; Italy and Benelux in seeking greater leverage for weaker states through a strengthened European Parliament. All the Twelve at times treated the European menu as 'à la carte' rather than 'table d'hôte'.

But a radical assertion of 'sovereignty' flew in the face of the facts about modern Britain. Thatcher herself had allowed the erosion of sovereignty over Ulster by signing the Hillsborough agreement with Dublin. As former Foreign Secretary Lord Carrington acknowledged, 'we have had quite a loss of sovereignty in Nato for years'.[85] And, in the case of the EC, every aspect of British government policy was constrained to some extent by Community directives. Each Whitehall department, even those apparently 'domestic' in function such as Agriculture or the Home Office, now has a European dimension to its work. This was particularly true for the FCO. Douglas Hurd, Foreign Secretary from November 1989, commented in 1981 that since the early 1950s,

> the biggest single change of diplomatic method stems from European
> Political Co-operation. In 1952 [when he was a young FO official] it was
> broadly speaking with the Americans only that we shared information and
> assessments; policy-making was a national preserve. Now in some areas of
> diplomacy our policy is formed wholly within a European context; and in
> no area is the European influence completely absent.[86]

In particular, Thatcherite insistence on national economic sovereignty was unreal. The recovery of the mid-1980s had not solved the fundamental problems of the British economy. There had been changes, of course. The most uncompetitive firms had gone to the wall, public monopolies had been sold off as private monopolies, and the values of enterprise promulgated. Yet Britain's industrial sector was too small and too pricey to satisfy domestic demand, let alone conquer foreign markets. By 1988 a serious balance of payments deficit emerged, masked earlier by North Sea oil revenues. On trade in manufactures Britain ran a deficit not just with Germany but with every EC country except Ireland.[87] Thatcher still asserted that growth was inexorable. 'My ambition is that we catch up France. And then we catch up with Germany'.[88] But West Germany now dominated the EC, with nearly 40 per cent of its manufacturing output and 35 per cent of its manufacturing exports. Britain, with about 12 per cent of both, was behind not only Germany and France but also Italy. Membership of the EC had done nothing to arrest its decline in economic performance (table 10.1). Indeed the progressive creation of a European free market had only enhanced the competitive advantages of the German economy and its currency.[89]

Table 10.1 Indicators of Britain's comparative economic performance since 1960

a) Percentage share of the EC 12's real manufacturing output

	1970	1977	1985	(1985 population)
UK	16.8	14.8	12.8	56.2 million
France	20.5	23.5	23.0	55.2 million
Italy	14.7	15.5	16.4	57.1 million
FRG	39.2	37.6	38.4	61.0 million

b) Percentage share of EC 12's manufactured exports

	1960	1970	1977	1985
UK	25.8	17.7	16.1	11.9
France	15.5	14.6	15.8	14.5
Italy	8.3	12.0	12.7	13.9
FRG	31.1	33.2	32.1	35.4

Source: Cutler et al. 1989: 11–12
(Note: EC12 means the 12 countries that constituted the European Community from 1986.)

Reiterated assertions of national sovereignty and of British economic strength masked these underlying realities of interdependence and even dependence. Privately Whitehall was coming to terms with them, particularly after the budget issue had been settled, and the evolution of the government's 'operational' policy towards the EC testified to this. Under Foreign Office pressure the language of Thatcher's 'declaratory' policy changed to some extent in 1984 and the British government played a significant part in pushing through the 'single market' programme. But this was not integration as understood by most of Britain's European partners, whose pressures for a radical interpretation of 1992 and for a more coordinated Community intensified as the 1980s progressed. And, despite the growing 'European' packaging of government declarations, policy instincts under Thatcher remained viscerally nationalistic. There was no attempt 'by the Conservative government to build a domestic consensus for its European policies'.[90] This reflected the Prime Minister's own outlook, the evident reservations of the public about many aspects of integration and, in consequence, the perceived political benefits of nationalist rhetoric about 'our money' and 'our Parliament'. By 1989, however, the political calculus began to shift. The new Europeanism of the Labour party was one factor, and the 1989 Euro-elections were a sharp warning to the Tories about the danger of being seen as narrowly anti-European. Equally pressing were the new international realities. For the ending of the Cold War was redrawing the map of Europe more profoundly than at any time since 1945.

BEYOND THE COLD WAR

As the 1970s progressed, superpower detente had become increasingly strained. The SALT II arms control agreement had taken years to negotiate and it was overtaken by events in 1979 when the USSR invaded Afghanistan to stabilise a client regime on its borders. Carter withdrew the treaty from the process of Senate ratification and imposed economic sanctions on Moscow. His successor from January 1981, Ronald Reagan, went further. Denunciations of the 'evil empire' were matched by increased defence spending and a new determination to confront communist expansion in Central America. The central arena of the new cold war became the question of European defence. In December 1979 NATO had decided to modernise its intermediate nuclear forces (INF) in Europe with 108 Pershing II missiles and 464 Ground-Launched Cruise Missiles (GLCMs). The intention was to counter the new SS-20 Soviet missiles and to reassure Western governments about American commitments to Europe. To avoid the impression of escalation, the decision was 'dual track' – modernisation backed by continued negotiation for arms control. But as deployment went ahead it set off a crisis that rocked the European pillar of NATO. Its resolution preoccupied Margaret Thatcher for her first few years.

Thatcher was a vehement anti-communist. This was an extension of her crusade against socialism at home, for she saw the two ideologies as points on the same spectrum.[91] In 1976 her warnings that the Soviet Union was bent on world domination earned her the soubriquets in Moscow of 'iron lady' and 'militant Amazon' and within weeks of taking office she insisted that 'Communism never sleeps . . . . It never changes its objectives. Nor must we. Our first duty to freedom is to defend our own'.[92] As premier she continued to warn of the Soviet danger and the need to maintain strong defences as a deterrent: 'a bully always goes for the weakest'.[93] Consequently, she was a firm supporter of the dual-track decision and accepted 160 Cruise missiles for basing in Britain.

Inseparably linked to her anti-communism was her faith in the American alliance. 'I feel no inhibitions about describing the relationship as very, very special', she affirmed in Washington in 1985.[94] Again domestic and foreign policy intertwined. The USA was the embodiment of liberal capitalism and its nuclear weapons were the centrepiece of NATO's strategy. Reagan himself would never have found a place within her own Cabinet. 'Poor dear, there's nothing between his ears', she once observed privately.[95] But he shared her beliefs in economic liberalism, anti-communism and the Soviet danger. And, more important, for all his limitations, he was president of Britain's principal ally, whose support she regarded as fundamental. She therefore cultivated Reagan assiduously – flattering in public, cajoling in private – the British conception of the 'special relationship' in its purest form since Macmillan.

As a convinced exponent of nuclear deterrence, she also moved promptly to renew Britain's unique nuclear ties with Washington by deciding to purchase Trident C4 missiles from the USA – the next-generation deterrent when the Polaris system secured by Macmillan became obsolete. Agreement was announced in July 1980. When, the following year, the Pentagon decided to develop the more powerful D5 version, the British had little option but to buy that instead. The new agreement, signed in March 1982, was a further reminder, albeit less shocking than the Skybolt fiasco of 1962, of what it meant for Britain to be dependent on US nuclear technology.[96]

The Cruise and Trident decisions, taking effect amid a new cold war, ruptured the bipartisan consensus on defence. New anti-nuclear pressure groups proliferated. The Campaign for Nuclear Disarmament (CND), which had been dormant since the mid-1960s, jumped in membership from 5,000 in 1979 to 100,000 in 1985, and the women's 'peace camp' around the US air base at Greenham Common gained an international reputation. The Labour party took up the argument. Swinging left after the 1979 defeat, its union paymasters had blocked the leadership pretensions of pro-NATO centrist Denis Healey and supported the left-wing Michael Foot. In the 1983 election Labour campaigned against Cruise and Trident, demanding a non-nuclear Britain, stripped of US bases and its own nuclear force. For Washington this was deeply alarming. Though diminished in power, Britain was regarded as the most secure supporter of NATO. Senior Pentagon figures warned of a snowball effect if Labour policy had been enacted, leading to an unravelling of the Alliance.[97]

Although some of these warnings were deliberate scare-mongering, they testified to the depth of NATO's crisis at this time.[98] The Cruise deployment, reluctantly accepted by the USA to reassure the Europeans, especially Germany, had become a test of NATOS's political will and very survival, as the disarmament crusade – tinged with strong anti-American sentiment – spread through Britain, Germany and the Netherlands. The Soviets played on this, refusing to negotiate (the other element of NATO's dual-track decision) until the new missiles were withdrawn, and cultivating the western peace movements in an effort to split the Alliance. The Government became locked in a protracted propaganda battle against CND.

The collapse of the defence consensus and the new Trident programme also raised questions about the wisdom and cost of Britain's whole defence policy. The Thatcher government inherited a NATO commitment to increase defence spending in real terms by 3 per cent per annum until 1986. In addition, to staunch the outflow of skilled personnel, it agreed to increase service pay by one-third. In 1982 Britain was spending about the same on defence, in absolute terms, as France or Germany – around $27 billion per annum or about one-sixth of the US defence budget.[99] Yet as a percentage of its GDP Britain was spending far more than any Western European power – 5.2 per cent in 1982, compared with 4.2 per cent for France and 3.4 per cent for West Germany.[100] For an economy in decline against its rivals, that was difficult to sustain. Given, at the same time, Thatcher's determination to reduce government spending, cuts in the defence budget were inevitable – whatever the Government's rhetoric about a strong defence.

The problem, as before, with any reappraisal of defence, was the multiplicity of roles that Britain supposedly fulfilled. Conventionally the Ministry of Defence identified four: the strategic nuclear force, the defence of the UK, land and air commitments in Germany, and the protection of NATO's Atlantic lifelines. In addition, there was 'half' a role outside the NATO area, for example in naval patrols to help protect oil supplies through the Persian Gulf. Although in Defence White Papers strategy supposedly determined force structures, it was often the other way round – strategic doctrine was a rationalisation for the services' existence. It was to cut through this bureaucratic web that Thatcher made John Nott Defence Secretary in January 1981.[101] With a ruthlessness reminiscent of Sandys in 1957, Nott imposed his will on the MOD and forced the services to justify themselves. His Defence White Paper of June 1981 insisted that, given the escalating costs of defence and Britain's declining resources, 'we cannot go on as we are'.[102] It argued that the Navy's work in the Atlantic could largely be carried out by submarines and land-based aircraft and proposed eliminating the carriers and cutting the destroyers and frigates from 50 to 40.

'What we need now is a small colonial war requiring a lot of ships', observed a senior officer after the cuts were announced.[103] His prayers were answered by General Galtieri the following spring. The Falklands war gave the Navy's surface fleet a new raison d'etre and made it politically untouchable. Nott resigned once the dust had settled. But the budget problem remained. Michael Heseltine, Nott's successor, was more interested in diagrams than doctrine. His recipe for saving money was to push through further unification of the MOD, including the abolition of separate service staffs, and the adoption of new systems of management and procurement.[104] These reforms, announced in the 1984 White Paper, were part of the long-term effort, since the 1950s, to create a unified and efficient Ministry of Defence out of three rival Services and they undoubtedly enhanced efficiency. But the basic discrepancy between roles and resources remained. Defence pundits argued about how long Britain could maintain a nuclear strategic force, a navy second in NATO only to the USA and an army of 55,000 men in combat-readiness in Germany, plus the new obligations of Fortress Falklands. Assuming Trident was inviolable, which should go – the 'maritime' role, as Nott had argued, or the 'continental'? The only agreement was that choices could not be delayed indefinitely.[105]

Nevertheless, these were debates among defence specialists. The Falklands war had saved the navy and forced defence cuts off the political agenda for the moment. Moreover, Thatcher's re-election in June 1983 with a majority of 144 ensured that the Cruise and Trident decision would go ahead. The victory of Helmut Kohl's Christian Democrats earlier that year also confirmed the Pershing deployment in West Germany. NATO had survived its worst crisis since France withdrew in the mid-1960s.

But then the policy of extended nuclear deterrence, on which Thatcher placed such emphasis, was threated in a new way, this time by Reagan's 'Strategic Defense Initiative' (SDI), announced without warning in March 1983. The programme, quickly dubbed 'Star Wars', envisaged a network of space stations and lasers to destroy enemy missiles in flight and thereby create a complete 'astrodome' protection for America against nuclear weapons. Although most US scientists scoffed at the idea, even limited US missile development could upset the nuclear balance of mutual assured destruction on which deterrence rested and prompt the Soviets into a new arms race in space. If America felt secure, it might also presage a decoupling of American security from that of Western Europe.

Thatcher's response to SDI was a good example of the British concept of the special relationship. Publicly she supported the President, while privately trying to divert his brainstorm in directions beneficial to Britain. This effort had two dimensions – security and economics. On the security front Thatcher wished to maintain nuclear deterrence while preventing a new arms race. In America in December 1984, she lectured Reagan for an hour-and-a-half ('as a chemist') on the implausibility of SDI and then extracted a joint statement.[106] Both leaders, against the wishes of the Pentagon, pledged that any attempt to move from SDI research to weapons deployment would 'have to be a matter for negotiation'.[107] For the first time the USA had stated its wish to keep the new weapons within an international arms control framework. The following March Howe gave a long and detailed speech on SDI. Although ostensibly supporting *research* into SDI, it posed so many questions about the wisdom of eventual deployment that it cast doubt on the whole programme, much to the Pentagon's fury. 'Research may acquire an unstoppable momentum', Howe warned, implying clearly that SDI would not make nuclear weapons 'independent and obsolete' – Reagan's dream – but would simply be another stage 'in the everlasting marathon of the arms race'.[108]

On the economic side of SDI, Thatcher followed what was a consistent pattern underlying her diplomacy. Ideology or theory had never been allowed to imperil British commercial interest. At the end of 1981, when Reagan imposed sanctions against the Polish government for its imposition of martial law, Thatcher publicly commended his 'excellent lead' but the actual British measures were extremely mild.[109] In June 1982 Reagan imposed sanctions on European firms engaged in building a Soviet gas pipeline from Siberia to Western Europe. Thatcher issued a rare public rebuke of US policy, calling it 'wrong . . . for one very powerful nation' to impede fulfilment of 'existing contracts that do not, in any event, fall under its jurisdiction'.[110] In the case of SDI, she judged that British commercial interests dictated co-operation. Whatever Thatcher's doubts about the strategic wisdom of the project, it seemed essential that British firms were not excluded from the high-tec bonanza. Britain became the first European nation formally to join the SDI, thereby enhancing the project's credibility in Congress. Although the Government had talked of £1.45 billion of business for Britain, by May 1988, when the project was being drastically cut by Congress, British SDI contracts had only amounted to £61.5 million.[111]

Thatcher's public loyalty to the United States was rarely breached. In October 1983 she was severely embarrassed when Reagan, partly for domestic political reasons, decided to send troops to restore order in the Caribbean island of Grenada. His failure to inform Britain, even though Grenada was a member of the Commonwealth and the Queen was its head of state, left Thatcher looking foolish. Labour's Denis Healey lambasted her as Reagan's 'obedient poodle'.[112] But she confined her fury to phone conversations with the President and in April 1986 Britain was the only European ally to allow its US bases to be used for raids on Libya, in retaliation for terrorist acts against US servicemen. Thatcher was privately unhappy about the raids. In January 1986 she had condemned the idea of 'retaliatory strikes that are against international law'.[113] But her Falklands debt to Reagan and her commitment to Alliance solidarity carried the day. Typically, in public she displayed no hint of these doubts. The USA 'has hundreds of thousands of forces in Europe to defend the liberty of Europe', she told the Commons. 'In that capacity they have been subject to terrorist attack. It was inconceivable to me that we should refuse United States aircraft and pilots the opportunity to defend their people'.[114]

Yet behind the public image of a strong Atlantic alliance against the Soviet threat, British policy in the new cold war began to change in Thatcher's second term.[115] As with the European Community issue, the initiative came from the FCO, unhappy about the rigidity of Thatcher's position and the deadlock in east–west relations. Its opportunity came in mid-1983 when Thatcher was unsettled by Reagan's star wars speech and had gained new political security after re-election. A series of meetings with Soviet experts in the FCO and academia in the late summer persuaded the premier to adopt a policy of 'differentiation' in Eastern Europe, cultivating the more open members of the Soviet bloc. An early result was her visit to Hungary in February 1984 – the first time in nearly five years as premier that she had toured any Soviet bloc state. Ten days later she made her first visit to Moscow to attend the funeral of Soviet leader Yuri Andropov, having not attended the obsequies for his predecessor, Leonid Brezhnev, two years before.[116] In 1984–5 Howe, who took a particular interest in the new British Ostpolitik, became the first Foreign Secretary to visit all the Warsaw Pact countries.[117] And in December 1984 the FCO arranged a visit by Soviet Politburo member Mikhail Gorbachev, then largely unknown in the West. He was the most senior Soviet politician to visit Britain since Alexei Kosygin in 1967, and it was also Gorbachev's first serious visit to a major Western state. Frustrated by the gerontocrats of the Kremlin, Thatcher found the lively, open Gorbachev, six years her junior, congenial and impressive. 'I like Mr Gorbachev', she announced. 'We can do business together'.[118]

Within a few months they were indeed doing business together. In 1985 various strands of previous policy came together to weave a new pattern. Gorbachev's accession to power in March brought into the Kremlin an energetic new leader, determined to reduce the arms race which crushed and distorted his backward economy. That was a lesson born from long education in the Soviet system, but it was driven home by NATO's survival of the INF crisis and by the fears of a new high-tec arms race launched by SDI.[119] The need for detente with the West seemed more acute than ever. Yet Reagan, the ageing cold warrior in Washington, hardly seemed a likely partner. In Europe both Kohl and Mitterrand were also hardliners. The 'Iron Lady', now willing to unbend a little, seemed a useful intermediary. For her part, Thatcher was eager to assume this role. Politically secure at home in her second term, she sought a higher profile on the world stage. And, although Cruise had been deployed, the continued domestic furore over defence made it important to present the Tories as a party of peace through negotiation from strength.[120]

In the 1950s and 1960s, British premiers had offered themselves as potential interlocutors between the two superpowers. This was the self-image of Churchill, Eden, Macmillan and Wilson. For a while in the mid-1980s Thatcher did function in this way. As America and Russia reached clumsily towards each other, Britain's special intimacy with US policymaking and its growing credibility with Moscow permitted it to play a role as intermediary. Thatcher's visit to Moscow at the end of March 1987 was a highpoint of this process.

Yet the momentum of superpower detente soon pushed all third parties out of the way. Reagan and Gorbachev met in Geneva in November 1985 and again in Reykjavik a year later. In December 1987 in Washington they agreed on the elimination of all intermediate-range missiles from Europe – Cruise, Pershing and the SS-20s. Although applying to only about 7 per cent of the world's nuclear war-heads, it was the first time that the superpowers had signed an arms *reduction* agreement. And their acceptance of new procedures for verification – involving surveillance and short-notice inspections – was a major breakthrough in the area that had bedevilled all previous efforts at arms control. Negotiations on reducing conventional and also long-range nuclear forces were set in train and Thatcher's own influence over events was further weakened by the end of the Reagan presidency in January 1989. Her relations with his successor, George Bush, were much less close and her input to US policy was thereby reduced.

Thatcher's reaction to the new detente was cautious. Although welcoming the reduction of tension, she was alarmed at the potential for weakening the security of Europe. At Reykjavik in 1986 Reagan and Gorbachev had seemed close to a deal cutting long-range strategic missiles by 50 per cent. That could disastrously weaken the credibility of the US nuclear guarantee of Europe. The French, fearful of American desertion, pressed for Anglo–French nuclear collaboration as the basis of European defence. And for a while Thatcher, shaken in her faith in Reagan, was ready to listen. President Mitterrand recalled that 'after Reykjavik, I saw Mrs Thatcher start to wonder. The European option seemed to come closer'.[121] But it was only a momentary flirtation. Over the next year she gradually emasculated projects for Anglo–French nuclear cooperation that were touted in the Ministry of Defence. All that remained was collaboration on an air-launched nuclear missile for British and French bombers.

Instead, her response to the dangers of 'decoupling' America's security from that of Europe was, as over SDI, to reaffirm NATO's strategy of nuclear deterrence. After Reykjavik she rushed across the Atlantic to bring Reagan back into the fold, much as she had done two years before. Their statement in November 1986 'confirmed that NATO's strategy . . . would continue to require effective nuclear deterrents' and that 'reductions in nuclear weapons would increase the importance of eliminating conventional disparities'. And she also made sure that, whatever the superpowers agreed about their own arsenals, Reagan 'confirmed his full support for the arrangements made to modernise Britain's independent nuclear deterrent with Trident'.[122] Once the INF agreement was signed, covering missiles of a range between 500 and 5000 kilometres, she demanded that NATO modernise its *short*-range nuclear forces (SNFs) including the obsolescent Lance missiles, stationed in Germany. A bruising NATO summit in Brussels in May 1989 went against her – testimony to growing West German influence within the Alliance. Instead of a commitment to modernise SNFs, NATO leaders expressed their readiness to negotiate their removal. And the question of a successor to Lance would 'be dealt with in 1992 in the light of overall security developments'. But Thatcher did secure a pledge that negotiations would aim only at 'a *partial* reduction' of SNFs – underlined at her insistence – and the new NATO strategy document reiterated the importance of nuclear weapons in effective deterrence.[123]

By the summer of 1989, therefore, Thatcher was engaged in a rearguard action over east–west relations similar to her campaign against the EC. In both cases the negativism of her first-term policies – 'our money' and the Soviet threat – had possibly helped to stimulate change in Brussels and Moscow. In both cases, too, the FCO had encouraged her in the second term to take a more constructive stance – the European single market and the new British Ostpolitik. But then both in their turn were overtaken by events – a renewed drive for European integration and rapid superpower detente – leaving Thatcher trying to check the drift towards a very different Europe. The revolutions of 1989 made her task even harder.

TOWARDS A NEW EUROPE

The second half of 1989 saw the greatest upheaval in Europe for four decades. The communist governments of Eastern Europe had become increasingly unstable – economically backward, riddled with corruption, hated by their citizenry and burdened by massive Western debts. From 1985 Gorbachev's reforms in the USSR challenged their legitimacy. Perestroika and glasnost – reconstruction and openness – became buzzwords in much of Eastern Europe and the pressures proved irresistible when it became clear that Gorbachev, unlike his predecessors in 1956 over Hungary or 1968 over Czechoslovakia, would not use force to preserve communist rule in eastern Europe.

The cracks became apparent first in Poland and Hungary, where the communist monopoly of power was broken in the early months of 1989. The communist regime in East Germany survived just long enough to celebrate its fortieth birthday in October. The Bulgarian hardliner, Todor Zhivkov, was removed in November, and by mid-December a broad coalition, with non-communists in the majority, had been formed in Czechoslovakia. The year ended with the bloody demise of the Ceausescus and their oppressive dictatorship in Romania.

The extent of these revolutions varied. In Romania and Bulgaria, former communists remained strongly entrenched, whereas in Hungary and East Germany they were swept off the political map in elections in 1990. For all the diversity, however, certain themes became abundantly clear. The 'iron curtain' had been torn down. The old communist order was dead and Western political and economic liberalism was the new fashion. More than that, the Warsaw Pact crumbled as national armies disintegrated and Soviet troops were obliged to leave. The countries of Eastern Europe were, in varying ways, turning to the West. Yet the problems they faced were enormous.[124] Few had any experience of 'civil society', market forces or pluralist democracy. Their economies were dominated by inefficient heavy industry whose unfettered development had created appalling environmental pollution. The end of communist rule released old ethnic rivalries – Czechs against Slovaks, Romanians against Hungarians – which had been suppressed for years. Assimilating these states into a new Europe would be a costly and unsettling task.

A similar process – with all the problems magnified enormously – was taking place within the Soviet Union itself. Perestroika had undermined the old corrupt economy, while putting nothing in its place. Glasnost gave Soviet citizens unprecedented opportunities to voice their dissatisfaction and, in ethnically diverse republics, to resume ancient genocidal quarrels. Gorbachev's popularity waned, his political base eroding under attack from left and right. And the revolutions in eastern Europe set an incontestable precedent for dissident republics within the USSR, particularly the Baltic states. The old Russian empire, taken over by the Bolsheviks and kept in a straitjacket by Stalin and his successors, was finally breaking apart. What would replace it and how stable the new order would be were the great imponderables.

From these eruptions in eastern Europe and the USSR emerged a new Germany. The post-1945 European order had been a response to the German problem – the wartime expansion of Soviet power, its control of eastern Europe as a buffer against a new Reich, the eventual division of Germany. Conversely, in 1989 the contraction of Soviet power and the emancipation of eastern Europe precipitated a rush towards German unification. The exodus of East Germans westward through now-open borders denuded their own economy of skilled workers and placed intolerable burdens on the West German social services. With free movement of goods and currency across the borders the East German command-economy simply collapsed. And the new mood of German nationalism was hard to resist, least of all by Helmut Kohl in Bonn who calculated that being the architect of unification would ensure not merely a place in history but, more immediately, continued tenure of the Chancellorship. The Christian Democrat victory in the East German elections of March 1990 paved the way for currency union in July 1990, political union in October and all-German elections in December. The short-term economic and social burdens for the old West Germany of absorbing the backward GDR were enormous. But in the long-term, the prospects for an enlarged Germany, now 65 million plus 17 million people, were alluring. Germany represented the heart of a new European body politic whose circulatory system was being fully restored.

Britain and all of NATO were simply astonished spectators of these events. Yet the result was a new agenda for British foreign policy, indeed a completely new context. That was both exhilarating and alarming. The sense that 'we had won the Cold War was pervasive and understandable. But, compared with the uncertainties of the future – the demands made by eastern Europe, the disturbing instability of the Soviet Union and the unification of Germany – for some the old Cold War order had a reassuring stability. Not surprisingly, Margaret Thatcher was in the vanguard of those resisting rapid change. At home, and now in eastern Europe, she declared a few days after the Berlin wall was breached, 'freedom' was 'on the offensive, a peaceful offensive'. The changes in the old Soviet bloc deserved 'every possible encouragement and support'. Yet her aim was the advance of freedom in a form that preserved 'stability in Europe . . . . The need now is to take a measured view of the way ahead'.[125] That was her policy for three crucial areas – NATO, Germany and the European Community – but the pressures were now even harder to resist.

Thatcher wanted to maintain the fabric of NATO, now that its evident rationale, the threat from the Warsaw Pact, had disappeared. She tried to resist the pressure for substantial US troop withdrawals from Europe: 'we must try to learn the lessons of past peace settlements. The Americans must not go home'.[126] And she personally favoured the maintenance of a substantial NATO nuclear capability, preferably forward in Germany, but, if not, using Britain as a major base. Trident, she insisted, remained non-negotiable. Yet superpower arms negotiation continued with growing momentum and the idea of keeping substantial forces on German soil was no longer politically feasible. At its summit in July 1990, NATO moved towards a lower profile, with reduced reliance on nuclear weapons and a smaller US troop presence in Europe.

The new Europe re-opened Whitehall debate about British defence policy – largely dormant since the Falklands war. In the early 1980s

Nott had tried to reduce the defence burden by cutting the surface navy. In 1990 radicals such as Alan Clark, Minister of State for Defence, attacked the 'continentalist' rather than the 'maritime' element in British strategy, arguing that the new German situation removed the need for a British Army of the Rhine. In the end, the 'Options for Change' review in July 1990 envisaged deep but balanced cuts. All the commitments remained, but at lower force levels. The continental commitment would suffer most – halved in Germany from four to two army divisions and from fifteen to nine RAF squadrons – but the Navy was to be cut from 48 to about 40 destroyers and frigates. Only the Trident nuclear force remained inviolate. Overall, Britain's armed forces were to shrink from 312,000 to about 255,000.[127] The review called for the most radical cuts since 1957, but it was more a case of taking advantage of the new international situation to reduce force levels that had already become economically unsustainable than a radical rethink of Britain's military roles.

On the second great issue – Germany – Thatcher was privately very disturbed by the prospect of unification. 'We must not forget', she told one senior Tory. 'We have had two world wars, haven't we?'[128] In January 1990 she wanted unification delayed until eastern Europe's democratic reforms were complete. But by February the pace of events had forced her round to the FCO view that rapid unification was inevitable[129] and that all that could be done was to try and achieve it within a modicum of international agreement. The American 'two plus four' formula provided a framework of sorts. This meant that as the two Germanies negotiated their unification, they would confer with the original post-war occupying powers (Britain, France, the USA and the USSR) on 'the external aspects . . . including the issues of the security of the neighbouring states'.[130] But the real decisions were taken by Kohl, culminating in direct talks with Gorbachev. Agreement on German financial aid to the USSR in return for Soviet acceptance of continued German membership of NATO paved the way for unification of the two Germanies on 3 October 1990.

The mood around Thatcher was summed up in a rambling press interview given by her close friend, Nicholas Ridley. Harking back repeatedly to the war, Ridley warned that Kohl would 'soon be trying to take over everything'. Monetary union was 'a German racket, designed to take over the whole of Europe'. The French were behaving as Germany's 'poodles'. And, as for handing over sovereignty to the European Community, 'you might as well give it to Adolf Hitler, frankly'.[131] These remarks caused an international furore. Ridley was obliged to resign as Trade and Industry Secretary and his language was

repudiated by Thatcher, although it was generally agreed that, privately, she shared his sentiments. Ridley's outburst illustrated the impotence of British policy. He had no alternative to offer – he was not
suggesting that Britain withdraw from the EC – but was simply railing
at the tide of events. Furthermore, in so far as the interview had an
argument, this was open to question. That Germany was now the
dominant European economy was indubitable. That Germany ran the
EC was much more debatable. Ridley's tirade pointed to the Thatcherite conception of the Community as a centralised superstate, run
by the bogeymen of the day – be it French socialists or autocratic
Germans. But whatever his sentiments or hers, in October 1990
Thatcher finally capitulated and accepted full British membership of
the European Monetary System. Her decision was probably motivated
by a desire to influence the imminent intergovernmental conference
on monetary union and by the domestic political need to improve the
Tories' European credentials as another general election approached.

The future role of the EC was indeed the most important question
arising from the European revolutions. With the Warsaw Pact collapsing and NATO contracting, the Community promised to be the
pre-eminent European institution of the 1990s. By 1989 Thatcher and
Delors were entrenched in their respective positions but the Eastern
European revolutions gave each new ammunition.[132]

In her Bruges speech in September 1988 Thatcher had reminded
her listeners that the EC was only '*one* manifestation' of the European
identity. 'We shall always look on Warsaw, Prague and Budapest as
great European cities'.[133] A year later those cities were coming back
within the Western orbit. Thatcher claimed that 'deepening' the EC
through further integration would make 'widening' eastwards harder
to achieve and that the latter was more important. As she put it in
August 1990, if the EC 'set off down the path of giving more and
more powers to highly centralised institutions, which are not demo-
cratically accountable, then we should be making it harder for the
Eastern Europeans to join. They have not thrown off central
command and control in their own countries only to find them reincar-
nated in the European Community'.[134] Thus, the need for association
with Eastern Europe gave Thatcher an additional argument in her
campaign for a loose European Community.

The Commission's view, supported by the Franco-German axis,
was to insist that, on the contrary, deepening was given further
validity by the new European situation. The Community had always
been in part a device to handle the 'German question' – how could a
strong German economy be an engine of European prosperity without

becoming a military threat to its neighbours? The surrender of national sovereignty inherent in the Coal and Steel community of 1952 and in the European Economic Community of 1958 had been a way of reconciling these aims. France had lost full control over its economy, but so had Germany, and this had made German recovery acceptable. In the same way, it was argued, deepening the Community in the 1990s would help 'anchor' the new Germany safely into a new and peaceful Europe. Moreover, with Germany already dominating the EC economically and financially, the other eleven would benefit from deepening, by further limiting Germany's freedom of action.[135] The Bundesbank's role would be 'Europeanised' through a European federal bank. Thus widening and deepening were seen in this view as mutually reinforcing processes, which should occur simultaneously.

For Britain, then, the European revolutions of 1989 set a new agenda for foreign policy. They raised policy dilemmas about the futures of NATO, British defence, Germany and the European Community. The resolution of those problems would be difficult and protracted. And they would also be addressed by new leaders. Disgruntlement with Thatcher had been growing among Tory MPs in 1989–90, centred on the unpopular poll tax and her autocratic style. But it was the European issue which finally brought to an end what one German paper called the Thatcher-Dämmerung.[136] In late October 1990 the European Council set a timetable for further stages of monetary union, including a central bank by 1994 and a single currency by 1997. Thatcher alone stood out, denouncing the EC for living in 'cloud cuckoo land' and calling sterling 'the most powerful expression of sovereignty you can have'.[137] For the long-suffering Howe, this was the last straw. His outspoken resignation speech in the Commons persuaded Michael Heseltine finally to come into the open and challenge Thatcher. In the two leadership ballots that followed, Heseltine was strong enough to force Thatcher to resign but not to stop the compromise candidacy of John Major. After two weeks of vicious Tory infighting, the Thatcher era ended on 28 November 1990. With apt symbolism, three days later, on 1 December, British and French tunnellers met beneath the Channel.

Major had been an obscure junior minister until given the Foreign Office and Treasury in quick succession in 1989. Despite his debt to Thatcher's patronage, however, in important respects his outlook on Europe diverged from hers. He was the first British premier with no meaningful memories of the 1940s. Born in 1943, 18 years after Thatcher, he did not bring to the job her intellectual baggage about Frenchmen and Germans, the Cold War and the special relationship.

His brief tenure at the FCO had convinced him that Britain
European country and that it must play a constructive role within th
EC or risk the Community drifting into dirigisme and protectionism.[138] Commentators therefore anticipated an end to the strident
negativism of the Thatcher years, which had undermined the credibility of any British alternative to Delors's vision of European integration. If so, Britain would be better able to act as a focus for the
disquiet elsewhere in the EC about the Commission's blueprints for
monetary and political union without automatically seeming a 'bad
European'.

Nevertheless, it was expected that, under Major, the substance, if
not the style, of British foreign policy would remain fundamentally the
same. A Labour government would probably favour more radical
defence cuts, nuclear as well as conventional. But, on the crucial issue
of the European Community, any British government – Tory or Labour – was likely to take a similar stance, favouring intergovernmental
cooperation rather than institutional union. It was equally probable
that such a stance would slow the process of change within the EC
but not prevent it and that Britain, as so often in the previous four
decades, would find itself obliged in the end to scramble aboard the
European bandwagon.

How do we explain this isolated position? – 'isolated and right', as
Thatcher proudly put it.[139] It was not simply a matter of Thatcher's
obstinacy. It was also the product of a distinctive history that had
made Britain in the end a member of the European Community, but
a resentful and ill-suited one. That history has been the underlying
theme of this book. It is now time to make its conclusions explicit.

REFERENCES

1.   Thatcher 1990a: 5–6
2.   H. Young 1989: 381
3.   c.f. *Independent* 13 July 1990: 3
4.   P. Jenkins 1989: 318
5.   Holmes 1985: 22–4
6.   Cmd. 8787 (Franks report); Freedman 1988; Dillon 1989
7.   Dillon 1989: 25–8, 96–8
8.   Commons 17: 856–7
9.   Hastings and Jenkins 1983: 380
10.   Cmd. 8787: paras 114–18

): 265–6

82: 115

nd Reynolds 1988: 314–15

1988: 100, 102

s 1989: 164–5

1. al. 1982: 262

18. rs et al. 1987

19. Freedman 1988: 100–4; Clarke et al. 1990

20. Little 1988: 148

21. Dillon 1989: 235 and Appendix

22. Low 1988: 65–9; Patel and Bhila 1988

23. Carrington 1989: 288

24. H. Young 1989: 175–83

25. Arthur and Jeffrey 1988: Appendix II

26. Ibid., 18

27. H. Young 1989: 470–2

28. Cmd. 9352: 11–12

29. H. Young 1989: 397, 431

30. Commons 65: 828

31. Cmd. 9407: para. 3.1

32. Commons 69: 395

33. Cmd. 9407: 82

34. Cheng 1987

35. Segal 1988: 124

36. H. Young 1989: 485

37. Carrington 1989: 292

38. H. Young 1989: 248

39. Dillon 1989: 27–8

40. M. Smith 1988: 15

41. Thatcher 1986: 100

42. H. Young 1989: 185

43. Kavanagh 1987: 250

44. H. Young 1989: 186–7

45. De la Serre 1987: 162

46. H. Young 1989: 190

47. El-Agraa 1985: 166

48. H. Young 1989: 190

49. De la Serre 1987: 154

50. Carrington 1989: 317

51. George 1990: 151

52. D. Allen 1988: 42

53. J. Barber 1983, 1988

54. M. Holland 1988: 53

55. George 1990: 205

56. Howe 1984: 187–8

57. D. Allen 1988: 40–1

58. Volle 1989: 38–41
59. Edwards 1984
60. George 1990: 176
61. H. Wallace 1989: 4
62. Pryce 1984
63. Commons 82: 185
64. George 1990: 183
65. Commons 96: 316–26
66. Commons FAC 1985–6, 3rd report, 442: 70
67. cf. Bogdanor 1989: 201–2
68. FAC, 1989–90, 2nd report, 82–1: xiv
69. Pijpers et al. 1988: 334
70. George 1990: 189–90
71. *Observer*, 14 Feb. 1988: 11
72. El-Agraa 1985: 174
73. Thygesen 1989
74. George 1990: 192
75. *Independent*, 26 July 1989: 19
76. George 1990: 192–3
77. *Independent*, 22 Sept. 1988: 29
78. Thatcher 1988: 5–6
79. Linklater and Leigh 1986; Freedman 1986/7
80. Commons 96: 326–7
81. *The Times*, 26 Oct. 1988: 16
82. *Independent*, 19 May 1989: 8
83. Curtice 1989: 220
84. *Independent*, 24 June 1989: 6
85. Ibid., 12 April 1990: 10
86. Hurd 1981: 383
87. Cutler et al. 1989: 20
88. *Sunday Times*, 25 Feb. 1990: A16
89. Cutler et al. 1989: ch. 1
90. D. Allen 1988: 52
91. Nossiter 1978: 42
92. H. Young 1989: 169
93. M. Clark 1988: 63
94. M. Smith 1988: 9
95. P. Jenkins 1989: 210
96. Baylis 1984b: 181–7
97. Dimbleby and Reynolds 1988: 319
98. Freedman 1982
99. Baylis 1986: 450
100. Chalmers 1985: 135
101. Grove 1987: ch. 10
102. Cmd. 8288: para. 6
103. Bowles 1985: 196
104. Hennessy 1989: 418–19

105. Baylis (ed.) 1983; Coker 1984; Roper (ed.) 1985
106. H. Young 1989: 398
107. ACDN 22: 31
108. ACDN 23: 13–14
109. Byrd (ed.), 1988: 16, 65–6
110. Blinken 1987: 105
111. *Daily Telegraph*, 25 Oct. 1985: 4; *Independent*, 25 May 1988: 6
112. Commons 47: 294
113. *New York Times*, 11 Jan. 1986: 1
114. Commons 95: 726
115. M. Clarke 1988: 66–75; H. Young 1989: 388–95
116. M. Clarke 1988: 68
117. Moreton 1987: 254
118. H. Young 1989: 393
119. Haslam 1989: 143–4
120. M. Clarke 1988: 71
121. Volle 1989: 74
122. ACDQR 4: 3
123. ACDQR 14: esp. 30–1; *Independent*, 31 May 1989: 10
124. Schöpflin 1990
125. Thatcher 1989: A6, Bl–2
126. Thatcher 1990a: 6
127. *Daily Telegraph*, 26 July 1990: 8
128. *Independent*, 13 July 1990: 3
129. Ibid., 7 Feb. 1990: 10; 9 Feb. 1990: 8
130. Keesing's 37259
131. *Spectator,* 14 July 1990: 8–10
132. H. Wallace 1989
133. Thatcher 1988: 3
134. Thatcher 1990b: 8
135. H. Wallace 1989: 28
136. *Frankfurter Allgemeine Zeitung*, 30 Nov. 1990: 16
137. *Guardian*, 29 Oct. 1990: 1
138. *The European*, 30 Nov. 1990: 1
139. *Sunday Times*, 25 Feb. 1990: A17

Conclusion

BRITANNIA OVERRULED

'Never, surely, except under the impact of overwhelming military defeat
. . . has a great country gone so rapidly from world power to extreme
helplessness', observed the American diplomat and historian George
Kennan about modern Britain.[1] That tone of surprise is misplaced.
Power is not a possession but a relationship. Britain's power in the
nineteenth century depended on a temporary equilibrium in continental Europe. This enabled the British to exploit their naval advantage to
consolidate their trade and empire. Unlike America and Russia Britain
lacked a vast, continent-wide state. It depended for population and
resources on its colonies, investment and trade across the seas. This, as
Adam Smith noted in 1776, was 'not an empire, but the project of an
empire'.[2] Nor did Britain have an intrinsically strong economy. Compared with its rivals it was under-industrialised and heavily reliant on
foreign trade. Progressively less competitive in export markets, it experienced growing difficulty in paying for its imports, despite the assistance of invisible earnings from investments, insurance and shipping.

These underlying weaknesses made it harder to cope with renewed
international rivalry as the long Victorian peace came to an end. The
most pressing threat was Germany, which repeatedly sought a territorial base in Europe to complement its advanced economy. Its bid for
world-power status in 1914 and 1939 was the prime cause of two
great wars, and the direct danger to Britain was exacerbated in the
1930s by the development of airpower, which diminished Britain's insular advantage. Moreover, Britain faced many potential adversaries in
the early twentieth century, a result of its extended and exposed posi-

tion. German aggression allowed other rivals to advance their claims, particularly America and Japan in 1914–18. And the collapse of the European balance of power in 1940 opened up a global crisis in which Germany and Japan briefly reigned supreme and which required the mobilised resources of America and Russia to defeat them. Faced after 1945 by a Soviet Union deep in Eastern Europe, armed with vast conventional forces and, soon, nuclear weapons, Britain had little choice but to shelter under the nuclear umbrella of the USA. And as its economy and influence declined, it reluctantly sought incorporation in the European Community.

Thus, British power was directly related to the weakness of others. And its security was relative to changes in the technology of warfare – airpower, missiles and nuclear weapons – which negated the geographical advantages of insularity and seapower. Coming to terms with these changing relativities of power was complicated by problems of policymaking. This is not an argument that can be pushed too far: all bureaucracies have problems of coordination, all armed services squabble between themselves for funds and status, all twentieth-century democracies have faced the conflicting demands of social security and national security on their budgets. But the British case seems unusual in several respects.

Politically, peacetime conscription was unacceptable, except for fifteen years after 1945. This diminished Britain's effectiveness as a land-power in the early part of both world wars, until forces had been mobilised and trained. That was arguably a factor of considerable importance in the crisis of 1940. Economically, British policy was skewed towards the protection of sterling rather than the promotion of growth. This reflected the precocity of *financial* as against *industrial* capitalism in Britain, and the influence of 'the City' was institutionalised for much of the period through the Treasury's deference to the Bank of England. Britain is unusual in having no Bureau of the Budget or separate economics ministry, and efforts to create the latter have been stamped on by the Treasury.

More generally, Whitehall stands out among bureaucracies in its ability to prevent sharp changes of policy. Most senior posts are held by career civil servants and there is nothing like the changeover of personnel that accompanies a new US administration or a new French ministry. Disputes are resolved consensually behind the scenes by senior officials, resulting in compromises in which everyone gets something. And the whole system has never been shaken by radical upheavals such as war, occupation and new constitutions, as is the case, say, in France and Germany. In consequence it may have been particularly difficult for British 'policy' to adjust to declining relative power. Radical decisions about empire, Europe and defence spending were harder to take, let alone implement.

In a broad sense, then, the limitations of British power and the structural constraints on policymaking explain a good deal about Britain's decline and the difficulties of successive governments in adapting to it. Yet neither of these arguments should be exaggerated. Other European states have experienced the same decrease in relative power during this century – economic decline, loss of empire and eclipse by the 'superpowers'. Yet their responses have been very different, as we shall see in a moment in the case of France. Likewise, all policymaking structures have their own inherent deficiencies. The American system, for instance, may be more open to outside ideas and influences, but the separation of powers is frequently a recipe for political deadlock and policy stalemate, as Congress and President square off against each other. So, broad determinist explanations – be they power-political or policy-centred – take us only so far in explaining Britain's current situation. As historians, our first question should be not 'What's the problem?' but 'What's the story?'[3], for Britain's *story* is a distinctive one. Above all, we should recognise that it is not one of steady, century-long decline.

It is broadly true that Britain enjoyed great-power status on the cheap in the nineteenth century, and that made it harder to cope with the challenges of the twentieth. On the other hand, it also meant that there was a good deal of slack to be drawn on if necessary – manpower at home and abroad, investments that could be liquidated and colonial resources susceptible of development. All these were essential in two world wars. Moreover, the relativity of power did not always work to Britain's detriment. At times it became weaker but so, at other times, did its rivals. France and Germany were enervated by both world wars, Japan by the second. Only the New World, in Thomas Jefferson's felicitous phrase, was on each occasion able to 'fatten on the follies of the Old'.[4]

Moreover, the limits of power were not insuperable. As Lord Halifax observed in 1938, they simply 'threw the burden on diplomacy'.[5] In one direction that suggested the tactic of appeasement, reducing the multiplicity of threats by satisfying the grievances of lesser foes. This was the theme of the 1900s and the 1930s. In the first case, accommodations were reached with America, Japan, France and Russia. In the second, Italy and Germany were approached, though with less success. In the other direction, diplomacy dictated ententes and alliances. Lacking its own standing army, Britain consistently utilised the power of others – a strategy dating back at least to the eighteenth century. The Indian army supplied the bulk of Britain's military manpower in the nineteenth century. France and Russia were used for as long as possible to contain Germany in the 1900s and 1910s. The naval agreements of the 1920s reflected a hope that Britain could rely on US seapower to control the Pacific. In the interwar years the British were ready, in the bitter French gibe, to fight to the last Frenchman. From June 1941 the Red Army served the same purpose, far more effectively, and after 1945 Britain tried to mobilise and direct the vast power of the United States, in a so-called 'special relationship' in which supposedly '*they* have the money bags, but *we* have all the brains'.[6] This use of proxies was a consistent policy, to compensate for the limits of British power.

Thus, the relativities of power ebbed and flowed – to Britain's advantage as well as disadvantage. And in the vortex there was room for choice, for policy. In the early 1900s appeasement, endorsed by most of Whitehall, was relatively successful in eliminating peripheral threats and enabling Britain to concentrate its resources on the naval race with Germany. The war of 1914–18 was a disaster for all of Europe, but Britain allowed its allies to bear the brunt of the land war and emerged with an enlarged empire and reduced enemies. The upsurge of colonial nationalism, though troublesome, could still be managed. In the renewed rivalries of the 1930s, however, diplomacy proved less successful. Airpower made the German challenge more menacing, while Mussolini's pretensions and the rise of Japan posed a global challenge that left British seapower fatally overstretched. At the same time, Britain's growing economic problems, especially the strains on sterling, made the government reluctant to embark on rapid rearmament.

In these admittedly difficult circumstances, policy failures were particularly evident. Appeasement of Germany was based on fundamental intelligence misconceptions about Hitler's benevolent intentions and exaggerated capabilities, while British policy towards Japan was paralysed bureaucratically between conciliation and confrontation. Rearmament priorities shifted as the 1930s progressed, with the only success being the belated concentration on air defence from 1938. That played a part in saving Britain in 1940, but, arguably, if the Army had not been so neglected throughout the decade, the Battle of France might have continued, making the Battle of Britain unnecessary.

Throughout the 1930s, bluff was never tried. German airpower seemed too menacing. In 1940, both by temperament and necessity, Churchill used little but bluff. It worked against Hitler in 1940 but proved disastrous against Japan in 1941. In the world war that followed Britain relied heavily on American wealth and Russian manpower. As in previous conflicts, the use of proxies proved in some ways remarkably effective. The Russians bore the brunt of the struggle against Hitler, and the British returned to their Asian empire behind the bayonets of the (somewhat aggrieved) Americans. In human terms, this truly world war cost Britain half the dead of the much smaller conflict of 1914–18. Yet the struggle for survival had required a much greater mobilisation of resources. The financial burden in particular was immense. Colonies were encouraged to develop a capacity and a will of their own. And, most significant, Britain's great allies – America and Russia – ended the war vastly enhanced in position and aspiration. In 1947, it seemed, Britain was teetering on the edge of economic and imperial collapse, as the Cold War took hold of Europe and India was granted independence.

Once more, however, we have to remember that power is relative. As Churchill lamented, compared with the 'huge Russian bear' and the 'great American elephant', the British lion seemed small indeed.[7] Within Europe, on the other hand, Britannia ruled OK. All the major continental states ended the war in far worse political and economic turmoil. Like 1918–21, 1945–7 was a crisis, but one of post-war adjustment rather than terminal decline. Britain emerged from it as the major economic and military power in Western Europe, with most of its empire intact. And its growing reliance on America did not preclude a degree of independence, particularly over the Cold War in Asia. In fact, at mid-century Britain was acting as a great power to a degree unprecedented in peacetime. Conscription, the atomic bomb, new commitments in Germany and a vigorous programme of imperial exploitation were evidence of this. These were all policy choices, reinforcing the now-advantageous relativities of power in Europe.

What followed was the progressive unravelling of these great-power strategies. The Commonwealth gradually disintegrated as a vehicle for British influence and its economic value waned. The relationship with America became more unbalanced, despite (or because of?) the unique nuclear alliance established from the late 1950s. The armed services jealously guarded a variety of military roles inherited from the days of global reach, and attempts to cut defence spending usually concentrated on reducing capabilities rather than cutting commitments – the worst possible outcome. Most seriously, fixation with its English-speaking orbits blinded much of Whitehall to the significance of moves for European integration, until it was too late and the Six had created a European Community.

The contraction of the old circles of power and Britain's failure to position itself inside the new one have dogged British policy ever since. Through its own reluctance and then the French veto, Britain did not enter the European Community until the latter's essential institutions had been created. If it had been present at the creation, Britain might have helped found a more congenial organisation, less geared to agriculture, more open to the world economy. Instead, it had to adjust to a fait accompli – a painful process, as the rows over agricultural policy and the budget show. The same pattern was repeated over monetary union: Britain standing apart for a decade from 1978 and then finally clambering reluctantly onto the bandwagon.

Inside or outside the Community, British governments, with the exception of Heath's, have preferred to take a stance of critical aloofness to much of what has gone on. Often they have exaggerated their capacity to divert events, only to be disabused with a shock. In consequence, the Community is frequently depicted in Britain as a centralised autocracy, run by socialists, the Germans or whoever is the latest bête noire. That is to underestimate its diversity and divisions. It is more accurately understood as 'a negotiating forum',[8] in which national governments and domestic interest groups are constantly manoeuvring for advantage at all levels of its fractured structure. This interplay provides recurrent opportunities for creative diplomacy to build coalitions and advance national goals, but success depends on being regarded as a full partner and not an obstructive troublemaker. British governments have been slow to play this new game of perpetual alliance diplomacy, often hankering after images of British power (as balancer, bridge-builder or special American ally) that are not merely outmoded but also exaggerations of what in reality was once the case. Acknowledging what have been the consistent limitations on British power may make it easier to approach the Community more creatively. Like NATO, it can be seen in terms of an older tradition – as an institutionalised extension of the policy of power by proxy.

HISTORY AND HEGEMONY

The theme of this story, then, is not one of steady decline. Rather the motif is one of 'decline, revival and fall'.[9] And in retrospect the years 1947–55 assume a special importance in defining future options and confirming a course that was then held for too long. Were Britain's post-war aspirations for a world role the result of hubris and blindness?

In part, yes. In May 1947, responding to criticism by leftwinger Michael Foot, Ernest Bevin told the Commons:

> His Majesty's Government do not accept the view . . . that we have ceased to be a Great Power . . . . The very fact that we have fought so hard for liberty, and paid such a price, warrants our retaining this position; and indeed it places a duty upon us to continue to retain it.[10]

This was what Jean Monnet dubbed 'the price of victory – the illusion', as he put it, 'that you could maintain what you had, without change'.[11] It was of particular significance in two areas. One, of concern to Monnet, was Britain's aloofness from the movement for European integration in the late 1940s and 1950s. This was seen by Britain as appropriate for the war's losers, not its victors – 'for them, not us', in Churchill's phrase.[12] The other area was the failure to embark on a radical programme of economic modernisation. That would always have been difficult, given the legacies of Britain's partial industrialisation, but the decade of relative advantage, 1945–55, offered a grace period that was not exploited. Instead British governments opted for a strategy of colonial development whose successes petered out by the late 1950s.

Yet to deride post-war British politicians and officials for illusions of grandeur[13] is too simple. An excursion into theory may make this clear. Their sense of a global 'role' can be understood, more positively, in terms of the concept of international hegemony. This applies at two levels – the economic and the strategic. Economically, an open, multilateral world economy is not, *pace* classical liberalism, simply the creation of market forces. It is a function of *political* economy, sustained by the power of a leading state.[14] In the period 1870–1914, these theorists argue, Britain played such a role – negotiating tariff reductions, maintaining foreign lending, using its own currency as the medium of international payments. After 1945 the USA assumed some of these tasks, promoting a new open economy outside the communist world, but in the interwar years 'America wouldn't and Britain couldn't' – hence the protectionist blocs and economic instability of the 1930s.[15]

These theories of international hegemony have been developed particularly with reference to economics. But they can also be applied to the strategic sphere.[16] Britain's international exertions in the Victorian era, both naval and imperial, were usually related to maintaining its trade and financial interests around the world. In the more 'anarchical' environment of the 1930s, that seemed as necessary as ever, yet harder to do, and in 1940–2 Britain faced its worst strategic crisis of the century. Gradually, after 1945, Britain sheltered under the Eagle's wing – reliant for security on the US nuclear umbrella in Europe and on American support to maintain its interests around the world.

Hegemonial arguments should not be pushed too far. The capacity of a single leading power can easily be exaggerated.[17] Furthermore, this book has stressed repeatedly the limits of Britain's intrinsic strength. Nevertheless, hegemonic theory helps account for the dilemmas of British policy in the 1930s, in the period of hiatus between a British-centred pattern of international power and an American one. In the realm of security as well as that of economics, it is broadly true to say that Britain couldn't and America wouldn't. Moreover, the argument can be applied to the post-1945 era. The Americans assumed a hegemonic role after 1945 less quickly than historians once believed. The period 1945–7 was one of flux and, even after the clarion calls of the Truman Doctrine and the Marshall Plan, British leaders were unsure about the extent of the American diplomatic revolution. The USA also took on this new role less fully than Britain had done, not least because America's own prosperity and security were much less bound up with world trade than was Britain's, given the size of its own vast internal market and its greater security from great-power attack in a pre-missile era. Thus, American internationalism was no panacea for Britain's post-war problems – hence the British insistence on the sterling area, conscription and their own nuclear weapons.

The limits of the American role were part of the explanation for Britain's superpower exertions at mid-century. Equally important was the instability caused by the expansion of communist power, at a time when colonial rule was being shaken by nationalist convulsions. Of course, it is clear that the Western powers, particularly the USA, at times exaggerated the monolithic communist danger. Relations between Moscow and Beijing were always strained, even before the formal Sino–Soviet split, and nationalist leaders such as Nasser or Ho Chi Minh had no wish to become the clients of any great powers, West or East. That said, there is no denying the appeal of communism in post-fascist Europe, nor its potency when exploited by anti-colonial nationalist movements in the developing world. And Britain – whose security in an age of air- and missile-power, was closely linked to that of continental Europe, and whose prosperity was still tied up with trade and investment in now-volatile parts of the world such as Southeast Asia or the Middle East – was bound to be particularly concerned about communist expansion. The point can be grasped most readily by considering the effect of the revolutions of 1989 in casting doubt on the historic rationales for NATO and for British defence policy. In the past the communist threat may have been exaggerated, but it was always a credible argument for maintaining global responsibilities.

Thus, Britain's great-power role after 1945 was partly 'the price of victory' – illusions of grandeur – but it was also the price of hegemony in a period of extreme global instability when the Pax Americana was neither readily forthcoming nor perfectly tailored to British interests. Understanding the relativities of power aright in mid-century, we can see why British leaders felt it incumbent to maintain economic, imperial and strategic positions that, in retrospect, seem excessive and enervating. That, after all, is 'the hegemon's dilemma'[18] – trying to maintain a congenial international system can sap the national power it is supposed to protect.

And this argument also helps us see more clearly the impediments to a strategy of managed decline, touted at various times in the 1950s. Of course, service rivalries made this difficult and insufficient grasp of the underlying shifts of economic power was also an obstacle. But in a volatile and unstable world the 'credibility' argument had genuine plausibility. The image of power was often as important as the reality – more exactly, image was a part of the reality, prestige was a form of power. This was Eden's claim in 1952, when dismissing the idea of abandoning any 'major commitments': 'the Russians would be only too ready to fill any vacuum' and British influence 'depended largely on our status as a world Power' and on a willingness to honour obligations.[19] In a Cold War atmosphere of global, zero-sum rivalry, it seemed that retreat could easily become a rout.

Examining this crucial period around the middle of the twentieth century allows us to define more clearly how and why Britain's story is different from that of other great powers, notably France, who experienced a superficially similar decline. First, empire mattered much more, economically, to Britain than to France. For the latter, colonies were marginal to its national wealth. At the beginning of this century France's empire accounted for only 10 per cent of its foreign trade and 9 per cent of its foreign investment, whereas 25 per cent of the latter went to Russia.[20] Britain's empire took a third of its exports and provided a quarter of its imports in the early twentieth century, and attracted a quarter of its total investment in 1865–1914.[21] Between the wars empire assumed an increased importance for the French economy, as it did for Britain, but France lost most of its colonies in the decade after 1945. Despite some imperial flourishes, its strategy for post-war economic recovery, unlike Britain's, rested ultimately on industrial modernisation and European integration.

Nevertheless, Britain's formal empire was not synonymous with its global economic interests. France's colonies – much smaller in extent – were intended, if not always operated, as a closed mercantilist bloc, whereas Britain's were always seen as part of a larger and more open system of world trade. Not only did Britain need imports from a wide range of foreign countries, but much of its wealth derived from acting as banker, shipper and insurer of international commerce. These abstract dictates of 'national interest' were reinforced by the political dominance within the country of groups with this bias, especially through the City-Bank-Treasury axis.* Thus, the interests of both the state and of influential groups within it prompted a desire to maintain a multilateral trading system. Even when forced into a more protectionist mode in the 1930s, with imperial preference and the sterling area, the intent was to maximise world trade to the largest possible extent compatible with British competitiveness.

So Britain's empire was an unusual blend of formal and informal imperialism, always viewed, moreover, within the context of world trade. It was, in short, a 'liberal empire'.[22] Yet these diverse global interests depended to an alarming degree on the maintenance of peace and order. It was not surprising, then, that Britain assumed a hegemonial role. Yet it was hegemony of a particular sort – concentrating on seapower to keep open trade routes, maintaining free trade as much as possible, and protecting the value of sterling even at cost to domestic industry. Abandoning those policies, even as circumstances changed, was a slow process.

Britain's retreat from empire was also distinctive.[23] Far more than the French, the British developed policies of informal empire and managed devolution as devices for maintaining the benefits of imperial influence without its burdens. Nor, with the principal exception of Ireland, did they have powerful lobbies within domestic politics to resist the process of formal decolonisation, as in France over Algeria. Consequently, the British crises of decolonisation were less protracted abroad and less bitter at home. Extrication from India in 1947 and Palestine in 1948 entailed horrific suffering for the inhabitants of those countries. But for the British, it happened more expeditiously than withdrawal from Indochina for France or the East Indies for the Dutch. Admittedly, Rhodesia dragged on much longer than any of these, but it was less bloody or divisive. On the other hand, a relatively smooth withdrawal from empire made it harder to engage in a radical policy rethink. If Empire could be transmuted into Common-

---

* As Gramscian theory suggests, hegemony has to be applied to relations within states as well as between them – (cf. Klein 1988: 134.)

wealth, if colonies could be transformed into clients, then the global orientation of British policy could still seem viable. And the heavier hand of French formal empire left a more durable mark on former colonies, particularly via the politics of culture and language, than did the lighter touch of British informality.[24] Consequently, French imperialism was more effective as a device for post-imperial influence.

Also unusual was Britain's mode of adaptation to a superpower-led world. The British had special cultural, ethnic and linguistic links with America, a former colony. By themselves these were not necessarily of determinative political importance – Anglo–American relations were aloof and often strained in the first forty years of the century. But the crisis of 1940 saw the creation of a literally special relationship, shaped by World War and cemented, after a hiatus in 1945–7, by Cold War. Although increasingly unbalanced, the relationship did give the British unusual access to US policymaking and yielded results, such as the nuclear alliance, that were unique.[25] For France, neither cultural links nor wartime experience suggested a close alliance with America – in fact, the very opposite.[26] In an angry row just before D-Day, Churchill told de Gaulle: 'Each time I have to choose between you and Roosevelt, I shall always choose Roosevelt . . . . Each time we have to choose between Europe and the open sea, we shall always choose the open sea'.[27]

This reminds us that Britain has also displayed a weak sense of European identity. In fact, that is almost a way of re-stating what has just been said about economics, empire and allies. Britain was oriented to a seaborne, global economy in which it played a leading role. The Atlantic focus of that economy favoured its west-coast ports and their hinterland industries, particularly textiles. Britain also benefited from the economic divisions of continental Europe, fragmented successively by national rivalries, the German question and the Cold War. Between 1850 and 1950 it was indeed a bridge between Europe and the wider world. But the progressive integration of post-war Europe – in the west since the 1950s and involving the east after 1989 – has left Britain literally on the margins of a single European market centred on Germany.

As a cultural and ethnic frame of reference, the empire also served to pull Britain away from continental Europe. As Eden observed in 1952: 'Our thoughts move across the seas to the many communities in which our people play their part, in every corner of the world. These are our family ties. That is our life. Without it,' he added in a poignant phrase, 'we should be no more than some millions of people living on an island off the coast of Europe, in which nobody wants to take any particular interest'.[28] And the American connection further reinforced the sense of alienation from the Continent. Aside from a conviction of special British influence in Washington, American cultural and business leadership, building on British imperialism, made English the world's principal language. These seemed the realities that mattered.

Geography was, and remains, fundamental here: the Channel is a psychological as much as a physical barrier. In an era of seapower the 'moat defensive' permitted greater security at lower cost than that enjoyed by continental states. In 1940 it was of critical importance for Britain's survival, and that experience divided Britain from continental Europe fundamentally for a generation. In the post-seapower era the Channel has became progressively irrelevant to security, while at the same time proving a major obstacle to economic integration within the emerging European economy. The Channel Tunnel, while important psychologically, will have minimal effect on these physical realities, especially in the absence of improved transport networks linking the northwest periphery of Europe to its German heartland.

Taken together, these peculiar features of Britain's story – economy, empire, America and Europe, underpinned by the facts of geography – go a long way to explain the country's distinctive fate compared with other European powers facing similar pressures. Merely to state them in this fashion – as a process of progressive marginalisation within a new Europe – may, however, be too negative. The positive gloss is that Britain has undergone this metamorphosis without the ruptures of invasion and revolution experienced by France, Germany or Italy. In one sense, that stability has been a major impediment to changes of attitude and institutions. Continuity has bred complacency and thus resistance to change. But against that are the 'colossal economic and political advantages of peace and stability'.[29] And these are not to be underrated as social goods. Being powerful may be desirable; being alive is surely more important. Viewing the century as a whole, Germany's 'rise' has been a good deal more unpleasant for the average German than Britain's 'decline' has been for the ordinary Briton.

Moreover, we should remember the distortions created by standing close to historical events. A week may be a long time in politics; a decade is certainly a short time in history. An observer in 2050, say, may conclude that Britain's adjustment to the rhythms of rise and decline was surprisingly smooth, given the extent of the world we had lost.

POWER, POLICY AND INTERDEPENDENCE

This book is a product of the late 1980s, however, not the middle of the twenty-first century. From where we are now, a final theme stands out as we sum up Britain's international position near the end of a turbulent century. Both power and policy are being redefined in circumstances of growing international interdependence.

First, the currency of power seems to be changing, within the developed world, away from military denominators. One reason for this is the nuclear revolution.[30] It seems likely, though unprovable, that the development of nuclear weapons has helped to restrain the great powers from pushing their competition to the point of conflict, as happened in the past. Indeed the threat of nuclear escalation has acted as a brake on all forms of military confrontation between the developed states. Furthermore, the disintegration of the Warsaw Pact is likely to make existing Western military postures irrelevant. If military force has been downplayed as a form of effective power, then, secondly, economic influence has become more important.[31] The magnetic effect of a strong currency, the political penetration achieved by exports and investment – these are the forms of power that now matter. Of course, it is arguable, on the basis of history, that economic power is eventually translated into military power.[32] But this precedent may be less applicable than it was, partly because of the nuclear revolution but also because of the growth of economic inter-dependence.[33] Multinational corporations, international banking and transnational capital markets tie Western nation states together in a complex matrix and undermine their independence.[34] In other words, we may have entered a different kind of international system, at least in the developed world.

The threat of nuclear extinction and the experience of economic transnationalism both point therefore to the growing reality of interdependence. This has been underlined by a third, more recent development – the sense of impending environmental crisis, which has helped redefine security in global rather than national terms. The effects of pollution and climatic change are likely to assume an ever-higher place on the diplomatic agenda in the future, helping further to make old definitions of international power outmoded and even counter-productive.

Britain has been short-changed by this re-coinage of power. As a hegemonial state in the first half of the century, it invested heavily in military systems that were intended to help protect an international

order. From that order others became the principal economic beneficiaries. Since the 1950s it has been slow to throw off these burdens
and adapt to the imperatives of transnationalism and modern economics. Never a radically industrialised society, its pre-occupations with a
great-power role consistently distracted it from necessary economic
modernisation. And although 'green issues' found a place in Thatcher's
worldview in the late 1980s, the economic costs of environmentally
safer policies are harder to bear for a country struggling to be internationally competitive.

Nevertheless, the extent of international interdependence should
not be exaggerated.[35] It applies mostly to the developed Western
world. The pattern of North–South relations remains one of economic
dependence.[36] Many developing countries in Asia, Africa and Latin
America are still reliant on the northern hemisphere for their markets,
manufactures and investment. Their resentment at this situation is likely to be the source of increased international tension in the future.
Allied to this is the ideological reaction against the West – its values,
property and citizens. The Islamic resurgence in Asia, the Middle East
and North Africa will be particularly challenging, linked as it is to the
shift in demographic balance away from the West and the problems of
nuclear proliferation to radical states of the third-world. Thus, outside
the developed world of growing interdependence, old-fashioned military challenges are likely to arise in sensitive areas such as the oil-rich
Middle East. The attack by Saddam Hussein's Iraq on Iran in 1980 and
his invasion of Kuwait a decade later in August 1990 were examples of
this. The latter prompted the exercise of American military might on a
scale unprecedented since Vietnam and elicited enthusiastic support
from Thatcher, including a major redeployment of British armour
from Germany. The short but devastating war to free Kuwait was
likely to exacerbate rather than solve the insecurity and instability of
the Middle East. In other words, the old forms of power will still be
in use alongside the new: military muscles will be needed as well as
economic sinews. That will make policy choices for countries like
Britain even harder.

But to talk of Britain's own power is itself becoming problematic.
The realities of 'complex interdependence'[37] mean that the concept of
national power must be redefined with reference to the adjective as
well as the noun. The Western nation state now lacks its erstwhile
capacity to assert itself alone. In part, this is because the transnational
economy has gouged deep into the body politic. Multinational corporations and international banks have undercut the power of any
national government to regulate its own economy. In addition,

international institutions have taken over some of the government's own functions. Since 1949 British defence policy has been inextricably bound up in NATO, and the European Community now has direct authority over large areas of British economic and social policy, especially with the Single European Act. The work of almost all Whitehall departments now has a pronounced European dimension. The EC's role in fact highlights the progressive blurring of the old divide between domestic and foreign policy – a central feature of the new interdependence.[38]

This blurring poses particular problems for domestic politics. In the course of this century in Western Europe, citizens have expected their governments to satisfy more of their needs – not just those of defence, law and order. Economic growth and social security have been added to national security. Yet at the same time the increase in international interdependence means that national governments have become progressively less able to respond to these demands by themselves. In other words, publics expect more from their governments at a time when those governments can deliver less. Although domestic and foreign policies are being blurred, the domestic politics of foreign policy have become more insistent.

Britain's problems of adaptation to the EC illustrate this very clearly. The budget issue was the classic example, but it was part of a general politicisation of foreign policy at the points where a country's external relations touch on bread-and-butter concerns. Except in war, the latter are what excite most of the population – not arcane matters of monetary regimes or defence procurement. In the past, they have been largely handled within the domestic arena – except on rare occasions when they impinge on foreign policy, such as the 1900s debate on tariff reform. Membership of the EC has changed that. Since the 1970s the price of foodstuffs, the composition of 'the British sausage' and whether 'our money' is used to bail out foreign farmers have become in practice what 'Europe' means to many Britons. 'Low policy' issues now intrude repeatedly into 'high policy', and that is one reason why the foreign policy implications of British membership of the EC have been so hard to handle.

More basic still is the appeal of the concept of 'sovereignty' itself in Britain. In part this is, of course, a cynical politician's ploy. Here, parliamentary sovereignty means in practice the ability of the government of the day to translate its wishes into legislation. It is, after all, only 'the government of the day' because it has a working majority in the Commons. And, given the tightness of party discipline, backbenchers usually do what their Whips tells them. So, naturally, political leaders of both main parties are loath to abandon a constitutional doctrine that dresses up their autocratic power in seemly garb.

But 'parliamentary sovereignty' is not simply a piece of politicians' humbug. It is central to the definition of British identity. Its roots lie way back in the struggles surrounding the Civil Wars of the 1640s and the coup of 1688 – the last breaks in English political history.[39] Those roots have not been torn up, as in continental Europe, by wars, revolutions and military occupations. Consider, for a moment, the individual experiences of the original Six who formed the European Community. France had new constitutions in 1871, 1945 and 1958. Germany was not a nation-state before 1871, and its political structure has been wrenchingly re-formed in 1918, 1933, 1945, 1949 and 1990. On the continent federalist principles have frequently eroded the sovereignty of a central government: Germany has been a federal state for much of its national history, while Belgium, the Netherlands and Luxembourg have been in the vanguard of European integration because two world wars demonstrated the meaninglessness of 'sovereignty' for small states surrounded by powerful neighbours. And in Italy, united only since the 1860s, the European Community has been seen as a way of overcoming the strong sense of regional identity and the weak sense of allegiance to the Italian state.

In none of these countries is *cultural* nationalism a puny force. Pride in being French or German remains intense. And the determination to advance national interests is no less keen than in Thatcher's Britain. None of these states intends to become 'identikit Europeans'. But continental nationalism, unlike Britain's, is not translated into a rooted attachment to existing political institutions – the Crown in Parliament. For the EC to challenge the sovereignty of Parliament is, to many, a threat not merely to national power but also to national identity.

But whose national identity? What we call in shorthand 'Britain' is actually three nations – England, Wales and Scotland – to which is added Northern Ireland to form the 'United Kingdom'. In other words, unlike the original Six (except bilingual Belgium), Britain is not a single nation. Parliamentary sovereignty is deemed essential because it alone constitutes the unity of the kingdom. And the coherence of the UK cannot be taken for granted. Ulster is the most obvious case, with no evident solution, but Thatcher's Anglo–Irish agreement of 1985 gave an external government rights over part of the UK and, in the long term, this may prove to have been a significant step along a long road towards Irish unity. Perhaps more pressing is the persistence of Scottish nationalism. The economic and political potential for a separate Scottish state should not be underrated, especially with the Labour party still inclined towards devolution.

It is often assumed that the end of empire applied simply to Britain's relations with the non-European world. Yet Sir John Seeley entitled his 1883 classic, *The Expansion of England*. In his account, England's imperialism within the British Isles created 'Great Britain' and then continued beyond Europe to form 'Greater Britain'. The contraction of the British Empire may well involve a reversal of the process, leading to a loosening of the bonds of the United Kingdom itself. This is why the issue of parliamentary sovereignty is so delicate – it affects not just Britain's relations with its European neighbours but also what we mean by Britain itself.

Where does this leave us? Britain has lost power. That, very crudely, is the story of the twentieth century. But, since the Second World War, concepts of power have also been transformed. British policy has been slow to adapt to *both* developments – slow to abandon a world role *and* to accept the imperatives of interdependence. Yet the new interdependence is complex and partial – military as well as economic forms of power will remain important in the future. This complicates policy planning. And although Britain must now play its power role within larger groupings – NATO and particularly the EC – the erosion of sovereignty this entails places strains on domestic consensus and strikes at its sense of identity.

This book has dwelt on the role left for policy within the parameters of power – the realm of choice available despite economic, imperial and international realities. It has also emphasised that for a country to make choices is a fraught business, involving politicians, bureaucrats, interest groups and sometimes the public at large. Frequently the essential promptings are instinctive rather than calculated. In the twentieth century Britannia was overruled, but when, how, and with what consequences was not pre-determined. Choices *were* made – actively or by default – for instance, in 1914 and 1939, in 1940, 1955 and 1971. The choices facing Britain in the 1990s are no less momentous or painful than any of these, as the later chapters of this book have tried to show. But, aside from such contemporary concerns, one may also think of the relationship between policy and power in another, more universal, form, of which Britain's current dilemma – however pressing for its government and people – is but a passing example. For policy as the pursuit of power is as old as human society itself. In the measured words of Thomas Hobbes, from the eleventh chapter of *Leviathan* (1651), 'I put for a generall inclination of all mankind, a perpetuall and restlesse desire of Power after power, that ceaseth only in Death'.

REFERENCES

1. Kennan 1977: 135
2. A. Smith 1976: 947
3. Neustadt and May 1986: 274
4. Reynolds 1981: 16
5. Middlemas 1972: 128
6. Gardner 1980: xiii
7. Colville 1985: 564
8. H. Wallace 1985: 261
9. cf. Gallagher 1982
10. Commons 437: 1965
11. Charlton 1983: 307
12. Fursdon 1980: 77
13. Barnett 1972: 592–3
14. cf. Rowland (ed.) 1976
15. Kindleberger 1973: 292
16. cf. Klein 1988
17. Stein 1984
18. Ibid., 384
19. CAB 129/53, C (52) 202
20. Andrew and Kanya-Forstner 1981: 14
21. O'Brien 1988b: 166–75
22. Beloff 1969
23. Andrew and Kanya-Forstner 1981: ch. 10; Kahler 1984
24. T. Smith 1981: ch. 3
25. Reynolds 1985/6 and 1988/9
26. Harrison 1981
27. Dimbleby and Reynolds 1988: 242
28. Carlton 1981: 311
29. M. Olson 1982: 145
30. Mandelbaum 1981
31. Keohane and Nye 1977: ch. 2
32. Kennedy 1988
33. Reynolds 1989b: 485–6
34. Morse 1970: 372–4
35. Smith, Smith and White 1988: 14–16
36. Spero 1981: 12–18
37. Keohane and Nye 1977: 24
38. Morse 1970: 374–7
39. Breuilly 1982: 53–7

Appendix 1
Principal Officers of State since 1895

Government	Prime Minister	Foreign Secretary	Chancellor of Exchequer
June 1895 Cons	*Salisbury*	*Salisbury*	Sir Michael Hicks Beach
		Lansdowne Oct. 1900	
July 1902 Cons	A.J. Balfour	*Lansdowne*	Charles Ritchie
			Austen Chamberlain Sept. 1903
Dec. 1905 Lib	Sir Henry Campbell-Bannerman	Sir Edward Grey	H. H. Asquith
April 1908 Lib	H. H. Asquith	Sir Edward Grey	David Lloyd George
May 1915 Coalition	H. H. Asquith	Sir Edward Grey	Reginald McKenna

Government	Prime Minister	Foreign Secretary	Chancellor of Exchequer
Dec. 1916 Coalition	David Lloyd George	A. J. Balfour	Andrew Bonar Law
Jan. 1919 Coalition	David Lloyd George	A. J. Balfour	Austen Chamberlain
		Curzon Oct. 1919	Sir Robert Horne Apr. 1921
Oct. 1922 Cons	Andrew Bonar Law	*Curzon*	Stanley Baldwin
May 1923 Cons	Stanley Baldwin	*Curzon*	Stanley Baldwin
			Neville Chamberlain Aug. 1923
Jan. 1924	Ramsay MacDonald		Philip Snowden
Nov. 1924 Cons	Stanley Baldwin	Austen Chamberlain	Winston Churchill
June 1929 Lab	Ramsay MacDonald	Arthur Henderson	Philip Snowden
Aug. 1931 National	Ramsay MacDonald	*Reading*	Philip Snowden
Nov. 1931 National	Ramsay MacDonald	Sir John Simon	Neville Chamberlain
June 1935 National	Stanley Baldwin	Sir Samuel Hoare	Neville Chamberlain
		Anthony Eden Dec. 1935	
May 1937 National	Neville Chamberlain	Anthony Eden	Sir John Simon

Government	Prime Minister	Foreign Secretary	Chancellor of Exchequer
		Halifax Feb. 1938	
May 1940 Coalition	Winston Churchill	*Halifax*	Sir Kingsley Wood
		Anthony Eden Dec. 1940	Sir John Anderson Sept. 1943
May 1945 Caretaker	Winston Churchill	Anthony Eden	Sir John Anderson
July 1945 Lab	Clement Attlee	Ernest Bevin	Hugh Dalton
			Sir Stafford Cripps Nov. 1947
Feb. 1950 Lab	Clement Attlee	Ernest Bevin	Sir Stafford Cripps
		Herbert Morrison March 1951	Hugh Gaitskell Oct. 1950
Oct. 1951	Winston Churchill	Anthony Eden	R. A. Butler
Apr. 1955 Cons	Anthony Eden	Harold Macmillan	R.A. Butler
		Selwyn Lloyd Dec. 1955	Harold Macmillan Dec. 1955
Jan. 1957 Cons	Harold Macmillan	Selwyn Lloyd	Peter Thorneycroft
		Home July 1960	Derick Heathcoat Amory Jan. 1958
			Selwyn Lloyd July 1960
			Reginald Maudling July 1962

Government	Prime Minister	Foreign Secretary	Chancellor of Exchequer
Oct. 1963 Cons	Sir Alec Douglas-Home (formerly *Home*)	R. A. Butler	Reginald Maudling
Oct. 1964 Lab	Harold Wilson	Patrick Gordon Walker / Michael Stewart Jan. 1965	James Callaghan
Apr. 1966 Lab	Harold Wilson	Michael Stewart / George Brown Aug. 1966 / Michael Stewart March 1968	James Callaghan / Roy Jenkins Nov. 1967
June 1970 Cons	Edward Heath	Sir Alec Douglas-Home	Iain Macleod / Anthony Barber July 1970
Mar. 1974 Lab	Harold Wilson	James Callaghan	Denis Healey
Oct. 1974 Lab	Harold Wilson	James Callaghan	Denis Healey
Apr. 1976 Lab	James Callaghan	Anthony Crosland / David Owen Feb. 1977	Denis Healey
May 1979 Cons	Margaret Thatcher	*Carrington* / Francis Pym Apr. 1982	Sir Geoffrey Howe

Government	Prime Minister	Foreign Secretary	Chancellor of Exchequer
June 1983 Cons	Margaret Thatcher	Sir Geoffrey Howe	Nigel Lawson
June 1987 Cons	Margaret Thatcher	Sir Geoffrey Howe	Nigel Lawson
		John Major July 1989	
		Douglas Hurd Oct. 1989	John Major Oct. 1989
Nov. 1990 Cons	John Major	Douglas Hurd	Norman Lamont

Note: italics denote peers of the realm.

Appendix 2
The Institutions of the European Community

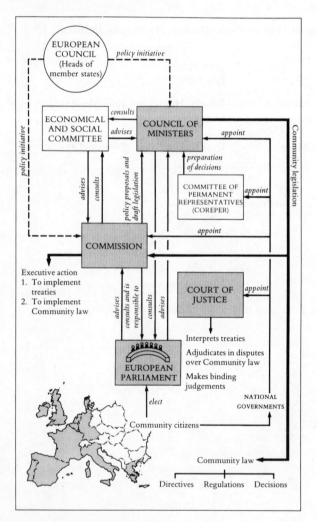

Source: Daltrop 1982: 52.

Bibliography

Place of publication is London, unless otherwise stated. Where appropriate, the date of original publication is given in brackets at the end of each entry. For abbreviations see pp. x–xi.

Abramovitz, Moses, 1986, 'Catching up, forging ahead, and falling behind', *Journal of Economic History*, 46: 385–406.

Ackrill, Margaret, 1988, 'Britain's managers and the British economy, 1870s to the 1980s', in Crafts (ed.) 1988: 59–73.

Adams, R.J.Q., and Poirier, Philip P., 1987, *The Conscription Controversy in Great Britain, 1900–18*.

Adamthwaite, Anthony, 1977, *France and the Coming of the Second World War, 1936–1939*.

Adamthwaite, Anthony, 1986, 'Britain and the world, 1945–1949: the view from the Foreign Office', in Becker and Knipping 1986: 9–25.

Adamthwaite, Anthony, 1988, 'Suez revisited', *IA* 64: 449–64.

Addison, Paul, 1975, *The Road to 1945: British Politics and the Second World War*.

Adelman, Jonathan R., 1988, *Prelude to the Cold War: The Tsarist, Soviet, and US Armies in the two World Wars*.

Aldcroft, Derek H., 1977, *From Versailles to Wall Street, 1919–1929*.

Aldrich, Richard, and Coleman, Michael, 1989a, 'The Cold War, the JIC and British signals intelligence, 1948', *INS* 4: 535–49.

Aldrich, Richard, and Coleman, Michael, 1989b, 'Britain and the strategic air offensive against the Soviet Union: the question of South Asian air bases, 1945–1949', *History* 242: 400–26.

Alexander, G.M., 1982, *The Prelude to the Truman Doctrine: British Policy in Greece, 1944–1947*. Oxford.

317

Alford, B.W.E., 1988, *British Economic Performance, 1945–1975*.

Allen, David, 1988, 'British foreign policy and West European co-operation', in Byrd (ed.), 1988: 35–53.

Allen, H.C., 1959, *The Anglo–American Relationship since 1783*.

Allison, Graham T., 1971, *Essence of Decision: Explaining the Cuban Missile Crisis*. Boston.

Amery, Leopold, 1951, 1969, 1969, *The Life of Joseph Chamberlain*, vols IV, V, VI.

Anderson, Olive, 1967, *A Liberal State at War: English Politics and Economics during the Crimean War*.

Anderson, Terry, H., 1981, *The United States, Great Britain and the Cold War, 1944–1947*. Columbia, Missouri.

Andrew, Christopher, 1985, *Secret Service: The Making of the British Intelligence Community*.

Andrew, Christopher M. and Kanya-Forstner, A.S., 1981, *France Overseas: The Great War and the Climax of French Imperial Expansion*.

Andrew, Christopher, and Noakes, Jeremy (eds), 1987, *Intelligence and International Relations, 1900–1945*. Exeter.

Arbuthnott, Hugh, and Edwards, Geoffrey, 1989, *A Common Man's Guide to the Common Market* (2nd edn).

Arthur, Paul, and Jeffrey, Keith, 1988, *Northern Ireland since 1968*. Oxford.

Aster, Sidney, 1973, *1939: The Making of the Second World War*.

Auden, W.H., 1976, *Collected Poems* (ed. Edward Mendelson).

Austin, Dennis, 1982, 'The British point of no return?', in Gifford and Louis (eds) 1982: 225–47.

Avon, the Earl of [Anthony Eden], 1962, *Facing the Dictators*.

Bairoch, Paul, 1976, 'Europe's gross national product: 1800–1975', *JEEH* 5: 273–340.

Bairoch, Paul, 1982, 'International industrialization levels from 1750 to 1980', *JEEH* 11: 269–333.

Balfour, Michael, 1982, *West Germany: A Contemporary History*.

Barber, James, 1976, *Who Makes British Foreign Policy?* Milton Keynes.

Barber, James, 1988, 'Southern Africa', in Byrd (ed.), 1988: 96–116.

Barber, James R., 1983, *The Uneasy Relationship: Britain and South Africa*.

Barclay, G. St J., 1977, 'Australia looks to America: the wartime relationship, 1939–42', *Pacific Historical Review*, 46: 251–71.

Barker, Elisabeth, 1983, *The British between the Superpowers, 1945–50*.

Barnett, Correlli, 1972, *The Collapse of British Power*.

Barnett, Correlli, 1986, *The Audit of War: The Illusion and Reality of Britain as a Great Nation*.

Bartlett, C.J., 1963, *Great Britain and Seapower, 1815–1853*. Oxford.

Bartlett, C.J., 1972, *The Long Retreat: A Short History of British Defence Policy, 1945–70*.

Bartlett, C.J., 1984, *The Global Conflict: The International Rivalries of the Great Powers*.

Bartlett, C.J., 1989, *British Foreign Policy in the Twentieth Century*.

Baylis, John, 1983, 'British wartime thinking about a post-war European security group', *RIS 9*: 265–81.

Baylis, John (ed.), 1983, *Alternative Approaches to British Defence Policy*.

Baylis, John, 1984a, 'Britain, the Brussels Pact and the continental commitment', *IA* 60: 615–29.

Baylis, John, 1984b, *Anglo–American Defence Relations, 1939–1984: The Special Relationship*.

Baylis, John, 1986, '"Greenwoodery" and British defence policy', *IA* 62: 443–57.

Bayly, C.A., 1989, *Imperial Meridian: The British Empire and the World, 1780–1830*.

Becker, Josef, and Knipping, Franz, 1986 (eds), *Power in Europe?: Great Britain, France, Italy and Germany in a Postwar World, 1945–50*. Berlin.

Beer, Samuel H., 1982, *Britain Against Itself: The Contradictions of Collectivism*.

Bell, David S. (ed.) 1985, *The Conservative Government, 1979–1984: An Interim Report*.

Bell, P.M.H., 1974, *A Certain Eventuality: Britain and the Fall of France*. Farnborough, Hants.

Bell, P.M.H., 1986, *The Origins of the Second World War in Europe*.

Belloc, Hilaire, 1970, *Complete Verse*.

Beloff, Max, 1969, *Britain's Imperial Sunset, vol. I, Britain's Liberal Empire, 1897–1921*.

Benn, Tony, 1987, *Out of the Wilderness: Diaries, 1963–67*.

Benn, Tony, 1988, *Office Without Power: Diaries, 1968–1972*.

Bennett, Edward W., 1979, *German Rearmament and the West, 1932–1939*. Princeton, NJ.

Berghahn, V.R., 1973, *Germany and the Approach of War in 1914*.

Berridge, G.R. and Young, John W., 1988, 'What is "a great power"?', *Political Studies*, 36: 224–34.

Best, Michael H., and Humphries, Jane, 'The City and industrial decline', in Elbaum and Lazonick (eds), 1986: 223–39.

Best, Richard A., Jr., 1986, *'Co-operation with Like-Minded Peoples': British Influences on American Security Policy, 1945–1949*.

Bialer, Uri, 1980, *The Shadow of the Bomber: The Fear of Air Attack and British Politics, 1932–1939*.

Bing, Geoffrey, et al., 1947, *Keep Left*.

Blank, Stephen, 1977, 'Britain: the politics of foreign economic policy, the domestic economy, and the problem of pluralistic stagnation', *International Organization*, 31: 673–721.

Blinken, Antony J., 1987, *Ally vs. Ally: America, Europe and the Siberian Pipeline Crisis*. New York.

Bogdanor, Vernon, 1989, 'The June 1989 European elections and the institutions of the Community', *GO* 24: 199–214.

Bond, Brian, 1972, *The Victorian Army and the Staff College, 1854–1914*.

Bond, Brian, 1975, *France and Belgium, 1939–1940*.

Bond, Brian, 1977, *Liddell Hart: A Study of His Military Thought*.

Bond, Brian, 1980, *British Military Policy between the Wars*. Oxford.

Bond, Brian, 1984, *War and Society in Europe, 1870–1970*.

Botti, Timothy J., 1987, *The Long Wait: The Forging of the Anglo-American Nuclear Alliance, 1945–1958*. New York.

Bourne, Kenneth, 1967, *Britain and the Balance of Power in North America, 1815–1908*.

Bourne, Kenneth, 1970, *The Foreign Policy of Victorian England, 1830–1902*. Oxford.

Bowie, Robert R., 1989, 'Eisenhower, Dulles, and the Suez crisis', in Louis and Owen (eds), 1989: 189–214.

Bowles, Nigel, 1985, 'The defence policy of the Conservative government', in D. Bell (ed.), 1985: 184–99.

Boyce, D.G., 1988, *The Irish Question and British Politics, 1868–1986*.

Boyle, Peter G., 1982, 'The British Foreign Office and American Foreign Policy, 1947–48', *JAS* 16: 373–89.

Boyle, Peter G., 1987, 'Britain, America and the transition from economic to military assistance, 1948–51', *JCH* 22: 521–38.

Bradshaw, Kenneth, and Pring, David, 1973, *Parliament and Congress*.

Breuilly, John, 1982, *Nationalism and the State*. Manchester.

British Documents on the Origins of the War, 1898–1914, 1926–38, (eds Gooch, G.P., and Temperley, Harold, 11 vols). Abbreviated as *BD*.

Brittan, Samuel, 1969, *Steering the Economy: The Role of the Treasury*.

Broadberry, Stephen, 1988, 'The impact of the world wars on the long run performance of the British economy', in Crafts (ed.), 1988: 25–37.

Brondel, Georges, 1977, 'The sources of energy, 1920–1970', in Cipolla (ed.), 1977, 5/1: 218–300.

Brown, Judith M., 1985, *Modern India: The Origins of an Asian Democracy*. Oxford.

Browning, Peter, 1986, *The Treasury and Economic Policy, 1964–1985*.

Bryant, Arthur, 1957, *Triumph in the West, 1943–1946*.

Bull, Hedley, and Watson, Adam (eds), 1984, *The Expansion of International Society*. Oxford.

Bullock, Alan, 1983, *Ernest Bevin: Foreign Secretary, 1945–1951*.

Burch, Martin, and Wood, Bruce, 1983, *Public Policy in Britain*. Oxford.

Burgess, Simon, and Edwards, Geoffrey, 1988, 'The six plus one: British policy-makers and the question of European economic integration, 1955', *IA* 64: 393–413.

Burk, Kathleen, 1979, 'Great Britain in the United States, 1917–1918: the turning point', *IHR* 1: 228–45.

Burk, Kathleen, 1982, 'The Treasury: from impotence to power', in Burk (ed.), 1982: 84–107.

Burk, Kathleen (ed.), 1982, *War and the State: The Transformation of British Government, 1914–1919*.

Burk, Kathleen, 1985, *Britain, America and the Sinews of War, 1914–1918*.

Burridge, T.D., 1976, *British Labour and Hitler's War*.

Butler, David, 1989, *British General Elections since 1945*. Oxford.

Butler, David, and Kitzinger, Uwe, 1976, *The 1975 Referendum*.

Byrd, Peter (ed.), 1988, *British Foreign Policy under Thatcher*. Deddington.

Cable, James, 1986, *The Geneva Conference of 1954 on Indochina*.

Cain, P.J., and Hopkins, A.G., 1980, 'The political economy of British expansion overseas, 1750–1914', *EcHR* 33: 463–90.

Cain, P.J., and Hopkins, A.G., 1986, 'Gentlemanly capitalism and British expansion overseas: I. The Old Colonial System, 1688–1850', *EcHR* 39: 501–25.

Cain, P.J., and Hopkins, A.G., 1987, 'Gentlemanly capitalism and British expansion overseas: II. New imperialism, 1850–1945', *EcHR* 40: 1–26.

Cairncross, Alec, 1985, *Years of Recovery: British Economic Policy, 1945–1951*.

Calder, Kenneth J., 1976, *Britain and the Origins of the New Europe, 1914–1918*. Cambridge.

Callaghan, James, 1987, *Time and Chance*.

Callahan, Raymond, 1974, 'The illusion of security: Singapore, 1919–1942', *JCH* 9: 69–92.

Calleo, David, 1978, *The German Problem Reconsidered: Germany and the World Order, 1870 to the Present*. Cambridge.

Campbell, Alan, 1982a and b, 'Anglo–French relations a decade ago: a new assessment', *IA* 58: 237–53, 429–46.

Camps, Miriam, 1964, *Britain and the European Community, 1955–1963*.

Cannadine, David, 1984, 'The past and the present in the English industrial revolution, 1880–1980', *PP* 103: 131–72.

Carlton, David, 1981, *Anthony Eden: A Biography*.

Carlton, David, 1988, *Britain and the Suez Crisis*. Oxford.

Carr, William, 1985, *Poland to Pearl Harbour: The Making of the Second World War*

Carrington, Lord, 1989, *Reflect on Things Past*.

Castle, Barbara, 1980, *The Castle Diaries, 1974–1976*.

Castle, Barbara, 1984, *The Castle Diaries, 1964–1970*.

'Cato' [Michael Foot, Peter Howard and Frank Owen], 1940, *Guilty Men*.

Ceadel, Martin, 1980, *Pacifism in Britain, 1914–45: The Defining of a Faith*. Oxford.

Cecil, Lady Gwendolen, 1921–32, *Life of Robert, Marquis of Salisbury* (4 vols).

Chalmers, Malcolm, 1985, *Paying for Defence: Military Spending and British Decline*.

Chamberlain, Austen, 1930, 'Great Britain as a European power', *Journal of the Royal Institute of International Affairs*, 9: 180–8.

Chamberlain, M.E., 1980, *British Foreign Policy in the Age of Palmerston*.

Chamberlain, Muriel E., 1988, *'Pax Britannica'?: British Foreign Policy, 1789–1914*.

Chandler, Alfred D., 1980, 'The growth of the transnational industrial firm in the United States and the United Kingdom: a comparative analysis', *EcHR* 33: 396–410.

Chandler, Alfred D., and Daems, Herman (eds) 1980, *Managerial Hierarchies: Comparative Perspectives on the Rise of the Modern Industrial Enterprise*. Cambridge, Massachusetts.

Charlton, Michael, 1983, *The Price of Victory*.

Cheng, Joseph Y.S., 1987, 'Hong Kong: the pressure to converge', *IA* 63: 271–83.

Chevalier, Michel, 1866, 'La guerre et la crise européenne', *Revue de Deux Mondes*, 63: 758–85.

Churchill, Winston S., 1948–54, *The Second World War* (6 vols).

Churchill, Winston S., 1974, *Complete Speeches*, 8 vols (ed. Robert Rhodes James). New York.

Churchill, Winston S., 1976, *The Collected Essays of Sir Winston Churchill*, 4 vols (ed. Michael Wolff).

Cipolla, Carlo (ed.) 1977, *The Fontana Economic History of Europe: 5 The Twentieth Century* (2 parts). Brighton.

Clark, Ian, and Wheeler, Nicholas J., 1989, *The British Origins of Nuclear Strategy, 1945–1955*. Oxford.

Clarke, Harold D., Mishler, William, and Whiteley, Paul, 1990, 'Recapturing the Falklands: models of Conservative party popularity, 1979–83', *BJPS* 20: 63–81

Clarke, Michael, 1988, 'The Soviet Union and Eastern Europe', in Byrd (ed.), 1988: 54–75.

Clarke, Peter, 1988, *The Keynesian Revolution in the Making*. Oxford.

Clarke, Sir Richard, 1982, *Anglo–American Economic Collaboration in War and Peace, 1942–1949* (ed. Sir Alec Cairncross). Oxford.

Clarke, S.V.O., 1967, *Central Bank Cooperation, 1924–1931*. New York.

Coghlan, F., 1972, 'Armaments, economic policy and appeasement: background to British foreign policy, 1931–7', *History*, 57: 205–16.

Cohen, Michael J., 1982, *Palestine and the Great Powers, 1945–1948*. Princeton.

Coker, Christopher, 1984, *The Future of the Atlantic Alliance*.

Coleman, D.C., and MacLeod, Christine, 1986, 'Attitudes to new techniques: British businessmen, 1800–1950', *EcHR* 39: 588–611.

Collier, Basil, 1957, *The Defence of the United Kingdom*.

Colville, John, 1968, [Memoir], in Wheeler–Bennett (ed.), 1968: 47–138

Colville, John, 1985, *The Fringes of Power: Downing Street Diaries, 1939–1945*.

Colvin, Ian, 1971, *The Chamberlain Cabinet*. New York.

Conservative Central Office, 1970, *A Better Tomorrow*.

Costigliola, Frank, 1984, 'The failed design: Kennedy, de Gaulle, and the struggle for Europe', *DH* 8: 227–51.

Cowling, Maurice, 1975, *The Impact of Hitler: British Politics and British Policy, 1933–1940*. Cambridge.

Crafts, N.F.R., 1985, *British Economic Growth during the Industrial Revolution*. Oxford.

Crafts, N.F.R. (ed.), 1988, *Long-Run Economic Performance in the UK*, published as *Oxford Review of Economic Policy*, 4/1.

Cromwell, Valerie, 1982, 'The Foreign and Commonwealth Office', in Steiner (ed.) 1982: 541–73.

Crossman, Richard, 1975, 1976, 1977, *The Diaries of a Cabinet Minister, 1964–70* (3 vols).

Crouzet, Francois, 1982, *The Victorian Economy* (translated by A.S. Forster).

Cuniff, M.G., 1903, 'British trade-unionists in America: what they saw', *The World's Work,* 1: 307–10.

Curtice, John, 1989, 'The 1989 European election: protest or green tide?', *Electoral Studies,* 8: 217–30.

Cutler, Tony, Haslam, Colin, Williams, John, and Williams, Karel, 1989, *1992 – The Struggle for Europe.* Oxford.

Daltrop, Anne, 1982, *Politics and the European Community.*

Darby, Phillip, 1973, *British Defence Policy East of Suez, 1947–1968.*

Darwin, John, 1981, *Britain, Egypt and the Middle East: Imperial Policy in the Aftermath of War, 1918–1922.*

Darwin, John, 1984, 'British decolonization since 1945: a pattern or a puzzle?', *JICH* 12: 187–209.

Darwin, John, 1988, *Britain and Decolonisation: The Retreat from Empire in the Post-War World.*

Davis, Lance E., and Huttenback, Robert A., with the assistance of Susan Gray Davis, 1986, *Mammon and the Pursuit of Empire: The Political Economy of British Imperialism, 1860–1912.* Cambridge.

Day, David, 1988, *The Great Betrayal: Britain, Australia and the Onset of the Pacific War, 1939–1941.*

De La Serre, Françoise, 1987, *La Grande-Bretagne et la Communauté Européenne.* Paris.

Devereux, David R., 1989, 'Britain, the Commonwealth and the Defence of the Middle East, 1948–56', *JCH* 24: 327–45 .

Dilks, David, 1969, 1970, *Curzon in India* (2 vols).

Dilks, David (ed.), 1971, *The Diaries of Sir Alexander Cadogan, OM, 1938–1945.*

Dilks, D.N., 1972, 'Appeasement revisited', *University of Leeds Review* 15: 28–56.

Dilks, David (ed.), 1981, *Retreat from Power: Studies in Britain's Foreign Policy of the Twentieth Century* (2 vols).

Dillon, G.M., 1989, *The Falklands, Politics and War.*

Dimbleby, David, and Reynolds, David, 1988, *An Ocean Apart: The Relationship between Britain and America in the Twentieth Century.*

Dingman, Roger, 1976, *Power in the Pacific: The Origins of Naval Arms Limitation, 1914–1922.* Chicago.

Dingman, Roger, 1982, 'Truman, Attlee, and the Korean War crisis', *International Studies* (LSE), 1982/1: 1–42.

Dobson, Alan P., 1986, *US Wartime Aid to Britain, 1940–1946.*

Dobson, Alan P., 1990, 'The years of transition: Anglo–American relations, 1961–7', *RIS* 16: 239–58.

Dockrill, Michael, 1988, *British Defence since 1945*. Oxford.

Dockrill, Michael, and Young, John W. (eds), 1989, *British Foreign Policy, 1945–56*.

Dockrill, Michael L., and Goold, J. Douglas, 1981, *Peace without Promise: Britain and the Peace Conferences, 1919–23*.

Dockrill, M.L., 1986, 'The Foreign Office, Anglo-American relations and the Korean war, June 1950–June 1951', *IA* 62: 459–76.

Dockrill, Saki, 1989, 'Britain and the settlement of the West German rearmament question in 1954', in M. Dockrill and J. Young (eds) 1989: 149–72.

Documents on British Policy Overseas, 1984, (eds Roger Bullen, M.E. Pelly, H.J. Yasamee, et al.). Abbreviated as *DBPO*.

Donoughue, Bernard, and Jones, G.W., 1973, *Herbert Morrison: Portrait of a Politician*.

Dooley, Howard J., 1989, 'Great Britain's "last battle" in the Middle East: notes on Cabinet planning during the Suez crisis of 1956', *IHR* 11: 486–517.

Douglas, Roy, 1977, *In the Year of Munich*.

Douglas, Roy, 1978, *The Advent of War, 1939–1940*.

Douglas, Roy, 1986, *World Crisis and British Decline, 1929–1956*.

Doyle, Michael W., 1986, *Empires*.

Drummond, Ian M., 1972, *British Economic Policy and the Empire, 1919–1939*.

Drummond, Ian M., 1981, *The Floating Pound and the Sterling Area, 1931–1939*. Cambridge.

Drummond, Ian M., 1987, *The Gold Standard and the International Monetary System, 1900–1939*.

Drummond, Ian M., and Hillmer, Norman, 1989, *Negotiating Freer Trade: The United Kingdom, the United States, Canada and the Trade Agreements of 1938*. Waterloo, Ontario.

Duke, Simon, 1987, *US Defence Bases in the United Kingdom: A Matter for Joint Decision?*

Dunning, John H., 1970, *Studies in International Investment*.

Dutton, David, 1985, *Austen Chamberlain: Gentleman in Politics*. Bolton.

Eddy, Paul, Linklater, Magnus, with Gillman, Peter, 1982, *The Falklands War*.

Edelstein, M., 1981, 'Foreign investment and empire, 1860–1914', in Floud and McCloskey (eds), 1981: 70–98.

Edmonds, Robin, 1986, *Setting the Mould: The United States and Britain, 1945–1950*. Oxford.

Edwards, Geoffrey, 1984, 'Europe and the Falkland Islands crisis, 1982', *JCMS* 22: 295–313.

Ekstein, Michael G., and Steiner, Zara S., 1977, 'The Sarajevo crisis', in Hinsley (ed.), 1977: 397–410.

El-Agraa, Ali, 1985, 'Mrs Thatcher's European Community policy', in D. Bell (ed.), 1985: 161–83.

Elbaum, Bernard, and Lazonick, William (eds), 1986, *The Decline of the British Economy*. Oxford.

Eldridge, C.C., 1978, *Victorian Imperialism*.

Eldridge, C.C. (ed.), 1984, *British Imperialism in the Nineteenth Century*.

Elrod, Richard B., 1976, 'The concert of Europe: a fresh look at an international system', *World Politics*, 28: 159–74.

Emy, H.V., 1972, 'The impact of financial policy on English party politics before 1914', *HJ* 15: 103–31.

Farrar, L.L., Jr., 1978, *Divide and Conquer: German Efforts to Conclude a Separate Peace, 1914–1918*. Boulder, Colorado.

Farrar, L.L., Jr., 1981, *Arrogance and Anxiety: The Ambivalence of German Power, 1848–1914*. Iowa City.

Feiling, Keith, 1946, *The Life of Neville Chamberlain*.

Ferris, John, 1987, 'Treasury control, the ten year rule and British Service policies, 1919–1924', *HJ* 30: 859–83.

Fieldhouse, D.K., 1973, *Economics and empire, 1830–1914*.

Fieldhouse, D.K., 1982, *The Colonial Empires: A Comparative Survey From The Eighteenth Century* (1966).

Fieldhouse, D.K., 1984, 'The Labour governments and the Empire-Commonwealth, 1945–51', in Ovendale (ed.), 1984: 83–120.

Fieldhouse, D.K., 1986, *Black Africa, 1945–80: Economic Decolonization and Arrested Development*.

Fink, Carole, 1984, *The Genoa Conference: European Diplomacy, 1921–1922*. Chapel Hill, North Carolina.

Fish, M. Steven, 1986, 'After Stalin's death: the Anglo-American debate over a new Cold War', *DH* 10: 333–55

Flint, John, 1983, 'Planned decolonization and its failure in British Africa', *AA* 82: 389–411.

Flora, Peter, et al., 1983, *State, Economy, and Society in Western Europe, 1815–1975: A Data Handbook* (2 vols).

Floud, Roderick, and McCloskey, Donald (eds), 1981, *The Economic History of Britain since 1700: vol. 2, 1860 to the 1970s*. Cambridge.

Foot, Michael, 1973, *Aneurin Bevan: A Biography, vol. 2*.

Foster, Roy, 1989, *Modern Ireland, 1600–1972*. Harmondsworth.

Fowler, Wilton B., 1969, *British-American Relations, 1917–1918: The Role of Sir William Wiseman*. Princeton.

Fox, William T.R., 1944, *The Superpowers: The United States, Britain, and the Soviet Union – Their Responsibility for Peace*. New York.

Frankel, Joseph, 1975, *British Foreign Policy, 1945–1973*.

Frankel, Joseph, 1979, *International Relations in a Changing World*. Oxford.

Frantz, Constantin, 1966, *Die Weltpolitik unter besonderer Bezugnahme auf Deutschland*, 3 vols (1882–3). Osnabrück

Frazier, Robert, 1984, 'Did Britain start the Cold War?: Bevin and the Truman Doctrine', *HJ* 27: 715–27.

Freedman, Lawrence, 1982, 'The Atlantic crisis', *IA* 58: 395–412.

Freedman, Lawrence, 1986/7, 'The case of Westland and bias towards Europe', *IA* 63: 1–19.

Freedman, Lawrence, 1988, *Britain and the Falklands War*. Oxford.

French, David, 1982, *British Economic and Strategic Planning, 1905–1915*.

French, David, 1986, *British Strategy and War Aims, 1914–1916*.

Friedberg, Aaron L., 1988, *The Weary Titan: Britain and the Experience of Relative Decline, 1895–1905*. Princeton.

Fry, Michael G., 1977, *Lloyd George and Foreign Policy: I, Education of a Statesman, 1890–1916*.

Fry, Michael G., 1989, 'Canada, the North Atlantic Triangle, and the United Nations', in Louis and Owen (eds), 1989: 285–316.

Fursdon, Edward, 1980, *The European Defence Community: A History*.

Gallagher, John, 1982, *The Decline, Revival and Fall of the British Empire* (ed. Anil Seal). Cambridge.

Gallagher, John, and Robinson, Ronald, 1953, 'The imperialism of free trade', *EcHR* 6: 1–15.

Gardner, Richard, 1980, *Sterling-Dollar Diplomacy in Current Perspective*. New York.

Gates, Eleanor M., 1981, *The End of the Affair: The Collapse of the Anglo-French Alliance, 1939–1940*.

Gause, F. Gregory, 1985, 'British and American policies in the Persian Gulf, 1968–1973', *RIS* 11: 247–73.

George, Stephen, 1985, *Politics and Policy in the European Community*. Oxford.

George, Stephen, 1990, *An Awkward Partner: Britain in the European Community*. Oxford.

Ghosh, P.R., 1984, 'Disraelian Conservatism: a financial approach', *EHR* 99: 268–96.

Gibbs, N.H., 1975, *Grand Strategy: I, Rearmament Policy*.

Gifford, Prosser, and Louis, Wm. Roger (eds), 1982, *The Transfer of Power in Africa: Decolonization, 1940–1960*.

Gifford, Prosser, and Louis, Wm. Roger (eds), 1988, *Decolonization and African Independence: The Transfers of Power, 1960–80*.

Gilbert, Martin, 1971, 1975, 1976, 1983, 1986, 1988, *Winston S. Churchill*, vols III, IV, V, VI, VII, VIII.

Gilpin, Robert, 1981, *War and Change in World Politics*. Cambridge.

Goldsworthy, David, 1990, 'Keeping change within bounds: aspects of colonial policy during the Churchill and Eden governments, 1951–57', *JICH* 18: 81–108.

Gooch, John, 1974, *The Plans of War: The General Staff and British Military Strategy, c. 1900–1916*.

Gordon, Lincoln (ed.) 1987, *Eroding Empire: Western Relations with Eastern Europe*. Washington, D.C.

Gore–Booth, Paul, 1974, *With Great Truth and Respect*.

Gormly, James L., 1984, 'The Washington declaration and the "poor relation": Anglo-American atomic diplomacy, 1945–46', *DH*, 8: 125–43.

Gorst, Anthony, and Lucas, W. Scott, 1989, 'The other collusion: Operation Straggle and Anglo-American intervention in Syria, 1955–56', *INS* 4: 576–95.

Gowing, Margaret, 1964, *Britain and Atomic Energy, 1939–1945*.

Gowing, Margaret, assisted by Arnold, Lorna, 1974, *Independence and Deterrence: Britain and Atomic Energy, 1945–1952* (2 vols).

Grenville, J.A.S., 1970, *Lord Salisbury and Foreign Policy at the Close of the Nineteenth Century* (1964).

Grigg, John, 1980, *1943: The Victory That Never Was*.

Grove, Eric J., 1987, *Vanguard to Trident: British Naval Policy since World War II*.

Gupta, Partha Sarathi, 1983, 'Imperialism and the Labour government of 1945–51', in Winter (ed.), 1983: 99–124.

Haack, W.G.C.M., 1972, 'The economic effects of Britain's entry into the Common Market', *JCMS* 11: 136–51.

Haggie, Paul, 1981, *Britannia at Bay: The Defence of the British Empire against Japan, 1931–1941*. Oxford.

Hall, Christopher, 1987, *Britain, America and Arms Control, 1921–1937*.

Hamilton, K.A., 1977, 'Great Britain and France, 1911–1914', in Hinsley (ed.), 1977: 324–341.

Hancock, W.G., and Gowing, M., 1949, *British War Economy*.

Hankey, [Maurice] Lord, 1961, *The Supreme Command*, 2 vols.

Hannah, Leslie, 1983, *The Rise of the Corporate Economy* (1976).

Hardach, Gerd, 1977, *The First World War, 1914–1918*.

Hargreaves, John D., 1988, *Decolonization in Africa*.

Harkness, David, 1983, *Northern Ireland since 1920*. Dublin.

Harley, C.K., and McCloskey, D.N., 1981, 'Foreign trade: competition and the expanding international economy', in Floud and McCloskey (eds), 1981: 50–69.

Harrison, Michael M., 1981, *The Reluctant Ally: France and Atlantic Security*. Baltimore.

Haslam, Jonathan, 1989, *The Soviet Union and the Politics of Nuclear Weapons in Europe, 1969–1987: The Problem of the SS-20*.

Hastings, Max, and Jenkins, Simon, 1983, *The Battle for the Falklands*.

Hathaway, Robert M., 1981, *Ambiguous Partnership: Britain and America, 1944–1947*. New York.

Hauner, Milan, 1978, 'Did Hitler want a world dominion?', *JCH* 13: 15–32.

Hazelhurst, Cameron, 1971, *Politicians at War, July 1914 to May 1915: A Prologue to the Triumph of Lloyd George*. New York.

Headrick, Daniel R., 1979, 'Tools of imperialism: technology and the expansion of European colonial empires in the nineteenth century', *JMH* 51: 231–61.

Heath, Edward, 1970, *Old World, New Horizons: Britain, the Common Market, and the Atlantic Alliance*.

Heath, Edward, 1988, 'European unity over the next ten years: from Community to union', *IA* 64: 199–207.

Henderson, Sir Nicholas, 1982, *The Birth of NATO*.

Hendrick, Burton J., 1927, *The Life and Letters of Walter H. Page, 1885–1918*, 3 vols. Garden City, New York.

Hennessy, Peter, 1989, *Whitehall*.

Henrikson, Alan K., 1980, 'The creation of the North Atlantic alliance, 1948–1952', *US Naval War College Review* 32: 4–39.

Hildebrand, Klaus, 1973, *The Foreign Policy of the Third Reich*, tr. Anthony Fothergill.

Hill, Christopher, 1988, 'The historical background: past and present in British foreign policy', in M. Smith et al. (eds), 1988: 24–49.

Hillgruber, Andreas, 1974, 'England's place in Hitler's plans for world dominion', *JCH* 9: 5–22.

Hinds, Alister E., 1987, 'Sterling and imperial policy, 1945–1951', *JICH* 15: 148–69.

Hinsley, F.H. (ed.), 1977, *British Foreign Policy under Sir Edward Grey*.

Hinsley, F.H., 1979, [with Thomas, E.E., Ransom, C.F.G., and Knight, R.C.], *British Intelligence in the Second World War: Its Influence on Strategy and Operations*, vol. I.

Hinsley, F.H., 1987, 'British intelligence in the second world war', in Andrew and Noakes (eds) 1987: 209–18.

H.M. Government, 1971, 'Britain and Europe: a short version of the Government's White Paper'.

H.M. Government, 1984, 'Europe – the future', *JCMS* 23: 73–81.

H.M. Government, 1989, 'An evolutionary approach to economic and monetary union'. H.M. Treasury.

Hobsbawm, E.J., 1969, *Industry and Empire*. Harmondsworth.

Hogan, Michael J., 1987, *The Marshall Plan: America, Britain, and the Reconstruction of Western Europe, 1947–1952*. Cambridge.

Holbraad, Carsten, 1970, *The Concert of Europe: A Study in German and British International Theory, 1815–1914*.

Holland, Martin, 1988, *The European Community and South Africa: European Political Cooperation under Strain*.

Holland, R.F., 1981, *Britain and the Commonwealth Alliance, 1918–1939*.

Holland, R.F., 1984, 'The imperial factor in British strategies from Attlee to Macmillan, 1945–63', *JICH* 12: 165–86.

Holland, R.F., 1985, *European Decolonisation, 1918–1981: An Introductory Survey*.

Holmes, Peter, 1985, 'The Thatcher government's overall economic performance', in D. Bell (ed.), 1985: 15–32.

Horne, Alistair, 1988, *Macmillan, 1894–1956*.

Horne, Alistair, 1989, *Macmillan, 1957–1986*.

Howard, Christopher, 1967, *Splendid Isolation: A Study of Ideas Concerning Britain's International Position and Foreign Policy during the Later Years of the Third Marquis of Salisbury*.

Howard, Michael, 1968, *The Mediterranean Strategy in the Second World War*.

Howard, Michael, 1970, *The Central Organization of Defence*.

Howard, Michael, 1972, *Grand Strategy: Vol. IV, August 1942 – September 1943*.

Howard, Michael, 1974, *The Continental Commitment: The Dilemma of British Defence Policy in the Era of Two World Wars* (1972). Harmondsworth.

Howard, Michael, 1984, 'The military factor in European expansion', in Bull and Watson (eds), 1984: 33–42.

Howe, Sir Geoffrey, 1984, 'The future of the European Community: Britain's approach to the negotiations', *IA* 60: 187–92

Hurd, Douglas, 1981, 'Political co-operation', *IA* 57: 383–93.

Hyam, Ronald, 1976, *Britain's Imperial Century, 1815–1914: A Study of Empire and Expansion*.

Hyam, Ronald, 1987, 'The geopolitical origins of the Central African Federation: Britain, Rhodesia and South Africa, 1948–1953', *HJ* 30: 145–72.

IISS (International Institute of Strategic Studies), 1964, *The Military Balance, 1964–1965.*

IISS (International Institute of Strategic Studies), 1972, *The Military Balance, 1972–1973.*

IISS (International Institute of Strategic Studies), 1987, *The Military Balance, 1987–1988.*

Ingham, Geoffrey, 1984, *Capitalism Divided?: The City and Industry in British Social Development.*

Ireland, Timothy P., 1981, *Creating the Entangling Alliance: The Origins of the North Atlantic Treaty Organization.*

Jacobson, John, 1983, 'Is there a new international history of the 1920s?', *AHR* 88: 617–45.

Jaffe, Lorna, S., 1985, *The Decision to Disarm Germany: British Policy towards Postwar German Disarmament, 1914–1919.*

Jenkins, Peter, 1989, *Mrs Thatcher's Revolution: The Ending of the Socialist Era* (1987).

Jenkins, Roy (ed.), 1983, *Britain and the EEC.*

Jenkins, Simon, and Sloman, Anne, 1985, *With Respect, Ambassador: An Inquiry into the Foreign Office.*

Johnson, Franklyn A., 1980, *Defence by Ministry: The British Ministry of Defence, 1944–1974.*

Johnston, W. Ross, 1981, *Great Britain, Great Empire: An Evaluation of the British Imperial Experience.*

Joll, James, 1984, *The Origins of the First World War.*

Jones, J.R., 1980, *Britain and the World, 1649–1815.*

Jones, Ray, 1971, *The Nineteenth-Century Foreign Office: An Administrative History.*

Jones, Raymond A., 1983, *The British Diplomatic Service, 1815–1914.* Waterloo, Ontario.

Jordan, A.G., and Richardson, J.J., 1987, *British Politics and the Policy Process: An Arena Approach.*

Judd, Denis, 1968, *Balfour and the British Empire: A Study in Imperial Evolution, 1874–1932.*

Judd, Denis, and Slinn, Peter, 1982, *The Evolution of the Modern Commonwealth, 1902–80.*

Kahler, Miles, 1984, *Decolonization in Britain and France: The Domestic Consequences of International Relations.* Princeton.

Kaplan, Lawrence S., 1988, *NATO and the United States: The Enduring Alliance.* Boston.

Kavanagh, Denis, 1987, *Thatcherism and British Politics: The End of Consensus*. Oxford.

Keiger, John F.V., 1983, *France and the Origins of the First World War*.

Kendle, John E., 1975, *The Round Table Movement and Imperial Union*. Toronto.

Kennan, George F., 1977, *The Cloud of Danger: Current Realities of American Foreign Policy*. Boston.

Kennedy, Paul, 1980, *The Rise of the Anglo-German Antagonism, 1860–1914*.

Kennedy, Paul, 1981, *The Realities behind Diplomacy: Background Influences on British Foreign Policy, 1865–1980*.

Kennedy, Paul, 1983a, *The Rise and Fall of British Naval Mastery* (1976).

Kennedy, Paul, 1983b, *Strategy and Diplomacy, 1870–1945: Eight Studies*.

Kennedy, Paul, 1988, *The Rise and Fall of the Great Powers: Economic Change and Military Conflict from 1500 to 2000*.

Kennedy, Paul, and O'Brien, Patrick K., 1989, 'Debate: the costs and benefits of British imperialism, 1846–1914', *PP* 125: 186–99.

Kent, John, 1989, 'Bevin's imperialism and the idea of Euro-Africa, 1945–9', in M. Dockrill and J. Young (eds), 1989: 47–76.

Keohane, Robert O., and Nye, Joseph S., 1977, *Power and Interdependence: World Politics in Transition*. Boston.

Kernek, Sterling J., 1975, *Distractions of Peace during War: The Lloyd George Government's Reaction to Woodrow Wilson, December 1916 – November 1918*. Philadelphia.

Kettenacker, Lothar, (ed.), 1977, *Das 'Andere Deutschland' im Zweiten Weltkrieg: Emigration und Widerstand in internationaler Perspektive*. Stuttgart.

Keynes, J.M., 1971, *The Collected Writings of John Maynard Keynes*, vol. 4 [A Tract on Monetary Reform, 1923]

Kindleberger, Charles P., 1973, *The World in Depression, 1929–1939*.

Kipling, Rudyard, 1933 ed., *Rudyard Kipling's Verse: Inclusive Edition, 1885–1932*

Kissinger, Henry, 1982, *Years of Upheaval*.

Kitchen, Martin, 1986, *British Policy towards the Soviet Union during the Second World War*.

Kitzinger, Uwe, 1973, *Diplomacy and Persuasion: How Britain Joined the Common Market*.

Klein, Bradley S., 1988, 'Hegemony and strategic culture: American power projection and alliance defence politics', *RIS* 14: 133–48

Koss, Stephen, 1981, 1984, *The Rise and Fall of the Political Press in Britain* (2 vols).

Koss, Stephen, 1985, *Asquith* (1976).

Kramnick, Isaac (ed.), 1979, *Is Britain Dying?*. Ithaca, NY.

Krieger, Wolfgang, 1988, 'Die britische Krise in historischer Perspektive', *HZ* 247: 585–602.

Kunz, Diane B., 1987, *The Battle for Britain's Gold Standard in 1931*.

Kunz, Diane B., 1989, 'The importance of having money: the economic diplomacy of the Suez crisis', in Louis and Owen (eds), 1989: 215–32.

Kyle, Keith, 1989, 'Britain and the Crisis, 1955–1956', in Louis and Owen (eds) 1989: 103–30

Lamb, Richard, 1987, *The Failure of the Eden Government*.

Lammers, Donald, 1973, 'From Whitehall after Munich: The Foreign Office and the future course of British policy', *HJ* 16: 831–56.

Landes, David S., 1969, *The Unbound Prometheus: Technological Change and Industrial Development in Western Europe from 1750 to the Present*. Cambridge.

Langhorne, Richard (ed.), 1985, *Diplomacy and Intelligence during the Second World War: Essays in Honour of F.H. Hinsley*. Cambridge.

Lapping, Brian, 1985, *End of Empire*.

Lapping, Brian, 1987, 'Did Suez hasten the end of empire?', *CR* 1/2: 31–3.

Lawlor, Sheila, 1983, *Britain and Ireland, 1914–1923*. Dublin.

Le Carré, John, 1969, *A Small Town in Germany*.

Lee, Bradford A., 1973, *Britain and the Sino-Japanese War, 1937–1939: A Study in the Dilemmas of British Decline*. Stanford, CA.

Lewis, Julian, 1988, *Changing Direction: British Military Planning for Post-War Strategic Defence, 1942–1947*.

Linklater, Magnus, and Leigh, David, 1986, *Not With Honour: The Inside Story of the Westland Scandal*.

Little, Walter, 1988, 'Anglo-Argentine relations and the management of the Falklands question', in Byrd (ed.), 1988: 137–56.

Lloyd, T.O., 1984, *The British Empire, 1558–1983*. Oxford.

Longford, Elizabeth, 1964, *Victoria R.I.*.

Louis, Wm. Roger, 1971, *British Strategy in the Far East, 1919–1939*. Oxford.

Louis, Wm. Roger, 1977, *Imperialism at Bay: The United States and the Decolonization of the British Empire, 1941–1945*. Oxford.

Louis, Wm. Roger, 1984, *The British Empire in the Middle East, 1945–1951*. Oxford.

Louis, Wm. Roger, 1989, 'The tragedy of the Anglo-Egyptian settlement of 1954', in Louis and Owen (eds) 1989: 43–71.

Louis, Wm. Roger, and Bull, Hedley (eds), 1986, *The 'Special Relationship': Anglo-American Relations since 1945*. Oxford.

Louis, Wm. Roger, and Owen, Roger (eds), 1989, *Suez 1956: The Crisis and Its Consequences*. Oxford.

Louis, Wm. Roger, and Robinson, Ronald, 1982, 'The United States and the liquidation of the British Empire in tropical Africa, 1941–1951', in Gifford and Louis (eds) 1982: 31–55.

Low, D.A., 1974, *Lion Rampant: Essays in the Study of British Imperialism*.

Low, [D.] Anthony, 1988, 'The end of the British empire in Africa', in Gifford and Louis (eds) 1988: 33–72.

Lowe, C.J., 1967, *The Reluctant Imperialists: British Foreign Policy, 1878–1902* (2 vols).

Lowe, C.J., and Dockrill, M.L., 1972, *The Mirage of Power: British Foreign Policy, 1914–22* (3 vols).

Lowe, Peter, 1977, *Great Britain and the Origins of the Pacific War: A Study of British Policy in East Asia, 1937–1941*. Oxford.

Lowe, Peter, 1986, *The Origins of the Korean War*.

Ludlow, Peter W., 1977, 'The unwinding of appeasement', in Kettenacker (ed.), 1977: 9–48.

Ludlow, Peter, 1982, *The Making of the European Monetary System: A Case Study of the Politics of the European Community*.

Mackay, Ruddock F., 1985, *Balfour: Intellectual Statesman*. Oxford.

Macmillan, Harold, 1969, *Tides of Fortune, 1945–55*.

Macmillan, Harold, 1971, *Riding the Storm, 1956–59*.

Macmillan, Harold, 1972, *Pointing the Way, 1959–1961*.

Macmillan, Harold, 1973, *At the End of the Day, 1961–63*.

McCloskey, Donald N., 1970, 'Did Victorian Britain fail?', *EcHR* 23: 446–59.

McCloskey, Donald N., 1980, 'Magnanimous Albion: free trade and British national income, 1841–1881', *Explorations in Economic History*, 17: 303–20.

MacDonald, C.A., 1972, 'Economic appeasement and the German "moderates", 1937–1939: an introductory essay', *PP* 56: 105–35.

MacDonald, Callum A., 1978, 'The Venlo Affair', *European Studies Review*, 8: 443–64.

MacDonald, Callum A., 1981, *The United States, Britain and Appeasement, 1936–1939*.

McDonald, Ian S. (ed.), 1974, *Anglo-American Relations since the Second World War*. New York.

McDougall, Walter A., 1978, *France's Rhineland Diplomacy, 1914–1924: The Last Bid for a Balance of Power in Europe*. Princeton.

McKercher, B.J.C., 1984, *The Second Baldwin Government and the United States, 1924–1929: Attitudes and Diplomacy*. Cambridge.

McNeill, William H., 1983, *The Pursuit of Power: Technology, Armed Force, and Society since A.D. 1000*. Oxford.

Maier, Charles S., 1981, 'The two post-war eras and the conditions for stability in twentieth-century Western Europe', *AHR* 86: 327–67.

Mandelbaum, Michael, 1981, *The Nuclear Revolution: International Politics before and after Hiroshima*. Cambridge.

Mandelbaum, Michael, 1988, *The Fate of Nations: The Search for National Security in the Nineteenth and Twentieth Centuries*. Cambridge.

Manne, Robert, 1974, 'The British decision for alliance with Russia, May 1939', *JCH* 9: 3–26.

Mansergh, Nicholas, 1982, *The Commonwealth Experience* (2 vols).

Marder, Arthur J., 1961, *From the Dreadnought to Scapa Flow: The Royal Navy in the Fisher Era: vol. I, The Road to War, 1904–1914*.

Martel, Gordon, 1986, *Imperial Diplomacy: Rosebery and the Failure of Foreign Policy*.

Mathias, Peter, 1969, *The First Industrial Nation: An Economic History of Britain, 1700–1914*.

Matthew, H.C.G., 1973, *The Liberal Imperialists: The Ideas and Policies of a Post-Gladstonian Elite*. Oxford.

Matthew, H.C.G., 1979, 'Disraeli, Gladstone, and the politics of mid-Victorian budgets', *HJ* 22: 615–43.

Matthews, R.C.O., Feinstein, C.H., and Odling-Smee, J.C., 1982, *British Economic Growth, 1856–1973*. Oxford.

May, Ernest R. (ed.), 1985, *Knowing One's Enemies: Intelligence Assessment before the Two World Wars*. Princeton.

Mayne, Richard, 1973, *The Recovery of Europe, 1945–73*. Garden City, NY.

Medlicott, W.N., 1981, *Britain and Germany: The Search for Agreement, 1930–1937* (1969), in Dilks (ed.) 1981: i, 78–101.

Meen, Geoffrey, 1988, 'International comparisons of the UK's long-run economic performance', in Crafts (ed.) 1988: xxii–xli.

Merrick, Ray, 1985, 'The Russia committee of the Foreign Office and the Cold War, 1946–47', *JCH* 20: 453–68.

Middlemas, Keith, 1972, *Diplomacy of Illusion: The British Government and Germany, 1937–1939*.

Middlemas, Keith, and Barnes, John, 1969, *Baldwin: A Biography*.

Mill, John Stuart, 1878, *Principles of Political Economy* (2 vols).

Milward, Alan S., 1970, *The Economic Effects of the Two World Wars on Britain*.

Milward, Alan S., 1977, *War, Economy and Society, 1939–45*.

Milward, Alan S., 1984, *The Reconstruction of Western Europe, 1945–1951*.

Mitchell, B.R., with Deane, Phyllis, 1962, *Abstract of British Historical Statistics*. Cambridge.

Moggridge, D.E., 1972, *British Monetary Policy, 1924–1931: The Norman Conquest of $4.86*. Cambridge.

Mommsen, Wolfgang, and Kettenacker, Lothar, (eds), 1983, *The Fascist Challenge and the Policy of Appeasement*.

Monroe, Elizabeth, 1981, *Britain's Moment in the Middle East, 1914–1971*.

Moon, Jeremy, 1985, *European Integration in British Politics, 1950–1963: A Study of Issue Change*. Aldershot.

Moore, R.J., 1974, *The Crisis of Indian Unity, 1917–1940*. Oxford.

Moore, R.J., 1979, *Churchill, Cripps, and India, 1939–1945*. Oxford.

Moore, R.J., 1983, *Escape from Empire: The Attlee Government and the Indian Problem*. Oxford.

Moran, Lord, 1968, *Winston Churchill: Struggle for Survival*.

Moreton, Edwina, 1987, 'The view from London', in Gordon (ed.), 1987: 232–68.

Morgan, D.J., 1980, *The Official History of Colonial Development* (5 vols).

Morgan, Kenneth O., 1979, *Consensus and Disunity: The Lloyd George Coalition Government, 1918–1922*. Oxford.

Morgan, Kenneth O., 1985, *Labour in Power, 1945–1951*. Oxford.

Morgenthau, Hans J., 1954, *Politics among Nations: The Struggle for Power and Peace* (2nd edn). New York.

Morse, Edward L., 1970, 'The transformation of foreign policies: modernization, interdependence, and externalization', *World Politics*, 22: 371–92.

Mowery, David C., 1986, 'Industrial research, 1900–50', in Elbaum and Lazonick (eds) 1986: 189–222.

Murray, Williamson, 1984, *The Change in the European Balance of Power, 1938–1939: The Path to Ruin*. Princeton.

Murray, Williamson, 1988, *Luftwaffe: Strategy for Defeat, 1933–1945* (1985).

Myers, Frank, 1984, 'Conscription and the politics of military strategy in the Attlee government', *JSS* 7: 55–73.

Navias, Martin S., 1989, 'Terminating conscription?: the British national service controversy, 1955–56', *JCH* 24: 195–208.

Neilson, Keith, 1984, *Strategy and Supply: The Anglo-Russian Alliance, 1914–1917.*

Néré, J., 1975, *The Foreign Policy of France from 1914 to 1945.*

Neustadt, Richard, 1969, 'White House and Whitehall', in Rose (ed.), 1969: 291–306.

Neustadt, Richard E., and May, Ernest R., 1986, *Thinking in Time: The Uses of History for Decision-Makers.* New York.

Newman, Simon, 1976, *March 1939: The British Guarantee to Poland. A Study in the Continuity of British Foreign Policy.* Oxford.

Newton, C.C.S., 1984, 'The sterling crisis of 1947 and the British response to the Marshall Plan', *EcHR* 37: 391–408.

Newton, C.C.S., 1985a, 'Britain, the sterling area and European integration, 1945–50', in Porter and Holland 1985: 163–82

Newton, C.C.S., 1985b, 'The 1949 sterling crisis and British policy towards European integration', *RIS* 11: 169–82.

Nish, Ian H., 1966, *The Anglo-Japanese Alliance: The Diplomacy of Two Island Empires, 1894–1907.*

Nish, Ian, 1972, *Alliance in Decline: A Study of Anglo-Japanese Relations, 1908–23.*

Northedge, F.S., 1983, 'Britain and the EEC: past and present', in Jenkins (ed.), 1983: 15–37.

Northedge, F.S., and Wells, Audrey, 1982, *Britain and Soviet Communism: The Impact of a Revolution.*

Nossiter, Bernard D., 1978, *Britain: A Future that Works.*

Nuallain, Colm O. (ed.), 1985, *The Presidency of the European Council of Ministers: Impacts and Implications for National Governments.*

Nunnerley, David, 1972, *President Kennedy and Britain.*

O'Brien, Patrick K., 1988a, 'The political economy of British taxation, 1688–1815', *EcHR*, 41: 1–32.

O'Brien, Patrick K., 1988b, 'The costs and benefits of British imperialism, 1846–1914', *PP* 120: 163-200.

Olson, Mancur, 1982, *The Rise and Decline of Nations: Economic Growth, Stagflation, and Social Rigidities.*

Orde, Anne, 1978, *Great Britain and International Security, 1920–1926.*

Ovendale, Ritchie, 1975, *'Appeasement' and the English Speaking World: Britain, the United States, the Dominions, and the Policy of 'Appeasement', 1937–1939.* Cardiff.

Ovendale, Ritchie, 1984, *The Origins of the Arab-Israeli Wars.*

Ovendale, Ritchie (ed.), 1984, *The Foreign Policy of the British Labour Governments, 1945–1951.* Leicester.

Ovendale, Ritchie, 1985, *The English-Speaking Alliance: Britain, the United States, the Dominions and the Cold War, 1945–1951*.

Ovendale, Ritchie, 1988, 'Egypt and the Suez base agreement', in J.W. Young (ed.) 1988: 135–55.

Overy, R.J., 1980, *The Air War, 1939–1945*.

Overy, R.J., 1982, 'Hitler's war and the German economy: a reinterpretation', *EcHR* 35: 272–91.

Overy, R.J., 1984, 'German air strength, 1933 to 1939: a note', *HJ* 27: 465–71.

Parker, R.A.C., 1974, 'Great Britain, France and the Ethiopian crisis, 1935–1936', *EHR* 89: 293–332

Parker, R.A.C., 1975, 'Economics, rearmament and foreign policy: the United Kingdom before 1939 – a preliminary study', *JCH* 10: 637–47

Parker, R.A.C., 1981, 'British rearmament, 1936–9: Treasury, trade unions and skilled labour', *EHR* 96: 306–43

Parker, R.A.C., 1983, 'The pound sterling, the American Treasury and British preparations for war, 1938–1939', *EHR* 98: 261–79

Patel, Hasu H., and Bhila, H.H.K., 1988, 'The last becomes first: the transfer of power in Zimbabwe', in Gifford and Louis (eds), 1988: 445–59.

Paterson, Thomas G., 1979, *On Every Front: The Making of the Cold War*. New York.

Peacock, Alan T., and Wiseman, Jack, 1967, *The Growth of Public Expenditure in the United Kingdom* (2nd edn).

Pearce, R.D., 1982, *The Turning Point in Africa: British Colonial Policy, 1938–1948*.

Pearce, R.D., 1984, 'The Colonial Office and planned decolonization in Africa', *AA* 83: 77–93.

Peden, G.C., 1979a, 'Sir Warren Fisher and British rearmament against Germany', *EHR* 94: 29–47.

Peden, G.C., 1979b, *British Rearmament and the Treasury, 1932–1939*. Edinburgh.

Peden, G.C., 1983a, 'Keynes, the economics of rearmament and appeasement', in Mommsen and Kettenacker (eds), 1983: 142–56.

Peden, G.C., 1983b, 'The Treasury as the central department of Government, 1919–1939', *Public Administration*, 61: 371–85.

Peden, G.C., 1984a, 'A matter of timing: the economic background to British foreign policy, 1937–1939', *History*, 69: 15–28.

Peden, G.C., 1984b, 'The burden of imperial defence and the continental commitment reconsidered', *HJ* 27: 405–23.

Peden, G.C., 1985, *British Economic and Social Policy: Lloyd George to Margaret Thatcher.*

Peden, George C., 1986, 'Economic aspects of British perceptions of power on the eve of the Cold War', in Becker and Knipping (eds), 1986: 237–60.

Pelling, Henry, 1970, *Britain and the Second World War.*

Pelling, Henry, 1984, *The Labour Governments, 1945–1951.*

Peters, A.R., 1986, *Anthony Eden at the Foreign Office, 1931–1938.* Aldershot.

Pierre, Andrew J., 1972, *Nuclear Politics: The British Experience with an Independent Strategic Force, 1939–1970.*

Pijpers, Alfred, Regelsberger, Elfriede, and Wessels, Wolfgang (eds), in collaboration with Edwards, Geoffrey, 1988, *European Political Cooperation in the 1980s: A Common Foreign Policy for Western Europe?* Dordrecht.

Platt, D.C.M., 1980, 'British portfolio investment overseas before 1870: some doubts', *EcHR* 33: 1–16.

Platt, D.C.M., 1986, *British Investment Overseas on the Eve of the First World War: The Use and Abuse of Numbers.*

Pollard, Sidney, 1985, 'Capital exports, 1870–1914: harmful or beneficial?', *EcHR* 38: 489–514.

Pollard, Sidney, 1989, *Britain's Prime and Britain's Decline: The British Economy, 1870–1914.*

Ponting, Clive, 1989, *Breach of Promise: Labour in Power, 1964–1970.*

Porter, A.N., 1980, *The Origins of the South African War: Joseph Chamberlain and the Diplomacy of Imperialism, 1895–99.* Manchester.

Porter, A.N., and Holland, R.F. (eds), 1985, *Money, Finance and Empire, 1790–1960.*

Porter, A.N., and Stockwell, A.J., 1987, *British Imperial Policy and Decolonization, 1938–64: vol. I, 1938–51.*

Porter, Andrew, 1988, 'The balance sheet of empire, 1850–1914', *HJ* 31: 685–99

Porter, Bernard, 1984, *The Lion's Share: A Short History of British Imperialism, 1850–1983*, 2nd edn.

Porter, Bernard, 1987, *Britain, Europe and the World, 1850–1986: Delusions of Grandeur*, 2nd edn.

Pratt, Lawrence R., 1975, *East of Malta, West of Suez: Britain's Mediterranean Crisis, 1936–1939.* Cambridge.

Pryce, Roy, 1984, 'Relaunching the European Community', *GO* 19: 486–500.

Reed, Bruce, and Williams, Geoffrey, 1971, *Denis Healey and the Policies of Power.*

Rees, Wyn, 1989, 'The 1957 Sandys White Paper: new priorities in British defence policy', *JSS* 12: 215–29.

Regelsberger, Elfriede, 1988, 'EPC in the 1980s: reaching another plateau?', in Pijpers et al. (eds), 1988: 3–48.

Reid, Brian Holden, 1988, 'The "Northern Tier" and the Baghdad Pact', in J.W. Young (ed.), 1988: 159–79.

Reif, Karlheinz (ed.), 1985, *Ten European Elections: Campaigns and Results of the 1979/81 First Direct Elections to the European Parliament*. Aldershot.

Remak, Joachim, 1971, '1914 – the third Balkan war: origins reconsidered', *JMH* 43: 353–66.

Reynolds, David, 1981, *The Creation of the Anglo-American Alliance, 1937–1941: A Study in Competitive Co-operation*.

Reynolds, David, 1985a, 'The origins of the Cold War: The European dimension, 1944–1951', *HJ* 28: 497–515.

Reynolds, David, 1985b, 'Churchill and the British "decision" to fight on in 1940: right policy, wrong reasons', in Langhorne (ed.), 1985: 147–67.

Reynolds, David, 1985/6, 'A "special relationship"?: America, Britain and the international order since 1945', *IA* 62: 1–20.

Reynolds, David, 1986, 'Roosevelt, Churchill, and the wartime Anglo-American Alliance: towards a new synthesis', in Louis and Bull (eds), 1986: 17–41.

Reynolds, David, 1988/9, 'Rethinking Anglo-American relations', *IA* 65: 89–111.

Reynolds, David, 1989a, 'Eden the diplomatist, 1931–56: Suezide of a statesman?', *History*, 240: 64–84.

Reynolds, David, 1989b, 'Power, wealth and war in the modern world', *HJ* 32: 475–87.

Reynolds, David, 1990a, '1940: fulcrum of the twentieth century?', *IA* 66: 325–50.

Reynolds, David, 1990b, 'The "Big Three" and the division of Europe, 1945–1948: an overview', *Diplomacy and Statecraft*, 1: 111–36.

Rhodes James, Robert, 1986, *Anthony Eden*.

Ricks, Christopher (ed.), 1969, *The Poems of Tennyson*.

Robbins, Keith, 1971, *Sir Edward Grey*.

Robbins, Keith, 1977, 'Public opinion, the press and pressure groups', in Hinsley (ed.), 1977: 70–88.

Robbins, Keith, 1985, *The First World War*.

Robertson, Alex J., 1987, *The Bleak Midwinter: 1947*. Manchester.

Rock, William R., 1988, *Chamberlain and Roosevelt: British Foreign Policy and the United States, 1937–1940*. Columbus, Ohio.

Rolo, P.J.V., 1987, 'Lansdowne', in Wilson, K. (ed.), 1987: 159–71.

Roper, John (ed.), 1985, *The Future of British Defence Policy*.

Rose, Norman, 1978, *Vansittart: Study of a Diplomat*.

Rosecrance, Richard, 1979, 'The Pax Britannica and British Foreign Policy', in Kramnick (ed.), 1979: 215–30.

Roskill, Stephen, 1970, 1972, 1974, *Hankey: Man of Secrets* (3 vols).

Ross, Graham, (ed.), 1984, *The Foreign Office and the Kremlin: British Documents on Anglo-Soviet Relations, 1941–1945*. Cambridge.

Rothwell, Victor, 1982, *Britain and the Cold War, 1941–1947*.

Rowland, Benjamin M. (ed.), 1976, *Balance of Power or Hegemony: The Interwar Monetary System*. New York.

Sainsbury, Keith, 1976, *The North African Landings, 1942: A Strategic Decision*.

Sampson, Anthony, 1971, *The New Anatomy of Britain*.

Sanders, David, Ward, Hugh, and Marsh, David, 1987, 'Government popularity and the Falklands war', *BJPS* 17: 281–313.

Sanderson, Michael, 1983, *Education, Economic Change and Society in England, 1780–1870*.

Sanderson, Michael, 1988, 'Education and economic decline, 1890–1980s', in Crafts (ed.), 1988: 38–50.

Sayers, R.S., 1956, *Financial Policy, 1939–1945*.

Scammell, W.M., 1983, *The International Economy since 1945*.

Schmidt, Gustav (ed.), 1989, *Grossbritannien und Europa – Grossbritannien in Europa: Sicherheitsbelange und Wirtschaftsfragen in der britischen Europapolitik nach dem Zweiten Weltkrieg*. Bochum.

Schöpflin, George, 1990, 'The end of communism in Eastern Europe', *IA* 66: 3–16.

Schroeder, Paul W., 1972, *Austria, Great Britain, and the Crimean War: The Destruction of the European Concert*. Ithaca, NY.

Searle, G.R., 1971, *The Quest for National Efficiency: A Study in British Politics and Political Thought, 1899–1914*. Oxford.

Seeley, J.R., 1883, *The Expansion of England*.

Segal, Gerald, 1988, 'Asia and the Pacific', in Byrd (ed.), 1988: 117–36.

Seldon, Anthony, 1981, *Churchill's Indian Summer: The Conservative Government, 1951–1955*.

Semmel, Bernard, 1960, *Imperialism and Social Reform: English Social-Imperial Thought, 1895–1914*.

Semmel, Bernard, 1986, *Liberalism and Naval Strategy: Ideology, Interest, and Sea Power during the Pax Britannica*.

Shannon, Richard, 1976, *The Crisis of Imperialism, 1865–1915*.

Shay, Robert Paul, Jr., 1977, *British Rearmament in the Thirties: Politics and Profits*. Princeton.

Shuckburgh, Evelyn, 1986, *Descent to Suez: Diaries, 1951–1956*.

Simonian, Haig, 1985, *The Privileged Partnership: Franco-German Relations in the European Community, 1969–1984*. Oxford.

Simpson, John, 1986, *The Independent Nuclear State: The United States, Britain and the Military Atom* (2nd edn).

Singh, Anita Inder, 1982, 'Imperial defence and the transfer of power in India, 1946–1947', *IHR* 4: 568–88.

Singh, Anita Inder, 1985, 'Keeping India in the Commonwealth: British political and military aims', *JCH* 20: 469–81.

Sked, Alan, 1987, *Britain's Decline: Problems and Perspectives*. Oxford.

Smith, Adam, 1976, *An Inquiry into the Nature and Causes of the Wealth of Nations* (1776), ed. R.H. Campbell and A.S. Skinner (2 vols). Oxford.

Smith, Malcolm, 1984, *British Air Strategy between the Wars*. Oxford.

Smith, Michael, 1988, 'Britain and the United States: beyond the "special relationship"?', in Byrd (ed.) 1988: 8–34.

Smith, Michael, Smith, Steve and White, Brian (eds), 1988, *British Foreign Policy: Tradition, Change and Transformation*.

Smith, Raymond, and Zametica, John, 1985, 'The Cold Warrior: Clement Attlee reconsidered, 1945–7', *IA* 61: 237–52.

Smith, Tony, 1981, *The Pattern of Imperialism: the United States, Great Britain, and the Late-Industrializing World since 1815*. Cambridge.

Spero, Joan E., 1981, *The Politics of International Economic Relations* (2nd edn).

Steele, E.D., 1987, 'Palmerston's Foreign Policy 1855–1865', in Wilson, K. (ed.), 1987: 25–84.

Stein, Arthur A., 1984, 'The hegemon's dilemma: Great Britain, the United States, and the international economic order', *International Organization*, 38: 355–86.

Steinberg, Jonathan, 1966, *Yesterday's Deterrent: Tirpitz and the Birth of the German Battle Fleet*.

Steinberg, Jonathan, 1977, 'The German background to Anglo-German relations, 1905–1914', in Hinsley (ed.) 1977: 193–215.

Steiner, Zara S., 1969, *The Foreign Office and Foreign Policy, 1895–1914*. Cambridge.

Steiner, Zara S., 1977, *Britain and the Origins of the First World War*.

Steiner, Zara (ed.), 1982, *The Times Survey of Foreign Ministries of the World*.

Steiner, Zara S., 1987, 'Decision-making in American and British foreign policy: an open and shut case', *RIS* 13: 1–18.

Stevenson, D., 1982, *French War Aims against Germany, 1914–1919*. Oxford.

Stockwell, A.J., 1984, 'British imperial policy and decolonization in Malaya, 1942–52', *JICH* 13: 68–87.

Stoler, Mark A., 1980, 'The "Pacific-first" alternative in American World War II strategy', *IHR* 2: 432–52.

Strang, William, 1955, *The Foreign Office*.

Strange, Susan, 1971a, *Sterling and British Policy: A Political Study of an International Currency in Decline*. Oxford.

Strange, Susan, 1971b, 'Sterling and British policy: a political view', *IA* 47: 302–15.

Swann, Denis, 1981, *The Economics of the Common Market* (4th ed., revised). Harmondsworth.

Swartz, Marvin, 1985, *The Politics of British Foreign Policy in the Era of Disraeli and Gladstone*.

Sweet, D.W., 1977, Great Britain and Germany, 1905–1911', in Hinsley (ed.), 1977: 216–35.

Sykes, Alan, 1979, *Tariff Reform in British Politics, 1903–1913*. Oxford.

Taylor, A.J.P., 1957, *The Troublemakers: Dissent over Foreign Policy, 1792–1939*.

Taylor, Paul, 1983, *The Limits of European Integration*. New York.

Temin, Peter, 1987, 'Capital exports, 1870–1914: an alternative model', *EcHR* 40: 453–8.

Thatcher, Margaret, 1986, *In Defence of Freedom: Speeches on Britain's Relations with the World* (ed. Ronald Butt).

Thatcher, Margaret, 1988, Speech on Europe, Bruges, 20 Sept. 1988, PM's Office printed text.

Thatcher, Margaret, 1989, Speech at Lord Mayor's Banquet, Guildhall, 13 Nov. 1989. PM's Office transcript.

Thatcher, Margaret, 1990a, Speech at Königswinter conference, Cambridge, 29 March 1990. PM's Office transcript.

Thatcher, Margaret, 1990b, Speech at Aspen Institute, Aspen, Colorado, 5 August 1990. PM's Office transcript.

Thorne, Christopher, 1967, *The Approach of War, 1938–1939*.

Thorne, Christopher, 1973, *The Limits of Foreign Policy: The West, the League and the Far Eastern Crisis of 1931–1933*. New York.

Thorne, Christopher, 1978, *Allies of a Kind: The United States, Britain and the War against Japan, 1941–1945*.

Thorne, Christopher, 1986, *The Far Eastern War: States and Societies, 1941–45*. (1985 title *The Issue of War*.)

Britannia Overruled

Thygesen, Niels, 1989, 'The Delors report and European economic and monetary union', *IA* 65: 637–52.

Tinker, Hugh, 1986, 'Burma's struggle for independence: the transfer of power thesis re-examined', *MAS* 20: 461–81.

Tomlinson, B.R., 1979, *The Political Economy of the Raj, 1914–1947: The Economics of Decolonization in India.*

Tomlinson, B.R., 1982, 'The contraction of England: national decline and the loss of empire', *JICH* 11: 58–72.

Trotter, Ann, 1975, *Britain and East Asia, 1933–1937*. Cambridge.

Turner, John, 1982, 'Cabinets, committees and secretariats: the higher direction of the war', in Burk (ed.), 1982: 57–83.

Ullman, Richard H., 1961, 1968, 1972, *Anglo-Soviet Relations, 1917–1921* (3 vols). Princeton.

Vaisse, Maurice, 1989, 'Post-Suez France', in Louis and Owen (eds), 1989: 335–40.

Venn, Fiona, 1986, *Oil Diplomacy in the Twentieth Century.*

Vital, David, 1968, *The Making of British Foreign Policy.*

Volle, Angelika, 1989, *Grossbritannien und der europaische Einigungsprozess.* Bonn.

Waites, Neville (ed.), 1971, *Troubled Neighbours: Franco-British Relations in the Twentieth Century.*

Wallace, Helen, 1985, 'The presidency of the Council of Ministers of the European Communities: a comparative perspective', in Nuallain (ed.), 1985: 261–79.

Wallace, Helen, 1989, 'Widening and deepening: the European Community and the new European agenda'. RIIA discussion paper, no. 23.

Wallace, William, 1975, *The Foreign Policy Process in Britain.*

Wark, Wesley K., 1986, *The Ultimate Enemy: British Intelligence and Nazi Germany, 1933–1939* (1985).

Warner, Geoffrey, 1984, 'The Labour governments and the unity of Western Europe, 1945–51', in Ovendale (ed.), 1984: 61–82.

Warner, Geoffrey, 1986, 'Britain and the world, 1945–1949: the view from the Foreign Office', in Becker and Knipping (eds), 1986: 27–44.

Warwick, Paul, 1985, 'Did Britain decline?: an inquiry into the causes of national decline', *JCH* 20: 99–133

Warwick, Peter (ed.), 1980, *The South African War: The Anglo-Boer War, 1899–1902.*

Watt, Alan, 1965, *The Evolution of Australian Foreign Policy, 1938–1965.* Cambridge.

Watt, Donald Cameron, 1984, *Succeeding John Bull: Americ*
Place, 1900–1975. Cambridge.

Watt, Donald Cameron, 1989, *How War Came: The Immedi*
of the Second World War, 1938–1939.

Weinberg, Gerhard L., 1970, 1980, *The Foreign Policy of Hitle*
Germany (2 vols to date). Chicago.

Wendt, Bernd Jürgen, 1971, *Economic Appeasement: Handel und Finanz*
in der britischen Deutschland-Politik, 1933–1939. Düsseldorf.

Wheeler, Nicholas J., 1988/9, 'British nuclear weapons and
Anglo-American relations, 1945–54', *IA* 65: 71–86.

Wheeler-Bennett, Sir John (ed.), 1968, *Action This Day: Working With*
Churchill.

White, Stephen, 1979, *Britain and the Bolshevik Revolution: A Study in*
the Politics of Diplomacy, 1920–1924.

Wiebes, Cees, and Zeeman, Bert, 1983, 'The Pentagon negotiations,
March 1948: the launching of the North Atlantic Treaty', *IA* 59:
351–63.

Wiener, Martin J., 1985, *English Culture and the Decline of the Industrial*
Spirit, 1850–1980 (1981). Harmondsworth.

Willert, Sir Arthur, 1936, 'The Foreign Office from within', *Strand*
Magazine, Feb. 1936, 398–405.

Williams, L.J., 1971, *Britain and the World Economy, 1919–1970.*

Williams, Marcia, 1972, *Inside Number 10.*

Williams, Philip M., 1982, *Hugh Gaitskell*. Cambridge (abridged edn).

Williamson, Philip, 1984, 'A "bankers' ramp"?: financiers and the
British political crisis of August 1931', *EHR* 99: 770–806.

Wilson, Harold, 1971, *The Labour Government, 1964–1970: A Personal*
Record.

Wilson, Harold, 1979, *Final Term: The Labour Government,*
1974–1976.

Wilson, Keith M., 1985, *The Policy of the Entente: Essays on the*
Determinants of British Foreign Policy, 1904–1914. Cambridge.

Wilson, Keith M., 1987, 'Grey', in K. Wilson (ed.), 1987: 172–97.

Wilson, Keith M. (ed.), 1987, *British Foreign Secretaries and Foreign*
Policy: From Crimean War to First World War.

Winter, Jay (ed.), 1983, *The Working Class in Modern British History:*
Essays in Honour of Henry Pelling. Cambridge.

Winter, J.M., 1985, *The Great War and the British People.*

Wohl, Robert, 1980, *The Generation of 1914.*

Woodward, David R., 1983, *Lloyd George and the Generals.* Newark,
Delaware.

Wormell, Deborah, 1979, *Sir John Seeley and the Uses of History*. Cambridge.

Wrigley, Julia, 1986, 'Technical education and industry in the nineteenth century', in Elbaum and Lazonick (eds), 1986: 162–88.

Wurm, Clemens A., 1989, 'Grossbritannien, Westeuropa und die Anfänge der europaischen Integration, 1945–1951', in Schmidt (ed.), 1989: 57–88.

Würzler, Heinz-Werner, 1989, 'Westeuropa im Kalkülbritischer Sicherheits- und Verteidigungspolitik (1945–1955/56)', in Schmidt (ed.), 1989: 141–67.

Young, Hugo, 1989, *One of Us: A Biography of Margaret Thatcher*.

Young, John W., 1984, *Britain, France and the Unity of Europe, 1945–1951*. Leicester.

Young, J.W., 1985, 'Churchill's "No" to Europe: the "rejection" of European Union by Churchill's post-war government, 1951–1952', *HJ* 28: 923–37.

Young, John W., 1988a, 'The Cold War and detente with Moscow', in Young (ed.), 1988: 55–80.

Young, John W., 1988b, 'German rearmament and the European defence community', in Young (ed.), 1988: 81–107.

Young, John W., 1988c, 'The Schuman Plan and British association', in Young (ed.), 1988: 109–34.

Young, John W. (ed.), 1988, *The Foreign Policy of Churchill's Peacetime Administration, 1951–1955*. Leicester.

Young, John W., 1989, '"The parting of the ways"?: Britain, the Messina Conference and the Spaak Committee, June–December 1955', in M. Dockrill and Young (eds), 1989: 197–224.

Young, Robert, 1978, *In Command of France: French Foreign Policy and Military Planning, 1933–1940*. Cambridge, Mass.

Young, Simon Z., 1973, *Terms of Entry: Britain's Negotiations with the European Community, 1970–1972*

Zakheim, Dov S., 1973, 'Britain and the EEC – opinion poll data, 1970–2', *JCMS* 11: 191–233

Zeeman, Bert, 1986, 'Britain and the Cold War: an alternative approach. The treaty of Dunkirk example', *European History Quarterly* 16: 343–67.

Zeitlin, Jonathan, 1987, 'From labour history to the history of industrial relations', *EcHR* 40: 159–184.

Ziegler, Philip, 1986, *Mountbatten: The Official Biography*.

Maps

1 Europe in 1871

Key:
- Lost by Germany 1919
- Saar: League of Nations control 1919–1935
- Demilitarized Rhineland 1919–1936
- Austria-Hungary until 1918
- Plebiscite areas
- Former territory of imperial Russia

2 European peace settlements, 1919–20

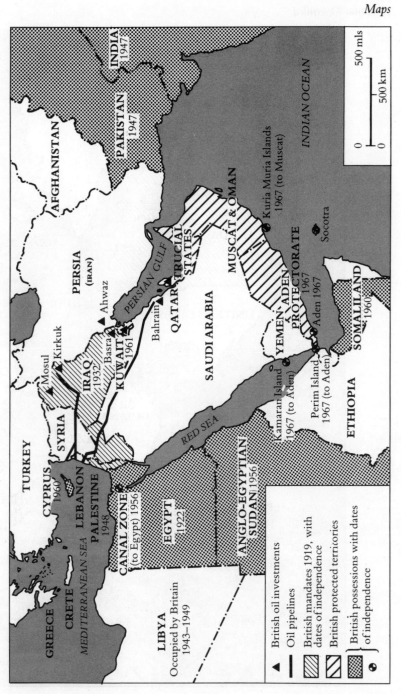

3 Britain and the Middle East, 1919–67

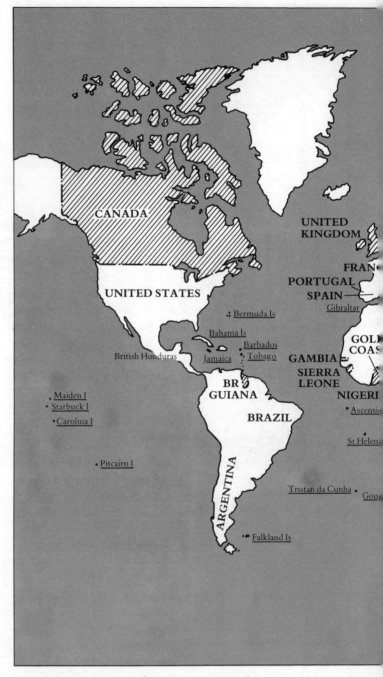

4 The British Empire after the First World War

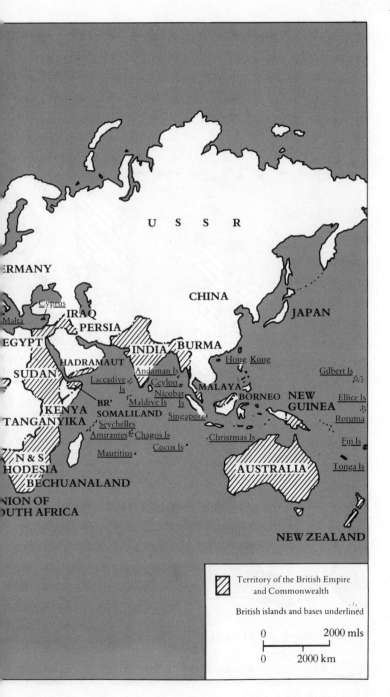

Territory of the British Empire
and Commonwealth

British islands and bases underlined

| 0 | 2000 mls |
| 0 | 2000 km |

5 Europe divided, 1949

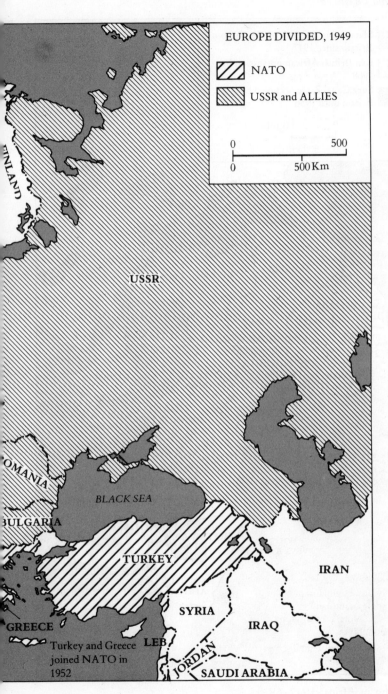

EUROPE DIVIDED, 1949

NATO

USSR and ALLIES

0 ———————— 500
0 ———————— 500 Km

FINLAND

USSR

ROMANIA

BULGARIA

BLACK SEA

TURKEY

IRAN

GREECE

Turkey and Greece
joined NATO in
1952

SYRIA

IRAQ

LEB

JORDAN

SAUDI ARABIA

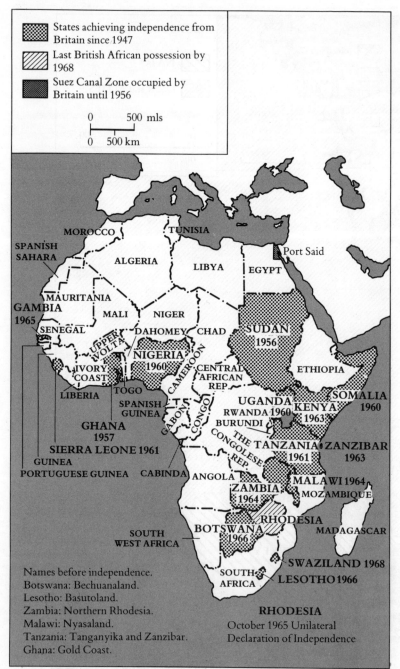

States achieving independence from Britain since 1947

Last British African possession by 1968

Suez Canal Zone occupied by Britain until 1956

0   500 mls

0   500 km

MOROCCO   TUNISIA

SPANISH SAHARA

ALGERIA   LIBYA   EGYPT   Port Said

MAURITANIA

GAMBIA 1965

SENEGAL   MALI   NIGER

UPPER VOLTA   DAHOMEY   CHAD   SUDAN 1956

IVORY COAST   NIGERIA 1960   CAMEROON   CENTRAL AFRICAN REP.   ETHIOPIA

LIBERIA   TOGO

SPANISH GUINEA   GABON   CONGO   UGANDA 1960   KENYA 1963   SOMALIA 1960

GHANA 1957   RWANDA   BURUNDI

SIERRA LEONE 1961   THE CONGOLESE REP.   TANZANIA 1961   ZANZIBAR 1963

GUINEA

PORTUGUESE GUINEA   CABINDA   ANGOLA   MALAWI 1964

ZAMBIA 1964   MOZAMBIQUE

SOUTH WEST AFRICA   BOTSWANA 1966   RHODESIA   MADAGASCAR

SWAZILAND 1968

SOUTH AFRICA   LESOTHO 1966

Names before independence.
Botswana: Bechuanaland.
Lesotho: Basutoland.
Zambia: Northern Rhodesia.
Malawi: Nyasaland.
Tanzania: Tanganyika and Zanzibar.
Ghana: Gold Coast.

RHODESIA
October 1965 Unilateral Declaration of Independence

6 Britain in Africa, 1947–68

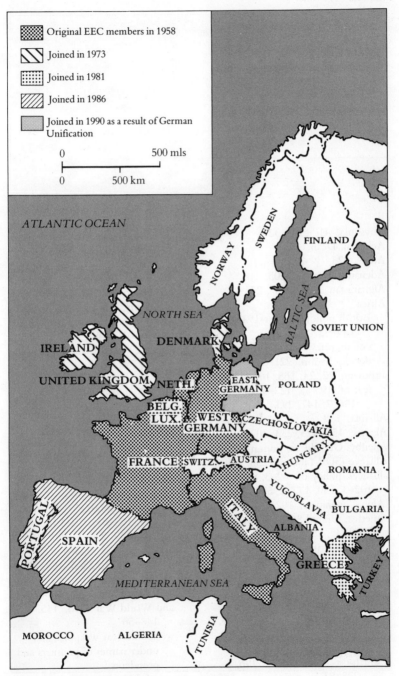

Original EEC members in 1958

Joined in 1973

Joined in 1981

Joined in 1986

Joined in 1990 as a result of German Unification

0   500 mls

0   500 km

ATLANTIC OCEAN

NORWAY

SWEDEN

FINLAND

NORTH SEA

BALTIC SEA

SOVIET UNION

IRELAND

DENMARK

UNITED KINGDOM

NETH.

EAST GERMANY

POLAND

BELG.

LUX.

WEST GERMANY

CZECHOSLOVAKIA

FRANCE

SWITZ.

AUSTRIA

HUNGARY

ROMANIA

YUGOSLAVIA

BULGARIA

ITALY

ALBANIA

PORTUGAL

SPAIN

GREECE

TURKEY

MEDITERRANEAN SEA

MOROCCO

ALGERIA

TUNISIA

7 The European Community since 1958

Index